Praise for
THE AMERICAN WAY OF EATING

"An indictment of America's industrial food system and a vivid,

T0071184

compassionate portrait of the working class."

—*The Portland Oregonian*

"Every time I find evidence of a massive forthcoming event to take away our freedom, I am going to warn you. And so now we have a book by Tracie McMillan . . . What is it with all of these young single white women, overeducated—doesn't mean intelligent."

—**Rush Limbaugh**

"This book is vital. [McMillan] has the writing skills to bear witness, the research background to provide context, and the courage to take on the challenging task."

—*Los Angeles Times*

"McMillan is a lively storyteller . . . her investigation pulls back the curtain on a host of unsavory practices along the food chain."

—*The Washington Post*

"Excellent."　　　　　　　　　—**Mark Bittman**, *The New York Times*

"With much courage and compassion, McMillan explores the lives of those at the bottom of our food system. Here is a glimpse of the people who feed us—and the terrible price they pay. If we want to change the system, this is where we must begin."

—**Eric Schlosser, author of** *Fast Food Nation*

"A compelling and cogent argument that eating healthily ought to be easier."

—*The Cleveland Plain Dealer*

"Valiant . . . McMillan's undercover work for *The American Way of Eating* takes readers on an educational journey."

—*San Francisco Chronicle*

"The genius, *genius* Tracie McMillan went from growing up eating a lot of processed foods to cultivating an interest in fancier, local cuisine, to even writing for high-end culinary publications including *Saveur* mag. Her personal journey led her to write this must read, which investigates our food system and what's exactly keeping Americans from eating well, and what we can do to fix it. (Did I mention genius?)"

—*Glamour.com*

"These pages will leave you with vivid, challenging images of how food is harvested, sold, and prepared."

—*Minneapolis Star Tribune*

"This is a voice the food world needs . . . her central concern, in her journalism and in this provocative book, is food and class. She stares at America's bounty, noting that so few seem able to share in it fully, and she asks: 'What would it take for us all to eat well?'"

"In her important new book, Tracie McMillan illuminates [a] murky yet vital sector of our economy. . . . McMillan has committed a brave act of immersion reportage, applying to the food system the techniques of Barbara Ehrenreich's classic 2001 chronicle of working-poor life, *Nickel and Dimed.*"

—Oneearth.org

"McMillan uses data to build her book's main argument, which is both clear and essential: In America, for a whole host of reasons, '[e]ating poorly is easier than eating well.' Until we change that equation, through policy changes large and small, no amount of telling people they should buy from their local farmer will make enough of a difference."

—*The Boston Globe*

"This is an amazing book. Tracie McMillan will take any reader into new territory. The implacable fierceness of farm work, the slovenliness behind the produce section at Walmart—prepare to be submerged in harsh little worlds and shocked. But McMillan keeps her cool, always presenting the context and the content of her struggles with enough analytic detachment to rough out a complete, and convincing, vision of food as a social good. Read her book and your dinner will never look the same."

—**William Finnegan, author of** *Cold New World*

"McMillan argues the local and organic food movement needs more empathy for consumers."

—*The Detroit News*

"A worthy book." —*Booklist*

"These tales lay bare the sinews, the minds, and the relationships that our food system exploits and discards. In a work of deep compassion and integrity, Tracie McMillan offers us an eye-opening report on the human cost of America's cheap food."

—**Raj Patel, author of** *Stuffed and Starved and The Value of Nothing*

"Personable, self-deprecating, elucidating, McMillan's account achieves an engaging balance between documentary and history, rich in the personalities of the people she works with and befriends while offering a smattering of research."

—*Publishers Weekly*

"McMillan provides an eye-opening account of the route much of American food takes from the field to the restaurant table."

—*Kirkus Reviews*

"Tracie McMillan is gutsy, scrappy, and hard-working; you'd have to be to write this book. *The American Way of Eating* takes us local in a new way, exploring who works to get food from the field to the plates in front of us, what they are paid, and how it feels. It's sometimes grim, but McMillan doesn't flinch; I especially appreciated her openness in telling us what she spent in order to get by (or not). A welcome addition to the urgent, growing body of journalism on food."

—Ted Conover, author of *Newjack* and *Coyotes* and Professor of Literary Reportage at NYU's Arthur L. Carter Journalism Institute

"To uncover the truth behind how our modern food system works, Tracie M. McMillan took jobs in a supermarket produce section, a chain restaurant kitchen, and the fields alongside migrant laborers. If you eat, you owe it to yourself to read this masterful book."

—Barry Estabrook, author of *Tomatoland*

"Three cheers for Tracie McMillan; this book is a revelation! It is the sort of engaging first-person adventure story that reads like a good novel, all the while supplying the facts and figures that make the larger picture clear. I'm grateful to her in equal parts for having the stamina and courage to undertake this undercover journey, the narrative skill that makes the account so digestible, and the commitment to social justice for both workers and consumers that infuses the whole project."

—Janet Poppendieck, author of *Free for All* and Professor of Sociology at Hunter College, City University of New York

"Tracie McMillan has written a remarkable book for right now—a book that smartly tells us what is wrong with what we eat and how we might improve it. But what is even more remarkable about the book is how deeply engaging it is. With her intimate and confident portraits of American food workers, she crafts a touching, emotional narrative that will stay with you long after you have finished the last page."

—James Oseland, editor-in-chief, *Saveur,* and author of *Cradle of Flavor*

"This is a wonderful introduction to the triumph and tragedy of the American food industry. Mixing compassionate participant observation with in-depth, up-to-the-minute background research, Tracie McMillan takes us for an eye-opening, heart-rending tour of the corporate food chain. Along the way we meet unforgettable people who, at great personal cost, labor hard so that we can eat cheaply and easily. Having seen what it takes to move our meals from farm to table, the reader will emerge shaken, enlightened, and forever thankful."

—Warren Belasco, author of *Appetite for Change* and *Meals to Come* Professor Emeritus of American Studies, University of Maryland

THE
AMERICAN WAY
OF EATING

❦

UNDERCOVER AT WALMART, APPLEBEE'S,
FARM FIELDS AND THE DINNER TABLE

Tracie McMillan

SCRIBNER

New York   London   Toronto   Sydney   New Delhi

SCRIBNER
A Division of Simon & Schuster, Inc.
1230 Avenue of the Americas
New York, NY 10020

First Scribner paperback edition October 2012

SCRIBNER and design are registered trademarks of The Gale Group, Inc.,
used under license by Simon & Schuster, Inc., the publisher of this work.

For information about special discounts for bulk purchases,
please contact Simon & Schuster Special Sales at 1-866-506-1949
or business@simonandschuster.com.

The Simon & Schuster Speakers Bureau can bring authors to your live event.
For more information or to book an event contact the Simon & Schuster Speakers Bureau
at 1-866-248-3049 or visit our website at www.simonspeakers.com.

Manufactured in the United States of America

9   10

Library of Congress Control Number: 2012372266

ISBN 978-1-4391-7195-0
ISBN 978-1-4391-7196-7 (paperback)
ISBN 978-1-4391-7197-4 (ebook)

"Holy Ted Nugent, We're All Foodies Now" originally appeared in the
Op-Ed section of the *Los Angeles Times* on March 4, 2012.

For those who aren't here to see this:

My mother, Charyl Kaye McMillan;
my grandmother Margaret Mary McMillan;
my grandfathers, John Alan McMillan and Donald Eugene Weddle;

And for my grandmother who, thankfully, is:

Katheryn Camelia Weddle

CONTENTS

BEFORE YOU READ THIS BOOK

This is a work of journalism, and an undercover one at that. Nobody I worked with ever knew that I was a journalist when I met them, and to protect their privacy I've changed all of my co-workers' names and, in rare instances, identifying details; most people who knew I was a journalist when they met me are identified by their real names. I tried a mix of strategies with regard to this, my rule of thumb being to never endanger my ability to maintain a job or to encourage preferential treatment. I succeeded on the first count, but even without revealing my "true" identity I seemed to fail abysmally at the latter. Much of that has to do with fixed variables (my inexperience, my youthful appearance, my gender, my language, my citizenship, my race) and not a little of it can be traced to something more fluid: the kindness of the people with whom I worked.

The basic story I used to get work was true insofar as it went. I said I had family problems, I needed to find work, I didn't want to deal with customers, I didn't mind working hard. The people I worked with met me as a single, childless thirtysomething white woman trying to keep her life afloat by, at various times, picking grapes, sorting peaches, cutting garlic, stocking grocery shelves on the night shift, stocking produce on the day shift, or expediting and doing prep in a restaurant kitchen. I didn't invent some other life, with other friends or work or family. On my applications I used real jobs and I talked about my real-life friends and family problems, and my actual likes and dislikes, as I would have with anyone else.

As a worker, I had a lot of advantages: good health, health insurance, education, a car, citizenship, the knowledge that this particular struggle would end in two months. As such, I can make no claim to having had an "authentic" experience. But I can tell you what I saw, and I can tell you what I learned from my co-workers, most of whom will never have the privilege to write a book about their work, let alone have people read it.

I began with a strict schedule in mind: two months in each job, with a startup fund equivalent to one month's wages, post-tax, of full-time work at minimum wage for the state in which I was living. Typically this meant somewhere between $900 and $1,100, which translates into a salary range between $10,800 and $13,200 a year. In each job, I found I had to fudge the rules a bit to keep afloat, figuring that if it had been my "real" life I would have done the same. I leave it to readers to judge what that says about me, or my work, or the story I tell.

THE
AMERICAN WAY
OF EATING

❧

INTRODUCTION

Eating in America

The first Brooklyn supermarket I ever walked into had a cockroach in the deli. Not one of those stealthy critters stealing along the crevices in the floor, or hanging out backstage in dry storage. No, this was a proud-to-be-here New York City roach, crawling openly up the wall's white tile before dropping, unceremoniously, onto the meat slicer below. I decided to skip the lunchmeat and headed for the produce aisle.

I sought out hard, pink tomatoes and pale spheres of iceberg lettuce, bags of Red Delicious apples and dusty sacks of potatoes. The contents of my grocery basket telegraphed my Midwestern upbringing. I'd been so busy putting myself through college by running errands for a fashion designer, tutoring rich kids, tutoring public high school kids, waiting tables at a barbecue joint, and a slew of other odd jobs that I hadn't yet made the city my home. I paid for the food and, to save $1.50 on bus fare, walked ten blocks, about half a mile, home. As I piled the groceries on the counter, I told my roommate about the roach.

That's pretty gross, he said. Maybe we can shop somewhere else?

But we never did. We were students, keeping rent low by living an hour from campus in a neighborhood thick with families headed by dishwashers and seamstresses, housekeepers and day laborers. Neighborhood signs were dotted with script in Polish, Chinese, and Spanish. If there were good ethnic shops I was too blind to see them; raised in rural Michigan, the only food stores I knew to look for were supermarkets. And the roach-in-the-deli was the only one we could walk to. We didn't cook much, anyway. We were too busy.

All of this—the chore of finding food, the lack of time to do anything with it when we did, the indifference to our meals—was familiar. I grew up in a small town outside Flint. My dad sold lawn equipment for a living. My mom was gravely ill for nearly a decade. Most of my family's time and money went to medical bills, and I grew up eating the kind of meals you'd expect from an effectively single working dad. Sometimes I helped make them, especially if it meant we'd end up with my favorites, like Tuna Helper, on the table. On nights when I couldn't sleep, I'd page through my mom's *Good Housekeeping* cookbook and bake cakes and breads to entertain myself while, ostensibly, helping out around the house.

We ate a lot of Helper meals and Ortega Taco Dinners when I was growing up, and I liked them. We had salads of chopped iceberg lettuce tossed with diced carrots, celery, wedges of tomato, and some Wish-Bone Ranch dressing. On weeknights, mashed potatoes came from a box, toast was brushed with melted Country Crock and sprinkled with garlic salt, and Miracle Whip held together the pasta salad. Time and convenience were important to our diet, just as much as taste and price.

That's not to say we didn't care for food that wasn't home-cooked or farm-fresh. My grandmother could summon forth tender roasts, rhubarb pies and crisp salads from her kitchen. When I spent weekends with her, we'd sometimes make a pre-dawn run to a crumbling garage-like building in Pontiac where farmers came to sell their goods. In the summers, my dad's garden, a grove of vegetable plants spiking up through black plastic sheeting and carpet of weed killer, would let us feast on tomatoes and peppers cheaply. And most Sundays, when my dad had relaxed from his week, he'd throw a roast in the oven, boil some potatoes, and steam some vegetables. But we still thought that regularly eating food that took that much time or money—or, most outrageously of all, both—wasn't for people like us. It was for the people my grandmother described, with equal parts envy and derision, as fancy; my father's word was snob. And I wasn't about to be like that.

No, here in Brooklyn I'd do the same thing my family had done in Michigan. I'd make do with my culinary lot in life. If I didn't have extra money to buy healthy food, or the time to prepare it, that meant the cheap and the processed. For a very long time, I couldn't see it any other way.

Like all myths, the idea that only the affluent and educated care about their meals has spread not because it is true, but because parts of it are. Healthier food is more expensive; that much is true. So is the fact that it can be hard to find in poor neighborhoods. And yet it requires an impossible leap of logic to conclude from these facts that only the rich care about their meals. "Food culture in the United States has long been cast as the property of a privileged class. It is nothing of the kind," wrote Barbara Kingsolver in

Animal, Vegetable, Miracle. She may be right, but for most people—myself included—seeing good food as a luxury lifestyle product has been so deeply embedded in our thinking about our meals that we barely notice it. I didn't until I met Vanessa.

I had been living in New York for nearly a decade, and was covering the poverty beat for a small magazine. I met people in welfare offices, child care centers, housing project courtyards, and after-school programs, and wrote stories about them; in doing so, I often ended up in their homes. I ate Jimmy Dean hamburgers in the kitchen of a fortysomething lady gang leader. I watched a Dominican home health aide run her four kids through math homework while spiraling the peel off an orange with a paring knife. I shared crackers and spreadable cheese during snack time at a child care center in a brownstone apartment. But I was there to write about welfare rules and crappy jobs, not food, so I hardly noticed it. What did food have to do with my work, anyway? The people I was writing about weren't fancy. Neither was I.

For years, I insisted food wasn't important to me. And yet, I had always made birthday cakes from scratch for my friends. In college, I shoplifted spices from an A&P to experiment with Indian curries. And while I kept my own grocery budget modest, my college years saw me working for an affluent family and occasionally cooking their dinner—leading me to stumble through a world of cookbooks and ingredients beyond Betty Crocker. In spite of myself, I started cooking fancy food: Moroccan stews, chicken breast and portobello mushrooms with balsamic vinegar, lentils green and red and yellow.

An internal debate began:

That's fancy food, for fancy people. Just who do you think you are? said my Midwestern upbringing.

But did you taste that tomato, that cheese, those spices? replied the burgeoning New Yorker. *It's* so *worth it.*

The Midwesterner always won, though, throwing down this gauntlet: *Even if it's worth it, I can't afford to eat like that.* I'd grown resigned to this annoyingly intractable debate over my meals. Fancy food was for the rich; box meals were for the rest of us, and there was no point in making a fuss about it. This idea was so ingrained in me that I never even bothered to see how much it would cost to cook better meals from scratch.

Vanessa was pure New York. She was short, still sporting a trace of baby fat, her tawny curls pulled into the same slicked-back ponytail as so many of the other girls filtering through the city's high schools. Mouthy and freckled. Brown eyes glinting with mischief. Vanessa was also ambitious enough that she'd gotten into a paid after-school internship program in Manhattan. The only requirement to get the stipend was that she attend one of several classes offered by a youth services agency. She had chosen a cooking class built around themes of health and environmentally friendly farming, and that's where I met her.

I didn't want to write about the class. I wanted to be writing about important things like the city's plan to close down child care centers. Or domestic violence programs that weren't getting enough funding. I didn't see the point in following a cooking class, much less one run by a young man who kept going on about yoga and greens and who—save for the fact that he was black—struck me as a well-intentioned hippie. I sat in the class, took notes, and paid extra attention whenever a kid declared a love of junk food or scowled at the mention of a vegetable.

Vanessa laughed in the first class, her brows raised matter-of-factly under a pink headband. "I love Popeye's. I love McDonald's," she said, naming two spots near her home in Brooklyn. "I think Manhattan's the best place for healthy food, but it's expensive."

Ronny, a rangy fourteen-year-old from Washington Heights, proclaimed his loyalty to McDonald's, too. "I'm not going to change the way I eat. I've got to live my life," he said, adding that he went there almost every day.

Good luck, hippie.*

I observed the class off and on for six months, and toward the end of it Vanessa agreed to let me come over to her house. She lived with her grandparents in a rickety two-family next to a vacant lot. Vanessa's grandmother cooked for a nearby Head Start program, and at home she refused to cave in to her granddaughter's taste for junk food. Instead, she fed Vanessa traditional Latin-Caribbean fare: pots of rice and beans, platters of *plátanos*, sticky and sweet.

"It's kind of hard to eat healthy around here," said Vanessa, and we went for a walk to Burger King, where she got a Whopper and washed it down with seven half-and-half creamers, grabbed for free out of the bin and squirted, one by one, directly into her mouth. This was not promising insofar as health went. But the more we talked, the clearer it became that Vanessa

---

*The class I profiled was run by Bryant Terry, now a celebrated food activist and writer perhaps known best for his cookbooks, which include *Grub*, which he co-wrote with Anna Lappé, and *Vegan Soul Kitchen*.

understood quite well that she should eat better. We were at Burger King for the same reasons her friends ate there almost daily: "They know it's not healthy, but it's what's there and what's easy to make." Vanessa told me that, inspired by the health component of her cooking class, she had stopped eating fast food every day and tried not to have it more than three times a week.

Vanessa took me to the nearest supermarket, a member of the same chain that had managed my roach-in-the-deli store seven years prior. She surveyed the offerings. "It's a lot of junk food," Vanessa said, gesturing at the cereal, cookies, soda, Rice-A-Roni and everything else lining the interior aisles. "They really just have, like, normal stuff. The grapefruit is bad. The apples are medium all right. The tangerines are gross, the lemons, the limes." Then she surprised me by professing, "I love tomatoes. I love broccoli and lettuce and peppers and onions."

Vanessa spent the afternoon telling me about the importance of seasonality in produce and then eyeing a *cuchifrito* stand hungrily; lamenting the lack of a farmers' market in her neighborhood, then reflecting that most people don't have time for it, since they go shopping before and after work. And then she posed a question—half rhetorical, half the genuine inquiry of a child expecting an answer from an adult—"If you want people to eat healthy, why make it so expensive?"

Vanessa hadn't said anything groundbreaking, she'd just made a series of observations that added up to the same truth we'd both grown up with: Eating poorly is easier than eating well. That's why she was eating badly. Vanessa didn't eat junk because she didn't know better, or because her family didn't cook, or because she didn't care about food and health. It was just easier to find junk in her neighborhood, her city, her life. And for the first time in my life, I began to ask why.

Once I posed that question, I found answers everywhere. There were obvious ones, like the fact that good, fresh food tends to cost more, especially in cities, making it difficult, if not impossible, for folks of limited means to afford it. Or the fact that New York's ubiquitous corner stores specialized in ice cream pints, Iced Honey Buns, and cola, not produce. These facts had been in the background of my entire life, but when I finally stopped to look at them, I saw this foodscape for what it was: an abandonment of America's great promise, implicit in every tale of rising fortunes and opportunity from Thomas Jefferson to Barack Obama, that it would always feed its citizens well.

If I lived in a land of plenty, how could the activists be right when they told me supermarkets, even scrappy ones, simply didn't open up shop in the city's poorer sections? That hadn't been *my* experience. I'd long since moved from my first Brooklyn neighborhood to a second, making my home at the edge of Bedford-Stuyvesant. This is the ghetto that birthed a lineage of black American culture from Richard Wright to Biggie Smalls, and a framed portrait of Biggie hung in our supermarket; neighborhood lore held that he had bagged groceries there as a kid. Leaning on a knob-topped cane and wearing a sleek black suit, this icon of New York rap looked out over shelves crammed with vegetarian options for rastas, halal ones for the Muslims, bottles of bitters for West Indian stews, and a wide swath of the Goya product line for Latinos. The produce didn't look great, but it was passable; I could still eat. This, I asked myself, was a lack of options?

I lifted my head up, looked past my neighborhood, and asked harder questions: Where were the city's supermarkets? How big were they? How many people did they feed? In the end, I compiled the first zip-code-by-zip-code guide to food access in the city, and *it was true:* Supermarkets were few and far between, and the city's poor had the fewest. In the arty-turned-affluent neighborhood of SoHo, each resident had more than seventeen square feet of supermarket space to shop in. Ten miles north in Washington Heights, where Ronny lived, family incomes were one-third of their counterparts' in SoHo—and they made do with one-half of one square foot of supermarket space per person, just 3 percent of what the SoHo-ites had. I had discovered what is now called a *food desert*: a community with insufficient grocery stores for its population.

How did this happen? Some grocery chains had joined the exodus known as white flight, heading for the suburbs after World War II and fleeing in earnest after the urban riots of the 1960s—taking with them all the systems for delivering fruits and vegetables into neighborhoods. Others had simply never planted their flag in urban soil, judging proposals for new stores by their likelihood of success in the suburbs—a method that made suburban neighborhoods, with high incomes, look like better bets than urban ones, where incomes were lower but there were far more customers to spend money. Either way, without big stores that would make big purchases, nobody had made a business of bringing fresh produce to the city's low-income neighborhoods: not distributors, not wholesalers, not grocers. Even if corner stores wanted to sell vegetables, there wasn't anyone to deliver the produce to them. If people wanted to spend their food stamps at farmers' markets, they found themselves caught in a technological black hole: Paper stamps had been replaced by magnetic cards, and farmers selling fresh collards and carrots didn't have the technology to accept them.*

The more I looked out on this vast landscape, the less I recognized any of it. And yet I couldn't stop looking, trying to figure out what had changed. Something had gotten under my skin; it changed how I saw the world. And the first thing that I could recognize as truth in this strange new place was what I learned at Vanessa's side: Everyone wants good food.

I'm not the only one who's found a new world through food. In the last decade, a burgeoning fascination with our meals has swept popular culture, finding its way into nearly every facet of public life. This is a new era in American food culture, pairing the rise of the cult of the chef with a celebration of the home cook, the stylized instruction of the Food Network with DIY dinner parties. There are countless books and blogs and websites that chronicle food obsessions. Whole identities have emerged around the contents of one's plate: locavores, flexitarians, Slow Foodies, freegans, and Chowhounds. Public figures of all stripes are drawing attention to eating well and living healthy. First Lady Michelle Obama has made childhood obesity her cause, encouraging us all to plant gardens, cook more, eat whole grains and fresh vegetables, get outdoors, and get some exercise. The cooking celebrity Rachael Ray has dedicated her nonprofit work to teaching kids and parents to cook and getting them to make better health decisions. Even Ted Nugent, an ardent pro-gun rocker best known for his 1970s anthem "Cat Scratch Fever," urges his fans to grow and hunt their own food, get plenty of exercise, avoid alcohol, and make "optimum health job number one."† Meanwhile, a growing pantheon of food philosophers from Alice Waters to Michael Pollan is coaching us from the sidelines, reshaping the way America thinks about its food and establishing new ideals for what people should be eating and how it should be grown.

---

* In the years since that work was published, local and federal officials across the country have begun to introduce wireless terminals at farmers' markets so that clients of the Supplemental Nutrition Assistance Program (SNAP; colloquially known as food stamps) can use their benefits to buy farm-fresh produce.

† "Our soul sandwich should be made from all-natural ingredients, well thought out and put together individually so we know exactly what goes into it and our belly. Whole foods or no food at all, I always say . . . by making optimum health job number one, we will be better prepared and equipped to live each day to the fullest, attaining great joy and happiness in our American Dream. Each meal should be a major ThanXGiving gitdown party, showing grand appreciation for these amazing gifts." (Nugent 2005)

All of this begets an obvious question: How do we put those ideals within everyone's reach? How do we transform them from luxury products into typical ones? How do we make a foodscape crowded with junk into an anomaly, and one flush with fresh, healthy food the norm?

We already know the stakes are high. Americans pay incredible costs—in terms of both our money and our health—for the way we eat. Obesity may soon outpace tobacco as the deadliest health threat in America. Today, nearly two-thirds of Americans are overweight or obese—a figure showing no signs of dropping. The resulting health problems, which cost the country $75 billion per year, are found most commonly among the poor, who account for 28 percent of the tab despite constituting only 16 percent of the population. Yet, so far, the dominant interpretation of this information has been to lament Americans' lack of understanding and commitment to our meals and health. "The main barrier between ourselves and a local-food culture is not price, but attitude," writes Barbara Kingsolver, neatly introducing a dominant theme in America's current food debates. "Career women in many countries still routinely . . . [head] straight from work to the market to search out the freshest ingredients."

There's another advantage other developed countries have when it comes to food cultures: money and time. Americans get derided for spending too little of both on their meals, usually with the observation that Americans spend about 13 percent of their take-home income on food, while the French spend about 20 percent. By spending more of their money on food, goes the thinking, the French have made food a priority—and they are also less fat. But it is also true that their government provides quality health and child care, higher education, and transportation at little or no out-of-pocket cost to its citizens*—not to mention mandating five weeks of paid vacation each year. The average American family may spend about 7 percent less of their paycheck on their meals than the French, but they also spend 7 percent more of it on education

---

* There are no comparable data between countries representing what individual households spend on child care. However, for comparative purposes, France spends 28.5 percent of its gross domestic product on social programs, and Italy, 25.5. Both countries offer free, public child care for infants until age three. The United States, by contrast, spends 15.7 percent of its GDP on social programs and the cost of child care is almost always the responsibility of the parents. Low-income American parents, for example, spend an average of 18 percent of their income per child in child care. (Organization for Economic Cooperation and Development 2011; Organization for Economic Cooperation and Development 2006a; Organization for Economic Cooperation and Development 2006b)

and health care. It's not just a gastronomic culture that leads the French to prioritize their meals, but a political and social landscape that makes it much easier for them to do so.

Today, America talks about its food culture as a set of choices made from equal footing—a vote, if you will, with our fork. Under this logic, it's as easy for me to choose to eat healthy food as for Vanessa, or for a rural migrant farmworker, or for a lawyer on the Upper East Side. And yet, if the decade that has passed since the declaration of an obesity epidemic is any indication, the primary strategy deployed to encourage us to "vote" differently—repeatedly lecturing at people, regardless of their income or work life or home life, to change their habits—has failed. Most of us know better, but we still eat poorly, and that leaves us with two basic reasons why: Either Americans are stupid and lazy, or we are dealing with a problem that won't be solved solely by lectures and individual choice. The question is, if lectures and leading by example don't work, what will?

For me, the concept of easy comes up again and again—and it's linked with good health choices as well as poor ones. For example, rates of obesity typically rise the farther people live from grocery stores—and for every additional supermarket in a census tract, fruit and vegetable consumption goes up by as much as 32 percent. Higher obesity rates correlate with spending less time preparing and eating our food. And when we make it cheaper (one form of easier) to buy produce, people do it. In 2010, farmers' markets across the country began adopting a program to match food-stamp clients' spending on local fruits and vegetables by up to $20 a week. In just the first year, food stamp spending at the markets increased by as much as five and six times—more than the matching funds would account for, indicating that people then supplemented the coupons with their own money, too. And 87 percent of clients say the coupons have enabled them to eat produce they would have otherwise done without.

So maybe we've been asking the wrong question. Instead of focusing tightly on the problems with America's food culture, maybe we should try asking the question behind all of Vanessa's ruminations: Why is it so difficult to eat well? A decade ago, asking this would have seemed tantamount to asking why the sky is blue. Today, it is simply the next logical step in the growing conversation about food and health.

* * *

Food has always been one of America's great paradoxes. Even before the vast abundance of industrial agriculture came to bear on our meals, our nation's affluent feasted on fresh vegetables and fine sweets while our poor made do with far less. In 1782, writing about the abundance of American agriculture, Thomas Jefferson noted that "the climate requires indispensably a free use of vegetable food. For health as well as comfort." Yet Jefferson, who dedicated much of his 5,000-acre Virginia plantation to agriculture, noted that even as wealthy landowners tended to thriving vegetable plots in excess of what they could consume, "the poorer people . . . [live] principally on milk and animal diet." This state of affairs, he added, was "inexcusable."

To be fair, food is only one of our nation's paradoxes—our founding fathers proclaimed a free republic even as some of them owned slaves; we extended the right to vote to men but neglected to include the women—but it is perhaps the most stubborn. More than two centuries after Jefferson wrote of the inexcusable divide between the meals of the poor and the rich, we've yet to solve what food historian Harvey Levenstein has aptly dubbed the "paradox of plenty." Put simply, our agriculture is abundant but healthy diets are not. The American way of eating is defined not by *plenty,* but by the simultaneous, contradictory, relentless presence of scarce nutrition in its midst. And though this conundrum may be seen most clearly in America's extravagant harvests alongside our declining health, it is slowly taking root across the globe.

This intransigent paradox has spread by many means, first and foremost by our industrial agriculture. Focused on grain that can be morphed into an endless array of food products, and using chemicals developed by U.S. companies, the American way of growing food has found its way to the humblest of African villages and the most sophisticated of South American farms, deposited there by our aid programs, our philanthropists, and international institutions. The paradox continued to grow as other nations followed the trail of our supermarket system, once considered an American idiosyncrasy and now so common abroad that Walmart isn't only the largest grocer in the United States, but in the world. And it has spread even further via processed foods—pioneered in American factories, kitchens, and board rooms—that rely on the cheap grain produced by our agriculture and are tailor-made for supermarkets and restaurants that demand shelf-stable foodstuffs. There are mounting pressures that may change all of this, intensifying climate change and declining soil health not least among them, but the pattern is unmistakably set: The American way of eating is on track to become that of the world, too.

In the pages that follow, you'll find the story of my investigation into just how America came to eat this way, why we keep doing it, and what it would take to change it. I spent a year working undercover in America's contemporary food system, from California to Michigan to New York, drawn to each place because I wanted to live and work inside three segments of our food system—farm, store, and restaurant—and learn how the whole machine works. I was looking, on one hand, to understand the internal logic that governs the movement of every apple and zucchini from the earth to a produce aisle and onto our dinner plate. Yet, to truly understand a system, you can't just examine its structures; you have to look at its effects, too. I wanted to know how dinner gets on the table for American families, how the pressures of work and economy get translated into their meals. This was not, I had to admit, something I could learn from my cozy single-girl-in-Brooklyn apartment. And the best way—really, the *only* way—to do this was to leave my regular life behind for a little while and live and work among the rest of America. In each job, I lived and ate off the wages I earned, paying rent and buying groceries as if it were, in fact, my real life.

I started at the lowest end of the economic spectrum, as a laborer in the fields where a healthy diet begins: harvesting fruits and vegetables (the one dietary priority that everyone seems to agree on). Fruits and vegetables receive less than 5 percent of the $18.3 billion we allocated in 2009 for federal agricultural subsidies, but they are crucial for a healthy diet; California's innumerable valleys are the cradle of their production, so that's where I looked for work. I harvested grapes, I sorted peaches, and I cut garlic, moving around—like a lot of farmworkers—in the hope of finding better work and better housing. Almost a year later, I visited the place where most food ends up, in a kitchen—though the job I took, as an expediter at a Brooklyn Applebee's, helps to produce a very specific kind of meal. I chose Applebee's because it's the biggest casual dining restaurant in America and the world, and because these kinds of restaurants are rarely equated with the fast food their meals so closely resemble.

Between the farm and the plate, I went to work in a part of the food system that's been curiously absent from most of today's food debates: the supermarket. I worked as a stock clerk in two Michigan Walmart stores, most notably one outside Detroit. When we talk about the problems with our food today, we tend to focus on how we grow it or what we eat. But there is another problem, just as big, that we tend to skip over: how we arrange for the food to get from the farm to the plate. And today, that role is played almost exclusively by supermarkets and supercenters, the latter being Walmart's term for its stores that include a supermarket.

Today, supermarkets and supercenters supply 85 percent of the food we eat at home while the rest comes to us via "nontraditional food retail" like convenience stores and discount shops on the industrial end of things, and farmers' markets and community-supported agriculture buying clubs on the artisanal end. In 2009, farmers' markets had grown to supply just over 1 percent of America's groceries; Walmart controlled nearly one-quarter of America's food supply, significantly more than the next three biggest competitors combined. This makes Walmart a massive produce locomotive, the single greatest conveyance delivering farm produce and myriad other products to millions of Americans.

It also highlights the fact that food is one of the only base human needs where the private market alone dictates its delivery to our communities. When we build a new city, the public sector works to make sure that certain needs are met safely and affordably: roads, water, electricity, telephones. But, for reasons that are just beginning to be publicly questioned, America has traditionally done nothing to make sure there is also food in that new city. Food deserts are one result of this agnostic approach to food distribution, and as a city of 700,000 without a single national grocer, Detroit has become that problem's reluctant (and in some ways undeserving) poster child. I lived there, commuting to a suburban Walmart—just as, I presumed, anyone living there might do for grocery shopping. The longer I stayed, the more I came to see that Detroit has as many lessons to teach us as problems to solve.

More than an investigation, though, this is also a book about how food works in our lives, how priorities around health and convenience and cost shift when resources are tight—and what we won't compromise on even when they are. Truthfully, it's mostly about how food worked, for a period of time, in *my* life, but it also traces the contours of the lives and meals of the people with whom I lived and worked. When I began this project, I was aware that much of the difference between myself and America's working poor had less to do with economics than education and geography. My life as a writer is flexible, giving me the ability to take extra time with my shopping. I belong, by virtue of geography and free time, to a cooperative grocery store, which keeps my food both affordable and of unusually high quality. I work from home, so I can cook throughout the day—and doing so is easy for me, since I started learning to cook around age seven. I am also a childless adult, free to eat whatever I want, whenever I feel like it. Even before considering income, my daily food reality is very different from what's available to most Americans whose incomes match, or fall beneath, mine.

That's a polite way of saying I believed that the way I thought about food was so deeply removed from the "rest" of America that it would be foreign—inapplicable, even—once I gave up the few rungs I'd gained on the class ladder, and particularly if I descended a few more. Implicit in that is the idea that the food culture I had chosen for myself was not only different from, but a little bit superior to, the others on offer throughout America's kitchens. Like most armors, this hubris protected me from feeling as if I didn't know what I was doing—something most of us need from time to time, and almost always when we leave home behind. But it also obscured my view and limited my movement. Eventually, I had to strip myself of it, and try to look at the world in a new way, asking the question, *What would it take for us all to eat well?*

I didn't know; there's no way I could have. But, luckily, I'm a reporter. What I don't know, I can go find out.

PART I

❦

FARMING

WAGES
Hourly, weeding and gleaning: $8.00
Per 20-pound flat of grapes: $2.00
Per 5 gallons of garlic: $1.60

POST-TAX INCOME
Weekly: $204
Annually: $10,588

FOOD BILL
Daily: $7.44
Weekly: $52.06
Annually: $2,707

PERCENTAGE OF INCOME SPENT ON FOOD
All food: 25.6%
Food at home: 11.8%
Eating out: 13.8%

CHAPTER 1

Grapes

By the time I meet Pilar, I've already spent a week looking for work, venturing out in increasing radii from the cheap hotel where I've holed up in Bakersfield. I've met with an organizer from the United Farm Workers, outside a rural gas station, to get the phone numbers of foremen. I've met with a community advocate, Felix, whose job entails helping farmworkers in one of the towns outside the city: recouping back wages, finding health care, and otherwise negotiating rural poverty. I've driven up and down the highway looking for onion crews to no avail, hindered by my ignorance of, in descending order, what an onion field looks like, how many people might be on a crew, and basic local geography. In every instance, I have been unable to find work in the fields of California's Central Valley. Accordingly, I've begun to feel the first strains of desperation that precede failure.

Pilar lives in the dusty trailer next door to the one I move into after a week in a hotel. I meet her in exactly the manner that had been suggested to me by Felix: I walk out my front door, go to the nearest trailer, and say hello.

When I come up to the yard, it's not Pilar but Alejandro, with whom she shares two children, who greets me. He and a boy are talking in the driveway, a narrow spit of gravel that leads to a black pickup, a grove of clotheslines, and, finally, a chain-link fence thick with vines. Beyond it lies another street of trailers holding the line against endless fields of grapes and almonds, and thirty miles beyond that a hot sun lowers itself toward the mountains at the valley's edge. Near the pickup, a diminutive woman paces under scraggly trees, a cordless phone clutched to her head. Her hair, knotted on her head in a series of loops, looks impossibly long.

Hi! I say, in Spanish, over the fence at the edge of their yard. I wave. I smile. The woman doesn't notice me, but Alejandro and the boy look up. I smile harder.

I'm Tracie. Alejandro looks startled by my Spanish, but recovers quickly and introduces himself and his son, Sergio. We begin conversing in Spanish. I explain that I am staying in the trailer next door, and when they nod as if this is reasonable, I add that I am looking for work in the fields and need to find a job quickly.

Alejandro raises his eyebrows and tells me his wife is a *mayordoma,* a forewoman, in grapes.

I try to maintain a measured voice. *Does she need workers?*

He nods, and dispatches Sergio to bring Pilar over. Sergio tugs at her arm, and she lowers the phone to listen to him. Then she looks at me and promptly bursts into laughter. She comes over.

You want to work in the fields?

Pilar looks at me over the fence, her eyes friendly but baffled. I try to smile naturally, as if there must be many white girls speaking stilted Spanish looking for work in California fields alongside indigenous Mexican immigrants. Then I try to project an air of economic desperation. *Yes, I am looking for work in the fields. Do you need workers?*

She pauses and looks me up and down again. *Why don't you apply for a job?*

I shake my head, taking this to mean applying for a job in a store or an office. *I don't want to have to talk to people. I have a lot of problems right now, and I just want to work hard and not think.*

Today is a Sunday, the only day most farmworkers here have off, so the park and its forty-odd trailers buzz with small-town activity. Mexican *banda* and *ranchera* music float down the street, mixed with hip-hop in Spanish; families are cooking meat and warming tortillas over heavy metal grills in their yards; little kids are playing soccer in the street, using speed bumps for goals.

I smile sheepishly and repeat my story over the low din behind me: *No, I want to work in the fields. I need to work hard so I don't have to think.*

OK, says Pilar. *I will have work the day after tomorrow or the day after that. Do you have scissors?*

I shake my head.

I can loan you some. Do you have gloves?

Yes!

What kind? Cotton or leather?

Leather.

Pilar shakes her head as if scolding a silly child. *I'll give you some cotton ones. Talk to me tomorrow, when I'll know if there is work.*

Thank you very much! I say, smiling, punch drunk on my luck. *Thank you! This is great. I will talk to you tomorrow.*

You're going to have to bring lunch, she adds firmly. Then her tone softens: *And we're neighbors—let us know if you need anything.*

Of course, you too, I say as I begin walking back home. Then Sergio calls out.

Wait! he says, in English. She wants to ask you something.

I turn back, and Pilar smiles shyly. *Maybe you can help me with my English?*

Of course! I'm not a teacher, but I can try to help. She smiles broadly, and we make plans to study the next night.

I say my goodbyes and float home, buoyed by the fact that I have not only just found farmwork but maybe friends, too.

My world, and thus my sources of food, now consists of three municipalities and the trailer park. My trailer is in a tiny rural town whose commercial tenants are limited to an intersection with a concrete block of a corner grocery, a taquería, and a gas station. Ten minutes away sits a slightly larger town, this one with a single main street, two strip malls, and a larger grocery store. Forty minutes past the town is Bakersfield, a city with a university, courthouses, a swath of corporate farm offices and a range of supermarkets. Before I moved to the trailer, Maria Vasquez, the paralegal whose parents have loaned me their trailer while visiting family in Mexico, offered me advice: Go grocery shopping in Bakersfield, at Foods Maxx.

So on my way out of town, I stopped at the discount grocer, which resembled a Mexican-themed Costco. My flour, bread, eggs, cilantro, tomatillos, tomatoes, peaches, lemons, and limes came to $10.34. The Vasquez family also left me some squash and watermelon, a basket of onions, and a half-full five-gallon jug of drinking water.*

---

* Most people in the area—at the southern end of the San Joaquin Valley, the southern half of the Central Valley—drank from five-gallon jugs they filled up at dispensing stations in parking lots and at grocery stores. Tap water there comes from groundwater, which is particularly vulnerable to nitrate contamination from fertilizers that percolate into the aquifer. (Cowan 2005) In 2007, three-quarters of violations of nitrate levels in California drinking water occurred in the San Joaquin Valley. (Ward et al. 2005) The Community Water Center, a nonprofit advocacy group based in the agricultural county of Tulare, found that valley residents spend up to ten percent of their income on water, five times the "affordable" limit set by the Environmental Protection Agency. (Community Water Center 2011)

From the outside, the trailer nearly resembles a house, with the carport and back porch on the north side and an addition and porch on the south. Its exterior is two-tone orange and white, the facilities basic. There's a narrow galley kitchen, a combination living/dining room that holds the refrigerator. There are three bedrooms and a large, clean bathroom that would be unremarkable except that the toilet tank is covered by a scrap of plywood and the floor buckles slightly under my weight. Some of the windows don't quite fit their frames, the back door sits high enough over the threshold that beetles scurry inside at will, and all the locks are flimsy, but I remind myself that a farmworkers' trailer park would be a poorly chosen target for robbery.

I turn on the swamp cooler to fight the heat that's baking the roof and soak some beans while I make a green salsa. I've only recently started cooking Latin American food, and this salsa is a simple one that I cribbed from a woman I lived with in Guatemala while studying Spanish; I had been thrilled by her tangy version and begged for the recipe, though "recipe" is overstating it—there was no card or cookbook, just the mixture she'd been throwing together forever.

After making the salsa, I sort through my handmade vocabulary cards for learning Spanish; any words I am confident about, I set aside to give Pilar. At around six, our appointed time, I knock on Pilar's trailer door. Nobody answers, and I am surprised at how disappointed I am. I leave her a note saying I stopped by.

A while later there is a knock at my trailer's door, a mom and her kids looking for Maria's mother, Andrea. She's surprised to hear they're gone, but walks off unfazed; she'll come back later.

The same story repeats itself later as dusk falls, and just as darkness overtakes the twilight, there's a knock at the door again. I open it to find a hunched, older woman with a plastic grocery bag. She's looking for Andrea, too.

No, I'm sorry, she went to Oaxaca to see her mother. Can I help you?

She's gone? Julio, too?

Yes, I'm sorry. I'm a friend of Maria.

She doesn't let me finish. *I brought these green beans for them. Do you want them?*

I look at the bag, bulging with several pounds of string beans.

You don't want them?

She shakes her head. *I picked them today in the fields, we took some. I can't eat all of it.*

Me neither, I say. She looks appalled, so I backtrack: *But I can take a little.*

Do you have a bag? she asks. She's very organized, this woman.

I do—inside—so I pull out a few handfuls of beans and drop them into a bag. *Thank you so much!*

No, take more! she says, forcibly adding beans to my bag. I manage to stop her around the halfway mark. I have no idea what I'll do with all these beans. I don't even *like* green beans.

That's enough for me, I say cheerfully, rapidly twisting the bag to prevent any unwanted additions. *Thank you so much. How do you know Andrea and Julio?*

Andrea is my cousin. When are Andrea and Julio back?

Maria told me two weeks.

She nods, makes a little huffing noise that sounds like approval, and turns to leave.

Thank you for the beans, I say, holding my bag aloft. She doesn't say anything, just waves her hand in the air as she closes the gate and walks into the dark.

Pilar doesn't show up, and I go to bed worrying that I've somehow missed my chance, but in the morning Sergio knocks on my door. Across the yard I can see Pilar watching from her doorstep as her son explains, in fluent English, that there is work tomorrow. Since we couldn't study last night, maybe I can come over tonight for an English lesson, and Pilar can talk to me about work?

I barely notice the quid pro quo at work, charmed by Pilar's mix of chutzpah and bashfulness. Of course, I say, relieved that my day of anxious unemployment has been transformed into a day off. By the time I go to bed that night, I'll have handed over a stack of vocabulary cards to Pilar, borrowed cotton gloves, and gotten my marching orders. I'm to report to the corner of Panama and Tejon at 5:30 a.m. sharp. I should bring my own lunch. Pilar will bring me the tools I'll need.

Cars are already creeping through the trailer park when I rise at 4:45 the next morning, just in time to hear Pilar's truck pull out of the driveway next door. Even at this early hour, the sky is fading from black to deep blue in the east, the Sierra Nevadas a dark silhouette against it. I throw the burritos I made last night into my cooler, along with two water bottles I'd frozen and a big water jug.

I am out the door at 5:15 and head east toward the dawn, careening over shoulderless two-lane roads crowded with farmworkers.* Nobody is at the appointed intersection, so I drive past it to a line of trucks and realize they're for the workers already in the field to my right: Bulging burlap sacks line up like soldiers, and white orbs litter the ground, nearly glowing in the early light. Onions. I turn around and go back to Panama and Tejon, and this time Pilar is waiting for me. She signals for me to follow her and we drive farther east, pull off the road, and wait. For twenty minutes I sit there, listening to the rapid-fire Spanish of Radio Campesina, a station run by the United Farm Workers, and watching Pilar and the woman she's carpooling with fix their work clothes. The woman riding with Pilar takes off her ball cap, folds a bandana in half diagonally and ties it over her nose and mouth. Then she folds a second bandana in half, into a rectangle, ties two corners together, and settles the narrow circle over the crown of her head. Then she puts her hat over all of it.

The sun is starting to rim the top of the mountains in gold, the sky above them turning to a silvery blue. More cars pull up behind me. A short, pony-tailed man with a Yankees cap and a Detroit Lions sweatshirt walks past my car to Pilar's. They talk for a while, and he looks at me questioningly—irrationally, I slink lower in my seat—then returns to his own car. Finally, around six, a big pickup pulling a trailer filled with hand trucks pulls up. This is the signal. Brake lights burn red, headlights switch on, and our caravan heads east, past oranges and grapes and almonds, down Panama Road, heading toward the mountains. Just as the sun crests the hills, turning the tops of the vines from deep green to chartreuse, we hang a right onto a road of washboard ridges. We turn down a lane, driving into the grape field, and when the truck finally stops, we all get out.

There is a flurry of activity. Men help the truck driver pull the hand trucks off the trailer, along with stacks of shallow plastic bins. Pilar helps me tie my bandanas properly; the extra layer of fabric makes my hat tight

---

* From 1994 to 1999, sixty-four farmworkers died while riding in farm labor transportation vehicles, leading Congress to appropriate $4 million to support licensed bus and group transport in 2000. Nonetheless, many workers carpool. Two years after Congress approved group transport funding, 42 percent of all farmworkers nationwide rode with others or with a *raitero*, someone who informally operates a taxi service to the fields, often a supervisor or fellow worker; carpooling was much more common among foreign-born newcomers, 77 percent of whom shared rides in 2001–2002. (Agricultural Worker Health Project 2011; U.S. Department of Labor, Office of the Assistant Secretary for Policy, and Office of Programmatic Policy 2005)

against my skull. Then she affixes her own: a pink gingham affair in which the hair cover and face mask neatly Velcro together, giving the appearance of a cheerful burka from the neck up. She wears a broad-brimmed straw hat, and I worry that my ball cap will be insufficient. Then she sets up a folding shade tent and a single Igloo cooler. And then: Nothing. We loiter. We are waiting for the containers to pack the grapes into, and until they arrive there's no sense in picking.

We wait nearly two hours, until eight o'clock, which gives everyone ample time to observe my presence. I had hoped that my bandanas would help me blend in; save for the sliver of face around my eyes, every inch of skin is covered, and my hair and eyes are both dark brown. But I still spend most of these idle hours explaining to them what I'd told Pilar: I need work, I have problems, I don't like working with customers, I'd prefer to be outside.

The tall, broad-shouldered man driving the truck and trailer, Pilar explains as we wait, is José, our *contratista*—farm labor contractor. Pilar works for him, recruiting workers to her crew and organizing basic support for them—water, shade—in exchange for a small premium. José has most likely been hired by Giumarra, one of the country's largest grape growers, to harvest the grapes. These are Giumarra fields, but while Giumarra is colloquially referred to as the grower, in industry-speak, the company is a grower-packer-shipper, a corporate entity that grows some kinds of food and handles the shipment and transport of others. This arrangement differs with every kind of produce, owing to the vast differences between crops. Grapes are usually grown and harvested by the company that sells them, an arrangement that makes sense with a long-term investment like a vineyard. Tended well, a vineyard will bear fruit for twenty-five years or more, giving growers a strong incentive to oversee production as closely as possible. Because grapes require a long-term investment, growers are more vulnerable to labor unrest. When Cesar Chavez and Dolores Huerta organized strikes in the 1970s, growers couldn't afford to rip out vineyards, or go a season without harvest. Timed well, a strike could threaten a grower with losing an entire season's crop and watching it rot on the vine. By contrast, annual vegetables, such as spinach, represent only a year's investment; a grower's success is therefore less dependent on skilled tending, and also represents a smaller long-term investment.

Pilar explains to me that we're here today because the grapes are nearly ripe enough for a full-on harvest, but Giumarra wants to make sure that they're ready. I don't know how frequently Giumarra brings in outside workers instead of the ones they've hired directly, but today they've brought in a farm labor contracting company to handle the harvest—represented, in this case, by José.*

I'm just beginning to contemplate forming the sentences in Spanish to ask Pilar what she gets for being a forewoman—the premiums vary, usually an incrementally higher wage along with the promise of more hours—when José gets a phone call. The packing boxes will be here shortly. We can start.

José leads us down a row, rolling up the sleeves of his button-down shirt, and walks maybe twenty yards before kneeling. We follow suit, falling to our knees at the base of gnarled vines as thick as my thigh, a leafy canopy blooming three or four feet over our heads. Taut bunches of grapes dangle down the center of the arch in a neat line. José reaches up and snips off a bunch with his *tijeras,* or pruning shears. These are going to be table grapes, he tells us efficiently, so they have to look good. We have to hold them gently, so that we do not bruise them or put fingerprints on them. We are to cut out the green ones, *verdes—snip*—the small ones, *chiquitas—snip*—and the rotten ones, *podridas—snip.* Does everyone understand? Everyone does. And then there is another burst of activity as everyone disperses. I spend a moment looking around before Pilar comes over and tells me that I will work with her and Juán, the ponytailed guy in the Lions sweatshirt.

Here are some cotton gloves, she says, handing them to me. *And your scissors. Are you ready to start?*

I think so, I say tentatively.

Oh, Tracie, she laughs. *Let's go.*

Pilar hands me a plastic tray. She and I will pick the grapes, and Juán will collect our bins using the hand trucks and pack them at a table at the end of the row, under a sun umbrella. She motions for me to get under the

---

* Using farm labor contractors, who in part play the same role for farmers that overseas factories play for clothing brands, became more popular with California growers in the 1970s after farmworkers began demanding higher wages. Today, between 50 and 60 percent of California farmers make use of contracted labor for at least part of their labor needs, with small farms spending more than half their labor budget on subcontracted labor, compared with about one-third of large farms. (Bon Appétit Management Company Foundation and United Farm Workers 2011) Workers for contractors typically make lower wages than do those employed directly by farms (Martin 2011b), but migrant workers may find themselves vulnerable to far worse situations: In September 2010, the U.S. Department of Justice filed the largest human trafficking case in American history against Global Horizons, a Los Angeles–based labor contracting company, for its treatment of four hundred agricultural workers in Washington and Hawaii. The conditions faced by those workers, wrote the *New York Times* editorial page, constituted "slavery without shackles."(*New York Times* 2011)

vines, then positions herself about fifteen feet farther down the row. *Are you ready?* she asks.

Maybe, I say dubiously, fear of failure suddenly streaking through me, and she laughs again as she clips a bunch of grapes off the vine. I turn away, reach up, cradle a bunch of grapes in my palm, and with a satisfying snip sever the tendril attaching it to the vine. I eye the bunch, tightly knotted in on itself, in my hand. I see a green grape peering out from behind a red one. I pilot the *tijeras* in, snip, and promptly pierce the skin of the red grape next to it. Juice soaks into my glove. Now I have to get rid of the red one and the green one as well. I try again, aiming for the now-damaged red grape, and hit a third grape instead. Frustration wells up in my chest, and I try to remember that I am learning. Slowly, so very, very slowly, I trim the bunch, lay it gently into the bin, and snip another from the vine.

I have been doing this for about a half-hour when José walks by, fingers the fruit in my bin and stops me.

Mira, look, he says, taking out a pair of *tijeras. Like this. No little ones, no rotten ones. Throw them out.* He picks up a bunch from my bin and snips into it efficiently. Grapes fly. Stems snap. He finishes, and holds up a finely draped, flawless bunch of grapes. It belongs on the cover of *Bon Appétit,* or maybe a wine label. *See? These are for the table, so they have to be nice.*

I nod and smile and try to figure out how to say "I understand how to do it, it's just that I suck at it," in Spanish, but before I can say anything José has moved on, and I see him give Pilar an approving nod as he fingers *her* grapes. I look at my bin: José's bunch sits atop a layer of grape bunches composed primarily of scraggly stems haphazardly ornamented with fruit.

It doesn't take long before I am cursing the entitled American grocery shopper: *Oh, sure, you just* have *to have a perfect bunch of grapes. God forbid you should have to pick out a few Raisinettes. You think those nice pretty bunches grow on trees?* The labels on the plastic cartons for the grapes are green and fancy, emblazoned with the name Nature's Partner—a brand, I later find out, of Giumarra Vineyards. By midday, I get more comfortable, and I admire the tight, trim bunches as I snip them off the main vine, surprised to find that their stems knot in on themselves so firmly that each bunch feels like a solid mass, so different from the loose, languorous piles of grapes in the supermarket. I find my rhythm and pick up speed. I get cocky and compare my speed with Pilar's. But she works twice as fast. Where her bins overflow with fruit, mine contain a prim, solitary layer. I try to speed up.

Through it all, Pilar and I chat a little, or I listen to her talk to other workers in Spanish. Some of them ask her about me, and more than once I interrupt their speculations on me—Am I a student? Just poor?—with *I can understand you. I cannot speak well, but I understand a lot,* which yields laughter. Later, I ask Pilar if we'll have work tomorrow, and she says she doesn't think so; the grapes aren't really sweet enough, they need to grow for another week. She must see my face fall because she asks if I want to do some other work tomorrow.

What kind of work?

Selling food in the fields, she says.

Maybe, I say. *Let's talk about it later.*

Toward the end of the day, Pilar shifts me onto packing duty, and I stand at a makeshift tabletop at the end of the row. I'm supposed to take the grapes from the bins and pack them into the plastic containers they will be sold in. I grab a handsome, taut bauble of grapes and place it in the container. Its firm, conical shape doesn't fit. I move it around, to no avail. I look around guiltily and cram the top down, squashing a few grapes, and place it quickly in a *caja.* Juán looks at me and, almost imperceptibly, rolls his eyes.

Look, says Pilar, grasping a bunch of grapes from one of her towering bins and laying it gently in a plastic container. The stems, cut loose and separate, accommodatingly curl into place, filling the box as if they had been poured in a liquid stream. Those tight clusters I'd admired as I laid them into the bins? Disastrous for packing. Pilar, I now realize, has been doing more than removing *chiquitas* with rapid-fire precision; she's also been untangling the stems of each bunch. It's as if she had been handed a knotted ball of rope and with a few quick nips and tucks, opened it to reveal a patch of intricate lace.

I want to apologize and walk off the field, stop wasting their time. I wait for Pilar to take me aside and politely explain that she won't be needing my help again. I decide that when the moment comes, I'll shake my head in embarrassment and accept my fate quietly.

But no.

Around 3:30, we finish packing up the last of the grapes we have picked in our row, and Pilar tells me to stop. *You worked very hard. Good job,* she says. *I'll pay you next week.* Juán barely conceals a glare. We have spent the last nine and a half hours in the field, all but the first two hunched under the green-roofed tunnels of grapevines. Pilar finally explains the specifics of our payment.

Ten of the plastic clamshell boxes fit in a cardboard *caja,* a flat, and for every *caja* the three of us fill, we earn $2. We count our haul for the day:

thirty-nine *cajas*. That's $78 divided by three: $26 apiece. We've been at work since 6:00 a.m. There was a half-hour lunch. Nine hours for $26.

I swallow nervously and ask how many *cajas* each worker usually fills in a day and Pilar tells me thirty. By working with me, then, my crew just lost a collective $42, more than half of what we earned. I try to fix it.

No, it's not fair to you and José. I am learning, so I should get less. I don't have kids. It's not fair to you.

Juán pipes up. *She's right.*

Pilar is undeterred. *No, Tracie, it's fine. You worked very hard.*

Pilar.

We'll see. Good work.

Juán sighs and lopes off to help another crew pack their boxes, but Pilar keeps smiling at me. *Go on, I'll see you later,* she says. As the *mayordoma,* she has to stay until everyone finishes.

Thank you very much, Pilar, I say, and climb into my car. There's only one word to define what just happened: *charity.* And I know I am in no position to refuse it.

As a farmworker, I do not have the same rights that I have when I work in an office. Under federal labor laws, I have no right to days off; I have no right to overtime pay; I have no right to collective bargaining.* I am lucky to be in California, though. The same way that each state can raise the local minimum wage above the federal standard, states can extend greater labor protections to farmworkers—and California has some of the country's strongest laws to protect them. Here, I have the right to a union; I must be given time for lunch each day and a day off every week; I am entitled to workers' compensation if I am injured on the job. All of this is by virtue of the fact that I am in California instead of, say, Texas.

Back when California decided to extend these protections to farmwork-

---

* Legislators excluded farmworkers, along with domestic workers—jobs that, in the East, had historically been the work of slaves and freed blacks—from the 1934 National Labor Relations Act, which established American workers' right to bargain collectively, and from the 1938 Fair Labor Standards Act, which established the minimum wage, as part of the political horse-trading required to get the laws passed. Until 1980, farmworkers had no federal right to the minimum wage. Since then, most—though not all—farmworkers being paid by piece are required by law to earn minimum wage. If I am unable to earn $8 an hour at piece rate, for example, my employer is required to pay me the difference—although they are free to fire me for my poor performance as well. (Martin 2011b; Marshall 1981; Bon Appétit Management Company Foundation and the United Farm Workers 2011)

ers, one of the biggest concerns was whether they would increase the price of food. Higher wages do change the price of food, but rarely as much as people fear they will. That's because, even for produce, most of the price tag at the store pays for the system that moves it from place to place—not the wages in the field. From a farm field, produce might go to a plant where food is stored or processed, or even directly to a store; the grapes I picked were packed directly into the cartons they were sold in, for example, so they'd either be kept cool in storage or shipped out immediately.

Usually, boxes of grapes that are packed in the field go directly to a cooling facility while the company figures out where to send them. They might go to produce brokers who buy from the farmer and sell to wholesalers, who in turn sell to other wholesalers or directly to supermarkets. Or, if the grower has a direct contract with a supermarket, they'll deliver it to one of the chain's distribution centers, where the produce is transferred to stores. All of that—the brokers' haggling over prices, the calmer negotiations between wholesalers, the advance contracts with supermarkets—adds cost at every step. By the time an apple ends up in the supermarket, the entire cost of growing it accounts for just about 16 percent of the price, while the other 84 percent goes to the complex infrastructure that got it there, what industry experts call marketing.

So if the farmer is only getting 16 percent of what we pay for food, what share is being paid to me, the worker in the field? Different crops have different needs; delicate fruit like peaches and raspberries, for instance, take more hand labor than something like onions or potatoes. (And most fruits and vegetables, when grown organically, take even more hand labor, since human hands take the place of weed killers.*) Generally, though, farm wages for much of our food are a very small fraction of what we pay at the store. Today, if you pay a dollar for a pound of apples or a head of lettuce in the supermarket, only about six cents covers the farmwork used to get it there; increasing farm wages by 40 percent would increase the average American family's produce bill by about sixteen dollars a year. The wages

---

* Broad studies comparing the labor costs of conventional and organic agriculture are just beginning to be done regularly by major research institutions such as UC-Davis. The most recent research shows that, typically, any crop that is harvested or weeded by hand in conventional agriculture will expand its use of hand labor when herbicides are removed from the process. The hand labor required to produce an acre of organic tomatoes, for instance, is triple that required for conventional; organic strawberries require more than twice as much hand labor as conventional; and the labor required for organic broccoli is nearly double that required for conventional. (Klonsky 2011)

my co-workers and I are earning could easily be higher without imposing ridiculous prices on shoppers. So why aren't they?

Mostly, wages are so low because growers don't have any reason to raise them. For one thing, any grower who hires a farm labor contractor like the company José and Pilar work for doesn't have any legal obligation to me or any of the other workers; that's the contractor's business, not theirs. What's more, labor law enforcement typically relies on complaints—people coming in and making a fuss over not having been paid. There are not, contrary to my initial belief, inspectors patrolling the fields to verify that the proper wages are being paid.* So far as I can tell, most of the workers I'm with are undocumented, giving them a compelling reason to keep quiet. Workers with the legal status to work here might be more prone to make a fuss, but if they did, growers might do what they've always done when the threat of higher wages looms: use machines instead.

Take the example of lettuce in the early 1960s. A notorious federal guest worker initiative that guaranteed growers a cheap labor supply called the bracero program was set to expire. The end of bracero threatened growers with the prospect of hiring local workers who would require higher wages—if they could even convince local workers to work in the fields at all. So growers and researchers at the University of California's agricultural extension office began developing robotic lettuce harvesters that would have done away with human labor in lettuce almost entirely. But in 1964, growers and their allies won changes to immigration policy that codified the presence of immigrant workers in the United States outside of a guest worker program. With a supply of cheap labor guaranteed, research on the harvester stopped, and the lettuce companies went back to paying pickers what they'd always been paying them.

Today, labor's become a primary concern all over again. "Every time the unions raised their flags, the growers and shippers looked at better ways to

---

* Workplaces are rarely subject to surprise inspections for wage and hour violations, primarily because the system revolves around complaints; inspectors seldom conduct investigations unless someone makes a formal complaint with the Labor Department—although surprise inspections for heat violations have increased in recent years. This is a function, in part, of the number of inspectors in comparison with the number of workplaces. In 2010, the state of California employed 48 inspectors in the state's wage and hour division at the Department of Labor, and another 395 people conducted similar work in the California Occupational Safety and Health Administration, for a total of 443 inspectors statewide. That year, among the state's 1.3 million workplaces—81,500 of which were farms—the agencies' combined staff conducted 16,169 inspections, hitting one in eighty workplaces. (Chasarik 2011; California Employment Development Department 2010).

harvest the crop," Frank Maconachy explains to me later. A board member of the Western Growers' Association—an industry group for agribusinesses and farms in California—Maconachy is also president of Ramsay Highlander, an agricultural manufacturer that introduced a mechanized lettuce harvesting machine in 2008. Growers and shippers, he says, "are tired of dealing with the labor . . . You have to put umbrellas out there and to have enough water out there, and it's impossible for someone to consume that much water—they would drown." And that's driving big growers to look at machines. The jet-stream lettuce harvester retails for about $650,000, but would make up for its cost, says Maconachy, in about thirteen months.

Once growers do make the switch to mechanization, it changes the whole equation. Fields have to be planted differently, to accommodate the machines—easy in most vegetables, which get replanted each year, but tricky for fruit trees or vineyards. Jobs dealing with the simple (though not easy) task of harvesting disappear, while more are created for machine operators and sorters. Machines do not get tired, and they can work through the night, so harvesting can be done more quickly. Both speed and productivity rise. When the bracero program ended, tomato growers and agricultural researchers set out to develop a machine to harvest the fruit for processing in the 1960s. With hand labor, it took more than five and a half hours to pick one ton of tomatoes, eating up nearly half the production costs; thirty-five years later, it took just twenty-four minutes to pick one ton of tomatoes—and labor was only 12 percent of production costs. Every acre produced more, too. Growers got twenty tons from every acre in 1965, but by 2000 were getting thirty-three tons from the same amount of land. There are certain trade-offs made in the process. Agricultural researchers had to develop a breed of tomato that could withstand machine harvesting, selecting for traits like durability and an ability to ripen well after being picked, rather than flavor. Fewer workers were getting paid for harvesting—though some jobs, usually better-paid, did open up for machine operators and sorters. But the work for those crews of sweating men, bent over and picking tomatoes from vines and putting them into buckets, running to the crates to dump them out? That all disappeared.

The new jobs in sorting and machine operating come with better pay, so labor costs don't disappear; they just shift toward fewer, higher-paid jobs. And the increased productivity means that there is more work to be done when it comes to packing, sorting, and transporting food. Prices at the store did go down—but by much less than you might expect. Between 1960 and 1997, efficiency in harvesting skyrocketed, with the time required to harvest a ton of tomatoes dropping by more than three-quarters. Prices at the supermarket dropped, too—but not by anywhere near as much. From 1960 to 1998, the cost of a can of tomatoes dropped by 43 cents, from $1.21 to $0.72. Yet the majority of those savings didn't come from the farm. For every can of tomatoes sold in 1998, farmers earned 9 cents less than they had forty years before. The other 34 cents in savings came from the marketing system responsible for everything that happened after tomatoes left the farms where they were grown. Lower field costs saved us a little money, but it was efficiencies in transportation and retailing and processing that really made tomatoes cheaper for us.

I know that mechanizing the fields comes with great, perhaps even untenable, risks: greater reliance on fossil fuels, the compacting of soil, the loss of jobs. But at $26 a day, I can't help but think, *Go ahead, mechanize my damn job,* because it's not just hard, but I suspect it will become boring, too, as the physical challenge loses its novelty. But that's the thoughtless luxury of a woman with an education talking: Even if I'm in the fields for now, I know I can go elsewhere. No, if I were really stuck here working in the fields, I wouldn't want machines. I'd want to know why, if the cost of food is such a great concern, we don't focus on figuring out how to make marketing cheaper. And I'd want to know why, if my wages don't change retail price much, I couldn't just get paid better ones.

When Pilar invited me to sell food to farmworkers with her, my assumption was that we would sell lunches. This sounded like a luxurious option: Cook at night, sleep in until 7:00, roll out around 8:00, hit the lunch hour at 9:00. Then Pilar explains to me that sales start around 5:30 in the morning, because that is when onion pickers finish their shifts.

Why onions? I ask her, standing on her steps. Surely there were crops with a later mealtime. *What about people in grapes? Or carrots?*

Pilar reminds me that there isn't any work in grapes, which is why we are selling food in the first place. And besides, she adds, it's only worthwhile to sell food to onion pickers because the crews are huge, maybe eighty or ninety people, and there are crews that work overnight. By morning everyone is hungry and willing to spend a little of the cash they are paid at the end of the shift. If you show up with a real Mexican breakfast—quarts of *avena,* milky oatmeal so thin you can drink it, sprinkled with cinnamon;

soft flour tortillas rolled around spongy pork *chicharrones* spiked with red chilies and jalapeños; hot coffee steaming in the morning damp—you can turn a profit.

I ask what I should make. I hope she wants to show me how to cook something. I also hope she doesn't expect me to do it at three in the morning.

You can sell soda! she says triumphantly, offering to loan me a small, handled cooler on wheels. She promptly dispatches Sergio to accompany me to the grocery store in town to make sure I buy the right sodas. It's a quick trip, and as we drive I thank Sergio for translating between me and his mom when my Spanish fails. He shrugs. He tells me he tries to help as much as he can and then proudly tells me he has been working in the fields with his mom for about three years now, since he was eight, usually during the raisin harvest later in the summer, when *contratistas* will let kids come in and help their folks.* The big companies won't let him work, he scowls, but the *contratistas* will. He helps his mom sell food in the fields, too, which is more interesting than sitting at home.

At the grocery store we begin eyeing soda specials. Sugar and caffeine are what people want in the fields. With Sergio's help, I decide on a mix of Pepsi, Mountain Dew, and Gatorade. I spend $25 on three cases and thank Sergio, planning to charge $1 for sodas and $1.50 for Gatorades. If I sell everything, I'll make about $23 in profit, nearly what I made picking grapes.

This is how I find myself scrunched into the fold-down chair behind the passenger seat of Pilar's pickup at 5:30 a.m. She and Sergio, who've been cooking since 3:00 a.m., are in the front, and I'm pressed into the corner, staring out the window at the fields racing by: almonds, cherries, onions, grapes, carrots, watermelons. Radio Campesina plays as we look for San Clemente Road. Half the roads splitting off the highway are signless, and we do a series of U-turns trying to pinpoint our turnoff, tension mounting

---

* Conservative estimates put the share of farmworkers under age eighteen at 9 percent, although this excludes those employed by farm labor contractors. Typically, child farmworkers start working adult hours during summers, on weekends, and after school around age eleven or twelve, with some starting on a part-time basis much earlier. As of late 2011, U.S. law allowed children of all ages to work on small farms with parental permission; at age twelve, children can work on any farm with parental consent; and after age fourteen they can work regardless of parental consent. There are no limits on the number of hours children may work in agriculture. Outside of agriculture, children are not allowed to work until age sixteen, with a handful of very specific and highly time-restricted exceptions. (Human Rights Watch 2010)

because we're racing against sunrise. Once the sun's heat starts to penetrate the valley, the crews will start to pack up and leave. In desperation, Pilar calls her cousin who's working in onions, and learns that we need to turn onto Meyer Road, which we've passed several times.

Ten minutes later we're rolling along a broad path between massive tracts of land that stretch for the length of many, many football fields. The ground is striped with endless rows of thigh-high burlap sacks, bulging with onions, emblazoned with the words Cal-Organic; we're in an organic field.

Pilar slows to a crawl, rolls down her window, and starts calling out to the workers: *Tacos! Avena! Soditas!*

No one looks up from their perches atop overturned construction buckets. Men and women wield scissors with blades that seem to approach a foot in length. I see one woman—a girl, really—in a Mickey Mouse T-shirt grasp an onion by the greens and bear down on the scissors, hard, to cut off the stringy roots. Then she suspends the bulb over a bucket, her long maroon nails bright against the green of the stalk, and—*snip*—it drops in. Other workers are dumping mounded buckets into burlap sacks. It takes three buckets to fill one.

Tacos, soditas, avena! Véngase! We roll along for several minutes like this before anyone signals for us to stop. Two men, middle-aged, paunchy, with bushy mustaches and cowboy hats, approach the truck. Pilar turns off the engine, and we climb out. The men speak with Pilar in a blend of Spanish and some indigenous dialect, probably Mixtec. They are asking about me.

Is she your daughter? they ask Pilar, and I redden; we're only a couple years apart in age.

No, she says. *But she speaks Spanish, and she's helping me with English.* She smiles like a game show assistant displaying a prize. *She's very smart: she gave me cards to memorize words with.* I smile at the men, and now I want to prove to them that I'm as smart as Pilar says. So I start in with Spanish.

Hi, I say.

Hi, they say back, munching on their tacos. There's silence.

So, I say, nodding at the sacks, trying to affect a "come here often" casualness, *These are organic fields?*

They look at me oddly. *Yes.*

Is that better than regular fields?

Why would it be better?

Because there aren't any chemicals. Is the work better?

The shorter of the two snorts. *No chemicals, but it's the same. Ninety-nine cents for a bag of onions,* he says, nodding at the sacks.

It's not better to work in an organic field?

It's the same.

We pack up and move on to the other side of the field, where Porta-Pottys bearing the name Maui Harvesting sit in the sun; the workers have stopped and are gathered in a huddle to collect their pay. We park in the shade of an almond orchard across the road and Pilar takes up her cry: *Soditas, tacos, avena!*

I try to strike up conversations with our customers and learn that most of them sleep in their cars and often in the field to save on rent. Around here, they tell me, it's not bad for this kind of living; in a town an hour south, there are snakes and scorpions in the field. *It's better in Bakersfield,* they say.

Pilar sells out quickly, pocketing $38 for her work; she tells me she spent $25 on ingredients. But earning $13 for the day is better than nothing—it adds up. She'll have put in six or eight hours by the end of this, which puts her hourly wage—at best—at $2.17. When Pilar continues hypothesizing about whether she can replicate this morning's success with an evening run to the fields, I realize that she's not thinking about income in terms of whether an hour of work is worth the trouble; what matters only is that she's amassing additional income.

The sodas are not selling well, owing to the early hour and the shade in which we're currently sheltered; it's still cool out.* Pilar asks me how much I've sold, and I shrug: *Not much, but it's OK. You're finished,* I say.

Pilar shakes her head. *Let's go!*

We get back in the truck and Pilar, without explanation, drives to another onion field. The sun has begun to burn its way across the valley, and the sodas sell well. This is due less to my skills than the generosity of Sergio and Pilar, who watch my pathetic attempts to convincingly yell out *Soditas* for roughly one minute before they take over. The earth is soft, tilled into mounded rows, and walking through it is like crossing a dusty beach; Sergio takes the cooler from me and trundles through the dirt, calling out to the workers. When he finds a customer, he signals to me, and I dash over with change.

Pilar, you don't have to do this, I say during a lull, eyeing Sergio's pudgy

---

* Daily temperatures in the Central Valley can range by 30 degrees or more. In June, the average daily low in Bakersfield is 63.7 degrees; the high is 91.6. (National Climatic Data Center 2011)

little figure trolling across the field. *He's only eleven.*

She waves me away. *He's a good worker!* And now I remember Sergio telling me about his work in raisins; he probably works most summers. *No problem, we're friends,* she says. *He needs to know how to work.*

By the time we give up, I've pulled in $39 in the four or five hours we've been out. Of my $14 profit, I give Sergio $4; I ask him, in English, if his mom would take any money from me and he shakes his head no. In my head I calculate: With my remaining profit, I can buy another five gallons of water in town and some rice and beans.

We close out our morning by gathering up onions left behind by the harvest. The field is littered with them, pearly spheres scattered in the dirt, and we fill every receptacle in the truck bed we can. Pilar grabs an errant Cal-Organic bag off the ground, and we fill it to bursting; she'll share them with her cousins, she says.*

And, it now goes without saying, with me.

I stay in the trailer only a few more days, rooted not by paid work or entrepreneurial food sales, but by Pilar's generosity. I'd planned on using my time outside Bakersfield as a dry run, a means of getting oriented to farmwork before I truly started my reporting. I never intended to stay, if only because—as a reporter—I'm more interested in vegetables than grapes. But I've struck up a real friendship with Pilar, and I feel guilty leaving. Yet here I am, telling Pilar how I'm going to head north to Fresno because the Vasquez family is coming back, and I don't have a place to stay.

In Fresno, I say dramatically, as if I am talking about some glorious wonderland, *I have free housing.* This is technically true, for I've talked to the owner of an agricultural services company, located on an old ranch, who's willing to put me in touch with some farm labor contractors who are hiring for the season. They'll tell the contractors what I'm up to as a writer and, provided I don't name any companies in this round, they're fine with hiring me. And, because the company is headquartered on an old ranch, there's a

---

* The extent to which farmworkers depend on each other for survival may help explain Pilar's generosity with me (though I also believe she is simply a kind person). An emerging body of psychological and sociological research suggests that because the poor must rely on others to provide a range of needs that the wealthy can pay for, they are also more empathetic and have stronger social skills. Correspondingly, those in the upper-income bracket are found to be less capable of reading others' emotions and hence are less empathetic. (Paul 2011)

house where I can stay for a few days while I look for housing and work.

You can stay with me. I have a sofa, says Pilar. *It's no problem.*

I haven't toured Pilar's trailer extensively, but I'm pretty sure it has just two bedrooms, neither of them large, one shared by Pilar and her two kids, the other occupied by a boarder—a young woman who also works in the fields. The last thing she needs is another body crowding into the bathroom and kitchen.

No, better to head north and start over again. If I found work this easily here, how hard could it be to find it in Fresno?

CHAPTER 2

Peaches

My new boss, Constantino, meets us alongside Conejo Avenue, a two-lane road reaching from the interstate to a gravelly terminus in the fields. Orchards crowd the roadside, confining its asphalt interruption to a sliver, and that's where we stand, alongside Constantino's looming white pickup. He was waiting for us in the hazy morning heat, stationed at the end of a lane, unsigned, that snaked between peach groves. He doffed his hat when we met.

I followed Jorge from the old ranch, where the offices for his agricultural services company are located, this morning, getting on the road at daybreak. Through a series of personal connections—a reporter who knew a reporter who knew a farmer who knew a contractor—Jorge had agreed to help me find work. So now here I am, listening to Jorge and Constantino trade rapid Spanish, watching Constantino dump a water cooler full of peaches into Jorge's pickup—a gift. They speak too fast for me to get every word, but the basics come through loud and clear: Constantino knows I am writing about working in the fields, that I will not name any companies, and that I'll change everyone's name. In exchange, he'll give me work on a crew, pay me as he does the other workers, and not tell anyone that I am actually a writer. Jorge shook my hand, wished me luck and left me with my new boss.

Call me Tino, he tells me when Jorge leaves us, again touching the rim of his *sombrero tejido.* And follow me.*

We disappear into the trees and all I hear is the padding of our feet in the dirt before the sounds of the field begin to register. I hear more than I see: distant shouts, leaves rustling, engines chugging, the clatter of metal striking metal. The trees stretch up, filtering the sun, and I see that their branches are bound with rope, pulled into a conical shape, to keep them from falling

---

* *Sombrero tejido* directly translates to "woven hat," but is typically made of fine straw, resembling a Westernized version of a Panama hat.

over with fruit. Tino explains the work. I'll help to sort peaches with a *cuadrilla*, or crew, he says. We sidestep a ladder with a man atop it, both hands wildly darting into the leaves.

Tino goes on. It's hard work; I need to make sure to drink water; do I understand? *Thud*: The picker we just passed strides ahead of us, wearing some kind of bag slung over his front like a backwards backpack and heading up the row where two tractors with low-slung trailers sit. Dust clouds puff around his feet. He steps onto the running board of the farthest trailer, fidgets with his backpack and, *swoosh*, unleashes a stream of peaches into a giant crate. Sweat has already soaked through his long-sleeved T-shirt and the band of his backwards baseball cap. He barely glances at us as he hurries away.

We come to two tractors, each with a trailer holding four crates, and we stand to the side, clearing a path for the pickers. Tino introduces me to Victor, whose outfit matches Tino's: white *sombrero tejido*, neat button-down shirt taut over his belly, a tooled leather belt, cowboy boots. He extends his hand, rings heavy on his fingers. *Welcome*, he says. He checks his BlackBerry as he talks with Tino. Every few minutes another man, sweaty and covered in a thin film of dust and peach fuzz, arrives to empty his backpack into the crate while an older man stands on the running board, bending into the crate after every addition, fingering the fruit and tossing a few out.

That will be you, says Victor, nodding at the man on the running boards. *You'll need one of these*, he says. *Un aro*. He turns a plastic ring, perhaps three inches in diameter, over in his hand, then holds it up. This is how I'll know if the peaches are big enough: If a peach passes through it, it's too small and should be thrown out. Do I understand? I nod.

The tractor suddenly sputters and starts. The fourth crate is full, and one of the pickers is now at the wheel, preparing to haul the crates away. Pickers have already begun to empty their bags into the second trailer. Over the grumbling of the engine, Tino tells me I can start work right now if I like. I hesitate.

Can I start tomorrow? I need to find a place to stay first, I say. The ranch where I had been staying is more than an hour away, too long and expensive a commute to make on minimum wage. Tino assents: If I come back to the same field in the morning, at 5:30, he'll take me to a crew. Can I be up that early?

Of course, I say. *I'm a white girl but I'm not lazy.*

Tino glances at me uncertainly before breaking into a smile.

* * *

Naturally, I get lost. Driving down Conejo at 5:20 a.m., before the sun has crested the hills, all the gates look the same; the orchards stretch for miles. After a few mistaken turns, I finally find the correct lane. I zip down it until the rows part and a swath of gravel the size of a parking lot opens before me, with Tino's pickup off to the side. It's 5:35—I'm late!—and when I get out of my car to say hello, he waves his arm out his window for me to follow him. We roll slowly through the orchard, passing trees silhouetted in the blue light of early morning, lanes lined with workers' cars: minivans with mismatched doors, faded Dodge Neons discharging five grown men, rusting SUVs, the occasional pickup. I see a few women, the young ones in fitted plaid blouses standing alongside trailers, ready to sort, the older ones with faces swaddled in bandanas, preparing to pick.

We come upon a line of cars and Tino motions for me to park. There are a dozen men loitering about in the unofficial uniform of a *pizcador:* sneakers, jeans, long-sleeved shirts, caps, and *botes,* the packs in which they collect fruit. Tino leads me to the only woman present. She's short and fat, heavy breasts resting on a thick ring of flesh around her midsection. This, explains Tino, is Lorena, my new *mayordoma.* I smile tentatively at her.

She barks. *You're here to sort? Work with Eduardo.* She points to a wiry man in his fifties. He's not wearing a *bote,* just gloves and a cap. He smiles, leads me into a row, and hands me a yellow *aro.* We walk past one tractor with four empty crates behind it and mount the running board on another in front of it, standing on either side of the first *cajón,* or crate. Lorena takes up her position at the tractor's steering wheel. Metal clangs, echoing down dewy, vaulted rows, as the men pick up ladders and dart between the trees.

For the first few minutes, there's little for us to do. There's the sharp din of ladders unfolding, the rustling of leaves. And then the first picker arrives, a mound of fruit glowing yellow in the bag on his chest. As he walks he unhooks the two ropes keeping the bottom of the sack closed, and Eduardo bangs his palm against the left-hand corner of the crate. In one smooth motion, the picker steps onto the running board and releases the ropes as he swings his torso forward, leaning over the *cajón.* A small avalanche of peaches pours into the corner that Eduardo has indicated, and before it is even finished Eduardo is bent over full at the waist, head below his hips, his hands flying through fruit. He pulls out branches and leaves, tosses out peaches that look perfectly fine to me, slides a few more into his *aro* to make sure they're big enough, and shows me a peach with a decomposing patch of exposed flesh, rotting in the sun, before tossing it. *Birds,* he says.

This is roughly what happens every thirty seconds until lunchtime. A picker, or two, approaches. They dump their fruit, and Eduardo and I try to snatch out anything that is too small, too green, or too rotten; as in the grape fields, I am on the lookout for *chiquitos, verdes* and *podridos.* Eduardo has a sixth sense for precisely where the rotten peaches from each load will land, and can see leaves and sticks where I'd miss them. The loads come fast, one right after the other, so that I spot a bruised peach only to have it covered by another forty pounds of fruit. These peaches are bound for the cannery, explains Lorena, so they don't need to be gorgeous, just big enough to suit the machinery and ripe enough to have some sweetness to them. (Later, a supervisor adds the caveat that if they are very big, it is better to pick them now, whatever their color, because by the next round of picking they will have rotted.) I have a hard time identifying the green ones until Eduardo takes pity on me and does a comparison. He holds up one yellow peach against another; side by side, the first has an unmistakable greenish cast. All the while, Lorena is loudly providing equal parts encouragement and pressure to the crew.

Véngase. Véngase. ¡Véngase las caritas! Cabrones, ¡no chiquitas! ¡Están tan chiquitas! ¡No verdes! ¡Dame las bonitas! ¡Dame las frutas buenas! ¡Ánimo! ¡Ánimo! Pinche cabrón, ¿qué son éstos? ¡No verdes! ¿Por qué me dan almendras? ¡No quiero pinche almendras! ¡Déjelos!

(Come here, come here! Show me your cute little faces! Assholes, no little ones! These are too small! No green ones! Give me the pretty ones! Give me the good fruit! Faster, faster! Fucking asshole, what are these? No green ones! Why are you giving me almonds?* I don't want fucking almonds! Leave them!)

All the sorting takes its toll: The row is becoming littered with fruit, most of it too green or too small, some of it rotted. Peaches line the irrigation ditches, dot the rows, smush under the trailer wheels.†

At lunch, I walk awkwardly toward the crew with my little cooler and am relieved when Lorena invites me to sit with her. Most people have brought portable gas burners, so they can toast tortillas over the flames. Lorena asks me where I live, and when I say that I'm in a motel in town, about twenty

---

* On the tree, unhusked almonds are roughly the size of a small egg.

† The USDA does not measure the amount of crops that are lost, for any reason, between farm and market. Independent estimates put the range anywhere from 13 to 29 percent. (Lundqvust, de Fraiture, and Molden 2008; Bloom 2010)

minutes away, she immediately asks me how much I am paying.

About forty dollars a night, I say, biting into my cheese sandwich. *But I need to rent a room.*

That's expensive! exclaims Lorena, waving her hand dismissively. She can see that I'm a woman in need of a bargain. She leans over her propane burner. *I have a room you can rent. It won't be that expensive.*

How much? I ask.

One hundred. It's in Caruthers.

That, I think to myself, is more like it. *Where is Caruthers? Can I look at the room first?*

Lorena nods, and we make plans for me to come by after we finish work; Caruthers is a small town fifteen minutes west of the orchard. Eduardo can ride with me, and make sure I find it OK; he lives at Lorena's house, too.

I have slept in a lot of places where sanitation was arguably a secondary concern: stranded on a cliffside trail in New Hampshire, fleabag hotels of various nationalities, a hippie trailer in Colorado. But my new landlady takes the cake. Raw meat in the refrigerator is left uncovered and uncooked; a wall in the bathroom is falling apart; there's the telltale scurrying sound of rodents at night; roaches skitter away when I walk into my room. The roaches were obvious from my first visit to Lorena's, when I went to inspect the room before agreeing to rent it. To her credit, when she saw the startled look on my face, Lorena darted out of the room and marched back a moment later, plunking down a can of Raid and announcing, *Hay muchas cucarachas.* There are a lot of cockroaches.

Nonetheless, I'm grateful that Lorena has rented me her second bedroom, which appears to typically function as a junk room. I didn't go into detail with Lorena in the field, but so far this place beats my first, and now only, night at the TavCam Motel in Kingsburg. There, the parking lot looked out on a cannery and the railroad tracks, and an anonymous man knocked on my door at 11 p.m. declaring, without explanation, "It's me." I had sufficient time in the sleepless hour that followed my firm rebuttal—"I don't know who you are. I'm not opening the door"—to rethink the wisdom of staying in a motel where I paid my four nights in advance through a half-moon window of bulletproof glass.

By my count, there are fourteen of us living at Lorena's. The house itself is a tiny ranch, just two small bedrooms, a bathroom, and a decent-sized kitchen that opens into the living room. I'm sharing the house with Lorena;

her husband, whom she introduces as Flaco ("skinny") but whose name is Raul; and a thus-far-nameless, shirtless man who lives on a single bed in the living room, which is otherwise empty of furnishings. The floors are wooden but unfinished, and while the bathroom has plumbing for a sink, there is nothing attached to it, just gnarled pipes coming out of the wall, which itself is rotting away; at night, light shines into my room through the holes at its base.

Initially, I thought that was it: four of us. But when Lorena concluded the basic tour of her house, in the kitchen, she slid a bolt and opened a door at the back. Beyond it sat a narrow makeshift galley kitchen with an open door at the end overlooking a small yard, and a doorway to the right. Lorena opened that door to reveal two sets of bunk beds; a young man looked at us, startled, from one of them. *Three guys live here,* she said. *They are on my crew.*

She closed the door to the bunk room and walked to the open doorway. We looked out on a small yard, surrounded by a tall wooden fence and crisscrossed with clotheslines. A brown wood cabin sat on the left. *That's the casita,* she said.

People live there?

Right now, seven, she said. *Eduardo lives there.*

And everyone is on your crew?

Yes. I drive them to work, too.

For farmworker housing, this is par for the course.* Pilar, for example, had been preparing to move to a new bungalow with a trailer in the backyard, which she offered to rent to me once she moved. As crowded as this may be, at least these are actual houses; farther south, in view of luxury subdivisions outside San Diego, farmworkers have built tent communities in the hills. In Florida, officials have found workers living in box trucks and

---

* Nearly half of all farmworkers live in housing considered to be overcrowded, where there is more than 1 person per room, and one-quarter live in conditions considered severe, where there are more than 1.5 people per room. (Villarejo et al. 2010) Forty-eight percent of farmworkers in the California Agricultural Workers Health Survey resided in a dwelling in which the number of persons per room (excluding bathrooms, but including kitchens) exceeded 1.0, corresponding to overcrowding. One-quarter lived in a dwelling in which the number of persons per room exceeded 1.5, the threshold for extreme overcrowding. (Villarejo and Schenker 2007) By these metrics, my new home, with four people in four rooms, would not be considered overcrowded, although the addition and *casita*—if they were included, despite not being part of the official house—would be considered severely overcrowded.

shipping containers.* Tight quarters come with their costs, most notably mental health and the potential for spreading disease.† But a place like Lorena's does two things. One, it's shelter in the most basic sense of the word. And two, it brings the cost of housing down to where someone earning $7 or $8 an hour could actually be sending real money back to family each month. There's no secret economy here, just a calculated trade-off.

We went back into our kitchen and Lorena rebolted the door.

This is always locked, so nobody can come in from the back, she said. I nodded. Of the twelve people to whom Lorena rents rooms, she and her husband drive ten of them to the fields and back each day; the shirtless guy doesn't seem to work, and I drive myself. Everyone seems nice enough, and as for the sanitation issue I'm hoping that a quick sweep-and-mop job in my room will take care of the worst of it.

Otherwise, I figure, I'll just have to remember to put my shoes on before getting out of bed.

My early days in the peach orchard are spent, as in any job, learning the essential tips and tricks for my new post: Don't stand near the trailer wheel without a wheel well, or else you might get your leg caught in it. Keep your bandanas as tight as possible, and tuck the bottoms into your collar, because the peach fuzz and dust will get into everything. Your clothing, impregnated with the fuzz, will turn to sandpaper on your skin, and thus cannot be worn twice without washing. These are all useful, insofar as they go, but the lesson that occupies most of my mental space is this: Stay on the shady side of the trailer.

I am no stranger to heat of the eastern variety, with its humidity, or of

* Since 1997, law-enforcement officials in Florida investigating forced labor have freed more than a thousand men and women in seven different cases of forced labor they have prosecuted in Florida, often in agricultural fields; living conditions in those cases have ranged from living in isolated trailers to being locked inside box trucks to living under the watch of armed guards. (Estabrook 2009)

† While establishing direct links between overcrowding and specific health problems is difficult, surveys of California farmworkers suggest that living in extremely crowded dwellings can be stressful and compel destructive behavior. Male farmworkers who lived in a dwelling with 2.5 or more persons per room used for sleeping were two and three-quarters times more likely to report experiencing *susto* (extreme fright) as compared with workers residing in a dwelling with a lower density of residents, according to the California Agricultural Workers Health Survey. The same study found that male participants who were unaccompanied by any family member and who resided with unrelated persons were two and one-half times more likely to engage in binge drinking. (Villarejo et al. 2010)

the beach variety, where ocean proximity cancels out the scorch of the sun. I have endured my share of steamy summer days. But the heat of the Central Valley is something else entirely. At night it's fine, but when the sun comes up the sky closes in and the temperatures begin to rise. The first few days of sorting, the thermometer tops out in the upper 90s. But then a heat wave begins, with the mercury edging north of the 100-degree mark by noon. I begin calculating which side of the row will have the least sun, and try to make sure I stand on that side. (Weeks later, I cringe when it dawns on me that this means I had been forcing Eduardo, twenty years my senior, into the hot sun.)

The heat poses the most immediate danger. Dust and fuzz are wreaking havoc on my sinuses, but that's the kind of thing that causes serious health problems in the long run; I have the distinct luxury of being here for only a short while.* But the heat can strike quickly. Since 2005, eleven farmworkers have died in California due to heat-related causes.† The most dramatic instance came in 2009, when a pregnant teenager picking grapes for a vineyard supplying Trader Joe's Two-Buck Chuck passed out and later died from heatstroke. The safest bet is to stay as hydrated as possible, but I have a hard time abandoning my post to drink water while trying to keep up with the flow of fruit.

The filth and heat drain nearly all my energy and replace it with apathy. When I finish my nine-hour day, I have little interest in doing anything besides taking a cold shower and lying on my bed—from roughly 2:30 until 4:00—with ice packs under my neck and back, a fan blowing

---

* Most farmworkers do this work for years, and the long-term exposure to chemicals can lead to serious health consequences for both workers and their families. A trio of studies released in 2011 found that pregnant women exposed to common agricultural pesticides produced children with diminished cognitive development and, in some cases, lower IQs. (Bouchard et al. 2011; Engel et al. 2011; Rauh et al. 2011) Meanwhile, the pesticides heptachlor and lindane, for example, have been linked to elevated rates of prostate cancers in farmworkers. Cancers of the lip, stomach, and prostate, as well as leukemia, non-Hodgkin's lymphoma, and multiple myeloma are found at such elevated rates among farmworkers that they are sometimes referred to as "agricultural cancers." (Mills, Dodge, and Yang 2009)

† Heat-related deaths are about 17 times as common among farmworkers, who post .39 heat-related deaths per 100,000 workers, as among all workers, where the average occurrence of a heat-related death is .02 per 100,000. (Luginbuhl et al. 2008) Even after enacting a heat-safety regulation for workers in 2005, the state of California saw 11 farmworker deaths tied to heat illness between that year and 2009. In 2009, the state conducted 750 inspections at the roughly 35,000 farms in the state, finding 40 percent to have violated safety regulations. (Khoka 2008; United Farm Workers 2009)

on me from the window, only leaving if I flee to the air-conditioned public library. Everything but keeping cool has plummeted in import. This morning, I woke, grabbed my toilet paper—our bathroom, I learned after my first visit to the facilities, is BYOTP—and found the tail end of the roll covered in baby cockroaches, a smattering of black confetti. I didn't flinch, just unrolled the paper to the ground and stomped on it with my flip-flops before peeling off a round with which to blow my nose.

I've lost all interest in cooking. I'm skeptical of the cleanliness in the kitchen, so I avoid using it. I know I should be eating something from the vegetable family, and that using soda for quick energy in the fields is foolhardy. I also know that eating out is wasteful, but I frankly don't care. When Lorena and her husband cook real meals, usually carne asada with rice and beans, they share with me—aggressively, in fact, not unlike Mrs. Vasquez's cousin with the green beans. But with my low rent, I can afford the gas to drive the twenty minutes to Kingsburg and splurge on a Carl's Jr. burger, fries, and soda, served in an icily air-conditioned and relatively clean dining room. I never get invited to visit the *casita*, so I don't know what the other boarders eat, just that they bring their portable burners to work to toast tortillas that they fill with rice and beans, sometimes adding a little grilled meat.

I don't work with Lorena for long. She tells me over the weekend that I'm switching crews—and warns me that Tino might try to say I didn't do the work and try to get out of paying me, something she's seen happen before. On Monday, Tino leads me to another crew, this one all men. My new co-sorter is a full-cheeked twenty-three-year-old named Carlos, who wears a faded Dolce & Gabbana cap sideways and is constantly making references to Daddy Yankee and Jackie Chan. He and his buddy, Luis, who wins my affection by wearing a Jimi Hendrix T-shirt, eagerly share the English they know with me: "Very nice, very nice," and "Be-yoo-tiful!" intentionally delivered, I realize when I listen closely, in the style of Borat. Carlos tells me he has worked in the United States for four years, and before that, for five years on farms in Mexico. They're both single, not yet bound by families of their own; Luis lives with friends up in Madera, and Carlos lives with his brother in the same town.

It's here that I begin to understand that the piece rate for peaches works differently from grapes. I'd noticed Lorena jotting down how many *botes* each worker brought in, and the foreman here does the same, but—I find out from Carlos—the crew is actually paid as a whole, based on the number of *cajones* they deliver. We count our day by *viajes*, or trips, made with full crates. For each half-ton crate, the crew is paid $22; each trailer holds four crates, or two tons, of fruit, so each trip yields $88 for the crew, about 2.2 cents a pound. We've been posting ten and twelve *viajes* a day, sometimes more, and this, Carlos tells me, means the pickers will make close to $9 an hour; he and I will earn minimum wage, $8. Carlos tells me he prefers picking but, he shrugs, sorting is OK too.

It's easier, right? I ask.

Yes, much.

A picker starts by setting up a three-legged ladder that's far wider at the base than at the top. Then, strapped into his *bote*—the few women I see are almost always *sorteadoras* like me—he climbs up, turns around, and begins snatching peaches from the tree. To do this, he'll need to have memorized, by touch, the size of peach that the company wants today, and to be able to tell, at a glimpse, whether the peach is yellow enough to pick; each field will get picked several times, and this is the first picking of the season, so it's better to leave small or green ones on the tree. He reaches up into the shiny leaves and grabs at the fruit they hide, removing them by grasping gently, twisting and pulling them off the tree. Grab too hard and he'll bruise them, fail to twist and he might end up with part of the branch. It takes a good picker about five to seven minutes to fill the *bote*, which holds about forty pounds. It's safer to pick while facing the ladder, the rungs snug against the belly, but this makes it harder to pick. Once the bag is full, the pickers descend the ladder and make their way to the trailer where the *sorteador* is waiting to assess their bounty.

The moment when a picker empties his bag into the crate is the obvious time for him to get water, since we keep a cooler strapped to the trailer's wheel well with paper cones to drink from. When it's hot, most pickers do take a coneful—about one-quarter cup of water—and as they walk away, Carlos calls after them about the state of the fruit they just deposited: your fruit is too small, too green, too rotten, or it is good size, good fruit. After 10 a.m., the heat intensifies, already in the 90s, and nobody pays much attention to what the *sorteador* is saying. It's just too hot.

Truthfully, I can only do half my job, on account of my limited language skills. The extra seconds it takes for me to convert a thought into Spanish, and then say it out loud, mean that I almost never join Carlos in his editorial comments to the pickers. And Tino, I learn, expected this. Lorena explains to me one morning that crews never have two *sorteadores*, not even to train them, making me even more unusual.

When our *pizcadores* empty their *botes*, Carlos shouts out encouragements that I cannot summon the confidence to offer:

Ahí está! Ahí está! Buen color y tamaño! Bueno!
(There it is! There it is! Good color and size! Good!)

Our supervisors do not feel the same way; they've been ramping up their visits to our crew, picking through the *cajones* and chastising us for having fruit that is too small or too green. They've also been worried that we're simply not picking enough fruit in the first place. The supervisors have done this so often that our foreman had our crew *stop picking* and called a meeting.

He pulled out a piece of paper. He'd been tracking how many loads each picker brought in for the last hour. Our best picker had filled seven *botes*. The worst? Three. They all, he said like a disappointed father, should be able to do five or six. And the size and color matter, he added, with a thinly veiled threat of unemployment: *Guys, you can't bring green ones or small ones. They don't want them and we can't work here if there are too many of them.*

He looked around at the fifteen pickers before him. *I'm not saying this for me, I'm saying it for you.*

The pickers all scurried off, newly motivated to pick well. If we don't all pull our weight, the whole crew could get fired. Carlos and I exchanged glances; we'd be trying harder, too.

If my floor had been clean, I might have made it to the toilet.

This is the initial thought that comes to me here, crouched on the bathroom floor, my face centered over a toilet seat and inches from a wastebasket filled with dirty toilet paper. Saliva and bile dribble from my chin, and I can see, off to the side, where the initial wave of vomit and dusty mucus splattered down the side of the tub. I'd felt the first heaving urge while lying on my bed and in my hurry had fumbled with my flip-flops before running for the bathroom, losing precious seconds to my obsession with keeping a barrier between my skin and the floor. Even now, with my digestive tract in open revolt, I squat instead of kneel on the bathroom floor, my arms gingerly bracing against the toilet for the next round.

The first signs that I was sick, I now see, came this morning. I'd barely been able to eat anything—in fact, I'd had the distinct urge to spit out my breakfast. I had blamed this on the heat wave, knowing that I often lose my appetite when it's hot, and besides, without an air conditioner I've been too hot to fall asleep until somewhere north of midnight. I resolved to drink enough water in the field, packed up my peanut butter and jelly and Pepsi, and went on to work. The day was slow, and after lunch we shifted to hourly pay instead of piece rate, charged with cleaning out overlooked fruit from a few rows. No longer paid by their output, the pickers' pace dropped dramatically. Carlos donned a *bote* and started picking, and I was left to sort on my own. Earlier in the week, we'd been filling between two or three *viajes* each hour. Now it took us the entire post-lunch shift, from 10:00 to 1:30, to fill one and a half.

Working alone, I didn't realize I was slowing down. I was drinking plenty of water, and the *mayordomo* was kindly making sure to park the trailer in the shade each time we moved down the row. It wasn't until he came over to spot-check my work and began to pick over the crate, throwing out peach after peach after peach, that I realized there might be a problem.

He looked at me balefully. The crate was almost full, and, I realized, probably needed to be sorted over again. I was hazy and tired, and felt an inkling that I ought to have been embarrassed. But when I looked down at the peaches before me, they were an indistinguishable mass of yellow fuzz. They all looked fine to me.

The foreman said something to me about the other tractor, one that was a few rows over. I barely understood any of it, my Spanish having disappeared along with my energy. I blankly stepped off the trailer, thinking he was telling me to go work at the other trailer.

No, Tere, stay here and sort this, he said deliberately. *Tell the workers to bring their fruit to the other trailer, over there.* He looked at me again. *Have a peach,* he said, handing me a piece of fruit. It occurred to me that if I could be fired, today would be the day.

I nodded, my head thick and foggy, and watched him walk away through the trees toward the other trailer. For the first time in two weeks, I sat down on the wheel well and bit into a peach. It was sweet and utterly unappetizing, but I ate it anyway. My head felt heavy and swollen. I made a nominal effort at picking through the fruit in the crate from my seated position. Whenever pickers came to the trailer, I would lift my head and say: *This one is full, you should go to the other trailer, over there,* and point after the foreman. Soon, the pickers stopped coming by at all.

Finally, I heard a series of cries: *Vámonos!* Literally, this means, "Let's go," but in the field it means "We're outta here!" There was nobody to drive the tractor away—Carlos tried to teach me, but I couldn't get the clutch to budge—so I left it sitting between the irrigation ditches and plodded toward the end of the row, emerging on a lane where there were no cars. For a moment I was confused. Where's my car? Then I remembered that we had moved our cars at lunch; they were at the other end of the row, a quarter or half mile; the distance didn't really matter because it all translated to "far." When I finally reached my car, I waved weakly at the worker whose car was next to mine.

It's very hot! I said, an attempt at levity. *What do you think, one hundred and four?* That's how hot it was yesterday.

One hundred and eight.

Really?

Yeah, I heard someone say so.

Damn.

The exhaustion became tangible, a solid force expanding through my body, centered between my shoulder blades and exerting a gravitational pull back and downward. I had the distinct urge to lie down in my car, but held off until I could pull myself into the house, take a cold shower, and pull three ice packs out of the freezer. It occurred to me that lethargy and confusion are classic signs of heat sickness, that the line between sickly and dangerously ill is an internal temperature of 103,* and that, being in possession of a thermometer, I would have been well advised to use it. But the thermometer was tucked away somewhere; to reach it I would have had to sit up. I stayed lying down.

Until, of course, my body demanded that I get to a bathroom, and so here I am, retching into the tub from a standing position, the shower curtain dramatically flung aside. Once my stomach quiets, nausea gives way to an irrational sense of abject failure. None of the other workers seemed to be getting sick, but here I am, turning my insides out.

I do what I can to clean up the mess and stumble back to my room to find the thermometer; the room is so hot it begins reading the air as soon as I turn it on. As for me, I'm at a prickly 100.7 degrees and I take this as a sign that I need, rather desperately, to get into some air-conditioning. I take refuge in the library, where I scoot my chair as close as possible to the vent

---

* Heatstroke can occur at body temperatures as low as 103. Typical warning signs include headache, dizziness, nausea, confusion, and unconsciousness. (Luginbuhl et al. 2008)

in the wall. Emboldened by the cessation of abdominal hostilities, I drink some water only to end up gagging over the library's toilet. I comfort myself with the reminder that it could be worse; I could be vomiting into the toilet in my own home.

There are other ways it could be worse, of course. I could have to keep doing this job indefinitely. I could lack the resources to pick up and move to a more temperate climate. I could be without a car. I could have a less friendly supervisor and could thus lose my job for spending an hour sitting in the shade and listlessly picking at fruit. I could be less educated about heat sickness and have somehow pressed on, working until I actually did collapse from the heat, or the dust, or the food poisoning, or whatever it is that has wrought havoc on me today. And I could be doing all of this without any legal status in the country, terrified that at any moment I'll be forcibly returned to the border.

There are so many ways it could be worse, in fact, that the part of me that insists I just take my lumps feels aghast to hear a question tinged with complaint arise from some deep corner of my psyche. Kneeling in a stall of the Caruthers Library bathroom, defeated at last by the heat and the dust, what I want to know is this: Whose fucking idea was it to grow food in a desert?

When I think of farms, I think of green: Green grass alongside a green field fighting against green weeds underneath green trees. Marketing likely plays some role in this, with all those food labels attempting to lure me with their charming bovines in green pastures. But after a few weeks in California, where green is found only within a tight radius from a water source, I realize this is a Midwestern way of looking at things. Where I'm from, water just falls from the sky all year, free and easy as air and sun. But that isn't how things work out here, in a land that Easterners never would have thought could yield food.* I am learning the truth in Bernard DeVoto's observation that, in the West, "water has exactly the value of blood."

When white settlers first crossed the Sierra Nevada mountains, what they found depended on the season. If they arrived in spring, they'd find a valley drunk on the water that came from the mountains' melting snowcaps.

---

* The early years of California agriculture, from roughly 1880 to 1930, wrote the historian Steven Stoll, exposed "a rural landscape that looked like nothing the United States had ever seen before." (Stoll 1998)

Meadows of wildflowers rioted on the banks of swollen rivers and crept to the edges of vast lakes; one, Tulare Lake, covered eight hundred square miles, never deeper than forty feet. But if settlers arrived a few months later, in summer, they'd find a land where rain seemed the stuff of fairy tales. By June, the terrain got sober, turning hard and dry beneath the sun. The valley in summer was little more than a dusty plain beset by wind.

My arrival in the Central Valley was in the middle of this dry season, which explains why it looked like a desert to me. The soil in the peach orchard is a mix of sand and loam, but to me it looks like nothing more than dust; its organic matter is below .75 percent, less than the 1 to 2 percent considered acceptable for farming in arid climates—and far below the 4 to 5 percent considered standard in fertile prairieland soils. Yet even with healthier soils, the field would likely still puff out in small clouds around my footsteps at this time of year, for the simple fact that this place will see not a drop of water from the sky between June and October. And yet it is our nation's Eden, accounting for a full third of its farmland. There's only one way to accomplish that Herculean feat: irrigation.

The initial efforts to grow food in the Central Valley mirrored the style of farming back east: using rainwater, or digging wells, or getting water from rivers that flowed nearby. Under this model, grain crops like wheat were the most profitable: They were planted anew each year, they could survive on the available water, and they could be shipped far and wide. They were also easy to mechanize. This allowed the landholders—speculators, really—who had amassed tens of thousands of acres apiece in what Joan Didion calls the "subsidized monopolization of California" to coax massive profit out of dry earth. By the mid 1880s, California outpaced the Midwestern bread basket in wheat production, growing more than any other state in the nation. Its wheat fields were so vast, and generated such massive profits, they were commonly referred to as "bonanza farms."

But then drought brought the bonanza to a halt, and large landholders fixed on a new enterprise. Growers started to hatch irrigation schemes. With the promise of more water came the notion that maybe the valley could grow something else.

Like, for example, peaches in Kingsburg.

The kind of irrigation needed for that—for transforming five months of desert into a garden lush with fruit—took more than adding a spigot along nature's pipeline. All agriculture requires changing what nature gave us, but the changes wrought in its name in California have been among America's most ambitious.* To build a garden from an inland valley that routinely flooded with snowmelt required wholly remaking the landscape. Farmers dragged crude precursors to the bulldozer across the valley and leveled its rolling plain into flat farmland. They built levees and dams to stop rivers and hold back the snowmelt, then dribbled it out onto fields over the course of the growing season.†

I'd see this legacy in action every few days, usually around the time we left the fields. The knee-deep furrows, thick with grass, that framed each row of trees would begin to fill with water sputtering from irrigation pipes, flooding up to the top. Getting that water doesn't just mean you can sustain your peach trees; it means you have reason to plant them in the first place. Crops like wheat or even tomatoes are a one-year investment, but tree crops—which typically fetch higher prices—are for the long haul. Peaches, for example, take three years before they'll even bear fruit (or profit), and the trees last for twenty years, but they take more than three acre-feet of water a year. There's no point in putting in crops where the payoff looms years down the road if you've no way to reliably water them in the interim.

Irrigation is a bargain we made with the natural world. All great deals come with a cost, and irrigation's is this: impoverished water and soil. Water running down from the mountains naturally gathers all kinds of minerals and salts along its downward rush, and it adds them to whatever soil it irrigates. If the soil has high salt and mineral content—as it does in parts of the Central Valley—they'll come along for the ride, too. Combined, the two phenomena can easily push the concentration of minerals in the soil beyond the level where crops can tolerate them, and as it filters down into

---

* California agriculture stands at one end of a very broad spectrum of cultivation practices. Farming, writes James McWilliams, "is the art of strategizing against the natural world," an observation that can be easy to cast as being in opposition to the observation of the poet, essayist, and farmer Wendell Berry that "we are not smart enough to recover Eden by assault, and . . . nature does not tolerate or excuse our abuses." Yet, rather than being mutually exclusive, these two observations are more like two sides of the same coin. All agriculture does require altering land to suit human needs, but rather than approaching food cultivation as a conquering of the land, it's possible to practice agriculture that makes use of land's natural advantages—and accepts its foibles. (Berry 2009, 3–10; James McWilliams 2009, 7)

† Tulare Lake, which would disappear in dry years, provides an extreme example. During drought years, farmers in the lake bottom would cultivate its rich soil, but when the snowmelt returned they'd be flooded out. Eventually, the farmers—massive landholders all—persuaded the federal government to dam up the four rivers that fed Tulare Lake so that it could be farmed consistently, even offering to pay for the cost of one of the dams themselves. (Arax and Wartzman 2003, 46–65)

the aquifer—taking fertilizers and other chemicals used in agriculture along with it—it can contaminate drinking water, too. There are ways to mitigate the problem, most of them centered on draining runoff away from crops and aquifers, but each comes with its own cost.*

Today, the farmers of the Central Valley are figuring out how to bear theirs. When there's nowhere for the water to go, or if it drains too slowly—a problem in parts of the valley where a thick clay layer impedes drainage—growers have few options. Some switch to crops that do better with high levels of salt. One grower I met had recently uprooted a mature almond orchard in favor of pistachios, because the latter can withstand higher sodium content in the soil. In some cases, the soil simply can't bear the toll that farming takes. In a part of the valley called the Westlands Water District, a hundred thousand acres now lie fallow, lain to rest because the land had become so depleted of nutrients and so rife with salts.

Societies have dealt with the consequences of irrigation since agriculture first took root in another dry, fertile valley: Mesopotamia. Located atop the current sites of Iran and Iraq, Mesopotamia was the world's first urban place, a new structure of daily life that was made possible by irrigation. Once people could control water, they created an agriculture that grew enough food to store and trade it. People no longer had to live near fields to eat. When wheat and barley and dates began to bloom across the once-barren valley around 3,000 BC, the population boomed and in turn required more agriculture. But salt, and silt, took a toll: A thousand years after inventing agriculture in the Middle East, feeding a population that peaked at 20 million, Mesopotamian fields produced just half of what they had in the beginning. "Clay tablets," writes the earth scientist David W. Montgomery, told "of the earth turning white in places as the rising layer of salt reached the surface"—something I saw in California. Agriculture crashed. Mesopotamia became "a backwater."

Is it any wonder, then, that I finally throw in the towel on this hot, dry irrigated garden that can be likened to Eden only by historical revisionists and salesmen? That's what I tell myself, anyway: Only a fool would stay here

---

* The Kesterson Refuge disaster provides a particularly dramatic instance of the need for appropriate drainage. In the 1980s, irrigation planners in the Central Valley directed crop drainage into a wildlife refuge consisting of shallow ponds that attracted birds. The crop water leached selenium and salts into the ponds, which evaporated quickly, concentrating the minerals to toxic levels and leading to extensive deformities in the birds. The drains were shut down, leaving growers to deal with an aquifer that was flooding upward, unable to percolate down. (Arax and Wartzman 2003, 398–399)

in this house, sick from the heat, if they had any other choice. It no longer matters that this valley produces one-quarter of America's food, and ships massive loads of it abroad. The Central Valley's grand bounty, all its oranges and grapes, onions and garlic; its almonds, cherries, pistachios, and pecans; its tomatoes, melons, and olives; anything grown here in this grand testament to man's struggle to conquer nature will have to get harvested without my help. I've been making a few phone calls in my off-hours, and I've gotten a lead on work in Salinas, over the mountains and safely in a coastal valley where temperatures rarely venture north of 90 degrees. I'm ashamed by my lack of fortitude, but there's something else, too, an aching knob of guilt pressing up through my bruised ego. I'm leaving the Central Valley, really, just because I can.

My last day in the orchard is a Saturday. Tino hands a stack of checks to the foreman, as is customary, to distribute to the crew, but hands me my check directly. Yesterday morning, still unable to drink water, I'd called in sick; Tino had been very nice and told me to get some rest. Today, as he hands me my check, he asks, with a knowing edge to his voice, if I want to work next week.

I shake my head. *No, I'm going to move to Salinas, I have free housing there.*

Today's another day of hourly-rate work, so I'm alone on the trailer. My conversations with the pickers have gotten comfortable enough that Luis, Carlos's buddy in the Jimi Hendrix T-shirt, asks if I can come up to Madera to teach him and his friends some English. I smile apologetically and say that I'm moving to Salinas.

When the *mayordomo* finally calls it quits, Tino offers me a ride back to my car, which is at the opposite end of the orchard, like everyone else's. I'm hot, and still feel a little queasy, so I'm in no shape to say no. I climb the running board and launch my frame into a seat that's easily three feet off the ground. Now looming above them, I can see my co-workers dousing their heads and faces in the water sputtering up through irrigation pipes; a few are drinking from it. The rest are traipsing back through the orchard toward their own cars, crosses of sweat soaked into their backs where the straps for the *botes* sat.

And this is how I end my time in the Central Valley. Not trudging alongside my fellow workers, not chattering in loose Spanish about the day, not quietly slipping away without anyone noticing a thing. No, the boss offered me special treatment, quite possibly out of sympathy but almost undoubtedly due to things I can't control—my skin color, my American passport, my fluency in English, my gender—and I didn't even pause. One glance at that air-conditioned, extended-cab F150, and I just climbed right in.

CHAPTER 3

Cutting Garlic

I have a good feeling about the Salinas Valley, and it all comes down to a bowl of soup. I'm talking about a rich broth bleeding with chiles and speckled with golden globules of fat, sweet slivers of onion floating alongside chunks of white, meaty fish. As soon as I agree to rent a room, Dolores, my new landlady, leads me into the kitchen and wordlessly ladles out a bowl of the stuff from a giant pot. Then she points to a stack of steaming hand-rolled flour tortillas and hands me half a lime and a salt shaker. *Eat!* she commands, pulling back a plastic lawn chair from the folding table in the kitchen. *Eat!* I hadn't realized how hungry I was for something fresh until I took the first spoonful. I barely stop to breathe as I empty the bowl, drinking down the last dregs of broth.

You like it? she asks, stifling a laugh.

Yes. I like it very much, I say. Then I think to myself, *This is going to be all right.*

I ended up here after three days of calling farmworker advocates and organizers from my bargain motel room in Salinas, a strategy that yielded an invitation to tag along with Francisco, a community worker. We drove forty minutes south to Greenfield, coming to a stop in front of a white bungalow. The sun was already behind the mountains, a chilly breeze tussling the treetops. In the yard, a cluster of men, maybe eight or ten, waited for us.

Francisco had already been planning a meeting, to explain to a group of farmworkers how to document that their boss is cheating them. The workers had noticed that the company rounds down the weight of the buckets of peas they pick each day to the nearest pound instead of paying for the excess ounces, a practice I'd read about in accounts of farmwork in the 1930s, but had assumed had long since stopped. Perched on the arm of a sofa,

Francisco opened the meeting in Trique, another indigenous language,* before broaching, in Spanish, the subject of helping me. He introduced me, as we had agreed earlier, not as a journalist but as a friend who's down on her luck. Eyebrows were raised, and then the conversation reverted to the singsongy patter of Trique. There was laughter, some pointing, and, finally, a skeptical glance by José, Dolores's husband, at a pair of French doors missing most of their panes and covered by a sheet on the far side. Their teenage son, Paulo, got up from the couch, opened the door, and held back the sheet to reveal a cubby-like room. There was a double mattress on the floor, a drawerless bureau, a window with a sheet for a curtain, and a rope strung diagonally over the bed, holding a few hangers with shirts and pants.

Everyone looked at the room and then at me.

This is OK for you? asked Francisco. You can pay them three hundred dollars?

I nodded, though the price was further into three figures than I'd expected. But while I'd be surprised to learn that the house meets building code requirements, it nonetheless met all of mine: It was clean; it felt safe; and it had a fully functional kitchen.

Francisco also canvassed the meeting—there were perhaps another eight or nine men beside José—for someone to take me along with them to work, but everyone balked. The best offer came from José, who said I could follow him to the fields and ask his foreman to take me on, but he wouldn't introduce me. I didn't ask why not; though they didn't know I was a reporter, showing up with a legal worker would draw attention to them,† something no undocumented worker wants. Francisco also explained that I can drive around to fields and ask foremen for work; that's how people usually do

---

* While migration to the United States from Mexico in the twentieth century came mostly from Mexican states where Spanish was the primary language, a growing share of the Mexican migration to the north comes from indigenous peasant communities. Data gathered by the U.S. Department of Labor in 2004 suggest that roughly 20 percent—128,000—of California farmworkers are now indigenous. (Aguirre International 2005)

† It is difficult to count unauthorized workers, since they don't reliably show up in formal statistics. Federal data indicate that by 2004, 57 percent of California farmworkers were unauthorized, up from 9 percent in the early 1990s. (Aguirre International 2005) The shift partly reflects tighter border security, which makes it more difficult for workers to travel between nations and gives workers who come to the United States an incentive to permanently make their home here. From 1996 to 2007, the share of farmworkers who had settled here, as opposed to migrating over the border for work and then returning, increased from 42 to 67 percent. (Carroll, Saltz, and Gabbard 2009, 6)

it. Whatever worries I had about finding work disappeared with the soup, which has left me food-drunk with optimism.

After I gorge myself in the kitchen, Paulo and his sister Inez help me move in. First we clear out the cubby, which I realize, belatedly, is where Paulo had been sleeping. Then they help me with the couple of bags I have; I squirm when I see Paulo tucking his clothing into shelves beneath the television.

Paulo speaks English well. He came to the states a few years ago, when he was big enough to make the crossing through the desert; Inez just came over this year. Paulo likes school, has been making the honor roll, and plans to graduate next year and maybe go to community college. During the summers he works alongside his parents, so he tells me the basics about working in peas: I should be up by 5:30 since we should all be out the door at 6:00. I should wear sneakers and jeans and a hat, and two bandanas.

Is the work hard? I ask.

As an answer, Paulo extends his hand and sticks out his thumb: The nail is half-gone, and the skin where it should have been is blackened and gnarled. To shell the peas in the field, he explains, workers glue scraps of tin over their nails, creating a stronger, sharper edge. He and his father had been trying to glue one onto his thumb, but something had gone wrong and he'd gotten burned.

Do I need to do that?

No, says Paulo. See if you get work first.

I spend my first week in Greenfield traipsing in the wee hours to the fields that carpet the Salinas Valley. On the first day, I try following José and Dolores to work, but when I approach the foreman he shakes his head at the dozens of cars already lined alongside the field and says he has enough workers. *Maybe you can find another crew,* he says.

I apply at the three farm labor contractor offices in town, and two more in other towns, putting my name on their lists. I call each office to follow up. *No work.* I drive to Salinas to case the shopping center parking lots on the south side, where farm labor buses congregate to take workers out to fields across the valley, but I arrive too late.

Every morning, I dutifully drive up and down Highway 101 in the early morning, searching for a crew at work in the fields that run alongside it. If I see any crews—which is to say, if I see a sprinkling of lights indicating a cluster of headlamps or a harvesting machine—I get off the highway at the next exit and try to maneuver my way back to it on the side roads. Once the sun rises, there's less chance of being hired—but the crews are easier to find. In any event, I get the same result each time I park my car, walk into the field and ask to talk to the foreman: *I don't need anyone right now, try another crew.*

The problem, I am gradually realizing, is that hardly anyone finds farm-work by showing up unconnected and unannounced. One foreman did tell me to apply at the union office up the highway, in Soledad, but that's the only time anyone mentions the word *application* to me. It seems like the most-worn path is to make your way to a town where you know one or two people and start asking for work; eventually someone puts in a word for you with the foreman and gets you on their crew; then you pass on the favor when you meet someone new to town, looking for work and in need of a little help. And since my landlords aren't willing to make that connection for me, I'm going to have to find someone who is.

I should note here that this is particularly tricky to negotiate as a woman—gringa and Mexicana alike. There's a presumed level of desperation for anyone seeking work in the fields—the unspoken rule is that anyone with better options would take them—and, as frequently happens when the vulnerable depend wholly on the powerful, episodes of sexual quid pro quo and even rape are not unheard of in the fields. In Monterey County, where I'm now living, federal lawyers heard workers refer to *el fil de calzón,* the field of panties, a reference to the rapes that occurred there.*

What I need, then, is to make friends with someone who can take me to the fields and introduce me to a foreman. I need them to be the kind of people who won't try to take advantage of my weaknesses, and might even keep an eye out for me while I'm there. And I need them to show me the ropes, and teach me how to pick whatever it is that we are picking.

Once I've identified this need, I feel oddly comforted. The world of farm-work, I'm learning, relies on the same thing that my "real" professional life does: connections. I just need to go make some.

---

* Rape and sexual harassment in the fields has been documented as a problem since the late 1990s, when advocates first began compiling reports. The EEOC in California has won a series of settlements in sexual harassment cases for $1–2 million. (Tamayo 2000; U.S. Equal Employment Opportunity Commission 2005b; U.S. Equal Employment Opportunity Commission 2005a; U.S. Equal Employment Opportunity Commission 1999) A 2010 survey of 150 Mexican and Mexican-descended farmworker women in California's Central Valley reported that 80 percent of respondents had experienced some form of sexual harassment; of those, 24 percent had experienced "sexual coercion," or being offered a quid pro quo in return for sexual favors. (Morales Waugh 2010)

* * *

It is Dolores who convinces me that following a stranger into an unknown field before dawn should be considered an absolute last resort. I am entering my second week of joblessness and beginning to feel desperate, enough that I've spent my afternoon negotiating an entrance to the fields that sounds increasingly sketchy as I narrate its terms in my head: *I met this guy, José, at the library and when he said he had a friend hiring cutters in garlic, I agreed to go meet them at the Fast Trip gas station at 4:30 a.m., and follow them down to the fields.* And when I admit to the particulars, it begins to sound dubious: Negotiating the arrangement involved visiting a garage where men were drinking forties and openly smoking and selling weed; an unsolicited display (by José) of a scar from a pit-bull bite, incurred during the purchase of illicit substances; and the vague rejection (by me) of an offer of a date in order to keep myself in José's good graces. So when Dolores comes home from her ten-hour day picking peas, I explain the situation.

Do you think it is a good idea? It is safe?

Her eyes widen and she shakes her head. *No.* Not a good idea.

But I can't find work, I say. By now, I've approached so many crews and told my backstory so many times that it has almost begun to feel true: Yes, I want to work in the field. I have a lot of problems right now, and I just want to work hard and not think. And though my earnings in peaches replenished my nest egg, I paid José my rent up front; my financial cushion now stands at about $300, with six weeks to go. I am quite serious when I repeat my plea in Dolores's kitchen: *I need to find work.*

Dolores's eyes brighten: She has an idea. She walks to the kitchen door and calls out to a group of men in the driveway. One of them, a cousin in his early twenties, comes to the door.

Talk to Guillermo, says Dolores. *He is working in the garlic fields, maybe he can help.*

Guillermo listens to me patiently. He looks sympathetic. And he leaves me hanging anyway. *I'll talk to my friends,* he says with an air of finality. I nod and thank him, then sigh inwardly. It will take an extra couple days to go through Guillermo. I will be going by the gas station in the morning after all, to at least feel out the situation; I can always turn around and go home.

I retreat to the living room to watch a *telenovela* with Dolores's kids: Paulo, seventeen; Inez, fourteen; Leonel, seven; Julieta, five; Maricia, two. Sal, a middle-aged neighbor, is watching, too. Paunchy and with a cap perpetually covering his balding pate, Sal has been eager to come to my aid, but it hasn't gotten me very far. (He speaks English, which helps.) After three days of phone calls to his friend who runs a farm labor contracting business, Sal had found me one morning of *limpiando,* weeding. Even at minimum wage, it wasn't enough.

As the drama unfolds on the television before us, Sal counsels me about my current conundrum.

Be careful, he says. I have a friend, and he meets this guy who tells him he has work and to come with him. So he go. And he get to the field, and there's another guy there, and they take all his money. You have to be careful.

I nod resignedly, knowing I'll be going to the gas station at 4:30 just the same.

Thanks, Sal, I say. I'll try to keep that in mind.

What?

The *ponchadora* looks up at me in the glare of the headlights, pen poised over a *tarjeta,* a punch card. For the third time, she repeats herself. *How do you spell your name?*

Tracie. T-R-A-C-I-E. I had hoped that, in the dark, my full-on *campesina*—farmworker—uniform, from sunhat to face bandanas to gloves, would let me pass into the field without incident. I hadn't thought about the way my name and accent would give me away.

The woman sighs and thrusts the stack of cards at me, hands me the pen. She watches me print out my name and asks, *Do you have shears?*

I shake my head and she sighs again. There may not be enough *tijeras* for everyone, and since I'm new I'll have to wait. Guillermo has already walked into the field, carrying two construction buckets that shimmer white in the dark. I wait, studying my *tarjeta.* There's a list of times down either side of it, starting with 5:00 a.m. on the left, running to 12:00, and going from 12:30 p.m. on the right, through 7:30; the *ponchadora* punched out 5:30 a.m. for me. The card is preprinted with the name of our employer, El Bajío Packing, and in the space next to *precio,* price, the *ponchadora* has written $1.60. The rest of the card is a grid of numbers stretching from one to two hundred.

Dawn comes as I wait, and I can see that we're standing at the edge of a massive field striped with rows of pale gold straw and dark, heavy earth. Workers kneel at the edge of the field, their hunched frames hugging the ground, strung between giant wooden crates like low-flung Christmas lights. There's a steady mechanical chatter from the dozens of snipping shears. In the distance, I see the familiar lush ripples of grape fields; in the dry hills beyond, oil derricks swing methodically in the damp morning light.

Teresa! Teresa! Guillermo is calling to me from the field, holding up his hands to say, "What's going on?" and I shake my head. Fifty feet away, he calls over the foreman and, after a short discussion, waves me over, then hands me a bucket and shears.

I kneel in the dirt, trying to observe without staring, *tijeras* idle in my hand. How do I even begin?

Así, Teresa, says Guillermo. Like this. He reaches into the thatch of straw before us, which isn't straw at all but the dried tops of garlic plants. Before drying, they would have resembled giant scallions, but now they are shoots of translucent white paper, a cousin of onionskin. He pulls out a handful of them, shakes the bunch, then hits it several times with the side of his *tijeras,* until the heads of garlic—there are maybe eight or ten—are clear of dirt. Then he grasps the bunch tightly, just above the heads, and pulls the stalks tight; it's an upside down bouquet, the heads gathered into a snug bundle. To trim off the actual roots, which jut from the base like a thatch of unruly hair, Guillermo steadies the bouquet against his thigh and unleashes a rapid-fire series of snips until they are all relieved of their roots. Then he holds the bouquet over his bucket, which is angled toward him in the dirt, and with a final, severe clip, releases the heads from their stalks.

Do you understand?

I think so. I think I can do it.

My bluster doesn't get me very far. I remind myself that a bucket an hour is respectable for my first day. After all, it's not much slower than Santiago, with whom I've been chatting. He lives at Dolores's, too, either in the garage or the *casita* that's built alongside it, along with four or five other men, and just arrived in the States five days ago after walking for fifteen days. There's no work in Oaxaca, the home state in Mexico he shares with José, Dolores, and Guillermo.* They're also all Triqui; for them, Spanish is a second language, making English their third. Back home, when the rare job does present itself, it will only pay only about $10 a day, which is what brought

---

* Experts consider a mix of displacement caused by NAFTA and Mexican agricultural reform to be a significant driver of indigenous Mexican migration. While the self-sufficient subsistence farming that characterized the economy in rural southern Mexico since colonial times had been declining since the mid-twentieth century, the introduction of subsidized American corn to the Mexican market decimated Mexican corn farmers. (Patel and Henriques 2004; Relinger 2010; Weiner 2002) The resulting economic dislocation fed outmigration, which rose rapidly in Mexico's corn-producing regions, including Oaxaca. (Nadal 2002)

Santiago to Greenfield. Like most workers from his part of Mexico, Santiago left behind his wife and four kids to come here.* When he started picking garlic three days ago, he says, he was slow like me. But now, he adds encouragingly, he's getting much faster.

I would go on like this, chatting quietly with Santiago, except that the foreman, Pedro, comes by, addressing me with a thickly accented, "Excuse me, please," before slipping into Spanish. *Give me your bucket.* I nod and smile while Guillermo interrupts with *She doesn't speak much Spanish.* I try to protest, eliciting a grin from Guillermo and the declaration *You speak a little,* delivered with the know-it-all swagger of a big brother. Pedro ignores our squabble and dumps my bucket out on the ground, examining the garlic I've cut. *Ah, it's all good, very good, it's clean.*

I'm slow, but good! I chirp in my baby Spanish, giving Guillermo a pointed look. Guillermo rolls his eyes.

Pedro calls lunch a couple hours later, and Guillermo unceremoniously dumps half a bucket into mine; two other workers, whom I had not even met, have already done the same. They waved away my protestations, barely acknowledging them.† Suddenly I am awash in garlic, and now that my buckets are full I need to take them to the *ponchadora,* Rosa. She sorts the garlic and punches our cards. For each bucket, she punches a hole through the next number. She smiles as I approach her.

You almost never see gringos in the field, she says, not unkindly. *Are you a gringa?*

More or less, is the only answer I can choke out as I hoist the first bucket, weighing a good twenty-five pounds, to chest level. *It's possible my grandfather was Mexican, but me? I'm a gringa.* I balance the bucket on the edge of the crate, then tip it in, a flood of garlic piling beneath, and repeat the process with the second bucket. I hand Rosa my *tarjeta. Click, click.* After three hours of picking and at least a bucket and a half of charity, my tally

---

* Among married immigrant men from southern states in Mexico living in California, 64 percent have left their spouses in Mexico, compared with 54 percent of Mexican men in general. (Mines, Nichols, and Runsten 2010)

† A few days later, I asked another worker why I was getting so many buckets of garlic. He explained that once lunch is called, people don't want to stay in the field—and if they are just starting a bucket, it's easier to give what's been picked to someone who really needs it. Usually, this is a friend of the picker, and it seemed particularly common to donate extra garlic to women and girls who were picking. Later, Rosa, the *ponchadora,* whose reliability you can judge for yourself, suggested to me that the men were trying to get my attention because I was a legal citizen and could therefore be of use, either in general or as a potential spouse.

stands at four buckets.

This, I find out, isn't unusual for a first day. There's little talk during lunch; everyone pretty much hunkers down and inhales their food before heading right back out, but I do manage to learn that the price on my *tar-jeta*—$1.60—is the amount paid for each five-gallon bucket of garlic we fill, which means that my four-hour morning will bring me $6.40. This isn't so far off from Santiago, whose tally of six buckets translates to $9.60; and it seems like the rate at which Guillermo picks, a dozen thus far (worth $19.20), is likely within reach.

After lunch, two supervisors stride over, kneel in the straw and begin cutting garlic alongside me. Hello, booms the woman in clear English, I'm Marta. This is my brother, José. They switch between Spanish and perfect English, asking few questions and explaining at length that this is their family's company, they've been working in the fields themselves since they were young. Later, I learn that farm labor contracting is the next step up the economic ladder for many farmworkers. Some move into management posts like Rosa, and others launch their own companies—as the owner of El Bajío has done with much success.

Marta and José, it becomes clear, know what they're doing with the *tijeras*. Upon kneeling next to me, Marta takes my *tijeras*, and between her and José, who has his own, a mound of garlic equal to half a bucket appears rapidly. They are making me nervous, both because they seem to think I can't cut my own garlic and because they're the bosses.

I can cut them, I say, straining to avoid sounding like a petulant child in my limited Spanish. I lapse into English: I know I won't make much money today. It's OK. I'm learning. I'll get better. Marta and her brother exchange glances and return the *tijeras* so I can keep cutting on my own.

This incident attracts some attention, though, and before I know it a young girl is asking, in flawless English, if she can cut next to me. She's very pretty, with almond-shaped eyes and smooth dark skin, and I say, Of course. Her name is Rosalinda, she says, and she can't speak Spanish very well either, just Trique and English. She has just started coming to the fields with her dad, but she kind of likes it because there isn't much to do at home besides chores; girls aren't really allowed to go out and do things, so this way, she at least gets to leave the house. She says this last bit just as her dad comes over and introduces himself as Diego. He settles in to pick next to Rosalinda, asks her something in Trique, and looks at me.

He wants to know if you're being paid by the hour, says Rosalinda. I have no idea, so I just say I think they're paying me like all the other workers. Rosalinda relays this, and Diego shakes his head, rattling off in Trique at breakneck pace. No, he thinks you'll get paid by hour because you're a citizen, she says. He and Hector—do you know him? I shake my head. He and Hector, another picker here, did some work in the community about that, because companies weren't paying them.

I shrug my shoulders. I don't know, I think they'll pay me the same as everyone else.

We hear a long, low siren and, looking up, I see an Amtrak passenger train sliding across the horizon. It's almost time to go, says Rosalinda, and half an hour later, around two o'clock, Pedro starts shouting that we're done for the day. When I hand my *tarjeta* to Rosa, she smiles and tells me I can work only twenty hours because I am paid by the hour. Do I understand? I'm startled, but nod and say *Vamos a ver,* We'll see. Rosa punches my card—ten buckets—and separates it along a perforation down the middle. I keep one copy for myself, she explains, and give the other to Pedro so the company will know how much to pay me.

If they pay me by piece, the eight and a half hours I have been here will translate to $16.00. If they pay me by minimum wage, I'll earn more than four times as much: $68.00.

After a couple weeks, I've made friends with most of the people I share a kitchen and bathroom with; I never get a solid count on the population in the *casita* and garage, but I'd put the total for the house and outbuildings at seventeen. Guillermo, who is around all the time even though he lives on the next block, is something of a buddy, though I wish he'd stop asking me about my marital status. He does this almost daily, as if I might have snuck out in the middle of the night and gotten hitched. Santiago is quickly becoming my go-to resource for interpreting interactions with Mexican men—an invaluable service, given the amount of attention my complexion and single status seem to attract in the fields.

Dolores is doing her share of interpreting for me, too, although it would have helped me if she'd explained in advance that I should never drive a married man to the store three blocks away. I learned that lesson the hard way, having taken Valentino—the married boarder in the second bedroom—to the grocery store only to have his wife begin screaming in Trique and swatting at him the moment we pulled up. It's unclear to me whether it was the case of Bud Light he had bought (after more time in the house, I realized he had a drinking problem) or me that was the bigger controversy, but Dolores took me aside and patiently suggested that I never do that again. In return, I do what I can to provide a little outside influence and help rein in the kids. We were in the kitchen one afternoon when Leonel ducked in and pulled a Pepsi from the refrigerator, drawing a protestation from Dolores. An argument ensued, and she turned to me plaintively and said, *Tere, what's better, soda or water?* Leo's eyes turned to me. *Oh, water, definitely,* I said emphatically. *Soda is terrible. I never drink it.* It worked, and Leo put down the can.

I'm falling in love with José and Dolores's children, all five of them, even Maricia, the baby, who hates me. Paulo endeared himself to me the night he turned seventeen, when family and friends gathered in the living room to celebrate not just his birthday, but his designation as the godfather of a cousin. He held the tiny baby girl reverently, oblivious to the conversation swirling around him. I've taken Inez on as an English student, swapping lessons in the English alphabet and numbers for tutorials in the kitchen. I usually get home around 2 p.m., an hour or so before Dolores and José, and to help relieve Inez of some child-care duties, I bring seven-year-old Leonel to the library some afternoons and take out books that we can read together in English, and I try to keep Julieta occupied, letting her comb my hair and coo *Teracita, mi mamacita, mi tía nueva, te quiero.* Tracie, my little mama, my new aunt, I love you.

While I melt at Julieta's sweetness, I'm aware that it's likely the source of Maricia's hatred for me. I waltzed in and all of a sudden her big sister had a new favorite, and now Maricia is hell-bent on eliminating me. She screams NO! at the sight of me, attempts to block my entry into rooms by forming a (very short) human barricade across the door, and, when all else fails, stands with feet planted wide, tongue peeping out, and jabs her index finger upward.

Leo, does this mean something for Triquis? I asked, demonstrating.

No, he grinned. Maricia's trying to do this, he said, and flipped me the bird.

We all find this hilarious. While her parents are quick to reprimand Maricia when it advances further—when she slaps at my thighs or throws a plastic toy square at my nose—it's hard to take her seriously, which she appears to realize and find all the more frustrating. It's also incredibly entertaining, and sometimes when I disappear into my room to read in the evenings, I hear them in the living room: *Maricia, where's Tracie? NO! Maricia, do you want to go with Tracie in her car? NO! NO! Maricia, we're going to send you away with Tracie! No, No, No, NOOOOOO!* Her little two-year-old voice gets stronger and angrier until Dolores finally relents. *Oh, Mari, I love you!* she coos, and I hear the sound of a dozen tiny kisses bestowed upon Mari's forehead.

For all the things I find startling about the Martinez house—Maricia feeds herself most of the time, the mess dribbling down her clothes; the kids eat things they drop on the floor; there doesn't seem to be an appointed bedtime or mealtime; baths are often self-directed, leaving a pool of water on the floor—I'm impressed with their parenting. I came home one day to find José painstakingly tallying his punch cards for the last year, at the request of Francisco, and paying no mind to Julieta's efforts to do his hair. There he sat, a stack of *tarjetas* and a notebook in front of him, pencil in hand, his brow furrowed beneath a headband, a hair bow, and multiple glitter barrettes.

Even my workplace is becoming more friendly and familiar. Pedro has begun to advertise my presence to new members of the crew, pointing me out to them: *And over there is Tracie, our gabacha,** in a voice equal parts pride and "Can you fucking believe this?" Rosa, in her fifties, has a daughter my age and acts like it, giving me bits of advice and pointing out potential suitors for me in the field.

The other set of friends I've acquired are Rosalinda and her father Diego, along with Diego's wife, Claudia, and their five other children, ranging in age from nine months to eleven years. Diego patiently answers my careful questions about farmwork and then, exposing his tendency toward community organizing, rapidly twists the conversation around to his favorite topic: Why Tracie Should Go on TV and Talk About Farmwork. *People will listen to you,* he says. *They will not listen to me.* I brush him off gently—and repeatedly.

Rosalinda is proving to be a smart, savvy, and complicated young lady. She wants to be a trilingual translator when she grows up, to help families like her own, and when I'd asked her what kind of music she listened to, she primly replied, mostly Christian music. But later, I pass her sitting in her family's van during lunch—her dad had stayed in the field to keep

---

* Although *gabacha* can be used interchangeably with other words connoting whiteness, it has a dual connotation suggesting both whiteness and *belonging* to that group, with all its attendant privileges. Though it can be used to communicate hostility, *gabacha*'s direct translation is neutral. This sets it apart from *gringa*, which carries a hostile connotation, and goes beyond *blanquita*, which is solely a comment on one's pale complexion.

picking—and I hear the distinct strains of Jay-Z wafting out of the stereo. I comment that it doesn't sound like Christian music, and she avoids my eyes. Her parents don't understand English, and they're very religious, she explains, so she just tells them that hip-hop is Christian music in America. I picture Diego, round-faced and smiling, driving around Greenfield, windows down, blaring Jay-Z: *If you're having girl problems, I feel bad for you, son; I got ninety-nine problems but a bitch ain't one.*

Really? They think this is Christian music?

Yeah. But I'm going to have to be careful. He's starting to take English classes.

Dolores and José have fed me nearly every day since I moved in. I handle my own breakfasts (coffee and bread), and pack my own lunches (PB&J and cheese sandwiches), but when the sun begins to drop behind the Coast Range and the evening breeze picks up, there's a loosely communal meal on offer, and I am always invited. Sometimes the other boarders eat with us, but rarely. There has been sufficient time since my inaugural bowl of soup for a little guilt to seep in about this state of affairs. Here I am, a single person, eating the food of a seven-person family with funds so limited that they fill their cupboards from an informal food pantry twice a week.

My own funds are limited, too, and my cash reserves are dropping steadily. By my calculations I'm spending about one-fifth of my money on food, and more than one-third on rent, but work doesn't seem steady enough to justify spending down what little of my reserves remain on groceries for dinner, particularly when the only barrier between me and the good, home-cooked meal in the next room is my pride.

Still, I want to feel like I'm contributing, so I'm focusing on helping Inez, Dolores's fourteen-year-old daughter, with her English. She has been in the States for about five months, and she spends her days cooking most of the family meals, watching the smaller children, and cleaning house. Teaching anyone English is no small task, but I find it particularly difficult with Inez because even her Spanish is weak; her English is nonexistent. Though she went to school in Mexico, Inez isn't going to classes here; we had to start with the alphabet. She's so self-conscious that teaching her anything requires an almost endless stream of encouragement. To help even our footing, I have asked her to teach me something in which she is fluent and I am not: tortillas.

Traditionally, Triqui girls learn how to make tortillas at the age of ten, in preparation for the marriage that's expected to come during their early teenage years.* Rosalinda, my young friend in the field, has told me that her mom got married when she was fourteen, though Rosalinda is adamant that she won't be getting married anytime soon; Diego and Claudia seem comfortable with that. But Dolores tells me she was fifteen when she married José, and Inez seems to be on a similar path.

Night after night, Inez emerges from the kitchen with a thick stack of steaming rounds the size of dinner plates, crisp at the edges and soft, nearly doughy, in the center. They will go stale by morning, so we eat them until they are gone, the pile disappearing under a flutter of hungry fingers. Inez makes a lot of the other things that parade out of the Martinez kitchen: pickled jalapeños and carrots biting with vinegar; burning green and red salsas; rice tarted up with flecks of tomato and onion; tender carne and pollo asada for tacos; salty greens that emerge from a foil packet on the stovetop; even simplified moles, Oaxaca's most famous culinary export, with pan-toasted spices ground into liquid velvet. But, for now, I want to learn tortillas.

Inez is just finishing mixing the dough when I get into the kitchen, but she explains that she uses an instant mix, pointing at a large paper sack not dissimilar to those used to pack concrete. It's just the mix and water, she says, displaying a pallid mound of dough in a large plastic bowl. She mixes it by hand until it's right, adding the water bit by bit.

How do you know when it's ready?

Inez smiles uncertainly and says, *It's just ready.*

She pulls a handful of dough, slightly larger than a golf ball, off the mound and slaps it into a rough sphere, then *splat*, throws it down into the center of a pink plastic circle the thickness of tissue paper. She pats it down with her hand, then brandishes the rolling pin, a narrow tapered length of plastic, and begins rolling out the dough. A minute later, there's a thin, flat circle with smooth edges. She tugs the pink plastic in one smooth motion, lifts it, peels the tortilla off and onto the palm of her hand, turns, and flips it onto the hot *comal*, a griddle, behind her. She does it again, flips the first

---

* Triqui immigrants, one of the most recent ethnic groups to enter California, still maintain many of their indigenous traditions, which sometimes lead to problems in the United States. In 2009, a Triqui man in Greenfield was jailed for arranging a marriage between his fourteen-year-old daughter and an eighteen-year-old man, and accepting a dowry in return. In Triqui culture, no formal marriage ceremony is performed; it is customary for a dowry to be exchanged and then the couple lives together. (Wozniacka 2011; Hollenbach 1998)

tortilla over on the stove, and then hands the pin to me. My turn.

The dough for flour tortillas isn't like the dough I'm used to. It's not elastic, but soft, like a looser version of Play-Doh. When I press down on the pin, dough bunches up in front of it in waves, and spreads thin in its wake. Fail. I scrape the dough back into a ball with my fingers, splat it down and try again. This time my fingernail catches the dough, digging a channel deep enough to tear it.

Again: scrape into a ball, splat, flatten, roll. I have a thick square. I can smell the tortillas on the stove cooking. I'm falling behind.

Inez, I don't know what I am did, er, what I am doing. I'm already so frustrated that I'm losing my Spanish.

She smiles at me kindly but does not take the pin from my hands. She's going to make me sweat it out.

I frown at the dough, which has come to resemble a Rorschach blot. I try rolling it out some more. The Rorschach blot expands but does not change shape. I attempt to mimic one of Inez's signature moves, peeling up the plastic liner just enough to separate the jagged edges of the dough from it and then folding them back in, smoothing the border. The consistency of the dough, I realize, is crucial here because it allows the folded edges to melt in seamlessly; make the dough too thick and the edges won't meld. Make it too thin, and it'll fall apart as you roll it.

In the meantime, Inez has been tending the tortillas on the stove, both of which have been neatly stacked and wrapped in a clean towel. The *comal* is nearly smoking with heat, the scent of hot metal wafting up from its empty plain—something that never happens when Inez makes the tortillas. I look at her resignedly, then hold out the pin.

Can you fix it?

She takes the pin from me, and with a calm efficiency of movement I associate with chefs, repairs the damage, flips it onto the *comal*, and makes two more. Then she splats another ball of dough down, unceremoniously hands me the pin, and says, *You need to practice.*

I nod and try locking the pin in place with one hand while spinning it out like a radius with the other. Bingo: smooth, round edges. I look at Inez for approval and she nods encouragingly. Better. She takes the pin and neatens my work, but it's a final once-over, not a redo.

We continue like this, with me rolling out the basic tortilla, Inez coming in to clean up the worst transgressions. Then Sal comes in.

Making tortillas, eh?

Sal is a good neighbor to the Martinez family. Most afternoons, he collects Maricia from the day-care school bus; later during my stay, he builds them a table from plywood and two-by-fours so they can eat in the living room. But, to my embarrassment, he has developed an obvious crush on me. To make matters worse, he speaks to me mostly in English, which means that, other than the two oldest boys, who speak English, the rest of the family can't understand what we're saying.

I keep my eyes on the tortilla and mumble, pointedly, *Estoy aprendiendo.* I'm learning.

It's good, you will learn.

Espero que sí. I hope so.

Good for when you get married, you can make them for your husband.

That's exactly what I want: to be locked up in a kitchen making tortillas, I say icily in English. Sal doesn't say anything back, just looks at me with surprised eyes.

My hostility recedes by the time the boarders start making their daily pilgrimage from the garage to the shower. When they see me with the tortilla pin in hand, they ask, *You're making tortillas?* And I reply with a wink to Inez, *I'm learning, but she's a professional.*

My tortillas never match Inez's, but she becomes more comfortable with me. That night, we get through the alphabet without her putting her head down in embarrassment. I am so encouraged by our progress that I figure we should start on words, and I ask what kind of vocabulary she might want to learn: What would be most useful? What does she need to know? But her face goes blank.

I try a different tack.

What do you want to do when you grow up? I ask her.

She smiles shyly and thinks for a minute. *I just want to help my mom.*

As it turns out, both Rosa and Diego were wrong. I don't get hourly wages, and my hours don't get limited. I'm paid by the piece, and less than minimum wage, just like everyone else. My first paycheck, handwritten on a company check, covers my first three days—about twenty-four hours of work, though that information isn't printed on the check—and comes to $54.40. Minimum wage would have yielded $192.

Paychecks, I learned on my third morning, are not the only way the company cuts corners. When I brought up my first load of garlic, Rosa presented me with a paper to sign: a sheet indicating that I had taken a food safety training course that week. There had been no such thing, but I was not inclined to point out this discrepancy, even with Pedro walking around in a vest emblazoned with *La Seguridad es Primera*—Safety First. I just signed it, like all my co-workers.

This lax stance on food safety aside, Pedro seems a decent enough foreman, and in the fields this goes a very long way toward making the work bearable. I see him going up and helping newcomers to the crew, especially—in a manner that suggests chivalry more than chauvinism—women. There's a day when a woman cuts herself and tries to keep working through it, but he forces her to put down her *tijeras* and sit under the shade tent—which, counter to regulation, stands only about three feet off the ground—while he helps bandage the wound. Not all foremen do things like this, and I hear workers talk in nervous tones about another foreman for El Bajío whose crews have been working alongside us—and who is known for firing anyone who can't cut at least twenty-five buckets a day, or just over three an hour.

By my second week, things settle into what seems a viable pattern. I'm giving rides to Diego and Rosalinda most days. Not only is their company welcome, but Diego knows the fields well enough that when we change location—which happens three or four times during my tenure there—he's a reliable navigator. I'm cutting thirteen, fourteen, fifteen buckets a day. The charity buckets from Guillermo stopped when I tried to argue that I could do it myself. *I'm not, I'm not . . .* I was searching for a translation for "a fucking baby," but before I could locate it, he interrupted me, smiling wickedly. *A princess?* I glared, then smiled. *Yes. I am not a princess!* He grinned and said, with equal parts generosity and condescension, *I know, I know.* He left me alone after that, so I've mostly accomplished this doubling of productivity through applying one simple rule: economy of motion.

Working by piece rate means that I've got to do everything I can to maximize my output. Like a tiny factory, I'm responsible for turning as much raw material as possible into the finished product. When I walk to a new section of a row, I set my bucket down at the beginning of the patch I want to claim and then walk maybe ten or fifteen feet. Quickly, I begin pulling the garlic up and standing it on its roots, working my way back toward my bucket, indicating to other workers that this is "my" garlic. The next worker will set up his "station" at the end of my territory, and in this way we'll leapfrog over each other until we clear an entire row. Once I've claimed my territory, I pull up a chunk of plants and pile it next to my bucket, so that I can easily reach over and grab it. The positioning of the bucket is important, too. I'm going to be reaching hundreds and hundreds of times for the garlic and the last thing I need to do is add another series of reaches, so I place the bucket just to the right of the garlic and grind it into the loose dirt at an angle, positioning it so that its mouth opens into my lap. With the garlic at my side and the bucket directly in front, I can reach once for the garlic, pull the bouquet tight, steady it against my thigh, cut off the roots, and then cut it from its stalk, barely moving at all.

For an industrial field, there's little machinery involved—our wages are still low enough, apparently, that investing in machines doesn't make sense—so I've just got the *tijeras,* the bucket, and my body. At first, nobody explains that I must maintain my *tijeras* by sharpening the blades and oiling the hinge. Once I figure this out, I am startled to realize that the lubricant is a neon-orange liquid in a bottle plastered with safety warnings—including to avoid contact with food; I've been spraying it liberally over the *tijeras,* enough that I'm sure it's gotten onto the garlic. I never really learn how to sharpen my *tijeras,* either, because I don't have my own file and whenever I ask to borrow one from someone, he inevitably extends his hand for my *tijeras* instead of handing me the file.* (Using higher quality *tijeras* is another option, but I don't pursue it after hearing they cost around $30— several days' pay.) But it's the machine of my body that proves to be more tricky. My thighs look as though they've been attacked by an enraged but weaponless toddler, peppered with dull reddish brown bruises where I've pressed into them again and again. My hands, swollen and inundated with blisters the first few days, have acclimatized, but there's a worrisome pain shooting up my right arm. And while I don't have a scale to gauge my weight, my clothing has become suspiciously loose.

The other cutters are still much faster than I am. Guillermo, for example, seems to average about twenty-two buckets of garlic a day ($35.20). Diego usually comes in closer to thirty ($48.00), and one day maxes out at thirty-four ($54.40)—a number practically unheard of on our crew. He achieved this by coming to the field well before dawn, around 5 a.m., and working through lunch. He ended up hurting his wrist in the process and couldn't work the next day. Claudia, Diego's wife, who joins us on some mornings,

---

* Here, as in most fields, men outnumber women. Across the United States, women make up about 21 percent of all farmworkers, and just 10 percent of recently arrived immigrant farmworkers. (Carroll et al. 2005; Aguirre International 2005)

picks in the mid-twenties. Rosalinda, the baby of the bunch, hovers around ten ($16.00). I poll my colleagues from the field, asking: What's the most a person can pick per hour? The consensus is four buckets.

None of us earn minimum wage, but you wouldn't know it from looking at our checks, where some curious accounting is at work. I start off getting simple company checks without payroll information, but Diego's family gets checks that have it. Each check lists the buckets picked and hours worked, but the numbers never match the information on their *tarjetas*. Each worker is paid for the number of buckets they got credit for; if Rosalinda picked ten buckets in one day, her check says she earned $16 that day, and she'll be paid that amount minus social security and taxes.

The problem is that, somewhere between the farm and our paychecks, the company is changing the number of hours for which it is paying us. Even though Rosalinda's *tarjeta* will show that she came in at 5:30 a.m. and left at 2:30 p.m., a nine-hour day, her check will say she was there for two hours—exactly the number of hours she would have had to work at minimum wage ($8) to earn what she made via piece rate ($16). Later, I ask advocates if this is unusual, and everyone shrugs: Not every contractor does it, but they see it regularly.

Earning minimum wage at our piece rate would require a speed that seems impossible: five buckets an hour. (In my month in garlic, I do not meet anyone who can average that for an entire day.) That would mean one person filled forty buckets—that's two hundred gallons, roughly half a ton of heads of garlic—in eight hours.

If the company names on the crates I pack are any indication, the garlic I harvest goes to two of the country's major garlic producers, The Garlic Company, which I see sold at Walmart, and Christopher Ranch, which is sold at Whole Foods.* Both companies hired a grower named Rava Ranch to plant and cultivate the garlic, and then hired their own harvest company, selecting from the state's 1,200 farm labor contractors. Contractors for farm

---

* In 2011, representatives of Christopher Ranch and The Garlic Company confirmed that they had contracted with El Bajío to provide harvest labor in the Salinas Valley in 2009. Both companies checked their paperwork from 2009, and said that all documents showed that workers were paid minimum wage. "We checked their invoice against their payroll detail reports, and can clearly see that whenever their employees make under minimum at piece rate they make up the difference," said Janette Codiga, a representative for Christopher Ranch, which has worked with El Bajío for several years. "That's as much as we can do without becoming investigative." (Codiga 2011; Layous 2011)

labor compete like any other on price, and the grower must balance cost against quality; they need skilled workers who won't leave good crop in the fields. At the end of each harvest, the crates get labeled with the company they're destined for, and a flatbed truck comes into the field. With a forklift, a worker will stack them two wide and six deep, two or three high, sending out ton after ton of garlic.

I'm not working in an area known for garlic. The Garlic Company is based at the southern tip of the Central Valley, the land responsible for almost all the garlic grown in America, while Christopher Ranch makes its home in Gilroy, the self-proclaimed "Garlic Capital of the World," about eighty miles north of the fields we've been picking in. American garlic growers will tell you, with some reason, that they've been struggling. Today, just under half of the fresh garlic we eat comes from American farms, with the balance coming from abroad—and most of it from China. That's a big shift from 1998, when American garlic represented around 80 percent of the fresh garlic we ate here, and imports from China accounted for less than 1 percent of it. But by the year after I leave the fields, American growers are producing half the fresh garlic they had grown in the late 1990s, and imports have more than doubled—with China's garlic accounting for the majority of them. The stray root hair left behind on each bulb by my *tijeras* brands it as a product of American fields; Chinese garlic, cut with knives, has a flat bald spot instead.

California is the heart of American garlic production, where its long, predictably dry summers make industrial-scale production possible; in wetter and less predictable climates, rain dampens the garlic while it's still in the ground, causing it to rot. Here, with no threat of inclement weather, growers have the luxury of letting the garlic dry out—cure—for storage while it stays in the ground, a stability that lets them plant vast fields on a grand scale that would never make sense anywhere else in America. Maintaining this scale is expensive, however, and so the American garlic industry is almost entirely dominated by the five packer-shippers who grew nearly all of the fresh garlic in California—and thus, in the United States—in 2009.

In my time with El Bajío I only pick for two of them. Christopher Ranch is smaller, selling whole bulbs and unsheathed cloves of fresh garlic, which is the way half of the garlic grown in the United States is sold. The Garlic Company is bigger; it grows garlic to sell fresh, but it's also a player in the other half of America's garlic market, processed garlic. That's the stuff that gets dehydrated to make garlic powder and garlic salt, flavoring the endless array of garlicky processed foods.* Between seasons, The Garlic Company imports fresh garlic from South America; after China, our neighbors to the south—Mexico, Argentina, and Chile—are our biggest sources from abroad for it. With all this competition from beyond our borders—particularly China, with its regular food-contamination scares—both companies market themselves as small, well-run places where you can trust the quality of their product because they grow and harvest it themselves.

Part of me wants to believe the stories I see on their websites: family farms, consistent control, high quality. Maybe, I reason, they really believe that farm labor contractors aren't likely to cheat workers; maybe it hasn't occurred to them that contracting out the work means they'll lose control over conditions; maybe they simply don't think very much about what goes on in their fields after the bulbs are planted. But when I look online at The Garlic Company's website, it's clear that their marketers, if not their contractors, know how important work conditions can be. If I'm to take them at their word, The Garlic Company prides itself on the close attention it pays to every detail, and its proximity to the fields it tends: "This closeness to the fields gives us better oversight over every aspect of garlic production, from the first planting to harvest, storage, and processing," explains the site. "We're one of the few garlic companies that actually controls everything, from field to shelf."

---

* For the 2009 season, the top garlic-producing counties in California were Fresno, Kern, Santa Clara, and San Benito. Fresno County accounted for 92.7 percent of the state's $163,896,000 in garlic production; Kern for 4.8 percent; Santa Clara (where Gilroy is located) for 1.5 percent; and San Benito for .9 percent. The garlic produced in other counties, including Monterey, cumulatively yielded less than 1 percent of the state's total, a testament to the massive scale of garlic fields in the north Central Valley, where Fresno is located. (California Department of Food and Agriculture 2010)

CHAPTER 4

Gleaning Garlic

Icatch a lucky break a week in, at our third field. This one is bigger than anything I've seen yet: three-quarters of a mile by one-fifth of a mile, roughly thirty-one acres of land ridged with straw and earth. The field is carved into a hill, so that on two adjacent sides the road looks down from ten feet above; on a third, a steep incline juts upward, nearly the height of a large building, a service road switchbacking its way up the side. (Later, I see a helicopter performing the tell-tale looped passes of crop dusting* and realize there's another field up there, too.) There are four, five, some days six crews in our field, each with several dozen cutters, each of us dumping our garlic into giant crates labeled "Christopher." Twenty minutes off the main road, and located along a series of private gravel drives that wind three and a half miles back into the fields, I never would have found it at 5:30 a.m. without Diego.

On our first day here, Marta, the *supervisora* who'd cut garlic for me the first day, pulls me aside.

Do you have a car?

Yes.

You can drive?

Yes.

You have a license?

Yes.

---

* Later, I learn that the field above us grew organic spinach and that the helicopter's passes distributed 1.45 pounds of Entrust spinosad, an insecticide; 23.21 pounds of Javelin *Bacillus thuringiensis,* a biopesticide; 3.78 gallons of Cueva Fungicide copper octanoate, a fungicide; and an organic air rinse over the twenty-one-acre field. All are approved for use in organic fields and were sprayed while workers stood alongside. Being far below the field, I could not observe closely enough to know when workers returned to the field; pesticide regulations prohibit entering a field within four hours of spraying these chemicals. (Monterey County Agricultural Commission 2009a; Monterey County Agricultural Commission 2009c; Organic Materials Review Institute 2011)

How old are you?

Thirty-two.

Marta stares at me. *I thought you were fifteen or sixteen.*

Tomorrow, she explains, they need people to pick up garlic at the field we left yesterday, and the two women to whom she'd already given the work do not have cars. Since I have a car, I can go, too, provided I act as chauffeur. It pays *por hora*, and the way her eyes widen I know I am being offered a plum position. *Of course*, I say. *No problem.*

So here I am, rattling thirty miles down Highway 101 to the second field we had harvested, just outside the town center of San Ardo, a village of about five hundred people. I've got Rosalinda in the passenger seat—Diego's eyes nearly jumped out of his head when he heard she could get paid hourly—and in the back are Ana, a thirty-five-year-old mother of two from Jalisco, and Graciela, forty-two, who goes by Cela. Our job is to pick up any salable heads of garlic that the cutters have left behind and add it to the bins, transforming us in local dialect from *cortadoras*, cutters, to *juntadoras*, gleaners. The task before us dates back to biblical times, but our purpose is entirely different from what is described in the book of Leviticus, which counsels farmers to "not gather the gleanings of thy harvest," but to "leave them for the poor and stranger." We're here today to scrape a little more profit out of the land.

At lunch we all sit in the dirt beneath a grove of towering black walnut trees and discuss the difference between *por hora* and piece rate. Cela starts us off with a little well-earned boasting; she picked thirty-one buckets of garlic yesterday, better than most men. We all *ooh* and *aah* appropriately.

Ana grins and pulls out her cell phone and clicks a few buttons. *$1.60 times thirty-one*, she says. *$49.60.*

And how much for today's work? asks Cela.

Eight hours at $8 an hour, that's $64. We all laugh.

And me, says Ana. *Twenty-three by $1.60: $36.80.*

The calculations continue. My twelve buckets amassed $19.20, and Rosalinda's nine yielded $14.40. We all agree that these are embarrassing figures. *It's like Mexico*, I say, and we all laugh again, because there isn't much else to do when eight hours of child labor will bring you fifteen dollars.

It's not fair, I say. *It's not legal.*

Do you want to say something to Marta? Ana asks me, laughing.

No, I don't want to say a thing.

Ana gives me a hard look and switches to English. Do I think working in the fields is hard? Well, a little, I say, but it's not bad, and I like being out-side. But why not work in a store, counters Ana, who doesn't seem to buy my response that I don't want to work with customers and talk to people. But the fields? Really? I shrug noncommittally. For now, this is best, I say, and then go on the offensive. Why does she work in the fields?

There's a brief hush, a tangible rise in tension, before Ana says, with just a hint of vagueness, Because most of us don't have papers.

That sounds hard.

Yes, she says. It's hard.

It's wrong that they don't pay more.

What do you think of that?

I think it's wrong.

Ana gives me a long, silent look before pushing herself up from the ground, announcing, *Let's go!* at the top of her lungs. She and I are working alongside each other, so we talk as we return to our buckets.

Your English is pretty good, I say, sticking to the basic vocabulary I know we share. Better than my Spanish. It must be hard to be far from home in a different language.

Yeah, it is. But the language, the papers. . . everything.

I don't know if I can even imagine.

And for me, I have a degree. I finished college to be a teacher.

Really? For what age?

First grade.

That's great. Then I pause. That must be really hard. Why did you come to the States?

Ana lets out a long, exasperated sigh. *How do I explain it to you?*

Was it for work?

No, no, it was . . . my husband. He said . . . she pauses, lets her voice trail off. He said to get a better life.

By the end of the day the four of us have added twelve more buckets, each of them holding about twenty-five pounds of garlic, to the bins that are still in the field. A semi with a double trailer rolls into the field around noon and collects most of them, strapping forty-two *cajones* on the flatbeds. Each of the bins has a label now, designating the grower—Rava Ranches—and the company for whom the garlic is being grown: in this case, The Garlic Company.

As a fieldworker, I can't entirely grasp the economic logic of paying four people minimum wage for eight hours—$256, a sum that now seems monumental—to get garlic that would have cost El Bajío $19.20 if it were picked during the regular harvest. From here, the garlic will be divvied up for different destinations. The prettiest heads—the largest, whitest, and cleanest—will go to retailers like Walmart and local grocers. Dirty heads will be stripped of their skin and turned into jars of cloves and minced garlic. Everything else, though, will head for dehydration plants, where more than half of American garlic ends up. There, the garlic we picked is turned into the flavored powder and salt that's found in bagel crisps and pasta sauces, marinades and frozen dinners. There's no guarantee what we just gleaned will be sold as the fresh garlic I see in grocery stores.

Later, I learn that growers like The Garlic Company pay a flat fee to labor contractors, who bid on jobs the same way construction contractors do. They negotiate a price to have the field harvested, and if they ask for someone to glean, El Bajío is obligated to provide the service—no matter if it hurts their bottom line as a contractor or not. Paying four workers eight hours of minimum wage for just twelve buckets doesn't make any sense in financial terms: In 2009, California garlic sold for an average of $51.20 per hundredweight; our twelve buckets will bring the farmer $153.60, about $100 *less* than it cost to fill them at minimum wage.

The hundredweight price is an average over the year, so there's no way for me to know how much a retailer pays for the garlic I've picked. That amount changes depending on the deal struck by a store with the brands or wholesalers selling it, a negotiation influenced not just by the growers' costs but by the import market, whether last year's stock has been sold off, and consumer demand. The same mix of forces are at play in the prices that retailers charge at the store, which means they vary dramatically. By the time a netted sleeve of heads from Christopher Ranch—just under a pound—reaches Greenfield's La Princesa market, a small grocery store, it sells for $1.99, meaning that the twelve buckets we picked would retail for about $600. But later, I see Garlic Company bulbs sold in Walmart's produce section for much more, $3.38. At that price, our twelve buckets would fetch $1,014.

Each week, I am placing myself further in the red, receiving a total of $726.20 in checks during my first month in Greenfield but spending $824.89. I am maintaining financial solvency not through hard work but via the tiny inheritance I afforded myself before entering the field. The sum I'd portioned out two months ago—$1,123, equivalent to one month of full-time, minimum wage after taxes—was intended to cover a security deposit and first month's rent. But there's been no deposit required and my rent is quite low, which frees up extra money for food—55 percent of my grocery budget, in fact.

Even after I pay for my rent and car insurance, I am spending more than a hundred dollars in cash each week,* which strikes me as extravagant, but when I look at my budget I am baffled as to how to cut spending. The fields I am driving to can be up to forty miles away, and my gas bill runs between $40 and $60 a week. Then there are the mundane expenses of being an adult: Refilling my cell phone card so that I can contact Diego and Guillermo about work costs $15. Antibiotic cream, peroxide, and generic Band-Aids to care for my cuts and blisters run me $11. The alternatives to spending down my nest egg—risking infection, getting caught without insurance, or giving up my cell phone—just don't seem worth it.

But when it comes to food, where I could economize more easily, rationality flies out the window when I'm hungry. I'm used to eating three meals a day, but starting an eight-hour day of manual labor at 6:00 a.m. has introduced the need for a fourth. With coffee and bread before work and lunch only four hours later, there's an empty stretch from 10:00 a.m. until dinner, around 7:00 or 8:00 p.m. I keep thinking that if I just exercise a little discipline, I'll be able to power through and hold out until supper.

I trim down the grocery list and plan to eat less only to find that, come 3:00 p.m., I can't concentrate on anything but finding food, and I run to the town bakery almost daily for coffee and sweet *pan*—bread—or a *torta*, a sandwich. I even justify this to myself by arguing that I can't afford to spend money to buy the meat, crema, jalapeños, onions, and fresh bread that make up the sandwich; this, I tell myself foolishly, is a deal.

There's a wisp of truth in the lie I'm telling myself. Buying meat, jalapeños (either canned or the fresh peppers, vinegar, salt and sugar required to cure them), a jar of crema, a bag of onions, and rolls would probably cost more than a single sandwich, and take up far more of my grocery budget than the three dollars it takes to buy a sandwich. The bigger problem, really, is that the kitchen is always crowded and busy—Inez and Dolores, the boarders, and Valentino's wife—and I'm anxious about taking up too much time or space, or somehow losing my food to the communal nature of the kitchen. Better to stick to my coffee-and-bread breakfasts, cheese-

---

* Since I paid my $300 in rent up front, during my fourth week in California, I don't feel its pinch, but—if divided up—it accounts for another $60 each week. Similarly, my monthly car insurance costs $88, due my first week, accounts for $22 each week.

sandwich lunches, and the meals Dolores and José share, filling in the hungry spots with fresh *tortas*.

Rosalinda and Diego regularly offer me a chimichanga from their lunch box, partly out of simple generosity and partly out of pity—though I can't say for sure if that's because I look malnourished or because my sandwiches are less appetizing than their fare. My guess is the former, since they called and invited me to the house on Twelfth Street.

We had left work an hour before, and my food intake for the day stood at two cheese sandwiches, a pear, and a Diet Coke. I was heading to the bakery when my phone rang. It was Rosalinda. Her mom had asked her to call me and see if I wanted to come with them to get some free food.

Like, a food pantry?

Sort of. Just come to Twelfth Street.

After a few wrong turns, I find the house, across the road from an unkempt vineyard ringed with farmworkers' beat-up minivans and patchwork sedans. Families hover in clusters, eyeing the driveway of a small house where women are unloading Rubbermaid bins and foam coolers from a large pickup truck. Rosalinda, standing with her parents and little brother, waves to me. We loiter amiably.

As soon as the truck pulls out of the driveway, a jagged sliver of a woman with white hair at the wheel, we swarm forward. Rosalinda's mom heads to the left, Rosalinda leads me to the right, and another twenty families do the same: moms with small children clustered at their knees, their teenage daughters fanning out among them. Later I learn that this is not a food bank in the formal sense of the word, nor a food pantry; there is no affiliate organization beyond the white-haired woman at the wheel of the truck. It is charity in the most basic sense of the word, a single good Samaritan making sure food that would otherwise go to waste goes to feed some of the people who helped pick it. We all hold out plastic shopping bags like we are trick-or-treating, and the three or four women who've been unloading the bins begin.

It starts with the bread, of which there is more than anything else. I get Buttermilk Sandwich Bread, a floury pouf called a Shepherd's Loaf from Safeway, and an artisanal brioche from Trader Joe's. All of us are trying to catch the eye of one of our benefactors, hoping to get a choice item.

Then comes the produce. The workers rip open bags of fruit and empty them into bins, parceling out a few pieces at a time. The real prizes are the berries, their skins still taut; I notice the workers—who look to be just as desperate as we are—squirreling away the best for themselves. Rosalinda makes a sad face at one of the workers and gets a giant container of blueberries (retail $9, Trader Joe's). I receive an apple, a clementine, and a pear. Vegetables come loose, too, and I get three yellow squash, plus a one-pound box of Blue Lake green beans. Then the women dive into long, narrow foam coolers of cheese, raw meat, and fish warming in the sun, with today as their expiration date: I get lamb tips in burgundy pepper (retail $12.49), a chunk of double-cream gouda, and a twenty-ounce precooked pot roast, while Rosalinda's family walks away with a package of Black Angus ground beef and a Trader Joe's triple-cream Brie. Desserts are next, boxes of cookies, bags of donuts, and even a few cakes. Last of all come the bulk items: pinto beans, rice, and oatmeal. I snag a two-quart jar of half-sour pickles, too, because no one else would take it. Having skipped the *torta* and come straight here, I am ravenous. I thank Claudia for thinking of me and bid my goodbyes, then duck into my car like a dog with a bone. I don't drive home. I don't even start my car. I sit in the driver's seat, open the Shepherd's Loaf, and rip off handfuls, eating great chunks of nearly stale bread so fast that I find myself short of breath. When I finally stop to breathe, a quarter of the loaf is already gone.

When I get home, I share the dry rice, beans, and vegetables with the family, and throw the lamb tips in the freezer, but I hide the bread in my room so I can have it for breakfast with my coffee. I've saved the best part for last—the fruit. I've been buying plums, but the triple choice offered by the food drop is exceptional. The pear, still hard, is an easy decision. Wait for it to ripen and save it for lunch. The clementine? Eat it now, which I do, disappointed to find that it's mushy—although not quite rotten—inside; beggars, I tell myself, can't be choosers. The apple is nothing but a disappointment, with a giant rotting bruise spreading across half its body.

I sigh, and nibble around the rotten parts.

The first indication that something unusual is afoot on Sunday is the living room: It's empty and quiet when I emerge from my room at the late hour of 7:30 a.m. After I shower and dress, Julieta pokes her head through one of the French door's empty panes and asks for my help. She wants to carry a twelve-bottle box of Coronas that nearly outweighs her into the backyard for her dad. We pass Maricia playing with a box of laundry soap in the driveway, which necessitates a brief poison-control intervention, and therefore a quick run to the kitchen, where we squeeze in alongside Dolores and Inez, busy at the stove, to wash off the detergent's residue. Disaster averted, I pick up the beers and follow Julieta outside.

The backyard itself is empty, just a stretch of furrowed dirt that looks ready for planting, ringed with tomato plants, onions, and herbs and a waist-high stone wall. An opening in the wall leads to a lot behind it. Fruit trees sprawl out in the corners, and a bigger tree shades the windowless *casita,* which I now see is little more than a shed, and the stretch of dirt where José parks his truck. And *this* is where everyone is, a full-fledged barbecue already in process on the far side of the wall. The center of attention is the grill, a square column of cinder block standing three feet high. Plumbing pipes arc up from the sides, and a heavy iron grill roughly two feet square is suspended from them, via pulley, over the coals.

The kids scramble in the dirt and hide in the bushes while the men— José, Guillermo, Sal, Valentino, Santiago—tend the pit. Four square feet of food smokes before them: thin sheets of beef crackling from the heat; corn tortillas softening and deepening to gold; plump, blistered jalapeños; foil-packeted green onions; tiny fowl coated in a red rub. More meat, at least twenty pounds, sits on a rickety wooden table, pulled from some corner of the garage or casita. I put down the beers. *Your beer, gentlemen.* There is a round of smiles, and someone dumps the beers into a cooler.

I sit down at the rickety homemade table that usually sits in the living room.

Do you want a beer? asks Guillermo.

No thanks, I say, *it's a little early for me.*

No really, have a beer. The guys quiet down, all looking at me.

No thanks, I chirp.

No, have a beer.

No thanks. Smile.

Really, have a beer.

No thanks. Smile harder.

We could have gone on like this indefinitely, but Valentino calls the question. He opens a Corona and thunks it down in front of me, top off.

Have. A. Beer. he says.

I relent. *OK, one, no more.*

There is a small round of cheers. Most of the men talk among themselves, but Guillermo begins quizzing me on English vocabulary. *Silla* is chair; *mesa,* table. I try to spell the words out for him with Spanish phonetics: C-H-E-R, T-E-B-U-L. I give him rides to and from work sometimes, and he has been asking me about where he might take classes to learn how to use a computer and how to type.

Then Inez and Dolores appear, bringing food out of the kitchen as if from a clown car: a tub of guacamole checkered with chile, onion, and tomato and thinned with water; a vat of ruddy beans, still bubbling from the stove; a mound of rice turned tawny with seasoning; a pile of Inez's tortillas verging on a foot in height; salsas glistening with spice. Everyone comes running, crowds around the tables, and piles food on their plates. We all settle into a wordless reverie save for José, who is chattering in Trique to a cousin in Mexico on his cell phone. Maricia clambers into Dolores's chair, nestling behind her, and promptly undoes her mother's braid, releasing a cascade of waves that stretch to her seat.

Have another beer, Teresa! This time it is Dolores egging me on, devolving into slang I can't fully comprehend: *You have two eyes, so you should have two beers.* I feel sluggish from the beer and the food, and as a response I get up from the table, shake my head, and begin chasing the kids around the yard. I want to go to Salinas later, and I need to do laundry. When the men finish, I help Inez clear the tables and do the mountain of dishes that have to be lugged back to the kitchen. Over the sink, I find myself yawning.

It has been a long day, I think to myself, but when I look at my phone it is 11 a.m.

It is unmistakable: Rosa, the *ponchadora*, is paying extra attention to me with a motherly concern for the size of my checks, which is to say my ability to take care of myself. The other day, she spent the morning explaining to me, whenever I was cutting within earshot of her, that I should find a man.

Teresa, you should have a working man.

Yeah? I looked up to see her gesturing at one, right there, a working man with a big mustache and a cap. *Not right now, Rosa, no. Not right now.*

But a man, he can help you: rent, food, clothes. Your checks are small.

Rosa looks out for me in other ways, too. Every once in a while, she lets me dump buckets that aren't entirely full, crediting me for a full bucket. And last week she heard Marta saying there might be hourly work, and relayed the information to me, prodding me to ask about it. *Teresa, they have work by the hour! Go ask Marta! Now!* Nothing came of it, but I was still touched by the concern.

She even reprimands me for talking too much when I get going with Rosalinda, whose translating skills between Trique and English have come in handy. One day, all the guys in the next row were laughing themselves silly, and Rosalinda cracked a smile.

What are they saying? I asked.

He's saying this is too hard, and he should get a donkey to carry his buckets.

A donkey?

Yeah.

To carry all his garlic buckets?

Yeah.

The giggles started then, a tickle in the back of my throat that seeded tears in my eyes.

Can you imagine, I cried, if you drove up in the morning with a trailer and unloaded your donkey, to help you pick garlic for $1.60 a bucket?

We were really cracking ourselves up with this one when Rosa walked past us. She glanced at Rosalinda and then gave me a stern glare.

You're talking a lot today, Tere.

In English, yes, I giggled, wiping my eyes with my shirtsleeve, grit scratching my skin.

She should teach you Spanish, she said, nodding at Rosalinda. *And you should talk less.* Pronouncement finished, Rosa walked on to her post at the *cajón.* We watched her go and collapsed back into giggles.

Two weeks in, I reach the pinnacle of my garlic career: seventeen buckets of garlic. That's roughly 425 pounds, contained in 85 gallons. I am so excited about this near-tripling of personal productivity that I gloss over the sharp, jabbing pain that my right arm began communicating to me around one o'clock. In an attempt to appease my right arm, I use my left hand to shift the car into drive.

This does nothing, of course, because it's not the shifting of my car that is the problem. I make further entreaties to my arm. I massage it with Bengay, I ply it with extra-strength ibuprofen and ice, I abandon typing and let it rest when I leave work. The next day, my arm stages a work slowdown. I pick twelve buckets, two of which come from workers who see me struggling and help. One of those is Rosa, and as she kneels in the dirt alongside me, she says I am lucky because other foremen fire anyone who can't pick twenty-five buckets a day.* The next morning, as I sign in for my *tarjeta* and *tijeras* from Rosa, she asks me how my hand is.

It hurts. I put Bengay on it, and I took Tylenol, but it still hurts. What should I do?

---

* Even picking twenty-five buckets a day would not reach the state minimum wage of $8 an hour, which would require five buckets an hour, or forty buckets in an eight-hour day.

Ask God.

I do not find this reassuring.

I take the *tarjeta* and scissors anyway, resolving to muscle through this like everyone else has to. The pain has become so intense that forty minutes into the day I've filled only about one-quarter of my bucket. At this rate I won't even make my gas money. Rosa stops by to see how I am doing and I look up at her helplessly.

I can't cut any more. This is a joke. What should I do?

You need to rest. Go tell Pedro.

I dump my garlic in Rosalinda's bucket, saying goodbye, walk over to Pedro and say that I have hurt my arm and I cannot cut any more garlic. I'm expecting—hoping, really—that he'll say something like *Thanks for trying, come back when you are better.* He'll be sympathetic but resigned to the frailties associated with a *gabacha* farmworker; there'll be more than a touch of, Well, what did you expect? And that will be the end of it until my arm heals, which, frankly, could well be after the two weeks I have left are up. Secretly, what I'm hoping is: This is the end.

Ah, but these are farmworkers I am talking to, and I am their pet *gabacha.* Pedro's eyes furrow in concern, he calls Marta to ask her what to do, and I hear the magical phrase *por hora* get batted around in rapid Spanish. Rosa's eyes go wide. *Tere, go, hourly work!* she says, pointing back to the beginning of the field, where we picked last week. Off in the distance I see two small, bandannaed figures trolling the ground with buckets: *juntando de ajo.* Collecting garlic.

I don't want to go. What I want to do is drive home, put ice packs on my arm, and read. A beer might even be in order. Instead, I squelch my sense of entitlement, nod, and say, with as much sincerity as I can muster, *Thank you.* Then I walk across the field to trade places with a woman whom Pedro has just demoted to piece-rate on my behalf. But here's the thing: I can't cut, period. I'm utterly surprised to find that my arm no longer works, that the pain is actually so great I cannot cut a single garlic stalk. This was all it took? Two weeks in the field and I'm debilitated. Yet I need the money, and I'm a quarter-mile from anyone else but the other gleaner, and there's nobody watching, so . . . I cheat. I walk through the straw, kicking it up as if I am looking for heads but instead covering them up. On the off chance that anyone is looking, I pick up stalks with heads attached, shake off the dirt, hold them on the far side of the bucket, and pretend to cut them, then drop the heads in the straw and cover them up. Later I realize that this is foolish; I could have gathered the heads and given them to the other gleaner to cut. But I'm in pain, and I'm tired, so I give up. I go back to Pedro, say that I'm very sorry but I can't possibly gather any more garlic, and I'm going to go home.

When Pedro relays this chain of events to Marta, she tells him I need to file for workers' compensation. I follow Pedro over to his truck, where he removes a giant white binder full of forms, and we fill out an accident report, which reveals that we are on Bella Vista Ranch. There's some information he doesn't know, so he calls Marta but gets her voicemail, and we wait, surveying the field. The sun is just beginning to flood it fully, rising high enough over the hills to light up the garlic straw and fade the dirt from soil to sand. Every few rows hold a line of *cajones*, stamped in large black lettering with "Christopher." I ask Pedro why the *cajones* say that and he tells me, *That's the company buying the garlic from Bella Vista.*

There's a big semi loading up *cajones* we filled earlier this week, and from here the garlic will hit the road, bits of its skin showering like snow in the truck's wake. Since garlic isn't packed in the field, it has to be sorted, so its first stop will probably be a packing house, or, if the company has enough garlic on hand for current orders, a storage facility. (Kept at the right temperature and humidity levels, garlic will keep for a year.) At a packing house, the garlic will travel down a packing line on a conveyor belt, where workers will pick out rotten heads, or send damaged ones to the processing factory. The rest of the heads will be shaken through a series of sifters resembling chicken wire, the largest holes up top, keeping the big heads separate from the smaller and smaller ones that keep falling to the level below. Once sorted they'll be readied for retail. Good-sized heads with clean, white papery skin that's survived the harvest intact go into thirty-pound boxes bound for grocery stores and wholesalers. Others get funneled into bags: netted sleeves for supermarkets, two-pound sacks for club stores like Costco.

From here the garlic will start on a path that's more or less the same for every fresh fruit or vegetable grown in the country. Once packed, it will go into storage, while company executives arrange its ride on America's produce superhighway: supermarkets, which control not just storefronts but the vast network that moves our food from farm to plate. Much of it will get sold directly to the supermarket chains that control most of the flow of food between farmer and eater, accounting for 85 percent of the food we buy. Sometimes grower-packer-shippers—the industry term for companies like Christopher—will agree on contracts with retailers well in advance; sometimes they negotiate deals on a weekly basis. However it's sold, the stuff that goes to the big chains like Walmart will travel by truck to an in-house distribution center, where workers will organize the delivery and then parcel it out, packing in onto trucks for delivery to specific stores. Whatever isn't sold to big chains is sold off to brokers, who sell it to wholesalers, who sell it to grocers too small to run their own distribution systems and truck fleets.

Pedro and I finish filling out the report, and he sends me to a clinic in King City, another fifteen minutes down the freeway, where I receive excellent medical care. A kind doctor has me rotate my arms in different positions and attempt different kinds of grasping, and pronounces that I have a sprain. (A follow-up visit gives me the more-precise diagnosis of extensor epicondylitis—tennis elbow.) I'm not to lift anything more than twenty pounds with my right arm, and I cannot do any repetitive grasping.

But my job is to cut garlic. All I do is grasp, I say.

Have them give you something else to do.

I'm just a farmworker. All I do is cut garlic.

Then it's up to them if they want to keep you on, he says, not unkindly. He gives me a prescription for high-dosage Aleve and tells me to come back next Tuesday.

Three days later, on Monday, I drive to Soledad to collect my check and get two surprises: First, they do not have my check, because Pedro has it in his truck. But, as it turns out, that's OK because I will see him tomorrow: They would be delighted to give me modified work and have been wondering where I was these last few days. The doctor was right after all. The company will give me another kind of work, picking up garlic, which I can do using only my left hand.

When I explain this chain of events to Diego later, his eyes widen in surprise. This never happens for farmworkers, he says, which is why when he hurt his hand earlier he simply didn't come to work the next day. There's no way for me to know how frequently workers go without the care they're entitled to, if it's because they never ask or because their employers refuse to comply. But Diego makes a persuasive argument for why he never tried: If he hurts himself and complains, he says, the foreman may not hire him again.*

I'm expected tomorrow at 6 a.m. I can show up after sunrise—how else will I see the leftover garlic?—at another field in San Ardo, just past Dead Man's Gulch Road, but well before the oil fields that spring up a few more miles west. This is great news for my bank account. Minimum-wage work! For days on end! A week of this and I'll be rolling in money. But all my middle-class conditioning, all those years of being told that money isn't everything, is working against me here. I do not actually care if I will make more money. I want to leave the fields while avoiding the affront to my ego that quitting would entail—and I want my arm back.

The next day, I meet someone who wants to help me with both.

I meet Juán on my first day back in the fields, this time *juntando* all on my own, flung out in the far corner of a field. There are crews here, including Pedro's, but they're a quarter-mile away and I spend my day trudging through the garlic refuse alone. My only task is to fill a bucket with uncut garlic and hike over to the crews, where I dump it out for someone to cut. I'm wandering in a resentful daze after lunch, convinced that I'm only making my arm worse, when one of the company's pickup trucks, momentarily untethered from the Porta-Pottys and shade trailers it drags around, stops a few rows over. An angular man in mirrored sunglasses leans out the window and calls out, in English, Hey, are you thirsty? Do you want a Diet Pepsi?

I'm a little skittish at first, aware that I'm small and female and quite far from the rest of my crew. Thirst wins out, though, and while I sip a can of soda, the man, who introduces himself as Juán, offers to drive my garlic over to the pickers and bring me empty buckets. The offer is enticing enough that I ignore both his comment that having kids takes planning and his gift of an aluminum coin with a psalm from the Gospel of John on it.

The next day, Marta sends Rosa, the *ponchadora*, out to gather garlic with me. Apparently the rancher came through after we left yesterday and was appalled at the amount of garlic left behind, particularly in the part of the field where I had already gleaned, so we have to start over. We get off to a

---

* All farmworkers are covered under California's universal worker's compensation law. Nonetheless, a 2003–04 survey found that only 65 percent of farmworkers knew they were legally entitled to it, which may explain how rare its use seemed among the workers I met—most of whom were recent immigrants to the United States. (Aguirre International 2005, 40–41)

slow start, owing to the fact that a spinach field, separated from the garlic by a gravel lane, is being sprayed; Pedro has us take lunch an hour early and orders us to stay in our cars while a bright yellow, bubble-cockpit helicopter makes several passes over the neighboring field, gliding three or four feet above the ground and leaving a heavy gray mist in its wake.* Then it's back to the garlic, where Juán takes it upon himself to deposit a cluster of buckets with the promise to pick up any we fill. He comes by a little later and starts gathering garlic with me; Rosa is halfway down the field.

Do I have kids? No, I say, and no, I'm not planning on having any soon, either, although I can understand why a man of his age, in his forties, might. And, yes, it does sound sad to be married to a woman who never told you she couldn't have kids and to all of a sudden be looking for a partner to have kids with. I keep up a steady stream of sympathetic, yet disengaged, commentary until Juán gets a bit more specific.

All my life, I am looking for a white girl, he says.

There's a long pause. I don't know what to say to this.

Maybe you think that is strange.

There is a hidden blessing in garlic gathering: It requires one to stare at the ground. Well, I say to the dirt below, it doesn't matter to me, people want what people want. I change the subject to Mexico, asking what state he is from, but this backfires. As it turns out, Juán owns a ranch in Mazatlán, near the beach, and he would like to invite me there, I will love it, it's very beautiful and he has a nice house, he spent $80,000 on it. Have I ever been to Mexico? Well, once on a family trip to Cancún, I admit, adding that it was very expensive, mostly people just got drunk. Ah yes, he says, I am poor but I am happy, and we agree that one doesn't need money to be happy. Then we're right back to where we started.

All my life . . . all my life, I am looking for a white girl . . . Like you.

I stare at the ground and Juán says nothing for a minute. Then he perks up, says he will bring me another bucket and he hopes I will think about what he said. When he returns a few minutes later with the bucket, he asks me solemnly if I have been thinking about what he said.

Juán, I am not going to have babies with you.

---

* Later, I learn that the helicopter was spraying phosphorous, spinosad, and permethrin on the field next to ours. It was not very breezy, which minimizes the chance of drift, but I am not pleased to learn that California pesticide regulations prohibit workers from entering a field for twelve hours after this mix of chemicals is sprayed. (Monterey County Agricultural Commission 2009b)

What? Who said that? asks Juán, complete surprise in his voice, and for a moment I wonder if there's been an error in translation. Then I remember we are—and have been—speaking in English. Juán, I say, I don't want anything to do with men right now. He looks hurt as he goes back to his truck and I curse myself, a little bit for having hurt his feelings but mostly for having jeopardized my garlic transport.

My compassion kicks in after Rosa interrogates Juán and comes back to me with a full report. She has been schooling me, to the best of her ability, in the kinds of men one finds in the field. Guillermo, for example, is a bad one: He's lazy, and he is talking to me only because he wants to get papers. But Juán, she explains after gathering intel, is a good man, a friend of José, the co-owner of the company. Not only does Juán have a house in Mazatlán but one in Chicago, too, and yes, he is technically married but he and his wife are separated. She is mean to him because she's American, a teacher, and she can't understand why he keeps working in the fields for so little money even though he has his papers now. Juán has an interest in me, she explains, because I'm a white girl who works hard, and he'd love for me to just go and relax in his house in Mazatlán or Chicago and let him take care of me. He's a good man, says Rosa. Don't you want to go to Chicago? Or Mexico?

In a way, this is exactly what I was asking for: A way out of the fields, with plenty of rest and relaxation. If Juán wants a white girl who'll work in the fields, I'm probably the only one he's met in years; in all my time as a farmworker, I've been the only white person I've seen in the fields, and women of any race are rarities here besides. No wonder Juán's paying so much attention to me. And there's a part of me that's curious. Could I do something like that? Be a kept woman? On a ranch? In Mexico? Near the beach? I know that this isn't my "real" life, but I can see how foolish my disinterest must look to Rosa. I am hopeless at garlic picking—but I insist on doing it anyway—and I'm a single woman: Why wouldn't I at least entertain the idea of pairing up with a man who wants to whisk me off to the beach?

There's no reasonable explanation I can give to Rosa, so I hide behind my impoverished Spanish: *For me, no thank you, I don't want anything of men right now.*

Juán doesn't entirely get the message, even when I tell him I'm going back to Michigan soon.

Oh come on, he says, don't go to Michigan. Come on.

Juán's continued interest, however, comes with considerable benefits. He continues to ferry my garlic to and fro; having made myself clear, I let the argument drop. The price I pay for my diminished protestations is a shower of unwanted, unreciprocated compliments and gifts. I lose a bandana one morning, and after lunch he shows up with two, pink and red; he suggests I wear the pink because it will look nice on me. (And what can I do, because my neck is already burning in the sun without protection; when I tie it on he says it looks beautiful on me.) He stops by and tells me he only wants to treat me like a queen, will I please be his queen? The last time I see him, he puts his truck in park for a moment and leans out the window.

Hello, Tracie. I just stopped by to hear your voice.

In the end, it comes down to my arm or the fields, that's how I see it. And with all the luxuries conferred upon me at birth, I choose the former. I had put in four more days of garlic-gathering by the time I had my follow-up appointment, during which the clinic doctor and I determined that my arm had not improved. Yes, I explained, I'd been given modified work: I was picking up garlic in a field using only my left arm, my right one swinging about and sometimes—on those occasions when I forgot—picking up garlic. He tsk-tsked at me and gave me a thick Velcro band to wrap around my forearm, near the elbow, and told me to rest more. I had planned to spend one more week in the fields. I could have kept gathering garlic, which didn't seem to be helping my arm. Or I could have found other farmwork that somehow didn't require a functioning right arm. Or I could quit. I could just not show up to work again and let El Bajío figure it out on their own.

I've slowly realized that farmworkers do this frequently, at least in garlic. Diego misses days to go to the health clinic with his wife, nine-month-old daughter, and Rosalinda, who translates. Guillermo and Santiago didn't give notice when they left garlic for onions a week ago—there, they earn 95 cents for every *costale*, a big burlap sack that holds three buckets' worth of onions, they can fill. So when Diego calls me the morning after my visit with the doctor to say he doesn't need a ride, he's not going to work, I think, *Why bother?*

Any reserves of patience I had stored up for persevering were drained yesterday when I got my first payroll check, which charts out how much I picked and how long I was present. There, in plain black and white, is proof that the company has not only been paying me less than required, but diligently cooking the books to do so. Every day I cut garlic, the company took the total I earned by piece rate and divided it by minimum wage to get the hours they would put on my check. So, on a day when I worked eight hours and picked twelve buckets ($19.20), my check says I worked two hours.

That settles it: I'm not going back to the fields, and I'll quit when I pick up my last check. By the time I leave El Bajío, the company will have underpaid me, a single worker, by $454. I briefly consider bringing a claim against El Bajío, in hopes of deterring further such behavior; I'd like to teach them a lesson about paying their workers the minimum wage, at least, and not taking such hard work for granted. But when I look into it, I realize this is foolish, presuming as it does that the law will somehow mete out enough of a punishment to avert the practice. I might get my $454 back, but the average fine levied against companies who cheat agricultural workers is far less: $342. Later, I relay this to a lawyer who's represented farmworkers in Ohio for decades. He doesn't flinch at the practices I describe; he's been seeing them for years. "It's cheaper to violate the law than to follow the law," he explained with a verbal shrug. "It's the exploding Pinto theory of labor management."

I spend one more week in Greenfield, waiting for my final check, which won't be ready at El Bajío until Friday. So I busy myself the way anyone leaving their temporary home might: I clean up, I pack, and I say goodbye.

I tell the two families I've befriended—those of José and Dolores, Diego and Claudia—that I'm actually a writer. Farmwork is so informal that I don't want to spread it around too widely and somehow alert El Bajío. When I tell Dolores and the kids, they look at me blankly and continue with dinner, exhibiting the same reaction when I carefully repeat myself.

When I tell Diego his face breaks into a wide smile. He knew something was going on! I have to talk to Hector! So he, Rosalinda, and I drive over to Hector's apartment, a few blocks away, where we sit in plastic lawn chairs on kitchen linoleum, and they tell me they had no idea I was a journalist. Then they lapse into Trique, expounding on the problems of farmwork, using Rosalinda to translate their concerns: They don't earn enough money, the contractors cheat them, they don't like being in fields next to cropdusters and, heartbreakingly, can I please, please tell people about what it's like? Surely, they say, people on the news will listen to me; I'm a citizen. This is even better than what had been their best guess—that I was a government inspector who had come to expose El Bajío. I tell them I'll do what I can.

Across town, there are changes afoot at the little white house, too. Days are much quieter now. Valentino and his family have moved out after a particularly violent spat—I'd come upon Valentino with his hands clutched around his wife's neck, and screamed at him to stop, threatening to call the police before I realized the heft of the words coming out of my mouth. Now there's a new couple, very young, with just one baby in the second room.

The bigger reason for the quiet is that school has started, so every morning Sal takes Julieta and Leonel to school and gets Maricia on the bus. Rosalinda is eager about her middle school classes; Inez is still at home, cooking, cleaning, and babysitting an infant cousin; with the little ones gone, she seems to get a little more peace and quiet. High school starts next week, and Paulo is endearing himself to me all over again with his excitement. The only class he's been struggling in is English, and he's pretty certain he can graduate this year, on time. He'll be the first in his family to make it out of high school and plans to go on to community college classes.

My last night in town, there's a forest fire raging in the hills outside Soledad, the next town north, and the smoke has been clogging the sky since the morning. We eat from a platter of carne asada and tortillas in the living room and drift outside to watch the sky, painted with sunset and smoke. I don't remember what we talk about, just that Inez is studying vocabulary on the low stone wall, Leo is busy pestering Paulo the way little brothers do, and that Maricia, for once in her tiny life, gives me a hug. (Julieta tells her to.) I talk with Dolores about Michigan, where I'm from—and where I'm going next—and she asks when I'll come back.

Not for a while, I say, *maybe next year, in the fall.*

That's a long time, she says. *We'll miss you.*

When the sky goes dark, we file back inside. It's getting late, and they have work in the morning.

PART II

❧

SELLING

WAGES
Hourly: $8.00–$8.10

POST-TAX INCOME
Weekly: $221.00
Annually: $11,487

FOOD BILL
Daily: $5.44
Weekly: $38.06
Annually: $1,979.32

PERCENT OF INCOME SPENT ON FOOD
All food: 17.2%
Food at home: 11.3%
Eating out: 5.9%

CHAPTER 5

Grocery

Early November finds me in southwest Michigan, traversing two- and four-lane highways under the silvery skies of late autumn and taking my first stab at getting hired to work at a Walmart supercenter—the kind with a supermarket—in Kalamazoo. I chose Kalamazoo in part because it's on the west side of the state, where agriculture is strong, generating much of the produce that ranks Michigan in the top ten states for fruit and vegetable production. This small college town also happens to be the home of my sister Shana, so it offers a few days of free housing while I get settled. And I chose Walmart not for its reputation as a union-busting machine, and not even because it's the nation's largest employer. I'm here because Walmart is the largest grocer in both the U.S. and the world.

Perhaps most important of all is the lure of Michigan's economy. I knew it was bad before coming here, but on my drives to put in job applications, I hear a concise summary in the form of an ad for a local radio station. Scanning through the stations, I stop on one broadcasting a woman calling, "Economy? Economy? Where are you?" There's a pause, the sound of a toilet flushing and the inevitable response, "I'm in the crapper!" This wouldn't normally recommend a place for relocation, and will probably make the job hunt challenging, but I am hoping it bodes well for low rent—and will help explain why a college graduate is applying to Walmart.

I begin looking on a Thursday at a supercenter on the outskirts of Kalamazoo. I ask the older gentleman manning the door where I go to apply, and he directs me to two computer terminals, which he calls application kiosks. The one up front is already occupied by a woman with a shopping cart piled with groceries, so I hike past produce, ladies' wear, and electronics, duck down an aisle between fabrics and shoes, and finally arrive at an alcove. This kiosk sits beneath two security cameras, near a pair of swinging doors, with workers passing through almost constantly. If anyone notices me, they'll see the look of befuddlement on my face as I realize that I am unprepared to apply at Walmart. After my summer in the fields, I am taken aback by the volumes of personal information required to be considered for a position: a résumé, personal and professional references, an address, a phone number. And that's without mentioning the half-dozen screens full of legal and important-sounding jargon about being able to prove that I'm not a convicted felon and that I have legal status to work in the United States. (This last part, I infer, at least means I'll be earning minimum wage, which in Michigan is $7.40.) Through the kiosk, I'm able to direct my application to stores within twenty-five miles. That, at least, should save me money on gas.

The next week dissolves into a mishmash of phone calls to eight personnel managers of varying personability and incessant driving to stores farther and farther from Kalamazoo in the hope of wrangling a live interaction with someone in management—a dream that goes unrealized. In the interim, I do manage to find a place to live, taking a room in a renovated Victorian about ten minutes' walking distance from the picturesque downtown, for $350 plus deposit, all utilities included—and prorated—since I'm moving in after the first of the month. As for work, some combination of luck and perseverance pays off a week in, and I get what turns out to be my only callback, from Debbie at a supercenter about twenty miles away. There's a position available for a part-time overnight stocker in grocery and general merchandise, and they'd love to interview me the next morning at 10:30; just come to the swinging doors in back.

The next morning I wait underneath a certificate honoring this particular store for avoiding food safety violations for five months running. I'm retrieved by Marlene, a pudgy blonde with bangs that have been hairsprayed straight up. We settle into the old smoking lounge, and just as Marlene sits down, she startles, then pulls a walkie-talkie from behind, unclipping it from her belt. Sorry, she says, my butt bling.

First things first, says Marlene. She is interviewing me for a part-time, third-shift stocking position, but, she adds, once I get in on the ground floor I can move around from there—transferring's easy. That's what she did, and now she's a department manager. Sounds good, I say. (And I mean it, too, since I want to work in produce, so I can learn how fruits and vegetables move between farm and plate.) What'll I be stocking? Everything, pretty much; everything inedible is in general merchandise, and then there's grocery, too. Wow, I say, Walmart sells an awful lot of things, and Marlene grins like we're in cahoots when she tells me that Walmart.com sells steel caskets for $2,000. What won't we sell? She chuckles, then lowers her voice to repeat, incredulously, Is there anything we won't sell?

Then comes the part I'm most nervous about: my résumé, which features an unexplained gap from 1998 to 2007, bookended by part-time jobs in college and more-recent freelance copyediting. Marlene wants to know about these lost years, and I smile with a hint of embarrassment and tell her that I've "bounced around a lot" and did some writing classes and just so many jobs for not very long that I figured it'd be best to put down the jobs that I'd hung onto for a while. Then I add, truthfully, that my family is in Michigan and my grandmother needs help now that my grandfather is gone. I just need to make some money while I figure out how best to help, and Walmart is hiring. Besides, I love to cook, and I think I'd really like to work in grocery. Marlene smiles; she loves to cook, too, it's what she does on her day off, and, more to the point, that all sounds fine. After a few rounds of inquiries about my teamwork and people skills ("Talk about a time when you had to get something right on the first try. What were your challenges, and how did you overcome them?"), Marlene hands me off to an assistant manager, Sally, who ultimately makes a job offer. I just have to sign a few papers, take a drug test within the next twenty-four hours, and if I pass, they'll call me about orientation. Do I have any more questions? No? Just take these papers to the medical offices that do the screening—it's about a fifteen-minute drive—and they'll talk to me soon.

Waltzing out of the store, I have an unsettling recollection of the end of my visit to Walmart a week ago. I had been scribbling down what information I'd need to fill out the application when the greeter who'd helped me find the kiosks walked past.

You know, he said without stopping, there's a Hindu proverb that says, "Be careful what you wish for, you might get it."

You trying to warn me off the place? I smiled.

No, no. I'm just saying: Be careful what you wish for.

I had turned to make another smart comment, but he was already gone, the black doors swinging behind him.

Food is a relatively new product line for Walmart. When Sam Walton founded the company in 1962, he did so with a conviction that flew in the face of the reigning business orthodoxy. Poor, rural white communities, long avoided by national retailers, he argued, wanted the same nice consumer goods that their urban and suburban counterparts had. All they needed was a store to buy them at. Televisions and coolers and sports equipment were what built Walmart; food came later.

By the late 1980s, the retail behemoth had nearly conquered the consumer goods market and needed new ways to grow. Company leaders began experimenting with another model, blending a full-service supermarket with their regular retail. Their first supercenter opened in 1988 in Washington, Missouri; by 1998 Walmart had entered the ranks of America's top ten largest grocers. Three years later, the company ousted long-standing grocers like Kroger and Albertson's to claim the top spot. Today, groceries make up more than half the company's sales, and the company's supercenters and club stores sell 22 percent of all groceries in America. (For comparison, that is well above the combined sales of the country's next *three* largest grocers, who accounted for 15 percent of all grocery sales in 2009.) As a general rule, Walmart is most dominant in smaller communities, like those that gave it its start, having usurped the business of whatever other retailer had been there before. It's not just a nostalgia for rural life that has centered Walmart's business in smaller communities, though; large, once-industrialized cities with relatively strong labor movements, such as New York, have fought tooth and nail to keep the anti-union giant from coming in.*

Wherever it is, every Walmart supercenter contains far less fresh food than processed. That's something that's been true of supermarkets since their very earliest days, and to really understand the way that Walmart sells food, you have to reach back before Walmart began. You have to go back to the first years of the Great Depression, when supermarkets were born.

King Kullen, the world's first supermarket, opened in 1930 in a six-thousand-square-foot bus depot in Long Island. The store was the brainchild of Michael Cullen, a veteran grocery manager. He had been trying to convince Kroger and A&P, the biggest grocers in the country (he had worked for them both), to give a new model a try. He wanted to buy lots of food, enough that he could get it discounted from his suppliers, and he was particularly interested in stocking up on processed items, which can sit on shelves until they sell. Price some of it at cost, to lure in customers. Price the rest of it on a sliding scale, and expect that adopting thinner margins—and thus, lower prices—will result in more sales. Let shoppers pick from prepackaged goods, rather than

---

* In early 2011, Walmart began an aggressive public relations campaign to build support for opening stores in New York City, hiring Mayor Bloomberg's former campaign manager, and by late summer, 63 percent of residents supported the opening of a Walmart in the five boroughs. As of August 2011, no decisions had been announced as to whether Walmart would be opening shop. (Newman 2011)

haggle with a clerk parceling out goods from bulk. Apply, in other words, mass marketing to food. Cullen was convinced that cost-conscious shoppers would flee the "high-priced houses of bondage" represented by regular grocers. In a letter he wrote pitching the idea to Kroger, he envisioned "a riot" at his doors as consumers sought out "the low prices of the house of the promised land."

When he finally opened the doors of King Kullen in 1930, the floor was scattered with towers of goods, mostly canned foods and dry bulk but also a little meat, produce, and a few household items. Most of the food for sale represented the spoils of a newly industrialized agriculture that generated massive supplies of grain, fruits and vegetables, more than could be sold before it went bad.* With so much food available, it had become necessary to figure out what to do with it before it spoiled—and how to keep it edible. Preserving all that food required the heavy application of salt or sugar, the original preservatives,† and modern food manufacturers and processors were just coming into their own.‡ They created vast stocks of foods that could sit for long periods of time without going bad, what we call "shelf stable" today; hydrogenated fats, for instance, were invented by the French in 1905

---

* Later attempts to spread the American model of food stores abroad failed, largely because Europe had neither the agricultural technology nor the suburban development that were necessary for its success, writes the historian Shane Hamilton. Case in point: In 1950, Max Zimmerman, founder of the Supermarket Institute, launched an International Congress of Food Distribution to communicate American food retailing methods to Europeans. In 1953, Marshall Plan monies sponsored a traveling Modern Food Commerce across Europe. And in 1957, an exhibition called Supermarket USA opened in Zagreb, Yugoslavia to build a market for American-style agriculture and food retail abroad. All of this, explains Hamilton, failed without the founding pillars of American supermarkets: suburbs and industrial agriculture. (Hamilton 2009, 137–59)

† Salting as a method of preservation dates back to ancient Egypt, where salt extracted from peat and seawater was used to preserve food and embalm the dead. Sugar was introduced later, primarily as a means of preserving fruit, in ninth century Persia. With the advent of industrial processing, which involved heating foods significantly, sugar and salt were added both for their preservative qualities and to make up for the decrease in flavor that often resulted from canning or drying them. (Tannehill 1973, 210-212; Kurlansky 2002, 19; Mintz 1985, 123)

‡ The "real heyday" of industrial food canning in America hit around 1920, a considerable statement given that food processing already accounted for 20 percent of American manufacturing in 1900. Contrast this to the 1870s, when the American food industry centered on small, independent producers growing and processing their wares. By 1914, processors realized they could sell to mass markets if they could buy enough agricultural products and standardize their processing methods to ensure consistent quality. Selling this way also required massive infrastructure—factories, workers, packaging—and thus gave rise to corporate food companies that could afford it. Food manufacturers began consolidating throughout the 1920s and by the end of the decade, food processing was the largest American manufacturing industry, bigger than even iron and steel. (Levenstein 1988, 36-41, 150-152; GPO 1873)

and introduced to the American market in the form of Crisco in 1911. (It's worth noting that high-fructose corn syrup was rapidly incorporated into food processing in the 1980s not just for its cheapness, but because of its capacity to prolong shelf life.)

Without the threat of spoilage, more food could be produced at once, lowering the cost per piece. Food could also be standardized and distributed nationally, in small, recognizable packages; you didn't just need a name for your product, but a brand, to distinguish it from other, nearly identical products.* In just a couple short decades, America had taken the industrial economies of scale and assembly-line efficiencies that had spawned a revolution in manufacturing and applied both to its meals.†

This was worlds away from how an average housewife stocked her larder in the early 1900s. Most women would go to the A&P for dry and canned goods, handing their shopping list to a clerk who would portion out everything from bulk bins and shelves, and hand back the goods over a counter. (This sounds charming today, but it was a sore spot for many shoppers, who found themselves at the mercy of the clerks and their preferences or prejudices.) Much of what was on offer came out of bins: pounds of flour and sugar scooped into sacks, crackers and cookies portioned out by the pound. But some of it was sold prepackaged and bearing a label from one of A&P's house brands, an innovation that saw A&P running seventy food factories at its peak, enabling the retailer to compete against other manufacturers and push food prices down. For fresh ingredients, housewives and domestic

---

* In the early 1900s, advertising, promotion, and brand names were increasingly influential, since most manufacturers used the same processing technology, and processed foods were "absolutely uniform in appearance, quality, and taste." This remained the case for a number of processed foods at least as late as the 1930s. (Levenstein 1988, 34–35; Levenstein 1993, 26) Interestingly, as food processing and manufacturing have shifted to developing nations abroad, where industrialization is still in its early stages, there have been a number of cases where the same product made by one manufacturer is marketed as different products under different labels. In 2007, melamine contaminated the wet pet food manufactured in a Chinese factory that sold to American pet food brands, including seventeen house brands at major retailers like Walmart, leading to a recall of one hundred fifty different brands in the United States. (Lynn 2010, 4)

† Two other technological advances were key to Cullen's success: the automobile and the refrigerator. Though Cullen's store preceded midcentury suburbanization by several decades, Henry Ford's Model T had been on the market—and sold affordably—since 1908, and the fifteen-millionth rolled off the assembly line in 1927, enabling shoppers to purchase greater quantities of food on each shopping trip. The refrigerator became widely introduced to consumers in the 1920s, while the freezer didn't achieve widespread usage until after World War II. (Ford Motor Company 2011; Tedlow 1996, 182–86)

workers shopped almost daily; at best, houses had iceboxes that might keep food cool for a day or so, but modern refrigeration and freezing hadn't yet entered the home. They went out to produce markets crowded with whatever local farms were growing and a smaller selection of produce grown elsewhere in the country, or to street peddlers selling from carts.

Those markets didn't crop up by themselves, though; cities paid for them. In the decade before King Kullen opened its doors, most medium and large American cities paid to maintain 174 municipal retail markets, where residents could shop from a variety of sellers. Those markets were like distribution centers, where farmers could set their goods on the myriad paths that led to people's plates. Grocers would go to the wholesale markets, but so would alley peddlers and jobbers, small-scale distributors who in turn sold to more peddlers; a third of all goods bought at Chicago's wholesale produce market in the 1920s were sold to these small conduits, who in turn sold their purchases to street corners and tiny stores. Even as giant meat packers dominated the market, most of their meat was still sold in neighborhood butcher shops.

For shoppers, the difference between markets and supermarkets was dramatic. Prices at King Kullen were lower than most stores by as much as 90 percent. A can of Campbell's tomato soup that cost four cents at King Kullen was seven cents elsewhere; a pound of sweet potatoes cost less than a penny at King Kullen, but rang up at seven and a half cents at traditional grocer A&P. The store was a phenomenal success, underselling every grocer in town and luring so many customers away from regular grocers that they tried to introduce legislation to shut Cullen down.

King Kullen never became a massive national retailer the way A&P had; in 2011, it remained a New York City–area chain of forty-five stores, still family-owned and operated. But under Michael Cullen's tutelage, a new way of getting food to Americans had emerged, built on a foundation of industrial agriculture, industrial food processing, and mass marketing. Supermarkets would change in the years to come—they'd leave cities and sprout up in suburbs, they'd vacillate between promoting big brands and manufacturing their own—but the next revolution in moving food into American homes was still six decades off. It wouldn't come until the end of the twentieth century, when Walmart entered the game.

* * *

Are you new, too? Where are you working?

A heavyset brunette—her name tag says Blanche—is smiling widely at me from her post several tables over. She's sitting with Charlie, one of my fellow orientees from a few days ago.

Yeah, I'm new. I think I'm in grocery.

Aha! Yes! she gloats to another woman, scrawny and severe, at her table.

Don't matter, says the scrawny woman, whose name tag says Sophie, smirking and tossing her hand; grocery, I learn later, encompasses many different aisles and departments. Doesn't mean she's in dairy with you!

It's just before 10:00 p.m., and the entire night shift is sitting around, waiting for the managers to come in. There are thirty or forty of us, stretched out at eight or nine long folding tables and looking pallid under the fluorescent lights. The truth is that I don't know if I'm in grocery or not. I finished orientation a couple days ago, having sat through two days of videos about the vision of founder Sam Walton (summed up neatly by the current marketing slogan, "Save Money. Live Better.") and twenty-nine computer-based learning (CBL) programs. Thus far, I've spent my visits to Walmart marveling at how much it differs from the grocery stores I grew up with. The ceilings are higher, aisles are wider and longer, there are more foods to choose from, the lighting is brighter. But, even though company executives are positioning the company as a leader in grocery, food itself is mentioned only once in my training, as refuse, in a video about cleaning up spills in the store.

Before I left orientation, Debbie in personnel handed me a work schedule and told me she thought I'd be good for apparel, since men never want to work there. I smiled and silently bristled at this assumption—one that was used, specifically, as an example of inappropriate stereotyping in one of the CBLs—and, smiling, communicated two truths: that I likely had no more interest in skirts and trousers than the men, and I'm color-blind. Could I please work in grocery? Debbie made no promises, but did share the disappointing news that I will not be in produce, as that is an entirely separate section from grocery. I had worried this might happen, but had taken Marlene's assurances about the ease of transferring at face value. No, Debbie informs me, stocking cereal and soup and frozen dinners is just about the same as putting Nerf footballs on the shelf, but produce can rot; working with it requires special training, and they don't have any openings available there.

There's no time to communicate my apparent limbo to my new colleagues, though, because Coach Dana—managers, in Walmartese, are called coaches—strides in and greets us, misleadingly, with "Good morning!" Then Coach Stacey reads from a clipboard to list the night's assignments. I'm not working, to my surprise, in either apparel or grocery, but toys. Once everyone has grabbed their pricing guns and dispersed to their respective aisles, I approach Coach Dana and explain that Debbie and I had talked about my working in grocery and ask if I might do so. (I am already plotting how to transfer to produce.) Well, probably, she says, though she'll have to look and see. But she thinks they can work with that.

For tonight, though, I'm to work with Kerrie, a wiry, seven-year veteran of Walmart who's built so small that, she says with a sigh, all her sneakers have pink on them because she has to shop in the kid's section. There are already several towering pallets at the end of our aisles, stacked with cases of toys, so we retrieve shopping carts from the front and begin sorting: Boys' toys go into one cart, girls' another, and the gender-neutral preschool into a third. Then we "stage" the carts, placing the cases on the floor in front of their rightful place, and, last, we stock them, cutting open the cases, pricing each item with a sticker gun—Michigan sucks, says Kerrie, stretching her wrist, we're the only state where you have to price every single thing—and then put it on the shelf. We have to watch out for overstock, since sometimes the folks in back send out more toys than we need, and the last thing you want is to be caught at 6:30 a.m., quitting time, with a pile of boxes you have to run to the back.

Between fortifying the supply of Clue and rearranging the Sit'n Spins, Kerrie offers up what helpful information she's gleaned about working at Walmart. Working nights is a better deal because you earn a fifty-cent premium right off the bat, and she's a single mom, so that matters. Besides, it's easier, since you don't have customers coming in all the time with questions. Working nights does make it hard to cook, but she lives with her parents and they help out, and besides, Walmart sure beats waitressing, at least for her, since the pay goes up every year and the longer you stay, the more benefits you qualify for.*

---

* Among the benefits offered at Walmart are incremental wage increases each year, ranging from 40 to 60 cents, depending on performance; employee discounts on select items, including fresh produce, of 10 percent, which kick in after 90 days; and health care coverage with deductibles ranging from $350 to $2,500, which is available to full-time associates after 180 days. In a later conversation, Kerrie also pointed out to me that by working at Walmart, not Meijer—a regional competitor—she doesn't have to pay union dues, which helps her take-home pay, and that after fifteen years at Walmart associates receive a discount card for life. (Walmart Stores, Inc. 2008a; Walmart Stores, Inc. 2008b, 61, 229; McMillan 2009)

Despite a long-standing phobia of cigarettes, I accompany Kerrie for a smoke on our two breaks, which come at 11:30 p.m. and 4:00 a.m. We duck into the cavernous concrete halls of the back to retrieve our coats, our coffee, and our companions. Sophie, the severe-faced woman who was talking with Blanche, barks out, Hello, Munchkin! to Kerrie as she grabs her coat. They call me that because I'm so little, says Kerrie, telling me not to mind Sophie's tendency to shout, she's a real sweetheart. And Christine warmly introduces herself with a smile. We walk four abreast down an "Action Alley," a broad aisle lit up like a soundstage, pass through the sliding doors, and half-squat, half-sit on a concrete curb beneath the neon Subway sign buzzing in the autumn damp. The vast plain of the parking lot stretches out before us in the dark, mirrored puddles throwing the lampposts' glow skyward. The conversation veers into a collective groan over Michigan's pricing law—and the physical consequences of tagging every item. Both Sophie and Christine are wearing wrist braces.

So, how do you like Walmart so far? asks Christine, taking a drag on her cigarette. I can't tell if it's a hint of challenge or boredom in her voice.

Oh, it's . . . very exciting.

The ladies exchange glances and a collective chuckle erupts.

You're going to fit in just fine, says Christine.

The next night, I'm smack-dab in the middle of grocery. Aisle 8, Baking Supplies, a.k.a. Ground Zero for the Holidays. Here sits nearly every baking ingredient known to America. My aisle's off-white tile stretches from the hip-deep freezers of meats to one of the store's Action Alleys—a kind of shopping-cart thoroughfare, clogged with a holiday baking center display. On the right are salts and spices; sugars white, brown, artificial, and unrefined; Jell-O products ranging from gelatin and pudding mixes to No-Bake Cheesecake kits and pudding cups; marshmallows of different flavors, colors, shapes, sizes, and, with the inclusion of Fluff, consistency; nuts in varying degrees of dismemberment; graham cracker crusts, chocolate cookies, and shortbread; canned pie fillings of fruit and pumpkin; chocolate chips, peanut butter chips, and baby M&Ms; dry milk powder; flaked coconut; cocoa; and canned milk that's been evaporated or sweetened and condensed. The left-hand shelves start out savory, with cornmeal, flour, gravy thickener, bread crumbs, and multiple variations on Shake'n Bake; veer into sweet with cornmeal muffin mix, nearly limitless cake mixes, cookie and bar mixes, flavor extracts, leavening agents and cornstarch; and terminate in fats with lard, shortening, and oils.

My first night in the baking aisle, Friday, is spent with Jan, who warns me that tonight will be a little nuts since we'll be stocking up for the weekend grocery rush. She's a twenty-five-year-old mother from Indiana, with a husband in grad school. He works here, too; Walmart, says Jan, is pretty good about scheduling shifts for families, which explains the surprising number of couples I've already met. Jan shows me the grocery version of what Kerrie taught me: The pallets of food are already at the end of the aisle, so we have to unload their contents onto carts, take the carts into the aisle, unload their contents, put them away, and "zone" each item, which is to say pull all stock to the front so as to emphasize overabundance.

Manning the food aisle differs noticeably from toys in only two ways. For one thing, no partial cases can be sent back at the end of the night, so if you can't fit everything on the shelf, don't bother with it. More important, all food has an expiration date, however many months or years it may be in the future, and thus must be rotated, old stuff at the front of the shelf, new at the back. As I become familiar with the aisles of Walmart, I see surprisingly little fresh food. The freezer aisles are full of frozen pizzas and Hamburger Helper and waffles, and there's the snack aisle, the cookie aisle, the soup aisle, the soda aisle, the cereal aisle, the bread and coffee aisle, the heat-and-serve-meal aisle, and all the rest. But onions, chicken, lemons, tomatoes, milk, and all the rest of what I'd use to cook at home are relegated to the sidelines, with every processed food known to man taking center stage.*

The baking aisle and its neighbor, the cereal aisle, are Ground Zero in this grand experiment in unfresh food. Cold breakfast cereal is widely heralded as the first processed food, engineered and first manufactured near Kalamazoo by an eccentric health evangelist, John Harvey Kellogg, in 1881 as Granola (fourteen years later, the Kelloggs began manufacturing flaked cereals, like corn flakes, as well). Cake mix, which takes up roughly a quarter of one side of my aisle, was another early convenience food, introduced in the 1940s by Betty Crocker. Cereal and cake mixes are both textbook examples of the kinds of food that supermarkets were designed to sell: sold in boxes and possessing long shelf lives, they're easy to stock and to sell, requiring

---

* Supermarket layouts are designed to stretch the items that shoppers must return for repeatedly—perishables like milk, eggs, and meat—along the perimeter, thus ensuring that shoppers see as much of the store as possible without "annoying you so much that you run screaming from the store," writes nutritionist Marion Nestle. This is based on market research suggesting that "the more you see, the more you buy." (Nestle 2006, 19)

no more skill to maintain than the sneakers and toys that Walmart made its first millions selling.

Even so, I'm finding myself slow on the uptake in the baking aisle. The primary issue I face at first is one of navigation. With each new case I slice open with my utility knife, I ask, Where does this go? Like any stranger in a foreign land, I'm overwhelmed by the landscape around me. But, once I've learned the continents of my new world, each new product is a country, province, or town organized by its volume of sales. Finding Great Value (the Walmart house brand) flour is akin to locating North America on a map, but locating the solitary strip of Great Value Sugar-Free Strawberry Banana Gelatin is more like being tasked with finding the capital of Bhutan. Eventually, I figure it out through trial and error, with a lot of muttering to myself: Green cherries for fruitcake, green cherries for fruitcake . . . top shelf!

As a supercenter, we're open twenty-four hours, and other than the skeleton crew of cashiers, nearly everyone working nights is either stocking something—produce, grocery, electronics, toys, home repair, automotive, camping gear, gardening, clothing, pharmacy, health and beauty, stationery—or organizing the store's on-site warehouse so the aisles can be stocked. It's a good thing that 3:00 a.m. grocery shopping, as a rule, is confined to a bedraggled and sleepless few. Most nights, every aisle is an obstacle course composed of pallets, carts, and discarded cardboard.

After my first two nights training in Aisle 8, I'm on my own. At first, I think this means it will be just me and the shrink-wrapped stacks parked at the end of the aisle, but then Lou, who stocks drink mixes and seasonal specials in Aisle 9, starts dropping by—to show me an underpriced packet of Crystal Light drink mix, to compliment me on what a great job I'm doing. I'd guess Lou is about twenty years older than I am, so at first I think he's just being friendly. Then he sidles up beside me as I put away Betty Crocker Classic Brownie Mix (99 cents!), and murmurs, People are going to start talking if we keep meeting like this; I don't care, let 'em talk. Apparently, I realize with a start, we've been flirting. I confide all of this during break to Kerrie, and she rolls her eyes in the glare of the parking-lot lights. He's married! He just does that with every young girl that comes in here, she says. Ignore him, she advises me. But if he gets out of line, you let me know.

You should come work in baking supplies, I tease, so Lou has someone else to hit on.

Kerrie shakes her head. There's too much pricing, she says. My pricing's not what it used to be, not after the carpal tunnel.* She exhales, sending a spiral of smoke into the dark. Baking supplies is the worst.

The room I'm renting comes with an unusual advantage. In addition to sharing a house with three well-behaved college students who seem to mostly do their homework, I'm renting from an endlessly generous land-lady who talks at the speed of light. Well-the-room-I-have-is-real-nice-not-too-small-and-I-can-leave-the-cot-in-there-for-you, she greets me with when I go by to look at the place. Sue is short and fat, with stringy gray-ing hair in a sloppy ponytail, baggy jeans and T-shirts, glasses perpetu-ally sliding down her button nose; her husband, Max, rangy and laconic, observes us quietly from his perch at the dining room table. They live a little way outside of town, using the house as an investment. We-renovated-everything-and-it-was-a-crackhouse-before. We-think-we-don't-know. How-would-you-know? But-there-were-used-condoms-in-a-hole-in-the-wall-with-dirty-underwear. What-else-would-it-be-right? Do-you-want-to-see-my-before-and-after-pictures-Max-get-the-album-for-her? She continues the conversation I thought I had ended as she changes rooms, closes doors, and even, once, when she goes to use the toilet. She also has an intractable mothering streak. To wit: She has provisioned the kitchen with basic dry goods, condiments, plates, pots and pans. For this generosity, I am happy to listen to her ramble.

So-I'll-just-get-those-groceries-for-you-guys-and-then-you-can-share-it-or-figure-it-out-or-whatever, she told me when I dropped off my deposit. Did-I-tell-you-I'll-buy-you-pizza-if-all-the-rent-comes-on-time? Nice-little-incentive-don't-you-think? Who-doesn't-like-pizza?

I'm in a poorer part of town. It feels safe, but there's a dedicated Nar-cotics Anonymous meetinghouse a block over, there's a stretch of Habitat for Humanity houses at the end of my block, and Sue gives me a heads-up that, since she's paid some of the homeless men in the neighborhood to rake leaves in the past, they might knock on the door looking for work. (Don't-freak-out-they're-real-friendly, she says, endearing herself to me even more.)

---

* In 2000, the most recent year for which data was available, repeated trauma cases accounted for 73 percent of the total number of illnesses (the designation which covers repeated trauma) in the grocery industry, considerably higher than the proportion for all retail trade industries (50 percent). Repeated trauma includes carpal tunnel syndrome and other motion-related disorders and usually involves the hand, wrist, elbow, or shoulder. The grocery store indus-try typically ranks among the industries with the highest number of repeated trauma cases. (Clarke 2009)

The closest supermarket, a local chain called Harding's, is about ten blocks away and looks to be in the same shape as my neighborhood: rough around the edges, but nothing to be worried about. It's part of the Spartan Cooperative, a type of grocery store that straddles the line between an independent shop and the behemoths like Walmart. Grocery cooperatives like Spartan perform the same functions that places like Walmart take care of in-house: They coordinate orders from major food manufacturers, contract with others to develop house brands to compete against the big national ones, and function as produce distributors, too, managing the flow of food from broker and wholesaler into each member store. This one's medium-sized, and inside, it's clean and well-kept. Amish, pesticide-free chicken thighs are on sale for $1.99 a pound. I buy milk, and olive oil, and some carrots.

After paying my deposit and rent, and buying a few household furnishings at thrift stores, my nest egg has dropped to $547.10 for the next seven weeks. With Sue's generosity, I can spend my grocery money on animal protein, vegetables, and whole grains, and I luck out by catching the tail end of the weekly farmers' market. At the market late that afternoon, I capitalize on the end-of-day sales and secure a pile of food for ten dollars: potatoes, apples, squash, onions, and even four small, beautiful heads of a pale green cauliflower called Romanesco. I also figure that my best bet is to stock up on dry goods (the ones not provided by Sue, anyway) in bulk, so I drive fifteen minutes to a strip mall with a health food store where I stock up on bulk spices to flavor the rice, beans, and oatmeal I buy. At the cash register I get a shock, realizing that I've churned through $17.68; I'm too embarrassed, though, to put any of it back.

In my first two weeks of grocery shopping, I spend $68.36—enough, I figure, to last me several weeks. Now that I'm earning real wages—$8.10 an hour with my night-shift premium—I figure I'll be free of the hunger that plagued me in the fields. But I know things will be tight, and I'm grateful when Sue drops by one day when I'm making bread and asks if I bake a lot; when I say yes, it's cheaper, I practically see the lightbulb go off in her head. Well-don't-buy-any-more-yeast-sweetie-I-can-just-bring-you-some. I-run-an-adult-foster-care-home-and-we-bake-all-our-own-bread-and-we-make-our-own-soy-milk-and-we-make-our-own-veggie-burgers. It's-so-much-cheaper-and-better-for-you-that-way. And-those-little-packets-are-so-expensive-and-if-you're-working-at-Walmart-you-don't-have-much-and-there's-no-reason-for-you-to-buy-it-when-I-have-so-much-of-it, she tells me. I-can-just-bring-you-a-jar-of-it-next-time-I-stop-by.

I've been working for a little more than a week when Thanksgiving rolls around and I realize that my excitement over $8.10 an hour was poorly placed. I spend the holiday—flanked as it is by two night shifts, which precludes me from having to navigate family obligations three hours away—grimly documenting my penury. I received my first check yesterday, a couple days early because of the holiday, and it was for around six hours fewer than I'd expected, creating a shortfall. (Later, I learn this is because pay periods begin at midnight on Friday, dividing my shift; my Saturday morning hours won't show up until the next check.) This presents a problem, as my accounting has been tight. My rent of $350 is due in six days, and I have about $180 in savings. I'd been expecting a $200 check to make up the difference—$170 was tagged for rent, $30 for gas—but my check is for only $164, and I can't even make rent, let alone fill my gas tank.

Looking back at my receipts for the early weeks of November, I see where I was careless: I socialized with my sisters. In three weeks, there have been two meals out with Shana (pub food, then sushi); a coffee date with our other sister, Johanna; and a cup of chili and a solitary beer (Land Shark Lager, long neck) at a local bar after filling up on free wine at a party. These extravagances came to about $47, a figure not too far removed from the sum I am short. There's no gray area here: I brought this on myself. In addition to failing to grasp the realities of life on $8.10 an hour, I refused offers from both of my sisters to pay for me. I suppose paying for a sibling who earns less than you is not uncommon, but I was feeling too proud (to either argue with the choice of sushi or to admit I couldn't afford it) as well as being, I now see, overly confident in my budgeting abilities. There are other luxuries I could have sidelined, like the mirror, desk, chair, lamp, and linens I bought at a secondhand shop to supplement the lumpy cot and bureau in my room; I could, after all, have typed while sitting on the floor. My strategy of stocking up on bulk groceries in the first couple weeks now strikes me as less of an example of thrift than of the truth contained in Gloria Steinem's observation that "planning ahead is a measure of class," by which she meant not poise or erudition but income. I may save money in the long run by buying dry beans and whole poultry, but it's left me so cash-poor that I'm unable to cope with basic expenses.

All I can do is take this as a lesson and figure out how best to move forward, and I make use of the credit card I have for emergencies. I had figured that emergencies would be things like getting my car towed or paying for antibiotics, not making up for my own crappy budgeting. That might be because I've never before lived without at least modest savings, a condition owing less to thrift than the generosity of my Depression-era grandfather who worked hard, spent little, and left his savings to family. If it were food I was lacking, I could go to a food pantry, but I have cabbage, oatmeal, potatoes, cauliflower, flour, yeast, apples, a couple sticks of butter, beans, quinoa, rice, four eggs, and a handful of frozen chicken thighs; the Walmart doughnuts put out for the night shift every other Friday; the jumbo boxes of Post cereal provided by a roommate's relative who works for the company; and the pizza Sue has promised, and I hope to stretch this out for ten days or so. I could explore public transit.* I could have borrowed money from a sibling, but I figure it's better to save that option in case I run into problems further down the road. For now, I'm turning to MasterCard.

A few days later, I take out a cash advance. Like most who turn to plastic to fill the gap between grocery bills and paychecks, I pay dearly for the privilege: $10 to get the advance, since I don't have a PIN number for the card and it would take two weeks to get one, and a 19.24 percentage rate. At least, I tell myself, I can pay it back as soon as I get my next check. And I'll only do it this once.

The day after Thanksgiving, arguably the biggest day for leftovers in the American culinary calendar, is not a big day for grocery shopping. So when 2:00 a.m. rolls around on Thanksgiving night, I am—like all the other grocery staff—deployed elsewhere to help manage the big sale. I've already fortified myself on the (free) coffee and (free) holiday meal provided by Walmart, which was initially rumored to be roast chicken but wound up being white bread and cold cuts. As a treat, Sophie even brought in Ritz crackers and a dip of cream cheese and ham, half-shouting, "Eat it! That's what I brung it in for!" when she sees me hesitate in front of it. Energized from my meal, I head to my post. It's on the opposite side of the store from baking supplies, along the outer rim between the petrochemical perfume of Tire Lube Express and the capacious tents in Camping Gear, where I help man the ticketed line for

* Public transit, I later learn, would not have trimmed my expenses. A day of car insurance and gas for the round-trip drive run me about $8, but there is no public transportation between Kalamazoo and the city in which I work. There is the possibility of cobbling together transit with Greyhound and local transit options in each city, but due to scheduling constraints, it would require round-trip fare of nearly $17, leaving Kalamazoo in the midafternoon, walking two miles to get to Walmart, and catching an 11:00 a.m. bus the next morning.

"Hot Item K," a 42-inch flat-screen television priced at $598.

The doors are open all night, and shoppers start coming in around 9:00 p.m., giggly with pie-induced sugar highs. By midnight, they're crowding into lines and tearing corners off the brown paper that shrouds stacks of products scattered in the aisles, not to be opened until the clock strikes 5:00 a.m. Alongside two co-workers, Roseanne and Jacqueline, I settle in to help manage the line and thwart any shoppers' attempts to get started early. "No funny business, ladies," I proclaim to the shoppers waiting in our aisle. "I'm tougher than I look."

Selling flat-screens might seem to be a world apart from selling food, but at Walmart it's not. Just as Walmart can transfer me to general merchandise, it can shift costs and profits between departments, too. Having a massive mix of products is precisely what lets them drop prices to rock-bottom levels.

If King Kullen's success came from applying the economies of scale of America's early twentieth century to food, Walmart's comes from applying those of the twenty-first. One of the central tenets of mass marketing is to spread cost and risk across the entire store, pricing some of the things you'll sell a lot of cheaply while keeping higher price tags on things that might not sell as well. In King Kullen's early days, the store sold around 1,100 items, pricing roughly one-quarter of them at cost to lure people in, and the rest at a range of markups from 5 to 20 percent. The goal was not to make a profit on each item, but to figure out a pricing cocktail where some items barely turned any profit, but others made a lot. In the world of retailing, this is known as loss leading—pricing some items at a loss, with the idea that those low prices will lead people into the store where they'll buy other things.

Say Walmart is selling canned pumpkin at a loss in November to lure in customers, losing—for sake of argument—five dollars on every case it sells. It can still turn a profit if it makes six dollars off every shopper who stocks up on cranberry sauce, yams, and stuffing—or, better yet, another seven dollars off the pair of postdinner sweat pants they pick up, too. The bigger the pool of merchandise, the more a retailer can play with its prices, and that's one of Walmart's most powerful advantages. A typical supermarket sells between 15,000 and 60,000 items; the average Walmart supercenter has 142,000, giving the company much more "wiggle room" on price than traditional supermarkets. What's more, the supermarket section—or specific items, like organics or produce—can function as what Walmart calls a "trip-driver," bringing in shoppers who come for the food and then wander to the other sections of the store.

Those high-profile low prices set a cycle in motion. More people go to the store, expanding the customer base, building what economists call market power. Anyone producing a good for sale, be it sneakers or strawberries, must deal with these giant stores for the simple fact that they sell to so many people. Today, Walmart's market power is so great that it can essentially tell its suppliers how to make their products, and what price will be paid for them. This kills a basic feature of competitive markets: that the company making a product, not the stores through which they sell it, can set prices. When retailers control so much of a market that producers' options for selling their product are limited, so much so that the store dictates the price a supplier will get, economists call it a monopsony. And it's one reason that business journalist Charles Fishman wrote that "Walmart is so large that it can often defy the laws of supply, demand, and competition."

We think of supermarkets as just places, blocks of bricks and mortar where we go to shop. But in the contemporary United States, they're transportation and distribution systems, too, veritable railways that move our meals from farm to checkout aisle—and Walmart is by far the biggest. Today, writes the business journalist Barry Lynn, firms like Walmart have grown so big that "their control over their own shelving systems essentially replicates the power once enjoyed by our nation's biggest railroads." And that goes for our meals as much as anything else, even fruits and vegetables. In 2007, the five biggest chains alone sold more than half of the produce in America. There aren't public figures available to tell us how much of it passes through Walmart's produce aisle, but it's probably around one-quarter, enough to provide the fresh produce consumed by 26 million American families each year. The shopping done in Walmart's produce section could feed about 105 million Americans—a population equivalent to America's *five hundred* largest cities.

There's something besides food that lures customers here, though, and looking around the aisles in the wee hours before Black Friday begins, I'd have to say it has something to do with the company's mastery of telling its story as the modern-day price wrecker. As the clock ticks towards 5:00 a.m., the crowd swells, and the mix of festivity and tension turns palpable. Teenagers lounge in the baskets of shopping carts, waiting in line for a television; a heavyset couple in jeans and sweatshirts are in line for Hot Item K; a NASCAR-capped dad is patiently eyeing the stack of Candy Jewel Factory Ovens shrouded in brown butcher paper in front of me.

Somewhere just shy of five o'clock, I'm chatting with Jacqueline and

Roseanne when we hear a wave of sound rumbling toward us down the aisle. We look at one another and step back. The customers fall upon the wrapped stacks, paper flying, giggling and shouting and grabbing. In fifteen minutes, the mayhem in our corner has subsided, and we're dispatched to clear garbage and pallets out of the aisles until the end of our shift. I later learn we had it easy. My next shift begins with an assistant manager, Coach Brennan, announcing, "Welcome to Hell, er, Walmart," an observation he backs up by explaining that there were three fistfights during the initial push, and the police threatened to shut down the store because the lines were so long.

But this, too, is just one more maneuver that could have been cribbed from the King Kullen playbook. An early circular published by King Kullen itself suggests that the store-as-megaevent has a history predating Walmart's Day After Thanksgiving run on consumer items. "Exposed! The Reason Why 150,000 Housewives Crash the World's Biggest Food Market," screams the headline of a circular distributed in the chain's early years above a photo depicting a throng of women. I would normally be skeptical about tales of a mob of 150,000 descending on a store in a fit of bargain-shopping, but after my Black Friday morning at Walmart, anything seems possible.

After a couple weeks on the night shift, four and five nights a week—not all consecutive—my circadian rhythms are off, and things begin to fall apart. Despite the fifteen and a half hours a day I do not have to be at Walmart, leaving me presumably with nearly eight waking hours to do as I like, my free time seems to evaporate. I leave for work at 9:30 p.m. and get back home by 7:15 or 7:30 the next morning. (I rarely get out right at 6:30.) Then I huddle into my sleeping bag on the cot, pulling it over my head to block out daylight, and sleep as long as I can, usually about six and a half hours. Then I shower and take notes, cook, nap again from about 6:00 to 8:00, make lunch and coffee, and start all over again.

The few daylight hours I have access to pass in a groggy blur that I'm unable to shake, even on my days off. One hazy morning, I put a pot of beans on the stove just before sunrise—and fatigue hits. I mindlessly lie down to snooze and promptly take a lengthy nap, saved from fire and ruined food by the good grace of an alert roommate.

I'm also, as Shana has unhelpfully observed, getting "negative." Part of this is a warped expression of my personal shame over screwing up my budget, but I'd trace most of the grumpiness to the lack of sleep and limited socialization forced upon me by the night shift. I keep hearing ads on the radio about "shift work disorder" that describe symptoms that sound strikingly familiar: irritability, lack of interest in doing things, difficulty sleeping. But is it really a "disorder" to be foul-tempered when you barely see daylight for days at a time, work alone in an aisle moving a ton of freight each night, can't regularly talk to friends or family since they're at work while you've got free time, and still can't make ends meet? Further fueling my angst are the perks that Walmart is withholding until I've proven my dedication to the company; most of my co-workers have worked here for years, so for them there's a tangible benefit in the profit-sharing program associates can join after a year on the job, not to mention the discounts that kick in after three months—10 percent off most store purchases, including fresh produce. (Those discounts, in turn, lure Walmart's wages back to the company; as the nation's largest private-sector employer, its 1.4 million American workers have an estimated collective gross income well into the billions.)

Shana says she has some mail for me at her house and invites me over for chicken enchiladas. This luxurious combination of meats and cheeses is a lure in and of itself, but she's throwing in another treat I've been unable to afford: beer. Dinner is around six, and in an attempt to lighten my mood, Shana starts listing some upcoming holiday events I can come along to. There's a Christmas potluck party at a friend's house where everyone will bring a dish to pass and an ornament for the host's tree, which should be fun, even if it is forty-five minutes away on a potato farm. Then there's her annual cookie-and-booze exchange, and for that I'll just need to bring six dozen cookies, homemade, and a bottle of the adult beverage of my choice. Some cookie exchanges online are crazy about the rules, she says dismissively, prohibiting drop cookies and bar cookies. This won't be anything like that. Just six dozen and the recipe. Normally, I'd be scheming about taking something good to the potato farm, searching out a cute ornament for the tree, and ferreting out an interesting new cookie recipe. But this isn't normal life.

Well, I don't know if I can afford the gas, I say, which is true, since the potato-farm party falls before payday. And, I add, I have to work that night. Besides, I probably can't afford an ornament.

Shana's eyebrows raise—a family trait that indicates displeasure—and she asks about the cookie exchange.

Six dozen cookies is a lot, I say, thinking of the two remaining eggs and solitary stick of butter I have at home.

It's only two batches!

I know, but . . . I trail off, faced with her raised eyebrows. What I want to say, but am embarrassed to, is that that's two batches more than I probably have money for.

So instead, I backtrack. Maybe, I say, envisioning the glossy envelopes of cookie mix I've spent hours arranging, I can just make one of the mixes from work. They're cheap.

The eyebrows go up one more time. Bar and drop cookies might be acceptable, but mixes appear to be over the line. I don't have the energy to explain myself further.

I'll figure it out, OK? It'll be fine.

The first party rolls around, and between my hunger for socialization and appreciation of Shana's invitation, I add to my growing pool of debt and drive the thirty miles, first on the freeway and then down unlit dirt roads, to the potato farm. I try to justify the gas money I've spent by eating its cost equivalent in vegetables, dip, and brownies. I've been relieved of ornament duty by Shana, who offered a few days ago to put my name on her ornament and food. I have to work at 10:00, though, so no serious carousing for me. I limit myself to one beer, and then drive the hour to work.

When I get to work, grocery is slammed since it's the first week of the month. Food stamp accounts get replenished this week, and Michigan—like the rest of the country—is hitting record numbers; the resulting workload keeps chatting to a minimum.* The disappearance of cheer extends to the break room, too. There were a few days of Thanksgiving leftovers crowding the microwave during "lunch" break, but as the holiday recedes, we go back to the regular routine. There's a lot of random snacking on the night shift, with about half the folks I work with bringing a meal: sandwiches, pasta, dinner leftovers. Barb, a grandmother who usually works in beauty supplies, mostly gets by with a bag of pretzels out of the vending machine, and Nate, the big guy who typically mans the soda-and-beverage aisle, favors a big bag

---

* This monthly crush of business has made it difficult for stores in low-income neighborhoods to establish stable supply chain relationships, particularly for perishable items, due to the dramatic difference in demand. In response to stores owners' complaints, a number of states—including Michigan—have begun staggering benefit issuance dates, to create a more even flow of income into stores. (Food and Nutrition Service 2011a) This is particularly important given food stamps' increasing role in the United States; by late 2009, one in eight Americans received food stamps, about 13 percent. The county where I worked saw significantly more of their residents relying on the program, with 16 percent of Kalamazoo County receiving food stamps; neighboring Calhoun County saw 22 percent of its residents participating in the program. (Bloch et al. 2009; DeParle and Gebeloff 2009)

of Kettle Chips and two liters of Mountain Dew, drunk straight from the bottle. When I ask him why he eats this for lunch, he tells me it's quick and easy and takes another swig of pop.

One night I pass Kerrie and Christine decimating a plastic container of pound cake from bakery and tease them about their healthy diet. (Not that I'm judging, given my dependency on the free Friday doughnuts.) Kerrie explains that she already had a real meal before work: porcupine balls, noodles, and green bean casserole. As a child of the Midwest, I have a soft spot for the casserole in question, but the porcupine balls are new to me. They're just ground meat formed into balls with rice in them, explains Kerrie; meatballs with rice, served with tomato sauce. I nod and say it sounds good and ask Kerrie for the recipe; she doesn't have one, she says, it's just meatballs with rice.

There are other signs of home cooks, like Kenny, a mild-mannered giant with a baseball-sized lump protruding from his elbow—bursitis, he tells me, a forklift accident at his last job. He used to live in the Upper Peninsula and cooked in a diner there, so he brings in plastic containers of heavy northern fare like potatoes, sausage, and cheddar, washed down with a forty-cent can of Mountain Dew from the staff vending machines. And Sophie even brings in a shepherd's pie one night to share with Blanche, a white casserole dish layered with ground beef, mashed potatoes made from a box and topped with American cheese roughly the same color as the break room walls. She offers me a taste and then laments that her doctor told her no more salt, so she'll probably have to stop making the dish. Well, I say, you could make it so it's more healthy; make the potatoes from scratch, so there's less salt, maybe. Sophie looks at me skeptically, and Barb pipes up in my defense. It's real easy, Sophie, honey. You could buy ground turkey instead, too. Sophie shrugs; she'll see if it tastes OK.

All jobs require a certain logic and intelligence to do well, and stocking shelves is no exception. In the baking aisle, I'm putting to use skills that I had vainly presumed were useful only in white-collar employment: prioritization, time management, multitasking. My shift begins with an assessment of the most barren stretches of shelving—invariably, flour, sugar, and marshmallows top the list—and then checking the pallets and carts for what's available there. But I'm not just moving boxes from cart and pallet to shelf. I'm also breaking down boxes and disposing of the waste, I'm sorting excess stock to either return to the back room or put on the holiday baking display in the Action Alley, and above all I'm trying to clear pallets out of the way before daybreak. The volume of freight is so high that, each night when I walk to the aisle, it's a given that I won't finish my job. With failure assured, the only thing that keeps me from slacking off entirely is the hope that doing well here will ease my transfer to produce. And it's that, more than anything, that compels me to spend a good share of my third and fourth weeks worrying about failure—so visibly that Lou, who still visits my aisle occasionally, tells me not to take my job so seriously. When I tell Christine that I worry about never being done at closing time, she counsels me that it will probably take six months before I'll have figured out a system that lets me finish before quitting time.

Six months, it appears, is precisely how long Walmart expects it to take for an associate to learn a job, because, as Christine explains to me while we huddle in the cold outside on break, nobody can transfer from job or store until they've been in one position for that long. She delivers this news without knowing, of course, that she's just informed me that this month on the night shift has all been for naught. With a sinking feeling, I realize that in the scheme of Walmart employment, six months is nothing; many of my co-workers have been here for ten, fifteen years, Walmart being one employer showing no signs of leaving, at least. At first, I can't believe the news; all I've ever heard about Walmart is that there's an excess of turnover. Surely I can bounce around. But the more I poll my co-workers about this, almost all of whom have been here for years, the clearer it becomes that those tales of turnover were likely from the boom years. With a sinking feeling in the pit of my stomach, I realize that the very thing that drew me to Walmart—its grand, corporate size and efficiencies—will also prevent me from circumventing the six-month rule. My social security number is indexed in their giant computer system, and even if I quit and try to go to a different Walmart, they'd know I'd just left this one.

Maybe, I tell myself, Christine is wrong; Marlene never mentioned anything about a six-month waiting period.

I'm stocking the Baking Center on a Wednesday night, trying to find a place to stash another twelve cans of white frosting, when Coach Stacey comes by with a clipboard to inform me that I'm about to hit overtime hours. I nod and tell her I've just been working my schedule, which, thanks to the holiday season has been edging over full-time. I did stay late on Thanksgiving morning to help out Coach Dana, but only by about twenty minutes.

She grimaces. Well, that may be so, but there's really no reason for me to be working overtime, so why don't I just take tomorrow night off—relieving me of eight hours of work (and pay) for having been scheduled to work a couple hours of overtime.* I try to finagle Friday night off instead, since that's when my sister's cookie party is, but no dice. The schedule resets at midnight on Friday, so that won't really help her out. Tomorrow night off it is.

A blizzard is just starting to hit as I drive home—alarmingly, there's a semi in the ditch at my exit—and by the time I get up in the morning, the roads and sky are thick with snow, tree branches bowered under white blankets. Radio announcers are recommending that everyone stay home.

It is with irrational resentment that I drop a little further into debt and purchase two envelopes of Betty Crocker Oatmeal Cookie mix ($1.50 each) and a pound of butter ($1.98) from a Walmart closer to my home. Combined with my last two eggs, this is enough to produce the requisite six dozen cookies. I do what I can to doll them up; I had splurged on a bag of dried cranberries and add that to the mix, and I roll the cookies in cinnamon sugar and press them down with forks like peanut-butter cookies. This ends up being a futile exercise: The cookies are hard and dry, sweet but tasteless, and all my efforts to dress them up have done little to improve them but probably added an hour to the time I spent making them. Some masochistic math streak in me forces me to offhandedly calculate that a basic sugar cookie would have been just as cheap to make from scratch—and probably better, too.

My sister, meanwhile, has been pulling out all the stops, and I use my night off to help her with advance preparations. Upon arriving at her now-snowcapped home, I find that she and a friend are making three different kinds of cookies—two of our grandmother's recipes and one from a holiday issue of *Cook's Illustrated*. I help them set up a full bar, plus bottles of wine. There are plans for chips and dips and warm appetizers, so we set up a red-tableclothed buffet beneath strands of colored lights. There's a Christmas tree in the front window of her little Cape Cod, reflecting off the snow in the yard. There's a table just for the cookies and recipes, and I help Shana

* During my time at this Walmart, the agenda during the shift meetings we reported to at 10:00 p.m. typically included a verbal listing of associates who were in danger of running into overtime hours. Those who would have soon run into overtime were often instructed to take long "lunches;" one night, Kerrie was told to take a two-hour lunch, from 1:00 a.m. to 3:00 a.m. For reasons I could never discern, coaches refused to let workers leave early instead. This sort of treatment of workers, the labor department later explained, is perfectly legal. (Value 2011)

arrange them before an artful display of cookie cutters casting shadows on the wall via tea lights. It's lovely, and I'm glad to be here, but I can't stop thinking, "How much did she spend on butter and sugar?"

I arrive early the next night to help set up, and sneak off for a prework nap in my sister's real bed as the party gets under way, but when the alarm goes off at 9:00 p.m., inertia and fear take hold. I'm not just groggy but wary of the roads. The temperature has stayed in the low twenties, so even the salt trucks have done little good against the two feet of snow dumped on us yesterday. Each set of guests that arrives as I begin saying goodbye recounts their adventures on the roadways. Faced with an idyllic holiday party or a white-knuckled drive down an unlit stretch of freeway to a job I not only dislike but also am unsure if I'll keep, I make a calculation. Walmart has a highly codified tardy-and-absence system, and there are no repercussions until an associate reaches their third unexcused absence—and even then it's only a "coaching," a finger-wagging talking-to. This would be my first absence. I decide, guiltily, to listen to my inner slacker on this one. I call in, feigning car trouble.

My last shift ends up being the night after the cookie party. I haven't yet decided for sure that I am leaving, so there are no warm goodbyes. When the shift starts, Kerrie asks me where I've been; she was worried when I didn't show up after the blizzard, knowing that I have to drive the twenty miles from Kalamazoo. I explain that Coach Stacey told me to take that night off, and then I had car trouble with the cold the next night; now, I say, laying the groundwork for the exit I suspect I'll be making, my grandma is having some trouble. She nods and says something like, "It's always something, isn't it?"

It's the one night I forget my lunch during my tenure, but I'm flush with my paycheck—which covers two full weeks of work, including a little bit of overtime: $516.48. I cash it at the checkout counter during break, though paying off the debt I've incurred in the last two weeks has technically already relieved me of $93 of it—so I take a cue from the other workers and buy my meal. I spend $2.98 on a Healthy Choice heat-and-serve meal of Szechuan beef and noodles, and another forty cents on a Diet Coke from the vending machine. The meal is bland and salty, but the bigger problem is that it leaves me hungry; I've been slammed tonight, transferring a half-ton each of sugar and flour in five-pound increments from pallet to shelves.

I have the next two days off, and spend them calling around to other

Walmarts about whether there are jobs available in produce: none. I've already surveyed each of the coaches about my transfer options, and they each told me to wait six months. Finally, I give up: I'm going to have to quit Walmart and return at a later date to a job in produce.

I can see how, if I were to somehow finagle my way into full-time hours as a regular thing—not just holiday excess—I might eventually scrape by. Each week, my expenses have averaged $237.92, and full-time checks, after taxes, are generally around $290, so that gives me a surplus of roughly $50 a week. Strictly by the numbers, I should be spending more on food. Edibles have averaged 16 percent of my spending, but most people in my income bracket spend nearly 40 percent—though I can't quite fathom how they manage to do that while paying for transportation and rent. In theory, some of my monthly $200 surplus could be spent on better food, though given the paucity of my cupboards, my inclination would be to simply buy more of it. I'd be especially keen to add more fresh fruits and vegetables, since I haven't been able to replenish that supply since the first couple weeks; instead I sate myself with bread, rice, beans, and oatmeal. But maybe, just maybe, this could work.

A week after I leave Walmart, my car's radiator dies, and although I know the mechanic, it still costs $229.02. Transportation is one route to failure; health care is another. Even if I eked my way into the health care plan by getting hired full-time, my co-workers routinely complain about the Walmart insurance for its miserliness. In Michigan, Medicaid shuts off assistance to single adults if they earn more than $408 a month, and I mistakenly assume food stamps will be little better. (Later, I learn that the income qualifications for the two programs differ, and I likely would have qualified for food stamps.) My corresponding economic vulnerability to the small tragedies I've heard about from co-workers—a broken foot from a runaway pallet jack, carpal tunnel borne of the rigors of pricing, ramming a guardrail on an icy exit ramp—leads me to conclude that my chances of improving my lot in life via Walmart, at least on my own, would be slim to none.

I call in on Tuesday, citing a family emergency, and then on Wednesday call again to say I'm not sure when I can come back, due to the aforementioned family emergency. Robin, Debbie's assistant in personnel, says that if I miss too many days I'll get fired, and I ask, Should I just quit, then? She says maybe that would be best, and then I ask the real question I'm worried about: Does this mean I can't work at Walmart again? I'd like to come back.

Oh no, she assures me, these things happen all the time. She'll put down that I left for family reasons and when I'm ready I can just come back. I'll still have to get hired, of course, but that should be easier now that I have a track record with the company. They'll mail me my last check.

It takes five months, two days, and one hundred fifteen phone calls to twenty-one stores (and two months of working at Applebee's in between) before I return to Walmart, this time to stock produce in the suburbs of Detroit.

CHAPTER 6

Produce 101

For all the things you can call Detroit, perhaps the most disheartening is its unofficial title of Food Desert Number One. Jobs come and go; public services like streetlights and snow plows, once gone, begin to seem like bourgeois accoutrements one can live without; a rash of break-ins drives you to purchase a loud and vicious dog. There is, in a way, room to negotiate. But there's something inescapably concrete about the prospect of living in a place where food is hard to find, a heft that brings the human experience down to the bones.

Foreign correspondent and food writer Annia Ciezadlo writes about the civilian experience of war as "a relentless accumulation of can'ts," going on to observe, "No matter what else you can't do, you still have to eat." Detroit is no abandoned city—its population of 714,000 still ranks it among the nation's largest urban centers—and Detroiters justifiably bristle at the comparison of their home with a war zone. Yet the city undeniably faces on a grand scale the hardships created by America's suburbanization and deindustrialization. It isn't war, but it bears a passing resemblance; whatever devastation may be found in Detroit says less about the people here than it does about the decisions made, and policies chosen, by the powerful on their behalf. Ciezadlo's maxim thus applies: Whatever problems it faces, Detroit still has to eat.

A decade ago, nobody had heard of a food desert; the term did not exist. The fact that some neighborhoods, usually poor ones, had far more liquor stores than supermarkets was so common it wasn't notable; it was just the way things were. Detroit could be seen as a city-sized version of the same trend, with supermarkets closing up shop as the city's economic prospects fell. By 2011, neither Walmart nor any other national grocery chain had a store within Detroit's city limits. The last Farmer Jack, a local chain operating as a subsidiary of A&P, closed its doors in 2007. For all this, Detroit *does* have grocery stores—eighty-one, according to a 2010 city survey*—but it doesn't have enough.† Food access isn't measured by number of stores, but by how much square footage of grocery stores is available or how far you have to travel to get to one.‡ On average, Detroit residents make do with about half the amount of grocery store space considered standard by the industry, about three square feet per person. (By comparison, New Orleans and Washington, D.C., fall short of the standard by about 25 percent.)

There is one abundant option for Detroiters who live far from one of the city's supermarkets: the liquor store. Ninety-two percent of the stores that accept federal food coupons in Detroit are liquor stores, gas stations, drug stores, and other "fringe" retailers, and Detroiters spend their food stamps at them more frequently than their counterparts elsewhere. Every store in the food stamp program is required to carry a basic array of foodstuffs; many also join the Women, Infants, and Children nutrition program (WIC), which has a more stringent grocery list to fill, requiring retailers to stock at least two kinds of fruits, two kinds of vegetables, and one whole grain cereal, as well as approved infant formula. In 2010, about 13 percent of all food stamps in Detroit were spent at convenience stores, a figure more than triple the national average. In local dialect, these shops are known as party stores, a term that references their preponderance of liquor,

---

* This figure comes from a survey commissioned by the city, done by demographic research firm Social Compact. In 2011, local planner and blogger Robert Linn put the number of actual grocery stores higher, at one hundred eleven, after doing an analysis of 2010 Department of Agriculture store registration records, lending some heft to local sentiment that the "food desert" label inaccurately reflected food retail options in Detroit. (Social Compact 2011; Linn 2011; Kavanaugh 2007; Griffioen 2011)

† This is likely to change in the next few years. In July 2011, the city announced that Whole Foods would be opening a store in the city's Midtown neighborhood with the help of $4.2 million in incentives. There have also been rumblings about a Meijer opening up shop on Eight Mile Road—the city's northern border with the suburbs, a half-hour bus ride from downtown—though no lease had been signed by August 2011. As for Walmart, the closest supercenter is in Dearborn, ten miles from downtown, though Walmart executives had announced plans in late 2010 to pursue stores in urban areas, including Detroit. (Duggan and Skid 2011; Oosting 2011; Trop 2010; Google Maps 2011d; The Week Fact Sheet 2010)

‡ The metric used to determine food access is decided by the research group using it, and each has its benefits. Square footage helps to control for the differences that emerge if there is one giant supermarket in a community as opposed to three small; distance measures ease of access to a supermarket, but not its breadth of selection. The latter metric is more tricky to measure, while the former can usually be accomplished by procuring a list of licensed food stores and comparing it with census data. Thus, square footage per person is the more dominant measure in use.

cigarettes, lotto, and junk food; the implications for relying on such shops as a food source are correspondingly grim. However much they redeem in food stamps, party stores rarely carry anything fresh, relying instead on products that can sit on shelves, unattended, for months without any threat of rotting.

Yet for years, convenience stores have been treated as the natural food supply for urban residents, while supermarkets were considered the feeding grounds for suburbanites. Supermarkets made a big splash in the 1930s, but they really took off when suburbanization took hold in the mid-twentieth century. Instead of walking to work and taking streetcars, people began driving big cars to larger homes with refrigerators and freezers, where they could store more food, especially fresh food. Our country's supermarkets were so emblematic of America's rising fortunes that when Premier Nikita Khrushchev of the Soviet Union visited the country in 1959, he famously included one in San Francisco on his itinerary.

Supermarkets were a showcase for America's industrial agriculture and abundance, but beneath the surface they were a system for distributing food. As they headed to the suburbs, supermarkets had to do more than sell food to housewives—they had to figure out how to bring food into communities that suddenly needed far more of it. They began to convince wholesalers to deliver to their stores and, over time, built their own distribution networks. They sought sites where they could build sprawling stores and parking lots cheaply, and looked for communities that were affluent and willing to drive, rather than working-class and inclined to walk. Every metric supermarket executives used to decide where to build a store was written with the suburbs in mind. Today, Detroiters reenact that exodus for much of their grocery shopping, heading outside the city to stock their kitchens and spending an estimated $200 million—nearly one-third of their grocery budgets—at suburban supermarkets each year. The food heads back to the city, but the profits generated by this $200 million stay outside the city limits.

Yet, if you talk to a marketing expert, the typical explanation for food deserts is a lack of demand, which is another way of saying there is nobody in the proposed market area who, well, *eats*. Really, what marketers mean is that there are either not enough people to support a supermarket—which, because it makes its money on volume, has to reach a certain level of sales—or that the people there are too poor, and won't generate enough sales per person. In the 1990s and early 2000s, supermarket executives told city planners in Chicago and New York that their stores would never be able to turn a profit in Manhattan's Harlem or Chicago's South Side; these weren't their markets or their customers. There were tens of thousands of shoppers, but the average income was lower than in the suburbs. It took planners years to persuade developers that the sheer number of shoppers, even if they had lower incomes, would make it worth the developers' while. The case the planners had to make boiled down to this: Food is not like fancy sneakers or high-end housewares. Everyone has to buy it. Everyone eats.

Two decades later, Harlem has a Pathmark. Back in the early 1990s, Harlem's 125th Street had yet to be made over; brownstones were still crumbling, and the drug trade was still brisk. It was in all likelihood what we'd call a food desert today, lacking in big, suburban-style supermarkets, but with a number of smaller, independent ones. Crime and poverty rates there were among the highest in Manhattan, but the city worked with Pathmark, an East Coast chain, to open a Harlem store in 1999. Today, it's one of the chain's highest-grossing stores, often cited as an early, essential piece of the neighborhood's redevelopment—and a beacon for other cities looking to replicate its success. When the project was first being discussed, *USA Today* called historic ghettos, like New York's Harlem and Washington D.C.'s Anacostia, a "land of opportunity" for retailers.

I wonder, as I set out for Michigan, whether this could be an apt way to describe Detroit, too.

My first weeks in Detroit prove a makeshift maxim of struggling economies that one of Pilar's friends had shared with me over tacos in California: Housing is easy, but work is hard. Before I get to Detroit, I find a room to rent from Christina Guzman, a Mexican American forty-seven-year-old single mom who prefers to be called Chris, born and raised in "the D." My furnished room, including utilities, costs $400 a month with off-street parking, and it's in Hubbard Farms, a stable neighborhood on the southwest side. My rent is a bit steep for Detroit, and in return I live in a part of the city where occupied homes outnumber the abandoned ones. Elsewhere in Detroit, whole apartments can go for $300 and sometimes less, and across the city rent beyond $600 is almost unheard of. This is a simple function of housing supply far outstripping tenant demand in a city that's lost nearly 1 million residents from its 139 square miles since 1950. The city still loses an average of 1,200 residents a month, making me—as a newcomer seeking housing—something of a statistical rarity.*

But as far as employers are concerned, I am no such thing. Wannabe workers are a dime a dozen and get treated accordingly. I'd lined up an interview at a supercenter out in the western exurbs, for produce, before I even got to town, but when I finish the interview on my second day in Michigan, I am surprised to find there is no instantaneous job offer, as had been the case before. I did just fine, says my initial interviewer, Randy, a sloppy, surprisingly young kid, but they have to do a background check and call my references, and they'll let me know if I clear those hurdles next week—at which point they'll schedule a third interview. Until then, I'm to wait. During the half-hour drive back to Detroit, where my steady speed of seventy-five miles an hour relegates me to slow lanes, it strikes me that expecting to waltz into a job in the Detroit metro area in 2010 is naïve. The city's unemployment rate stands at 14.7 percent, nearly 50 percent higher than the country's as a whole. I am one tiny fish swimming in an ocean of applicants. This is going to take some time, dedication, and luck.

Chris's house, and therefore my home, is technically in Hubbard Farms, but really, we live in Mexicantown. Mexican immigrants first came to Michigan around 1900, many of them working in sugar beet fields; some ended up in Detroit with industrial jobs. The Great Depression saw many return to Mexico, but as the midcentury economy flourished, jobs began drawing immigrants once again. Detroit lured people on a 2,300 mile journey with the promise of jobs at the sprawling factories built by Ford and Chrysler and in its cavernous steel plants; the intersection of Springwells Street and Vernor Avenue, west of Chris's house, was the center of 1940s Mexican migration to the city. Chris's father left behind a thriving Mexican ranch at twenty-one to come north, as much for adventure as for money in the 1950s, settling in to work at a steel plant a few years later. (The family began renting the duplex I'm living in somewhere around 1960, buying it in the 1980s.) Today, the plants here are silent and empty, like most of the industrial-age behemoths that dot the city. They sit along the neighborhood's edge, monoliths of corrugated steel reaching skyward from asphalt prairies

---

* Numerically speaking, I am an outlier but the last five to ten years have seen an influx of young, educated, and creative people moving to Detroit, drawn by its cheap rents, vast available space, and urban agriculture. City population estimates have shown that neighborhoods popular with this demographic—notably Midtown, Woodbridge, New Center, and Corktown—are actually increasing in population. (Wilkinson 2011; Neavling 2011)

decaying around them, the radii of bars and diners that used to feed their workers shuttered for years.

But that is the edge of the neighborhood, and both Mexicantown and Hubbard Farms have done a better job than most of the city in avoiding the heart-wrenching blight that's slowly been allowed to creep across Detroit since 1950. Two blocks west of my new home, families crowd Clark Park for soccer practice and playground visits in the evenings, with the Ambassador Bridge to Canada in the background. Two blocks north, up a street canopied with oaks and maples, a string of businesses dot West Vernor: a coffee shop, an ice cream parlor, a neighborhood development group, a bakery, a laundromat, a small grocer, and a taco truck. As elsewhere, there are arson-ravaged shells and boarded-up storefronts, apartment buildings with plastic-sheeted windows and shin-high grass, but they don't dominate. There are entire blocks where well-kept homes with mowed lawns and tidy gardens consistently line the street, though it of course says something about Detroit that such stretches are the kind of thing you mention rather than take for granted. The best thing about my new neighborhood, hands down, is the supermarkets. Detroit is known for its lack thereof, but Mexicantown is different, home to what I am told—over and over and over again—is the best supermarket in the city: Honey Bee Market/La Colmena.*

Chris sent me there my first day in Detroit. I needed to get cash for her; as soon as I'd arrived Chris had insisted I needed a security "club" for my car—and she could get one for me, cheap, with her student discount. I pointed out that Ford Escorts weren't particularly hot sellers on the black market, but Chris would have none of it. Her car was stolen out of the driveway last year: They'll take anything that's not nailed down, don't leave anything in your car!

Is there a grocery store nearby? I asked. I could just get some food and do cash back?

Her eyes lit up: Do you want to make ceviche? I have fish in the freezer, so you just need to get lemons and limes. Her eyes got bigger, excited. You can go to the Honey Bee, you'll love it. There are a half-dozen supermarkets in the neighborhood, she added, but this is the best one; everything is really

---

* *Colmena* means hive, and was the name of the original corner market established by the family of one of the current proprietors when they first moved here from Mexico, selling basic groceries, including a modest selection of produce in a single refrigerated case, to Mexican factory workers. In 2006, the corner market was expanded into a full-service grocery store with an extensive produce section.

fresh. We live within a mile of four, making our non–food desert status official; three of the markets specifically cater to the Mexican American families
who form the backbone of the neighborhood. She handed me a list: eight
lemons, eight limes, onion, cilantro.

Off I went, about one mile, following Chris's directions: Up West Vernor's four lanes, past La Mexicana grocery with the taco truck in the parking lot; past the liquor store offering a free two-liter bottle of pop with every
ten dollars in WIC or SNAP purchases; keep going; cross over the Fisher
Freeway, and then, just after the shuttered police precinct being turned into
art studios and an urban farm supply shop, but before the road dips under
the colossal, abandoned skeleton of Detroit Central Station, go right. Then
left. Two blocks, past the tortillería, and the Honey Bee'll be on the right.

The market wasn't huge, but the produce section teemed with fruits and
vegetables, including eleven different kinds of fresh chile. And this was
before I noticed several different brands of fresh tortillas; house-made salsas
and guacamole; a sprawling meat counter; bags of dried, pale green Peru-
vian beans and earthy speckled pintos; and a fresh food counter with *barba-
coa* and taco specials. I was fingering the bags of lemons, six in each, when
a young man working in the section stopped me.

They're $2.49, he said. I see you looking.

Thank you, I said, adding two bags to my basket.

On the way home, I passed one more landmark Chris had mentioned: a
community garden, part of a citywide network of food gardens that began
with about 80 plots in 2003. Focused on producing food in a city where
procuring affordable, farm-fresh produce can be difficult for everyone, the
network grew to 1,234 in 2010, with more than 80 percent of the gardeners
returning each year. Our neighborhood garden was carved out of an empty
stretch of land behind a series of boarded-up row houses, sitting across from
the vacant lot opposite my duplex and visible from my bedroom window.
Garlic tops shot up in crisp rows, lettuces were starting to leaf out. It wasn't
yet May, and everything was just beginning to grow.

My first few weeks I am jobless, and I spend much of my time either cadg-
ing tours of the city from friends of friends or sitting in Chris's living room,
chattering with the constantly rotating series of visitors. Her twenty-one-
year-old daughter, Bianca, lives a mile deeper into Mexicantown and comes
by, like most children, to take advantage of the material comforts now
beyond her reach: in-house laundry and a full(ish) fridge. Chris's parents

live next door, along with her sister, Brenda, and Brenda's four-year-old son, Adrian; their kitchen has somehow ended up without an oven, so Brenda pops over with some regularity to make use of Chris's. Then there's Gabriel, a young lawyer she befriended during her bachelor degree studies in the early 2000s, and a sometime-suitor, whose name I don't manage to catch when he knocks on the door one night to see if she's home. (She's not, but I don't divulge that she is on a date with someone else.)

Brenda is one of the Detroiters who commutes for her groceries the same way I expect I'll be commuting for my job. I used to be a Meijer girl, she says, watching Adrian scramble around the duplex in his pajamas, a mass of inky curls atop his head. But now that she's divorced and going back to school, she's a Walmart girl, through and through. It might only be a difference of thirty cents here, twenty cents there, but that matters to a family, she says, and the smaller stores in the city are too expensive. She won't go to the Walmart just outside the city limits, though; that one is dirty and crowded. Instead she drives a half-hour to get to a good one, in a wealthy suburb, where the store is clean and the produce is fresh.

I don't ever go shopping with Brenda, but I do notice in my own shopping that La Colmena isn't as expensive as I would have expected—and the quality is excellent. Onions, potatoes, zucchini, and oranges, for example, are all *cheaper* at La Colmena than at Walmart, by a range of 16 percent (zucchini) to 54 (oranges). Later, I learn that small grocers are much more competitive when it comes to the price of fresh produce, which for all of its industrialization retains a stubborn agrarian trait: It rots. Since fresh food can spoil, the economies of scale of industrial grain are simply not possible; there's no profitable way to consistently buy massive quantities cheaply and then sell it off over time. In fresh produce, one of the large supermarkets' biggest competitive advantages—scale—doesn't get them very far.

Processed food is a whole different story. You can buy an entire warehouse full of box meals and sell them off over the course of a year, enabling a different kind of calculation. The biggest companies sell their own line of private-label products, and most have contracts with food manufacturers who manage the manufacturing process. Walmart doesn't actually make its house brands; for most of its Great Value products, it likely picks a recipe from an existing supplier's offerings and puts its own label on it. That's why, when it became clear that Walmart's Great Value peanut butter was at risk for salmonella contamination in a 2007 outbreak, it was ConAgra— the manufacturer—that first issued the recall, not Walmart. Today, having a house brand means that Walmart can compete viciously, both pushing down the cost of its inventory by guaranteeing suppliers access to its huge market, and conceding ever-thinner margins in the interest of drawing more people into its store for their remarkably low prices. Walmart might not win in produce, but it cleans La Colmena's clock when it comes to processed food. Of sixteen common canned and frozen items, every single one is more expensive at La Colmena than at Walmart. A fifteen-ounce can of Dole pears costs $1.99 at La Colmena, but a can of Walmart's Great Value pears, twice as big, costs 98 cents; ounce for ounce, Walmart's canned pears cost less than one-quarter of those at La Colmena.

Research commissioned by Walmart, as well as some academic work, suggests that it beats other retailers by between 14 and 16 percent on price, but it's important to look at this research closely. The report commissioned by Walmart, for instance, excludes random weight items and meats, which is to say produce and fresh meat. Most studies take an average across multiple store items without detailing the differences between departments; the few studies that look at specific, rather than average prices, suggest that meat and produce are categories in which Walmart is—as I saw at La Colmena—the least able to compete. And aside from the Walmart-backed study, any research looking at the company's prices is operating with a large handicap: Walmart doesn't report its sales figures or prices to any of the national data agencies, and, as a private corporation, it has no obligation to do so.* Instead, researchers either base their work on prices at supercenter-format stores—which Walmart dominates—or focus on very tight geographic areas, compiling store-by-store comparisons in a single metropolitan area. Either way, they're dealing with information that can never tell them what they want to know: The precise degree of power Walmart yields in our food system.

Much of the research draws on broad averages, not just across store items, but often across different kinds and sizes of grocery stores. The difference between prices at a Walmart and small stores can be quite dramatic, but the difference between Walmart and other big chains—Albertson's or Kroger, for example—is much smaller, about 2 or 3 percent. Size changes the game significantly. In traditional supermarkets, stores are competing against each

---

* Given Walmart's market share within our food system, the omission of its data hinders accurate assessment of trends within it, particularly regarding price. The omission is so serious that in 2004 the National Bureau of Economic Research published a paper subtitled, "Does the Bureau of Labor Statistics Even Know That Walmart Exists?" (Hausman and Leibtag 2004)

other on price, trying to find the sweet spot where a price is low enough to bring in more shoppers and high enough to turn a profit. But places like Walmart don't think like this: They have so many customers, and such a big share of the market, that massive sales volume is a given. Instead, the big guys focus on how to cut costs—things like distribution systems, and contracting out their own food manufacturing. Lower costs, in turn, mean they can charge lower prices when competition dictates it—or turn bigger profits when it doesn't.

The undeniable king of private infrastructure is Walmart, which means that it is almost always possible for the company to intensify competition, and lower prices if it chooses. In order to stock a huge selection of products, Walmart has always maintained a hypersophisticated inventory and transportation system, building a private satellite network in the pre-techie 1980s that allowed it to manage a massive product line. When the company shifted into grocery in the 1990s, it could leverage that inventory system to develop a pricing scheme* where key items would be cheap enough to lure people into the store, but other items could make a profit. And as people flocked in for affordable groceries, Walmart's share of our food supply grew at an unparalleled pace; at 22 percent, it now sells more than twice as much as the next three largest stores combined. If there is any store that *can* win on price, it's Walmart.

One of the more persuasive arguments Walmart offers when it comes into a community is that its low prices are good for everyone. Not only are the prices at Walmart good for consumers who shop there, goes the argument, but they're good for the people who don't, too; Walmart's lower prices beget competition and force down the prices at other stores. Most existing research suggests that Walmart's presence causes a drop in local grocery prices of between 1 and 8 percent. There's an important caveat to this, though: Without access to data over time, most research focuses on "snapshots," examining prices at different stores over a very short period in time, seeing whether prices at local grocers are higher than supercenters' over the course of, say, a month. Research has yet to delve deeply into the question of whether supercenters lower local food prices for the long haul, but in 2007 researchers in Wisconsin found something surprising. In their study

---

* Walmart typically refers to its pricing strategy as "everyday low price," the idea being that instead of pricing items promotionally they stick to one consistent range of markup. As any visit to a Walmart will show you, EDLP is in practice more of a simplified take on the promotional model supermarkets began with, employing the same tactics of loss leading and mass marketing but paring them back. (Ellickson and Misra 2008; Volpe 2011)

of twenty-three cities from 1993 to 2003, they found that the addition of a supercenter had no discernible effect on local prices over time. The same researchers also found something that *did:* market concentration.

It's an old rule of economics that the fewer competitors in a market-place, the higher prices will be—and that's what these researchers found. The fewer stores there were in a metropolitan area, the higher food prices were. To gauge concentration, economists use a metric called the C4 ratio, looking at the market-share held by the four largest competitors in a market. By this measure, America today has the most concentrated food retail market in the last century, a trend that has spiked in the last two decades, likely driven by Walmart. In 1992, the four biggest supermarkets in America controlled 17 percent of our groceries; by 2009, they accounted for more than twice that: 37 percent. The Walmart where I work, I later find out, is one of two huge grocery stores in town—which might explain why its prices aren't as jaw-droppingly low as I had expected.

In many cities, Walmart is so dominant that it has little incentive at all to drop prices, and for millions of Americans, it is far and away the biggest game in town. By 2010, the retailer accounted for between 50 and 70 percent of grocery purchases in twenty-nine cities, a collective population of more than five million. This doesn't necessarily bode well for local shoppers. "It appears that consolidation led to higher prices," wrote the Wisconsin researchers, "and any merger-related cost gains during this period were not passed on to consumers." For all of stores' talk of ever-lower prices, once one or two stores control enough of the market, they have no reason to charge less*—and we have no definitive proof that they do.

Today, Walmart is poised to become an even bigger player in our food. In early 2011, First Lady Michelle Obama appeared at a Walmart press conference to applaud the company's four-prong plan to work toward her goal of ending childhood obesity in a generation. Part of the plan involved Walmart making its house brands healthier by lowering their sugar and sodium con-

---

* A USDA study published in 2010 found that the price difference between nontraditional stores—the category of stores that includes Walmart—and traditional supermarkets was markedly smaller in cities with a high share of nontraditional stores. The average price difference in Atlanta and San Antonio, where supercenters dominate, was 5.3 percent, while in cities with low levels of supercenter retail, like New York and Philadelphia, it was 11.5 percent. This, said researchers, could indicate that traditional grocers lowered their prices in a bid at competition; or it could indicate that supercenter retailers, responding to the diminished competition, raised their prices to that of their remaining local competitors. (Leibtag, Barker, and Dutko 2010)

tent, a goal with which it is difficult to disagree. Another pillar of the initiative included making healthy food more affordable, saving Americans $1 billion on fresh fruits and vegetables. "No family should have to choose between food that is healthier for them and food they can afford," said Bill Simon, president and CEO of Walmart U.S., sharing the stage with First Lady Obama. He made it sound like a $1 billion discount for the poor, but Walmart wasn't reducing its *own* prices. That figure is derived from comparing Walmart's prices with those of other stores, not by estimating future reductions to Walmart's. The way Walmart plans to "save" us $1 billion is not by reducing the grocery bills of its own customers, but by selling its wares to new ones—by gaining market share.

The third piece of the initiative was the most interesting. Officials announced Walmart's intent to solve the problem of food deserts by building stores in urban neighborhoods—many of which have actively sought to keep the retailer and its downward pressure on wages out. "We are focused on bringing our mission of 'save money, live better' to these underserved areas," said Walmart's senior vice president of sustainability, Andrea Thomas, at the press conference announcing the program. "We believe that our initiative can make healthy, affordable food more accessible in the nation's food deserts."

I'm fairly confident that Brenda, Chris's sister, would not mind having a Walmart closer to home: She'd save on gas, and many of the prices are cheaper. (Taste, I later decide, is a wholly different matter.) And if the prices would *stay* cheap and the quality high, I don't know that I'd be able to work myself up about it, even after it occurs to me that in competing with the city's eighty-one supermarkets, Walmart would be taking business away from eighty-one individual entrepreneurs, all of whose profits repatriate into metropolitan Detroit. As Walmart gains more and more market share—by putting competitors out of business, by entering urban markets—I can't see why they would keep our food affordable.

You have to sit on the porch; it's a neighborhood institution.

Gabriel has just come over to visit, and he is insistent, all but pushing me out the front door to a brick patio overlooking the street. We sit on plastic chairs with Bianca, who's visiting from her apartment nearby, and her friend, Inez. Flowering baskets sway from the porch eaves in the humid spring twilight as we talk, and Bianca calls out greetings to everyone who walks past; she knows them all. It's Saturday night, my first one in Detroit and the night before the city's Cinco de Mayo parade. I'm still waiting to hear from

Walmart about a third interview, so my weekend plans are to spend as little money as possible, which makes the porch an attractive option. There's a festive anticipation humming through the neighborhood as glossy lowriders cruise the block, countered by the more sobering elements of the celebration: a cluster of candles that cropped up beneath a photo labeled "R.I.P.," next to the telephone pole down the street; the police surveillance unit that took up residence across from the park; the police helicopter thundering in broad circles overhead. All of this, explains Bianca, is because four people were shot during last year's celebrations, including the young man memorialized in the shrine on the corner.

The neighborhood, adds Gabriel, is one of the best in Detroit, but it's still Detroit; he might be Mexican, but he wouldn't walk around at night by himself, and definitely not on Cinco de Mayo. We keep talking: about Detroit, about how the city services keep diminishing, about work and the local lack thereof, about family and dating and school, about how drinking and driving is so accepted here that the police won't pull you over unless you're waving a gun out the window—and even then, says Gabriel, you'd probably have to be pulling the trigger.

The evening lazes on, and it might have just faded into bedtime except that Martina, Christina's younger sister, shows up, striding up the sidewalk, kissing Gabriel on the cheek, and introducing herself to me. Gabriel leans over to her.

You have to tell her about the foodie!

Oh, are you a foodie? she asks me, a hint of challenge in her voice. After a few days of living with Christina, once it was clear that being honest about my work wouldn't endanger my undercover status at Walmart, I explained that I'm actually a writer. Gabriel already knew all about it when we met, so I'm sure Martina's already heard it, too.

Well, I like food. I like to cook.

She sighs and tells me a story.

So, I work at the radio station, and there's this guy I work with, he's younger, white, and he was talking and talking about these people called "foodies"; he's one of them. So I ask him what that meant, "What's a foodie?" And he goes, "It's someone who's really, really into food, and grows their own, and then does things like make preserves and pickles and cans their food." Martina sighs again.

"They're like, really, really into food." And he's a foodie. And so I say, "Oh, like my mom, she does that." Or, says Martina, leaning closer, she did, but now she's old. But, when I was a kid, she used to grow all these herbs and tomatoes and chiles and everything, just like back on the *rancho* in Mexico.

Gabriel looks at me. You've seen the garden, right? I nod: In back of the house there are two long strips of flowers and herbs, and plenty of room to grow food.

You mean she would pickle jalapeños and salsas from scratch? And you could eat it all year? Just from the backyard? I ask, remembering the meals I ate in Greenfield.

Yes! says Martina. That used to be all food. And it was a pain, man, to help with that. But it was real good, too.

I nod. Right. That's totally the same thing!

Right! says Martina. And so this guy, he says, "Oh no, not like that." and I can't get him to tell me what the difference is, he just keeps saying, "It's just, like, you really, really like your food," and I keep saying "Like. My. Mom." And we go back and forth like this, and finally I just told him, straight up, "That's classist, you just don't get it." And all he could say was, "Foodies really care about what they eat."

What does that even mean, says Gabriel, that you really care about food?

I mean, I'm like, right, everyone likes food, says Martina. I like food, but I ain't a fucking foodie, you know?

I know, right? I like food, says Gabriel, slapping his belly. Look at my *panza*!

We all laugh at this because he doesn't have any belly to speak of, but they're talking back and forth quickly now, old friends who can all but finish each other's sentences. They nearly forget about me. Then Martina looks over at me.

I'm sorry if we're being too . . .

Oh no, she's fine, says Gabriel, winking at me. I think she's a kindred spirit.

Well, in that case, says Martina, smiling wickedly, we have to take her to El Chaparral. She turns to me, eyes sparkling in the streetlight. You want to see a real Mexicantown bar?

I do, of course, and even though it's only four blocks away, we drive over in Martina's hulking Mercury sedan. We park on the street in front of a building I'd seen on my walks around the neighborhood. I'd thought it was abandoned, but now the door is open, and from the sidewalk we can hear patrons chattering in barroom Spanglish. All through Mexicantown, I don't hear Spanish so much as its Anglicized hybrid, words swapped and traded and blended as they trickle out onto the street, sail out apartment windows, and roll out car doors.

Inside, we sit at the bar and Gabriel buys our drinks, PBR longnecks for him and me, and an iced shot of vodka for Martina, who takes a dollar from the bartender to feed the jukebox. She summons a flurry of guitars and trumpets threaded with deep masculine voices crooning in Spanish, and she and Gabriel throw their heads back and grin conspiratorially: I love this song! they say in unison. I smile, listening to lyrics I can understand but not translate, losing them in the hazy space between comprehension and definition.

Gabriel nudges me to turn around, smiling, his eyes directing me to a couple swaying together over the beaten floor. The man, old, is missing a few teeth beneath his white mustache. His thick head of white hair is slicked back neatly, and his lips move softly with the song. He's holding a woman who's younger but not young, thickly built, her skin dark against a fuchsia tank top and denim miniskirt. He spins and leads her in some approximation of salsa, the soccer match on the television behind them drowned out by the trilling of mariachi trumpets.

We're sitting there in our tipsy reverie when a Spanglish exclamation yanks us back to reality. A woman at the end of the bar is holding her purse and slapping the counter, settling her tab.

Ya me voy, porque I gotta work tomorra.

The drunken lilt to her voice says it all, and the three of us cackle like teenagers at the back of the classroom. But when we finally stop laughing, I realize she's at least got one up on me: I wish I had work to go to.

It takes three weeks in Detroit before I finally start at Walmart. There's a third interview, where I accept the job; a drug test, at a remote medical office in an industrial park near the airport; waiting for results, and waiting, and waiting, for the store to schedule an orientation, a process that takes so long I begin calling other stores in case it doesn't pan out. But finally, just past the middle of May, I get a call saying I am wanted in at 9 a.m. sharp for orientation on Tuesday.

As before, orientation passes in a blur of group activities, slickly produced video tutorials and a few personal lectures from staff about our roles on the floor. We're a mixed bunch of orientees: There are two girls in their late teens who'll be working in deli, a young, heavyset guy heading for lawn and garden, a clean-cut athletic type bound for asset protection (that is, antitheft), and an intense, tattooed young woman who'll be doing receiving at night. For produce, there's me and Nick, a pudgy college kid who claims to be proficient in mixed martial arts. This is a brand-new orientation program, we're told, since Walmart is shifting its focus onto customer service with the mantra "The Customer Must Win." This does not mean customers are always right, just that they should always get what they want.

There have been some other changes to the orientation since the one I had outside of Kalamazoo. Today, we're earnestly informed that we should think about the store like Disney World: On the sales floor, we are "onstage," and in the back rooms we can be considered "offstage," except for the break room, since nobody wants to hear you talking about your job and what you do or don't like about it while they're trying to enjoy their lunch. This is also, I can't help but notice, an excellent way to discourage employees not only from discussing their lives and forming friendships, but also from ever discussing work, wages, or conditions. It is, in other words, a way to keep us from ever whispering that dreaded word, *union,* which we learn in the brand-new *Protect Your Signature* video, is just another word for someone trying to steal our signatures by putting them on union cards.

The other thing I learn is that, as Walmart workers, we may well be responsible for our own injuries. During a safety presentation, we're informed that if we get hurt on the job, the safety expert at Walmart will be sure to pull up the tapes. My concern about being branded a troublemaker is no match for my curiosity about this idea that workplace injuries—particularly in supermarkets, where injuries are more frequent than in construction*—are the responsibility of individual workers.

So, if you lift something wrong, Walmart won't cover it? I ask, picturing a harried scramble with the pallet jack, my knee wrenched, a pinched-faced woman hitting instant replay. Well, it varies, but you know what I mean, says Matt.

Well, no, I don't, and I'm pretty sure this flies in the face of basic workplace injury law, but I don't say anything of the sort.

She's going to watch the video and see if it was your fault, says Randy.

---

* In 2009, more than 99,000 workers at supermarkets and grocery stores were injured, giving the job an incidence rate of 5.6 percent. The rate of injury for construction workers, by comparison, stood at 4.3 percent. (Bureau of Labor Statistics 2010a; Bureau of Labor Statistics 2010b)

Don't try to be a macho man, a macho woman.*

Before I can hit the floor, there's a parade of Computer Based Learning modules to slog through. I come in at 7:00 a.m. two days after orientation, as instructed, and find that I'm in better shape than most of the new hires, since a good share of my training from before has carried over. Most of my time is spent watching a series of videos that pertain directly to produce. All of them underscore the basic tenet of produce sections everywhere: If it's not fresh, it won't sell. This is an elegant bit of market-based logic that I find reassuring.

In *Produce Operations*, I learn that produce is a living commodity rapidly approaching its demise, and the produce section is nothing less than an expansive life-support system. There can be no slacking off over here, because 70 to 80 percent of purchases in the produce section are made on impulse—and "Mom," Walmart's target shopper, does not impulsively buy rotten lettuce. Naïf that I am, I had thought that most of the work in produce would be rotating stock in the back room and throwing out anything rotten, but there's a hidden world of preparation and presentation—Trimming! Crisping! Merchandising!—with the singular goal of presenting our food as fresh, no matter when it came in the door, and thus boosting sales. This is important because profit rates can be considerably higher in produce than in the average store department.

But I'm not just handling produce, I'm handling food, just like everyone else in the Fresh Section—Walmart's term comprising produce, bakery, and deli—so I sit through a double-feature dealing directly with food safety. The films—*Food Safety 1* and *Food Safety 2*—seem mostly geared toward people preparing fresh food in deli and bakery, given the initial video's focus on basic concepts like using a thermometer to check temperature and the vectors for delivering food-borne illnesses, though it occasionally dips into more broadly applicable topics like proper handwashing techniques and how to affix a hairnet. Part 2 goes into greater detail, highlighting the

---

* This line of discussion warning was not part of my orientation at the first Walmart, and I have no way of knowing if the presentation is representative of those made at other Walmart stores or was just one person's mistake. That said, all injuries in the workplace are covered by workers' compensation law, regardless of whether they are the result of poor judgment on the part of the worker or not. "They can tell you that you won't get workers' comp, and that's not true," explains a representative of the Michigan Department of Labor. "If everybody who was injured at work had their claim denied because of—and I'm not going to say the way they do their job, lift wrong or whatever—nobody would ever have a workers' comp claim. It just isn't going to happen that way." (Workers Compensation Agency 2007 Employee, MI-DHS 2011)

"Danger Zone" for fresh food—the temperature range between 41 and 140 degrees—and the importance of not leaving anything fresh in said zone for more than four hours, max. Little of this feels useful for produce—am I supposed to check the temperature of a cantaloupe?—but toward the end, everything starts to feel strangely familiar nonetheless. Then I realize why. I've heard bits and pieces of this before, in snippets from farmworkers and *mayordomos,* kitchen managers and line cooks. But in all the food jobs I've taken over the last year,* this is the only time I've ever been given an actual lesson in food safety.

My education concludes with *Food Safety and Handling,* a sort of greatest hits of everything that's come before. It opens, like a lot of Walmart videos, to a soaring U2 guitar riff from "Beautiful Day" and cuts between shot after shot of comfortably middle-class families of varying ethnic backgrounds cavorting in their well-appointed homes, yards, and kitchens. Then we move to a joyless pair of corporate heads of something-or-other explaining why food safety is important. They offer two reasons. The first is that food safety is important because it's the law, and if we don't follow the law, we might have to pay a lot of money. The implication, of course, is that they might otherwise dispense with the food safety, an observation that inspires in me a new appreciation for food safety legislation. Once they've covered this ground, the talking heads proffer the same motive that I'd like to think they kept in mind all along: We care about food safety because it's the right thing to do.

Awesome! We need people so bad!

This welcome comes from my new department head, Randy, the same befuzzed kid who interviewed me. Erica in personnel has just walked me to the produce section with a five-page handout listing, in arcane detail, what I am to be taught. Randy doesn't look at the papers, which Erica says need to be returned within a month, checking off the different skills I've learned by one-, two-, three-, and four-week milestones. Instead, he begins to explain what he is doing with a chain of plastic labels bearing the names of different countries.

We're working on our COOL labeling, he says.

Our what?

* As outlined in the introduction, I did my reporting for the final section, Cooking, in between the two Walmart reporting stints.

Country of origin, you have to have these up for any fruit or vegetable where 52 percent or more do not have a label or tag, it's state law, and you can get a $25,000 fine if you don't have it up, so it's really important. Randy recites this apparent fabrication* in monotone as he positions labels for Mexico under the peppers, Canada under cucumbers, then chuckles: I'm not losing my job over something like that.

From there, we're off on a whirlwind tour of the section, which consists of three major landmarks. We start at the back of the section with the unappetizingly named wet wall, the refrigerated shelves that get misted with water to freshen the bulk vegetables—collards, kale, red and green leaf lettuce, turnip greens, mustard greens, broccoli, leeks, zucchini, cilantro, parsley, yellow squash, bell peppers, poblano peppers, tomatillos, jalapeños, and all the rest. The wall continues with salad dressings, bagged salad, and mushrooms before terminating at a crouton display. Directly opposite the wet wall is the second landmark, a pair of big "mods," two-sided modular displays, separated by a short aisle. The mod opposite the wet wall's vegetables is stocked with fruit—domestics like apples and citrus on the vegetable side, exotics like papaya and plantains on the other. Opposite the mushrooms and salad is another mod full of potatoes, tomatoes, onions, and garlic—including some jars of minced garlic, from The Garlic Company, which I'd picked for in California.† The final major line of display begins closest to the front door with the farmer tables, hip-high shallow containers nestled atop deep bins so that from afar it looks as if there's a giant square barrel mounded with tomatoes, or corn, or blueberries. There's also a massive banana display—they're the number one item in the section—a short refrigerated island where we stock grapes, berries, and cut fruit near the deli counter, and a tiny mod for bagged nuts. Do I have any questions, Randy wants to know, and there's really just one: What do you want me to do?

Randy leads me to a pair of swinging black doors, and we duck into the back room, where we are confronted by a half-dozen pallets stacked high

---

* Since the introduction of Country of Origin Labeling in 2008, which requires grocers to identify the country from which produce comes with signage, no retailers have been fined for failing to follow the guidelines. The maximum fine for a violation is $1,000. (Samuel Jones 2011)

† During my last week at Walmart, I stocked fresh bulbs of garlic from the same company, although—it being June, before the California crop came in—the garlic had been imported, in this case from Argentina. To see the wholesaler crate label for that shipment, visit www .americanwayofeating.com.

above my head with crates of food, a narrow passageway carved between them down the middle of the room. Watermelons bulge against giant cardboard bins, snarls of corn husk press through their plastic crates, and strawberries loom in a tower seven feet tall. A short, stocky woman with hair the color of steel is shaking her head at all of it. Her name tag says Jean.

Can you believe what they left us? Jean says to Randy, who introduces us. She turns around, facing the pallets, then throws a glance over her shoulder at me. Oh, you don't know what you've gotten yourself into, she says, but we can sure use you.

It's crazy back here, says Randy. We're short-staffed, and they bring in so much food. It's all supposed to be put away in four hours. That's their nice little idea, he says, making air quotes with his hands, and it doesn't happen very much.

If the department is so short-staffed, I later ask Randy, why did Walmart just hire two part-time people? He shakes his head again and tells me that Walmart doesn't really like to hire full-time workers; co-workers from other departments tell me the same thing, unprompted.

But for now, there's the back room to deal with. The ceiling is high, and there are heavy steel wire shelves, five or six feet deep, flanking either side of the room. The food that doesn't need to be refrigerated—potatoes, tomatoes, bananas, onions—lives on the shelves, "the steel," out here; good luck getting to it, since the new pallets block all access. Along the back wall is a heavy canvas shade in lieu of a door. It rolls up and down with the push of a button to reveal the walk-in, a refrigerated room with more steel shelves down either side and with enough room between them to leave a line of pallets in the middle. A ventilation shaft bisects the ceiling, its two fans blowing out cold air and leaking water onto the pallets below.

Randy finishes the tour by showing me the food prep area, a narrow hallway along the outer wall of the walk-in. There's a triple steel sink and a food prep table on the left, for crisping and trimming. On the right sit crates of miscellaneous rotting food—"returns" that have been culled from the floor, and which have to be inventoried, using a hand-held scanner called a Telzon, before they can be thrown away. There's a door at the back for deli's dry storage, so I shouldn't worry if I see deli people coming through, though sometimes we put the returns back there, and it can get to be a real mess.

I watch Randy and Jean eye the pallets skeptically. There's some discussion of pulling the pallets onto the floor, or maybe not, and where is the pallet jack, and how are they going to get it under that pallet, and how long would they leave the pallets on the floor anyway? They're not really talking to me—this is a conversation to which I can contribute no insight—so I interrupt as politely as I can with my original question, What should I do?

Randy shakes his head as if I've woken him from a nap. He hands me a brand-new pricing gun, tells me to guard it with my life—I'm not joking, people will steal that, he says—and begins piling crates of tomatoes and small boxes of elephant garlic onto a flat rolling cart. I can take these out and price them while he and Jean get situated, I just need to look at the price tags below the displays. I finish around the time I'm due for break, so I tell Randy that's where I'm going, but when I come back after my fifteen minutes, neither Randy or Jean are anywhere to be found.

I've always prided myself on being self-directed, but here, I have no idea what I should do. Do I take food out of the walk-in or from the pallets? Should I be helping in the back room, and if so, what does that entail? Is there crisping or trimming to be done, and if so, how do I do it? I vaguely recall that there was something in the videos about what to do when you don't know what to do, some task that is so endless it is always an option. I can't remember it, though, so I roll a cart onto the floor and spend a few minutes staring blankly at the wet wall, pricing gun in hand, and try to look as if I might be busy.

This charade persists for a few minutes before Gabe, an intimidatingly fit redhead who—I find out later—used to manage produce, catches me.

Do you know what culling is? he asks. I nod guiltily, and the lightbulb goes off: That is the endless task I was looking for.

Look at this, says Gabe, picking up a white mushroom, wrinkled as a nonagenarian sunbather. This is disgusting. Would you buy that?

I think, *Well, I've cooked with things like that, and you could use it for stock,* but the correct answer is clear: No. I would not buy that.

So throw it away. Don't worry about throwing things away. If you wouldn't buy it, don't even hesitate. I mean, come on, look at this, it's disgusting. Gabe continues picking through the bin and snatching out desiccated fungi. If it doesn't look fresh, nobody will buy it.

Right, I say, and purpose begins to percolate up through me. I have a job to do, and since there's no obvious life-support function to perform on the produce before me, I can at least carry the casualties to the morgue. I will clear the shelves of the unfresh and unsalable, do my part to bring the

masses the healthy, quality food they seek and deserve. Then Gabe bursts
my bubble.

Of course, Walmart doesn't always have the freshest stuff, he says. That's
how we keep the prices low.

Gabe pulls out a few more mushrooms, tosses them onto my cart, and
walks away, unclipping a walkie-talkie from his belt and calling for Randy
over the airwaves.

Supermarket produce sections have long been one of America's underappre-
ciated wonders. We think of supermarkets as being the places where food is
bought and sold, but they are simply the most visible part of the massive,
hidden network that sprawls out beneath them—and this is especially true
when it comes to produce. Today, supermarkets control and coordinate the
sale of 95 percent of our fruits and vegetables, and roughly one of every four
dollars Americans spend on fresh produce ends up at Walmart, a feat less
about sales than its mastery of logistics. "The misconception is that we're in
the retail business," Jay Fitzsimmons, senior vice president and treasurer of
Walmart, told investors in 2003, fifteen years after the company had begun
selling groceries. "[But really] we're in the distribution business."

Stores have always distributed goods, of course, but when supermarkets
first began, distribution of fresh food was intensely local. In the 1930s,
most farmers sold their goods by setting a price and haggling over it—with
individual customers at public markets, with wholesalers and brokers, or
with grocery stores. If produce was shipped across the country, the equation didn't change much; a big California farmer would set a price with a
Detroit wholesaler or broker and ship it out. There were lots of farms; in
1930, America had 6.3 million of them; about half of which grew fruits or
vegetables. Just as important, there were many ways to sell what they grew.
In 1932, about 70 percent of the food sold in New York City, for instance,
went through the decentralized mish-mash that defined that era's food economy: public markets and jobbers, small stores and wholesalers, peddlers and
vegetable stalls. Like a wave of immigrants coming to America, food came
from myriad farms, moved through slightly fewer channels, and, once here,
spread out to myriad dinner plates.

In those early days of food marketing, every farmer and buyer was negotiating in a hectic market. If a buyer tried to lowball a farmer, the farmer had
plenty of other places to sell; similarly, if a farmer tried to price-gouge, buyers could go to other farmers. Most food, therefore, was priced according to

the oldest rules in the book, supply and demand. The system for distributing fresh food in the 1930s wasn't perfect,* but the decentralized way food stores got their produce meant that it approached what most Americans think of when we think "free market": producers and buyers, negotiating a fair price from equal footing.

Food stores in 1930s America were, for the most part, just stores. They specialized in selling things to make a profit, handling distribution as a matter of course but not focusing on it. As supermarkets matured, this changed. Marketing research showed that the more items a store carried, the more things people actually bought, so supermarkets began to stock more products (and more brands of products). Today, the average supermarket sells nearly 50 times as many items as the first King Kullen store, and a Walmart supercenter sells 135 times more. But all those products had to get to the store somehow, and eventually supermarkets realized it would be cheapest to coordinate the distribution themselves. By 1998, forty-nine of the fifty largest supermarkets in the country were running their own internal distribution networks and saving as much as 60 percent on operations costs as a result.

Once the supermarkets had built their own infrastructure for cheaply delivering huge volumes of food, they had every reason to keep doing it. By lowering their cost of doing business, big food stores could drive prices down so far that they put smaller competitors out of business. And by making massive internal infrastructure a prerequisite for competing, the big stores made it nearly impossible for new ones to open up. The only way for smaller stores to compete was to merge into companies big enough to build an internal infrastructure, something only huge businesses could afford. Meanwhile, the easiest way to keep stores stocked with produce was to contract with growers big enough to meet the demand. In the 1990s, as food retail got bigger and consolidated, agriculture did the same. From 1987 to 2007, large farms more than doubled their share of agricultural sales in the United States, and today account for nearly 60 percent of farm sales. Over the same period, the market share of small farms† dropped by two-thirds;

---

* Among early food wholesalers' imperfections, as documented by the Federal Trade Commission, were: collusion to fix charges among the handlers who controlled the limited receiving and marketing facilities; produce being destroyed to keep prices high; and new entrants being excluded by "rules that were occasionally enforced by threats, sabotage, and even violence." (Tedlow 1996, 209–10)

† While the number of small farms has risen in recent years, their overall market share has not. In 1987, there were roughly 1.85 million small farms, accounting for 22 percent of farm sales. Ten years later, in 1997, there were 1.6 million small farms, accounting for 13 percent

midsized farms' share decreased by one-third. As with supermarkets, most communities are fed not by a diverse and flexible web of farmers, but by a shrinking number of ever-larger farms. By 2007, just under 6 percent of farms accounted for 75 percent of farm sales in the United States, at an average acreage of 2,216 (three and a half square miles); the average American farm is 418 acres.

Both sizes are likely bigger than what Thomas Jefferson had in mind when he wrote, "the small landholders are the most precious part of a state." The idea was at the root of our republic's expansion, and when Abraham Lincoln signed the Homestead Act in 1862, he set the maximum acreage per family at 160 acres. The same benchmark helped shaped the fields I worked in California. The 1902 National Reclamation Act, President Theodore Roosevelt's massive dam- and irrigation-building effort that brought water to California's great valleys, limited access to irrigation water to farms of 160 acres or less. (Industrial farmers largely flouted the rule until they convinced President Reagan to sign the Reclamation Reform Act in 1982, increasing the limit to 960 acres and making provisions for exemptions to it.)

In hindsight, this progression from pastoral small farms and quaint produce stalls to supermarkets and agribusiness seems inexorable: Industrial agriculture creates one economy of scale, enabling a new way of selling food to consumers—supermarkets—at lower cost. Once in place, this new delivery system applies economies of scale to transportation, again making it possible to lower costs, thereby conferring advantages to anyone who can control transport as well as sales. This in turn favors suppliers who are capable of functioning on this larger scale, prompting a wave of consolidation among suppliers seeking to match the one unfolding in retail, and reconfiguring the rules of the game such that only the biggest players can compete. Inevitably, the number of players shrinks until only the strongest remain, controlling more and more of the market. Some marketing experts describe the modern supermarket industry a "natural oligopoly," where we find not only that a handful of players control the game, but that it wouldn't work any other way.

There is actually nothing natural about this system. To walk through Walmart's cavernous aisles is to walk through a landscape created by a century's worth of decisions America has made about its food. We prized agri-

---

of farm sales; and by 2007, the number of small farms had bounced back to 1.8 million—but market share had dropped to 7 percent. (Author's calculations, based on National Agricultural Statistics Service 2007, 10; National Agricultural Statistics Service 1997, 12–15) cultural bounty; we valorized mass marketing; we made transportation and distribution into a science. We've built a massive infrastructure capable of taking whatever we grow and delivering it wherever we choose, on a scale heretofore unseen; this much is true. And yet I'm reminded, in a small way, of what John Steinbeck wrote when he visited migrant labor camps not far from where I picked grapes: There is a failure here that topples all our successes. It is far easier to eat well in America than in most of the world, but we've done little to ensure that fresh and healthy food is available to everyone.

If there's one thing the Walmart training videos impressed upon me, it's that produce is fresh and must be maintained as such, which, surprisingly, gives me and Walmart a common purpose. I find myself internalizing one of the turns of phrase in the Walmart videos: "We want a better life for our customers; after all, we're just like them." I want the food to be good for the customers, because I want the food I buy to be good, too. I'm therefore struck by something I didn't feel when I worked in grocery: a mission, a grand social responsibility to provide fresh, high-quality produce. Most of our work here centers on removing food that is not fresh and replacing it with the stuff that is. But there's a smaller, though no less important, task we're required to perform, and Randy introduces me to it on my second day on the floor: crisping.

There was a whole segment about the practice in my *Produce Management* video. The basic concept is to rehydrate limp greens so that they appear fresh. I do this on occasion at home, though I realized after watching the video that I was going about it all wrong. First, I'd never bothered to trim off the ends of anything—not the base of the lettuce, not the stems of the cilantro, not the slender ends of kale. Second, I'd always submerged them in cold water and thrown them into the fridge. It's better, I learn, to cut off the very ends of the plant. Slicing off the most desiccated tissue allows the plant to more readily absorb water. What's more, the water should be luke-warm, so that cell walls open up and let more water in. Then, after draining the water off, I should wrap a labeled twist tie around it for identification purposes before rushing it into a cooler so that the cell walls close up, plump with water, and yield crisp leaves. Randy doesn't really explain this process to me, though. He just tells me to take anything that looks bad off the wet wall and bring it back and crisp it.

I find the crisping itself to be curiously pleasant. I'm squirreled away in the back room in a hairnet, gloves, and an apron, splashing around in warm water and methodically trimming lettuce and greens. There are yellow leaves to pull out of cilantro bunches and rotting ends to cut off their stems, slimed turnip greens to separate from their roots, and browning leaves to remove from the romaine. It's crisping, I realize, that yields the wide variety in size I see among bunches of herbs and heads of lettuce. For example, it is likely that the shorter the bunch of cilantro, the more times it has been crisped, and small heads of lettuce often start out large—they've just lost most of their leaves to rot. Fresh heads of lettuce are my favorite to crisp because they give evidence of having been alive; when I slice slender coins off the bottom of their stems, milky sap—rumored since ancient Egypt to have aphrodisiac properties—leaks out.* Once they've been put to bed in the walk-in among all the other greens, I pull out fresh ones to put on the floor.

Later, Jean and I are working the salad wall—the section of the wet wall where all the bagged, chopped lettuces are displayed, a grid of spring-loaded shelving boasting fifty-two offerings from Dole and the Walmart house brand, Marketside. This corner of the floor represents two of the biggest shifts in American supermarkets in the last generation: bagged salads and private-label produce, which is to say brands that originate with the store itself. Twenty-five years ago, bagged salad didn't even exist; by 1997 it accounted for nearly 10 percent of produce sales. Similarly, house brands for produce—a product that requires massive infrastructure to process and distribute on a national scale—were unheard of before the early 1990s. In 1994, for instance, only 2 percent of bagged salad was sold via store brands; nearly all the rest came from big agricultural producers like Dole. But by 2008, private-label salads represented 15 percent of the market.

Back on the wall, though, all that variety means people have a lot of questions, explains Jean. People will always ask where they can find different salads, but they don't know what they're called. So if anyone asks for shredded cabbage, she says, we hand them the coleslaw mix. When I comment that some of the salads seem expensive—ten ounces of Dole chopped romaine leaves costs $2.50, marked up 85 percent from the $1.35 Walmart paid for it, while a head of the stuff costs 88 cents—Jean waves me off. She buys all her lettuce this way because then she almost always eats it, which she doesn't do if she just buys a whole head of it. Then Jean confides one of her frustrations

---

* The name lettuce actually derives from the Latin *lactuca*, or milky, a reference to its sap, which contains a hypnotic similar to opium. For an excellent discussion on the history of lettuce, see *Much Depends on Dinner*. (Visser 1986, 194–99)

with the produce section: Randy doesn't understand about the freshness.

If there's an expiration date, there's a reason for it, you know? He'll just say, Oh, it looks fine, but if you look close, it doesn't.

This isn't the first sign that Randy's produce acumen is in disrepair. Yesterday, when I was helping him stock the tropical fruits, he asked me if I knew how to cook plantains. I nodded and explained that they're sort of like starchy bananas, prompting his eyes to go wide. They're related to bananas?

Now, I realize that Randy can't be more than a few years out of high school, and if he doesn't know anything about plantains it could well be because the white Midwestern diet rarely includes them and besides, he eats a lot of fast food from the chain where he has his second job since it lets him save money on groceries. But while youth and lack of education might explain why the plantain surprised Randy, or why he might keep food around longer than we'd like, they do little to answer the question I now put to Jean: If Randy doesn't know anything about produce, and he doesn't seem to care about freshness, how did he get to be a manager in produce? As with many small towns where Walmart operates, it's one of just three supermarkets, and only one of those even comes close to Walmart in size—which puts Randy in charge of half the town's produce supply. Jean shrugs. The job opened up, he applied for it, and you know how *that* goes.

There's no way for me to know if every Walmart is this casual in its hiring of produce managers; no reason, really, to believe that Jean was doing anything other than talking smack. But I do notice that the basic set-up of the section— something that's fairly consistent across stores—includes a raft of waist-high "farmers' tables." We pile all manner of perishables on top of them—cucumbers, lettuce, raspberries, strawberries—despite the fact that they have no refrigeration system. For some stuff, this is fine; strawberries on sale fly off the tables so quickly I sometimes stock them twice in a shift. But cucumbers begin to wilt after a few hours at room temperature, and the raspberries linger for days, enough that I grow accustomed to needing to dig down to the bottom layer on the table, assured of finding plenty of moldy containers.

I spend most of the afternoon hunting and pecking my way across the salad grid. My flat cart is stacked tall with cardboard cases of varying salads, and I'm humbled by the difficulty I find myself having with the task at hand. It's not complicated—I just open a case, remove the bag and try to match it to its mates on the grid—but visual matches have never been my thing, and I repeatedly find myself muttering, "Dole Very Veggie" or some such title, scanning the same shelves over and over again like some displaced contestant on *Classic Concentration*. Sometime near the end of my shift, a lanky young man attired in a style somewhere between hippie and punk approaches me for advice, a bag of Dole Classic Romaine in his hand.

Is this the same as a head of lettuce? This is better than a head of lettuce, right?

Well, I say, honestly, it depends on what you want to do with it.

I mean this is really cheap.

It depends on what you're after, I say, wary of explaining my preference for head lettuce—uncut lettuce doesn't dry out as quickly, it often stays fresher longer, and it can be used for sandwiches as well as salads—in case it could be construed as poor salesmanship. He thanks me and walks away, then comes back a minute later, snapping his cell phone shut.

My mom doesn't want this, she wants a head of lettuce 'cause you can do what you want with it and it doesn't go bad as quick, he says. Then, I notice appreciatively, he puts the bag back exactly where he found it.

Fair enough, I say.

You have a blessed day, he says, startling me with his Christianity as he walks off to get his lettuce.

In my normal life, I might be inclined to lament the lack of cooking knowledge that I see in my customers, and Randy, and Jean. But if I know more about preparing food, I quickly learn that I'm incredibly ignorant when it comes to buying quality produce. I learned to cook from a mix of box dinners and cookbooks, supplemented by a grandmother who let me help in the kitchen; along the way, I picked up intangible tips like the proper thickness of pie dough, the lightness of butter creamed properly with sugar. But the rest of the skills required to feed myself—avoiding wrinkled skins on tomatoes, planning when and how to eat—came from my father, who juggled an invalid wife, three small children, and limited cooking knowledge. No wonder I stammer whenever Gabe stalks through the section, asking me my opinion on whether something should be thrown out or not; I never really learned what to look for.

Truthfully, the bulk of my food literacy comes from one broad source: my family. This is how it has worked for nearly everyone, for as long as anyone can remember. Even in the 1950s, when home economics was a mainstream class for female students, only about a quarter of all high school students took it, the same proportion as today. For decades, then, three-quarters of us—myself included—have relied almost entirely on the skills we could easily learn at home. Our parents' ability to teach us about our meals shrank dramatically when mothers began entering the workforce in the mid-twentieth century. It wasn't just that our parents cooked less because they had to work; the more time-strapped they were, the less time they had to pass their knowledge on to their children. In the process, we left the learning of a vital skill up to chance.

There's no formal government or scholarly survey that tracks Americans' cooking literacy; correspondingly, there's little academic research on it. But private industry keeps an eye on how much we cook (less so the reasons behind it)—mostly to identify potential markets for new food products. For decades, these studies have typically found that Americans' willingness to cook is on the decline, as well as their ability to do so. In 1996, more than half of all Americans reported they had less knowledge and fewer cooking skills than their mothers and grandmothers. The same year, more than two-thirds of eighteen- to twenty-four-year-olds said they could not fix a meal. The best evidence of America's waning kitchen skills may come from career cookbook editors and recipe writers, who've found themselves adjusting instructions to reflect the shift. "Add two eggs," was the directive that Bonnie Slotnick, a longtime cookbook editor, said she used at the start of her career in talking to a *Washington Post* reporter in 2006. "In the '80s, that was changed to 'beat two eggs until lightly mixed.' By the '90s, you had to write, 'In a small bowl, using a fork, beat two eggs,' We joke that the next step will be, 'Using your right hand, pick up a fork and . . .'"

Twenty years ago, my customer at the lettuce rack would have had one option if he wanted lettuce: Buy a head, wash it, dry it, cut it. But food companies saw that Americans were losing both time to cook and fluency in the kitchen, so they began offering ways to avoid using the kitchen at all. America's great exodus from the kitchen is on display all around me in produce: whole potatoes sheathed in plastic, ready for the microwave, with a price tag of 88 cents apiece, cost the same per pound as the Idaho potatoes in the bin next to them. Just under three ounces of apple slices, hermetically sealed along with a packet of caramel sauce, cost $1, putting the per-pound cost above $5; a pound of whole Gala apples costs $1.47. Eight ounces of shredded cabbage and carrots retail for $1.39, or $2.78 a pound, while an entire head of fresh cabbage costs 58 cents a pound and a pound of carrots retails for $1.66. In my more affluent days, I've made use of these as much as anyone—which is why it disturbs me to realize that by industrializing the preparation of produce, we've made it more dangerous to our health. Bagged lettuces, for example, typically run through giant industrial processing systems, mixing crops from different fields in giant proportions. Pre-cut fruit gets exposed to more sets of human hands and utensils. All of that creates opportunities for contamination, and modern distribution networks make it easy for such problems to spread far and wide.

Outside the produce section, aisle after aisle reminds me that America has become a nation that *watches* cooks far more than it imitates them. The biggest proof is in the rise of meals like Hamburger Helper, which has been copied into numerous brands since my childhood, many of which no longer even require one to brown meat. I could pop over to frozen foods and buy a bag of Great Value frozen noodles, meat, vegetables, and spices, pop it in the microwave, and have dinner for two in thirteen minutes for $4.98. But going that route could be dangerous for my health in the long run. Most of the processed food we turn to in lieu of cooking is so high in salt that it accounts for about three-quarters of Americans' sodium intake (a fact owing as much to salt's preservative qualities as to our taste for it). A single serving of Hamburger Helper Beef Stroganoff supplies more than one-third of the recommended daily intake of sodium; Walmart's bagged sausage and peppers provides 40 percent.

The fastest way to solve this conundrum is money. The affluent can readily avoid the kitchen while still eating well simply by paying more: for processed foods with less salt or fat, for premade meals that are neither deep fried nor slathered with mayonnaise (as is much of what I see come out of deli). Without cost as a central concern, buying healthy, fresh, pre-prepared meals is a no-brainer. But when cost *is* a concern, that $5 sack of a frozen meal lets people like me and my co-workers avoid the kitchen anyway, freeing us from needing to know how to cook at a price we can afford.

There are two strategies currently in use to battle this money-time crunch while maintaining our health. One is to make options like Hamburger Helper healthier by lowering their salt and sugar content. The other is to make these ultra-easy options less necessary. When cooking instruction is paired with basic nutrition education, Americans cook more and eat more healthfully—even when money is tight. Organizations that run cooking classes with the poor have begun surveying their students. Nearly four in five low-income adults who participated in two-month-long cooking classes in twenty-eight cities, run by national nonprofit Cooking Matters, reported eating more nutritious meals after leaving the class; nearly two-thirds also reported saving money on their grocery budget. In 2010, university researchers undertook a close assessment of a cooking class for twelve low-income adults, taught by a chef. The themes that emerged among the students were consistent: They felt more comfortable cooking, more aware of the importance of eating fresh fruits and vegetables, and more capable of planning healthy, affordable meals.

I don't know where most of my Walmart peers fall on this question, and since breaks are staggered in my department, I never get to eat with the people I work with—the folks I could easily strike up a conversation with and see whether they cook much or care about their health, or eat many fruits and vegetables. But I see a lot of actual food brought in for meals, and far less guzzling of two-liters and potato chips, than I did on the night shift. Mostly people bring in sandwiches and yogurt, or leftovers from dinner the night before: spaghetti and salads, lasagna and chicken breast. And I do notice one thing: Whatever they might bring from home, everyone's eager to partake of fresh produce when it doesn't cost anything. Every other week, "Free Fruit Fridays" play the same role on the day shifts that doughnuts did on the night, crowding the break room tables with grapes, apples, grapefruit, oranges, bananas. And by the end of the shift, the bins of fruit have been picked clean.

There's one offstage area that my orientation leader forgot to mention: the produce back room. Unlike pretty much every other inch of Walmart, there's not even a security camera back here. There's nothing risqué going on, unless you count our unabashed snacking on pilfered bits of new shipments—We have to know if it's good or not, Randy explained to me—but it does mean that when it comes to conversation, all bets are off. Brent and Sam, the two young black men I work with, delight in reciting dirty rap lyrics to each other, trying to see who can outdo the other. The rapping stops if Pam or Jean, the middle-aged women, are around, and on the few occasions when it gets too raunchy—when specific acts are being described in detail—I just clear my throat, smile, and say, I'm right here, guys. Right over here. Watch it.

This is also where I get to know my co-workers. It's when we're stripping down moldy corn, out of view of the customers, that I hear about Jean's intense interest in flyball—some sportlike activity involving her dog and, she implies but never explains, a ball—and how everyone talks about being afraid Walmart will fire them, but she did military service before coming here, and Walmart doesn't scare her. While I hand crates of tomatoes to Brent, lifting them over my head so he can get them from his perch on a ladder and secure them in steel shelving, I learn that his girlfriend just moved to Hawaii, and he charms me with the loss in his voice when he says, I mean, at the airport, serious, I was bawling. And when I dash into the back room, pulling my cart a little too quickly behind me, Bob, a quiet, rail-thin steelworker who came to Walmart ten years ago when his plant closed down, tells me, Watch it, hot rod. Sam is less chatty, but he's probably the most helpful, always explaining what he can to make work easier: If I don't know the price for something, I can just walk across the Action Alley to the scanner in health and beauty, that's easier than getting Randy to check it, and he seems to know the most about produce, calling me over to display a perfectly ripe pineapple, pointing out the gold hue gridded over its skin.

Really, the only co-worker I struggle with is Pam, a married mother who keeps me on my toes by sharing my frustration with Randy while issuing comments prompted, so far as I can tell, by our shared skin tone and the economic advantages it might imply. When we're busy at the start of the month, she greets me in the back room saying, It's real crazy out there, all those people spending their free money from the government. Later, when she suggests I use gloves to remove fruit from its crates and I say it's a good idea—all those pesticides—she corrects me. No, the reason I should use gloves is all those people picking it piss all over the food. At this I protest, saying as vaguely as I can that I've worked in the fields, and I've never seen anyone pee on the food, which she takes as an invitation to extol the virtues of a new law passed in Arizona allowing police to stop anyone at random and check their immigration status, and her excitement at a similar one being considered in Michigan. It's about time, she says, because then the farmers would have to pay real wages.

I can only say I don't think that would happen—historically, growers have either mechanized or moved their fields to cheaper territory. I don't tell her that when I worked in fields I was the only white person I ever saw out there, even as California grappled with an economic downturn nearly as bad as Michigan's; that would only raise questions. So there's really no reason for Pam, who came to Walmart after the manufacturer she worked for shut down, to believe that I'm doing anything besides pulling this out of my ass, and she treats me as such. She ignores the comment.

They wouldn't move all of them, she says without glancing up from the pineapple she's coring.

They wouldn't move all of them, she repeats. And we need the jobs here.

CHAPTER 7

Produce 201

Detroit, I realize about a month in, would be a far bleaker place if I had a different roommate. Christina, as Gabriel tells me over PBRs one night, will give you the shirt off her back, though you may endure a little TMI while getting it. She's run political campaigns in the neighborhood as well as a nightclub—right now, she's working reception at a gym while she works on her master's degree in bilingual education—so she knows everyone and wastes no time offering up her expertise. I want to make friends? She knows someone in the neighborhood starting a recreational soccer league, here's his email, he's great, you'll love him, tell him I sent you. I have a flat tire? Here's a can of Fix-A-Flat, and drive west on Vernor until you see Arandas, you might need to use your Spanish but they'll fix it for twenty dollars, you'll love it. I don't have plans and I have no money? There's a civic event about the future of Detroit tonight and there should be some free food, too, you'll love it.

Christina quickly sizes up that I'm not bringing in much money and begins—like the mother that she is—quietly forcing help upon me. First she recruits me as a sous chef for batch after batch of ceviche, where she provides the fish and I get the citrus, onion, and cilantro. She tells me to eat whatever I want in the house: We might be broke, but we can eat! she says, prancing out the door to a date with a fireman. And a few weeks in, she asks if I'll run to the store and get basic groceries if she pays for them; if I do the shopping, of course, we'll share everything. Money's tight for her, too, so it's nothing gourmet—rice, beans, tortillas, crema, fixings for salsa, and some squash—and I'm still expected to contribute, usually in labor rendered in the kitchen, but what else do I have to offer?

My weekly food bills average around $40, which includes about $15 on coffee and cheap pizza and beer with friends, and the rest of it dedicated largely to rice, beans, tortillas, and the discount just-about-to-go-bad rack in La Colmena's produce section, where they stack green beans, squash, mangoes—anything that's within a day of rotting. A small foam tray piled high with produce on the verge of going bad goes for 50 cents, and if I cook it immediately I can eat off the resulting dish for a couple days. (Walmart, I've noticed, doesn't do this. Instead, we leave things on the floor until they begin to rot and then simply throw them away.*) Combined with Chris's trips to Sam's Club for econo-size boxes of cereal bars, ice cream sandwiches, and meat, I eat decently—and far more than I would have if left entirely to my own budgetary constraints.

The other way that Chris saves my broke white ass—as we've come to refer to me—is that she lets me shift to a weekly rent payment instead of a monthly one. I'd been without work for most of the first month, and even with my first paycheck—which, covering only my first three days of work, I knew would be small—I wasn't going to have enough to cover rent. I'm not used to asking for favors so I didn't bring it up until Chris asked about next month's rent.

So, Tracie, are you staying for another month? She was standing in the bathroom, curling her hair in the mirror before going to work.

I stayed in the hall, out of eye-contact range. Um, yeah, how much was the rent again?

Four hundred, chica. Did you get paid yet?

Uh, no, I get my first check this week. Chris, would it be cool if I gave you a hundred a week for the first couple weeks instead of the four hundred all at once? My first check is going to be tiny, so I won't have enough until I get the next one.

Oh sure, no worries, she said without pause, releasing the curling iron and teasing a wisp of hair into place. I know you're good for it. Besides, she said with a sassy lilt in her voice, I know where you live.

* * *

* In 2005, Walmart announced it would be pursuing a "zero waste" strategy, and by 2011 it had instituted composting programs in stores scattered among forty-five states. Food waste in American produce sections varies widely depending on the food. Stores usually throw away 63.6 percent of all the mustard greens they every buy, but only 11.9 percent of peaches, averaging an 8.4 percent loss rate for both fruits and vegetables in 2006, according to USDA estimates. More broadly, while stores do not typically publish their food loss rates, a small Massachusetts chain, Roche Bros, released its audit on food waste to the author Jonathan Bloom in 2009. Each store in the chain threw out more than 800 pounds of food a day. Similarly, an interview by Bloom of an executive at southeastern chain Harris Teeter put their average store waste between two to three tons each week, a range of 571 and 715 pounds a day. (Fleming 2007; Walmart Stores 2011b; Jean C. Buzby et al. 2009, 8,12; Bloom 2010, 150)

For a store known for its ruthless efficiencies and economies of scale, Walmart's produce section—at least the one I'm working at—strikes me as a caricature of the opposite. This isn't apparent at first, and part of the delay in recognizing the dysfunction can be traced to my status as a new employee. I figure that, as before, everything will seem confusing at first, but will make sense as I learn the ropes. The problem with this is my presumption about the ropes—of rules and priorities and a semblance of order.

The first clear sign that Walmart's efficiencies might be more myth than reality, at least regarding this particular store, comes on a Saturday. I'm out on the floor stocking the salads, standing near a little sampling booth that's been set up to persuade customers to buy a sprayable version of I Can't Believe It's Not Butter. There's a man, about my age but black and pudgy, microwaving chunks of corncob, spraying them with the featured product, and setting them out in little plastic cups.

Hey, are you a vendor, too? he asks me during a lull.

A what?

A vendor, like me? he says, gesturing at his setup.

I work for Walmart, I say. Don't you?

Oh no, he says, though his apron has the Walmart logo and his nametag is an orange version of a Walmart tag. I work for a company that tries to sell products, he says vaguely. I'm Carlton.

I remember, now that he mentions it, that there are whole aisles of the grocery section where food companies—vendors—send in their own staff to stock the shelves: Keebler and Kellogg are two name tags I've seen on folks. (Later, I learn that the practice is called direct-store delivery.) I introduce myself to Carlton and turn back to the salads.

Hey, you should do something about that bird, says Carlton.

Bird?

Carlton nods and points: There's a black bird with a yellow beak contentedly pecking at the fresh lettuces.

I'm surprised to remember that birds, the retrieval and removal of, actually were covered in our CBLs. Do not attempt to remove the pest on your own, the narrator had intoned. Inform a supervisor and they will contact a pest control specialist.

I spot Sam talking to the girl at the bakery counter. Maybe he'll know which manager to talk to. I point out the bird to Sam and ask him what we should do.

Well, we can find a manager, but . . . his voice trails off.

Good luck with that, says Jenea, the bakery girl.

We had one in here for a month and nobody did anything, says Sam.

Yeah, says Jenea, it was landing on the pizzas and poking through the plastic to eat. She nods her head toward the open cooler where Walmart sells prepared, uncooked pizza. (The same pizza, I notice, that my landlady in Kalamazoo fed us for paying rent on time.)

But we have to tell someone, right? I ask.

Yeah, but I'm telling you: It won't matter, says Sam.

I shake my head. So who do I find, the bald manager? Bill?

Yeah, that's the one.

I guess I'll do that.

Jenea smiles at me. Let me know how that works out for you.

I can't find Bill, so later I mention the bird to Randy and he tells me not to worry about it. Walmart doesn't like to call pest control for stuff like that 'cause it costs $6,000 to have someone come out and get it. We can get someone to open the skylight so it can fly away if it wants; it's best to just wait for it to go away or die.

This explains a lot of other things about the department. Like the leak I saw on my first day, which both limits our capacity to refrigerate produce and boosts the humidity level in the cooler; food has been rotting rapidly. One day I threw out two hundred pounds of asparagus, the base of every bunch coated in thick moldy layers. An entire pallet of fresh corn, still in its husk, became too consumed with mold for sale, so we stripped off the offending layers of husk and sent more than twenty crates of it to a food bank. And then there's the moment when Mary, in deli, comes over and quietly says that she is sorry to bring this up, but she bought three green peppers here that looked fine but when she cut them open at home, every single one was filled with mold.

When we find rotten food—on the sales floor or in the cooler—we can't just throw it away. We have to inventory it—it's called doing returns—so there's a perpetually growing stack of crates next to the food prep area crammed with rotting lettuce, moldy berries, slimy greens, expired bags of salad, and wrinkled mushrooms, not to mention vast stores of food that are still edible but not pretty enough for sale. Save for Gabe, who pokes his head over every once in a while, nobody besides Sam seems to know anything about produce: what keeps longest, what needs to move quickly, what a fresh artichoke looks like, how to tell when a pineapple is too ripe to last another day on the floor. And nobody's ever assigned returns, a time-consuming job, so the food sits there for a day or so until the fruit flies and putrid juices get to be too much and can no longer be ignored. When Walmart introduces a composting program toward the end of my tenure, the situation gets worse. Before we can take the rotting produce to the compost bin, it has to be removed from all the packaging, which increases the workload even though we've had no increase in staff. The return crates begin to number in the dozens.

No wonder everyone in produce eventually ends up resigned to this state of affairs, though the newer among us are still working our way from recognition to acceptance as if advancing through the stages of grief. Pam, who came to produce a month ago, still seems to be in the anger phase, openly frustrated with the lack of organization in the section. Nick seems placidly settled into denial, though in all fairness that could be because—as a guy— he gets drafted into putting away freight, arguably the least dysfunctional practice within the department since it does get done every day. Bob counsels me to never work harder than necessary because it won't do me any good, putting him squarely in the "acceptance" camp, along with the rest of my departmental peers. Jean, Sam, and Brent all repeat Bob's advice in different forms.

For myself, I'd gauge that I'm in the denial phase. Someone should do something about the state of the department, but badmouthing my manager doesn't seem a sound bet. If I just keep my head down, work hard, and don't make too much of a fuss, maybe everything in the produce section will be all right.

The more time I spend traversing the divide between Detroit and its suburbs, the more I realize the term "food desert" isn't quite right. Massive amounts of food floods into Detroit every single day, through its produce terminal and wholesale markets. Starting at midnight, semi after semi comes in full of produce, bringing loads from the nation's eastern ports: Chilean plums and grapes through New York, Honduran melons through Miami. In the mid-twentieth century, Detroit had four wholesale markets, sprawling conglomerations of market stalls and loading docks where farmers and brokers sent their wares to be sold, and where stores and restaurants came to buy it; today, two remain. Other places, like thriving New York City, have seen their market districts erode as property values shot up, while the most lauded market preservation projects, like Philadelphia's Reading Terminal, have focused on developing retail food shops. Either way, those cities have lost most of something that Detroit still has intact: food infrastructure.

Food pours into the city every day, and the wholesale markets here are its first way station. It's impossible to know exactly how much comes through the Terminal and Eastern markets, though, because nobody keeps an eye on the volume of sales. (The USDA tracked wholesale market sales until the late 1990s, but stopped when private distribution centers grew so large that officials realized they only had part of the picture—and couldn't compel private companies to divulge their sales figures.) Organizationally, markets like the Produce Terminal and Eastern Market work like shopping malls: The market provides a building and basic infrastructure, but each vendor operates independently of the market itself, and of other vendors. Compliance with food safety and fair business practices is the business of each vendor, each of whom deals individually with the government agency responsible for oversight; the market itself is little more than a landlord.

I visit the Terminal market just after Memorial Day, riding along with Marvin, a gravel-voiced produce buyer who starts off our 3:30 a.m. jaunt with tales about the barbecue he and his wife had put on over the weekend and offering me culinary advice: If I want my ribs tender, for example, it's best to soak them in cider vinegar first. Marvin works for Peaches and Greens, a tiny new grocery that's opened up in an old drycleaner's in a neighborhood where more than one-third of the residents have no car, leaving many to make do with the stores they can reach on foot—liquor stores. Chip manufacturers and soda companies deliver goods direct to corner stores, and independent distributors—called jobbers—deliver small orders of dry goods, like pasta, to small stores. Yet there's never really been an equivalent for produce;* corner stores typically specialize in shelf-stable items that don't need the constant attention that a case of lettuce does, making small-scale produce distribution a dicey entrepreneurial pursuit.

In a lot of ways, it still is, but in early 2010 federal officials introduced a

---

* Peaches and Greens is not the only entrepreneurial effort aiming to fill the gap left by the absence of small-scale produce distributors, spurred by the new WIC coupons. In Detroit, I also met a University of Michigan business student selling prepacked produce to liquor stores under the label Get Fresh Detroit, and organizers at Detroit's Eastern Market were beginning to develop other small-scale distributors for local produce. Other cities are experimenting with similar efforts, most notably Minneapolis, where advocates brokered a relationship between a traditional corner-store supplier and a produce distributor. (Berkenkamp 2010; Kimmelman 2011; Johanon 2011).

new coupon for WIC clients, which could only be redeemed for fruits and vegetables. In Michigan, then, any small store that makes the investment in produce has access to the $16 million market created by these new vouchers. This is where Marvin and I come in, barreling down the Lodge Freeway in a converted milk truck before dawn. Peaches and Greens had launched a mobile market in 2008, opening up the store about four months later. When the WIC program changed its rules, they hit upon an idea: Instead of stocking only their own store, they could help justify the hassle of these early morning trips by functioning as a small-scale distributor for other stores. Most of what we buy today will go to the Peaches and Greens store and truck, but when Marvin returns to the market in a couple days, he'll be buying stock for a number of corner stores that have begun selling produce, as required by the WIC program. Peaches and Greens's sales pitch is simple: With the dedicated WIC funding, stores need to get their produce from somewhere. (Modest produce distribution efforts like these are starting up across the country, spurred by the new WIC vouchers and slowly redeveloping small-food infrastructure.)

We rumble into the terminal's loading lot, a block of asphalt ringed on three sides by tall concrete walkways, twenty minutes later. The terminal building looks about like what you'd expect for one erected in 1929: a few stories of tawny brick, art deco flourishes across the windows, and of a scale suited to the rickety-wheeled trucks and horse-wagon pairings that would have been common when the railroad built it. The walkways that frame the lot, free of rails and several feet high, are far enough off the ground that the distance between bumper and sales floor becomes manageable. (I'm grateful for this later, when I help Marvin stock his truck.) Metal garage doors sit open, one after the other, revealing long hallways and sales floors. The market, I am told later, has a strict rule against journalists and photographers, a policy that emerged after a Los Angeles television station visited that city's terminal in 2007 and found produce stored inches from rat-infested dumpsters and Porta-Pottys. I figure I can always just put the notebook away.

Inside, the food is as modern as it gets: One stack of crates displays lemons in boxes labeled 75 or 95, another displays mangoes tagged with 10 and 12—figures that denote the number per box, and thus their size. Workers riding forklifts play Tetris with pallets of grapes and towering stacks of tomatoes. Marvin makes his rounds, eyeing the produce on offer, negotiating prices, and telling the wholesalers where we're parked; they'll pull the produce out for us and bring it to the truck. Like most of the grocers I've visited in Detroit, Peaches and Greens stocks basic supermarket fare, and we load up on bananas and apples and onions. Throughout the market, I see far more: Asian long beans and mangoes and yucca, pomegranates and Holland chilies and Persian cucumbers that are smaller and sweeter than the ones I grew up on.*

The other trucks in the parking lot bear names from all over the tristate area, some coming from Ohio and Indiana; others from Windsor, across the river in Canada; and still more from the suburbs, including some of the area's toniest markets. What I do not see, though, are trucks for any of the big national chains, which may have fled Detroit but still do plenty of business outside the terminal's reach. They all operate their own distribution channels, either contracting directly with growers or relying on longstanding relationships with brokers; many big corporate buyers don't even leave their desks, buying food, sight unseen, over the phone. Still, most chains maintain a relationship with wholesalers, using them to fill in gaps; for example, Rocky's Produce, one of the wholesalers here, delivers to the Walmart I'm working at a few times a week. As the big chains developed more and more of their own infrastructure, independent distribution such as what's found at the terminal has withered to a fraction of what it was a century ago; along with it went the innumerable smaller food businesses and wholesalers that relied on it.† Detroit has lost nearly two-thirds of the produce wholesalers it had eighty years ago. While it's true that the city today is about half the size it was in 1930, the market reach of its wholesalers is much bigger. The Detroit metropolitan area, including the postwar suburbs, today has about 4.3 million residents.

Marvin and I have unwittingly arrived in a post-holiday crush of activity, and as one of the smaller accounts, we wait, and wait, and wait for our deliveries to come. By the time the last load gets dropped off—watermelon,

---

* To see photographs from my visit to the Detroit Produce Terminal, visit www.the americanwayofeating.com.

† Local food infrastructure, and the jobs associated with it, is so vulnerable to mega-chain stores that when Walmart began campaigning to open stores in New York City in 2011, it discussed agreeing to buy a set share of its produce through the New York City Terminal Market in Hunts Point. "Walmart . . . isn't interested in a single supermarket in New York," City Council Speaker Christine Quinn told *Crain's New York Business.* "If one store becomes eight stores . . . then you have the risk of having a significant portion of the [city's] food not going through Hunts Point. That could destabilize the market in a way that could have enormous job impacts and enormous food system impacts." (Massey 2011)

a must for the start of summer—the sun has already come up, intensifying the humid spring air. This isn't the end of our morning, though, because there are a few things Marvin needs to get at the other market, so we settle into our seats and head for the city's east side.

Seven miles across town, at the end of a once-abandoned rail spur turned bike path, sits Eastern Market, still home to five massive brick-and-steel sheds that have sat here since opening in 1891. During growing season, farmers from all over the region come here from midnight to the early hours of the morning, and sell their wares at a nightly produce market under the yawning rafters, everything grown within a few hours' drive. On Saturdays it's open as a farmers' market, thronged with Detroiters and suburbanites alike. The mix of sellers changes, with some resellers coming in, removing ruby tomatoes from their Dole boxes and placing them in charming straw baskets. Local farmers are out in force, too, from a cooperative of community gardeners in Detroit to the larger growers from agricultural counties. Marvin and I aren't hitting up actual farmers on our visit, though; it's early in the season, so the few who come out for the night market are only selling early spring flowers (and, given the hour, we would have missed them anyway). Instead, we buy from one of the wholesalers operating out of a warehouse on the market's east side, stocking up on vegetables we couldn't buy in small quantities at the produce terminal.

After spending my morning watching food arrive in Detroit from every direction, I find it hard to consider the place a food desert. Detroit's problem, like a lot of urban neighborhoods, isn't that there isn't any food. The problem is that, for decades, nobody—not Walmart, not anyone—has been making sure that the food that is here ends up in neighborhoods. Instead, suburban grocers come in to the wholesale market, load up their trucks, and take the freshest stuff back to their shelves north of Eight Mile. Truckload after truckload of food comes into Detroit in the night and leaves by midmorning, rarely bound for shelves within the city limits. If Detroit is a food desert, it's an entirely artificial one, created by a series of dams and channels built to take the produce flooding into the wholesale markets and direct it elsewhere, usually to stores in the suburbs.

However you describe Detroit's foodscape, Eastern Market is one of its unmistakable gems. In early October, nearly six months later, I visit the place in full swing (my Walmart schedule kept me busy on Saturdays). By then I'm no longer living on my Walmart wages, doing straight-up reporting on a program called Double-Up Food Bucks that will match up to twenty dollars' worth of food stamps if it's spent on Michigan-grown produce at the market. First I talk to a woman who's shopping for her ninety-one-year-old mother. Then a woman who drives a shared van for Medicaid clients. Then a mother of four. They all like the program, and they all say they buy more produce because of it. But it's Patti, who helps manage checkouts at Kmart, who really makes an impression. She's here with her sister, Teri. They're both in their forties, I'd guess, and look like a lot of the mothers of the friends I grew up with: Long straight hair, loose. No makeup. Jeans and formless t-shirts and nondescript sneakers. They are not people, I realize with a start at my own snobbery, that I would guess care much about food. But when I ask Patti about the produce coupons, she can't say enough. It's too expensive to eat fruits and vegetables much, she says, and "you can't afford that stuff all the time," though she does enjoy an orange if she feels like splurging. When I hear that an orange is something she considers a splurge, I don't bother to ask her if she buys organic; more than half of the people who say they're interested in "earth-sustainable foods" don't buy them because they're too expensive. Later, I learn that lower-income households *value* organic produce more than the wealthy, even if its price—which on average is 29 percent higher than that of conventional fruits and vegetables—keeps them from buying it.*

Teri chimes in for a minute, telling me that she wishes she knew more about how to prepare different foods, too. "That's what holds me up," she says. "It looks good, it smells good, but what do you do with it?" Patti nods, then starts rattling off everything she buys like a music fan chronicling set lists: Honeycrisp apples, potatoes still smelling of earth, paper-skinned onions, and Brussels sprouts still on the stalk.

"Last year," she smiles, "I was even able to get a pineapple. That was really great." Then she paused. "Like I said, it's the affordability."

* * *

---

* There is reason to think that the appreciation for good produce shown by Patti and Teri may be somewhat typical of lower-income shoppers. A study published in the *Journal of Agriculture and Industrial Organization* found that lower-income, and less-educated, people actually *value* organic production more than higher-income people (whether they buy it is another matter). While 51 percent of respondents with less than a high school diploma place very high or extremely high importance on organic production systems, only 35 percent of those with a college degree or more education think similarly. Likewise, respondents with an annual household annual income under $40,000 place greater importance on organic production systems when deciding what food to eat than do higher income groups. (Bellows et al. 2008)

Patti and Marvin reminded me how much people care about their meals. There were signs of it all around me in Detroit. There was Chris and her ceviche, for instance. The woman largely subsisted, so far as I could tell, on high-fiber breakfast bars, quesadillas, and Michelob Ultras, but she would also spend an hour cutting through five pounds of raw fish so that we could eat it all week. Then there was my new friend, Michael, a writer and self-made city historian who insisted he didn't care for fancy food but then proudly took me to his favorite corner of Hamtramck: Bozek's, a Polish grocer complete with its own meat room and bulk sauerkraut, before we crossed the street to shop at Al Haramain, an Arab market overflowing with produce, hummus, and olives. We feasted on city chicken, a Polish-American specialty—chunks of veal and pork, breaded, threaded on a skewer, and then deep-fried—and feathery triangles of baklava.

Really, though, all I would have needed to do was look out my bedroom window. In the balm of springtime evenings, I'd watch my neighbors work in the community garden, crouching low to yank out weeds or ambling up the sidewalk behind a creaking wheelbarrow in the long shadows of twilight. Our garden wasn't that big, maybe half a lot, but there were hundreds of them throughout the city in backyards, vacant lots, and parks, most of them growing food not in the city soil but in raised beds atop it—a bid at doing an end-run around any industrial contamination that gets past a standard soil test. Since the early 2000s, Detroit's limited supermarkets and an overabundance of vacant land have inspired city residents to start growing their own food, in gardens ranging from tiny corner lots with collards and tomatoes to a four-acre expanse complete with a mushroom patch. They've churned out such an abundance of greens, herbs, and tomatoes that the most prodigious among them have formed a cooperative, Grown in Detroit, to sell their excess at farmers' markets and restaurants around town.* In all, Grown in Detroit grossed around $60,000 in produce sales in 2010. One neighborhood gardener, Greg Willerer, was so enthralled by urban farming's potential that he founded a farm in 2010, using his own yard before expanding to a couple vacant lots to grow an array of herbs and salad greens. He started selling to restaurants, got himself a stand at Eastern Market, and in 2011 he launched a community-supported agriculture project catering

---

* The Grown in Detroit cooperative was launched as an effort of the Gardening Resource Program, itself a collaboration between several urban farming organizations in the city, including the Greening of Detroit, Earthworks Urban Farm, Detroit Agriculture Network, and Michigan State University Extension. (Garden Resource Program Collaborative 2011)

to city residents. In exchange for greens and vegetables all summer long, locals pay Willerer in a number of ways: in full in March, piecemeal through the season, or even by donating labor. Across town, on the city's east side, Carolyn Leadley and Jacob Vandyke founded Rising Pheasant Farms in 2009, selling produce wholesale through Grown in Detroit. In 2011, they expanded and paid for a retail stand at Eastern Market, where they sell sprouts next to Willerer on Saturdays.

In the Detroit of 2010, even people whose primary concerns were profit and jobs had begun to think pairing the city's vacant land with large-scale agriculture could make sense.* In 2009, a local financier, John Hantz, announced plans to establish a 50-acre pilot project to establish large-scale commercial farming in the city, arguing that it would gobble up vacant, blighted land while generating profits. A local drug-treatment organization has begun drafting ambitious plans for Recovery Park, an agriculture, housing, and community development project designed to employ recovering addicts and other residents in living-wage jobs growing and processing food. And Majora Carter, a renowned urban advocate for green space, announced plans to recruit the city's urban farmers for a new produce label, American City Farms, conceiving of the effort primarily as one of economic development and job creation.

All of these larger players will be capitalizing on Detroit's long history of urban agriculture, which has been a part of the city's fabric for more than a century. In the 1890s, poor Detroiters were encouraged to grow food on 430 acres of vacant land by the mayor, Hazen S. Pingree. Precursors to the Victory Gardens of World War I, these early plots were dubbed Pingree Potato Patches, and by their third year, the value of food grown in the patches outstripped the cash aid distributed to the city's poor. Backyard gardening has always been strong in Detroit, a city where 79 percent of all homes are single-family, but local urban agriculture got a boost in the 1970s from a federal program that set aside money to encourage food production in urban settings. The brainchild of a liberal New York City congressman, Fred Richmond, the Urban Gardening Program gained the support of conservative southern representatives in 1976, when Richmond made them a

---

* By 2011, local officials worried that the state's Right to Farm law, designed to protect rural farmers from nuisance lawsuits, could limit the city's ability to regulate any farms within its limits. As this book went to press, advocates and lawmakers were negotiating to develop policies that would protect both farmers and community residents in the city. (John Gallagher 2011; Laitner 2010; Mogk 2011)

pitch they couldn't refuse: Help people in cities grow food and they'll start to appreciate how hard it is to grow it—and they'll be more open to the issues that matter to agricultural states. In 1977, the program launched in six cities, including Detroit.

The program revived a link between the nation's agricultural extension offices, the public venue for America's agricultural policies, and urban soil. During World War II, extension offices had helped to set up Victory Gardens in cities, but after their demise, extension's agricultural efforts became strictly rural affairs. A joint program between the country's land-grant universities and the USDA, extension offices can offer advice to anyone who wants to grow food. At the biggest universities, extension offices run massive research and resource programs; the extension at University of California–Davis, for example, helped develop the tomato harvester machine. Extension, as it's called colloquially, is where America's public agriculture gets made and shaped. Typically, it supports and expands on the conventional methods already in practice, further refining the industrial agriculture that has fueled America's food supply for generations. Techniques outside that purview do sometimes trickle up into extension's repertoire, but only when people push for them. That's how sustainable agriculture got a toehold in a handful of offices in the 1970s, a move that amounted to minor but official acceptance of the practice. Even so, extension offices have rarely led the pack on new ways of farming, focusing instead on refining existing ones and responding to farmers' current needs—which are, of course, defined by the way they already farm.

Truthfully, it's left to the outlying innovators—the organic pioneers, the urban farmers—to come up with a meaningful agricultural practice outside the industrial model. Big, industrial growers have to persuade extension services to help them, too—but they're often the ones funding research, which gives researchers a strong incentive to meet big growers' needs. (Most big agribusiness companies have their own research departments as well.) Accordingly, extension has had little incentive to suggest radical changes like leaving behind pesticides, adopting new labor practices, or making small-scale growing profitable. For seventeen years, the Urban Gardening Program, small as it was, bucked that trend and put money toward figuring out how to use city land to grow food instead of flowers and shrubs.

In 1994, the Urban Gardening Program ended, a victim of a funding reorganization that made it an optional part of another agency, instead of having its own specified place in the budget. Some cities continued to promote urban agriculture for food production, rather than beautification; in New York City, the local cooperative extension figured out how to keep its urban agriculture agent, John Ameroso. Now retired, Ameroso proved to be a relentless advocate for food production over recreation in garden spaces, pointing out that gazebos, after all, take away growing space. In the federal program's final year, the gardens grew $16 million-worth of food, the last year official records were kept. It was considered a nice, but ineffective, effort; all well and good, but not worth its own place in a budget. Productive agriculture was big; you could never make money doing it any other way.

I first meet Malik Yakini on a warm morning in May, at D-Town Farm, two acres tucked within a massive city park on the city's northwest side. (By 2011, they had expanded to four acres.) Yakini, the founder and principal of an Afrocentric charter school, founded D-Town Farm in 2007 as chair of the Detroit Black Community Food Security Network. The idea was to provide access to fresh, healthy food grown without chemicals while putting vacant land to good use, as well as to encourage the city's black community to "do for self" by providing jobs and income. Giving people the means to feed themselves, went the thinking, was one way to help mitigate the city's sometimes sparse options for fresh food.* At first D-Town was more an idea than a place, with Yakini and fellow activists farming one plot of land one year, a different one the next. In 2008, after two years of negotiations with city officials, Yakini and his colleagues managed to strike a deal for two acres tucked into a park on the city's northwest side.

The day I visit is perfect spring: blue skies, breeze rustling through glossy poplar leaves, sun pouring down. Yakini meets me at the farm's gate, near a little wooden signpost with a placard explaining the city's food access problems—and the hope that D-Town's fields can provide a partial solution to them. Other signs dot the property, stopping points for the volunteer tour guides who take visitors like me around. He gestures at the tall wire fence encircling the growing area, adjusting the knit cap keeping his dreadlocks in place as he looks up at it. "We had a pretty severe problem last year with inventory shrinkage," he says wryly, explaining that both humans and wildlife helped themselves. We pad around on tilled earth inside, his shell-top

---

* This is a goal that shares some form—if not inspiration—with Ted Nugent's philosophies of food.

Adidas sinking into furrowed ground between adolescent greens. When a half-dozen urban gardeners from New York show up, in town for a conference, I tag along on their tour of the mushroom patch and beehives, where our guide, Aba, informs us that they are "raising some strong Detroit bees that'll make it through the winter."

Much of what has kept urban agriculture from generating money has been its small scale; it's hard to make up the cost of growing food, which requires daily work no matter how little you grow. Commercial production requires balancing larger-scale production (which means more food to sell) against the cost of the inputs required to grow it (compost or fertilizer, tractors or pitchforks). The conventional wisdom about selling food just the way it comes out of the ground is that to do so profitably requires either massive, Walmartian scale or very high prices. Trimming back the vast network between farm and plate—the marketing system—is one way to get around that equation; that's why growers like Willerer, who sell directly to the customers eating their produce, can charge affordable prices. Another way to boost profits is by making food more appealing to customers—or, to use food-business lingo, to add value to it. "Once you wash something, cut it, put it in a bag, it gains a lot of value," says Yakini.

Currently, very little of the produce grown in Detroit has much done to it at all. For the Grown in Detroit label, produce has to follow basic industry standards; you don't wash raspberries, because the delicate fruits will disintegrate, but you do wash lettuce—a step that in turn requires facilities in which to do the washing. Then it's taken to market as quickly as possible, because the only cooling facilities available tend to be people's home refrigerators. "Growing produce is our thing, we've gotten fairly good at that," says Yakini. "But you have to be able to move it, move it quickly, and clean and pack it, and that side is kind of underdeveloped. We need to work much more on the infrastructure."

That's already on the agenda for the Grown in Detroit farmers, who have begun remediating a few acres of soil a few blocks over from Eastern Market, planning to use the space as a training facility, producing food for market. They also plan to build a packing house and cooling shed, and with that infrastructure in place, they expect to harvest and prepare even more food for sale. At the same time, they'll be operating as something of a de facto extension office, expanding on established agricultural practices for urban areas and developing new ones; testing different varieties of crops that suit the city's hot, wet summers and can be grown in tight spaces; and using intercropping so that one stretch of land can grow two kinds of food. Although there's little real estate pressure in Detroit, land still costs money, and spreading multiple inputs like water and compost over vast acreage can be tricky.

The question comes up again and again: Could you feed Detroit from farms within its limits? In 2010, researchers at Michigan State University decided to try to answer it, and they found that urban growers might not be able to supply the city with everything it eats—but they could make a significant contribution. Nearly half the nontropical fruit eaten by city residents could be grown here, and three-quarters of their vegetables; a similar study of Cleveland suggested residents could meet *all* their produce needs by cultivating vacant land and industrial rooftops. In both studies, the most interesting finding of all was how little land these farms would require. Take Detroit, for example. Researchers estimated that if growers practiced conventional industrial agriculture, they'd need 3,600 acres of land to produce that much food—nearly three-fourths of the vacant city-owned land in Detroit. But if they practiced biointensive agriculture—the kind in use at most of the urban farm plots, with compost, intercropping, and diverse crop plans—researchers found they'd need 568 acres, about 12 percent of the city's vacant land. (For comparison, Manhattan's Central Park is 843 acres.) Feeding Detroit most of its fruits and vegetables wouldn't require remaking the city into the endless cornfields of the Heartland, or the massive vegetable monocrops of California's Central Valley. Instead, it'd look more like a giant backyard garden, with lettuces giving way to tomatoes giving way to spinach in the same plot.

Yet urban farming gets pitted against redevelopment constantly—at least in Detroit. In 2011, a successful dog day care in the city's redeveloping Midtown neighborhood ousted a longstanding community garden, buying the city lot on which the garden sat so that it could expand. The two abutted each other on a stretch of Cass Avenue, a one-time thoroughfare now lined with boarded-up storefronts. Officials jumped at the opportunity to turn it into a tax-paying property; the garden was more of a neighborhood effort than a commercial farm plot. "If we all think about where we want Detroit to go . . . we don't want it looking like a farm in Kansas," said Councilmember Ken Cockrel. "We want it looking like Manhattan."

Yet most of the farmers I met in Detroit aren't envisioning Kansan cornfields so much as they're hoping to bring truly good food into their neighborhoods and maybe eke out a living doing it. Over toward City Airport, in one of Detroit's roughest neighborhoods, Mark Covington farms a couple blocks of land down Georgia Street from his house, the same one he grew up in. He moved back home a couple years ago, after losing his job as an environmental technician, cleaning oil tanks and commercial buildings. To keep busy, he started growing food for himself and his neighbors. Covington is something of a local celebrity for his work, but that hasn't made him sanguine about farming's prospects in his hometown. "Urban agriculture won't save Detroit," Covington told me matter-of-factly when I visited. But after seeing the work being done here, it seems possible that the city's farms could go a long way toward meeting the city's demand for fresh produce. They might even begin to help answer the biggest question of all when it comes to everyone's meals: How are we going to grow food for more people with the same amount of land? Either way, it seems a good idea to me.

What's the plan, Randy?

Luis, a trim, bespectacled man who dropped in from some distant perch in the Walmart bureaucracy this morning, is standing between us and a wall of pallets looming with produce, clipboard in hand. There must be twelve pallets, three rows of four that prevent us from even walking around the back room.

Randy blinks rapidly, a deer in headlights.

Um, I'm, I'm going to help put things out and Brent and Nick can work the truck.

Let's get more carts out. We need to fill this floor, now.

Luis turns around efficiently and pushes his way out the black swinging doors, leaving us staring at the pallets. Randy mutters something about who does Luis think he is, but he doesn't look at any of us—Pam, Brent, Nick, or me—and starts stacking crates onto carts to go out to the floor.

Pam and I are dispatched with a cart piled high with tomatoes, potatoes, and bags of peanuts. In hushed tones we discuss the saga that's been unfolding in the department this morning. Two pallets actually left out on the sales floor—that never happens, Pam tells me, because customers might trip on them—and the bank of twelve in the back room waiting to be put away. The store manager, Leo, is trolling around the section, conferring with Luis, eyeing the produce bins disappointedly. They've brought in a woman from another store and recruited a second from another department here, to help put out all the freight.

A couple weeks ago the department had a surprise audit from the state agricultural department about its country-of-origin labeling. Once management figured out the inspector was here, they accompanied her on her rounds—enough to see that we were missing a lot of our COOL labels. The inspector only reported one infraction, but the rumor on the floor is that the COOL problem is why we're getting a price audit—an inspection making sure that everything is displayed and priced correctly—from corporate next week. For that, upper management wants every bin to overflow with produce and has been putting in orders for more than usual. There's also a new "mod" layout—a complete reconfiguration of where and how each piece of produce is displayed—to implement. It would be a lot of work for anyone, but, as Pam and I cattily agree, Randy, who's shown little talent for organization or expertise in his field, is pretty ill-equipped for the job.

Luis and his minions disappear the next day, but the tension in the department doesn't relent. We've got eight more pallets from central distribution to put away, though that should be a little easier since maintenance—after a month—has finally fixed the leak in the cooler. Then two more pallets show up in the afternoon, special orders from the wholesaler at Detroit's produce terminal market where Walmart sometimes sources food. (Walmart's internal produce chain doesn't always carry exactly what we need, and sometimes we run out of things before our next scheduled delivery.) Still flustered from yesterday, Randy's been trying to call in more help, but Brent and Sam aren't answering their phones. Finally he gets Brendan, who'd normally come in at 10:00 p.m., to come in early.

You must have really freaked out when you came in, says Brendan, hefting sacks of potatoes into a table display. You must have thought this was a real mess.

What I thought was, *Randy's not very good at his job,* I say. But if I was hoping to ingratiate myself with Brendan, I've done just the opposite, revealing myself for the foolish snark that I am.

He's so young though, says Brendan. And then he tells me: It's Leo ordering all of this, when we don't have people to put it out. The store management here just doesn't get it.

Really? I say. I hadn't really thought about how we placed orders, how we got the food, or who made the decisions. I'd just noticed that our department was in disarray.

Really, says Brendan. It's really not his fault.

* * *

I spend my final shift, a Sunday afternoon and evening, putting away freight, a first for me. I'm working with Jean and Nathan, a voluble twenty-year-old from meats who explains that he's picking up extra hours over here. Since Jean has seniority over us, Nathan and I are tasked with organizing the walk-in and putting what we can up in the steel.

Nathan makes a newcomer's gaffe early on by asking me what our system is for organizing the crates of produce that are stashed in the walk-in. System, I ask? What system? We put the new stuff behind the old stuff. Nathan begins to explain that in meats there is a system, something about the newest stuff is always in front and then on the bottom of the pile behind it, or maybe it's the top—I never do entirely understand what he's trying to explain to me because he talks in fast-paced, ever-widening circles. Why don't we have a system here? They have one in meats and it works out real well, his boss really knows his stuff. We should have a system for produce. So why don't we have a system here? I don't want to risk engaging Nathan in substantive conversation, so I refrain from telling him that I've asked myself the same question many times since arriving here. Instead I repeat, slowly, that we have no real system other than making sure the oldest stuff is in front so that goes out to the floor first.

There's a whole pallet of apples and pears bound for the top shelf, and Nathan gamely offers to be the one on the ladder; I'm handing him crates of apples and pears and plums, lifting boxes over my head to reach him on his perch. I don't have a scale to weigh them, but several seem likely to be over twenty pounds, heavy enough that we're supposed to do a "team lift," but there's no practical way to do that. This goes all right until Nathan decides he needs to put a box behind a column of crates significantly to his left—far enough over that he needs to move the ladder. I bend over to get another box and when I stand back up I find he's left the ladder and is clambering across the steel, monkeylike, balancing his feet on the middle shelf, holding on to the top shelf with one arm and trying to shift a hundred pounds of fruit with the other. I have visions of him toppling to the ground, and there is a tense minute of my repeating in rounds of increasing volume, *Nathan, get back on the ladder; Nathan that's dangerous,* until he finally returns to the ladder. You're right, he says, that was a bad idea.

When I finish my shift, I go grocery shopping at Walmart, a first for me at this store. This marks me as something of a Walmart outsider, since many employees seem to take advantage of the employee discounts. I see a lot of people selecting from our bins while wearing the blue shirts and khaki pants we all don as our uniforms. People even come in on their off-hours; one Saturday, I recognize a young assistant manager, Toya, pushing a cart through the department in a strapless denim romper and espadrilles.

It would be reasonable to assume that, by now, I'd know better than to expect everything to be fresh. Still, some synapse fails to connect, and as I wheel my cart into the produce section I'm still clinging to the fiction that I'll be able to grab what I'm after. I'd eyed some Kirby cucumbers earlier in the week, but they've since gone soft; I suspect we have better ones in the back, but if I go back there I fear I'll never get out of here. The cilantro I wanted to get for salsa all has blackened greens in the center and mushy bottoms on the stems. I grab a package of mushrooms, realize they're slimed with age, and reach around to the back to get a fresh container.

At least the bagged spinach hasn't expired yet, and the kale, I know for a fact, just came out of its icy bed in the walk-in; I put it out myself. The cantaloupes look iffy, but Chris and I have been enjoying melon in the mornings so I pick out the best one I can find—I'm not entirely sure what I'm looking for, but weeding out the bruised ones narrows the field considerably. I can't bring myself to sort through much more produce, whether it's because of information overload or an actual flaw in the products on offer. I just grab some onions and tomatoes—the latter on sale for 99 cents a pound, which likely makes them one of our loss leaders*—and then putter over to canned goods and get some beans, chiles, and jalapeños.

My final bill looks just as I should have expected: The prices on produce aren't all that competitive, but Walmart blows away my neighborhood grocery's prices on canned and processed food. Take, for example, the garlic. At $3.38 a pound, it's considerably more expensive than the market near my place in Detroit, where it sells for $2.69 a pound. The canned goods are always cheaper—a jar of pickled jalapeños costs $1.99 in Detroit but $1.24 at Walmart. But then there are things like Walmart's vine ripened tomatoes, on special today for 99 cents a pound—which usually cost $2.19. At the Honey Bee on most days, I'll spend $1.99 for a pound of tomatoes that are redder, riper, and less wrinkled, making my local store a better deal. Yet this supercenter is twenty miles from my home; the closest is ten, and both would take me more than hour to reach on public transit if I were among the one-fifth of Detroiters living without a car.

* According to Walmart inventory documents, a shipment of tomatoes on the vine from May 26, 2010, cost Walmart $1.11 a pound, but would retail for $1.98, giving Walmart a gross profit of 87 cents per pound and a gross return of 78 percent. (Walmart Stores 2010c)

When Christina and I work our way through the food I bring home, we agree that La Colmena wins, hands down. The cantaloupe at Walmart was seventy cents cheaper, but it tasted like water. The jar of jalapeños had disintegrated into mush by the time we opened them. The tomatoes—OK, today Walmart won on the tomatoes, at least on price. When I cut into them at home, the tomatoes are rubbery and bland compared with what I've gotten at La Colmena—and I'd have to buy three pounds of them before the money they saved me canceled out the cost of the gas it took me to get to them.

I don't officially quit for a few days, pulling the same routine that got me out of the first Walmart. I call in for a family emergency the next day I'm scheduled to work, and plan to quit the next time I'm expected in. The problem comes when I'm so relieved to know I won't be returning that I even forget I was supposed to go in, resulting in a voice-mail message from the assistant store manager.

Hi Tracie, this is Toya, I'm just calling because we see you haven't been coming to work and just wanted to make sure everything was all right, give us a call.

When I call back to explain to Toya that I'm not going to be coming back, I start off by apologizing—less to Walmart than to my co-workers, for the additional headache I'm causing them—but she stops me. No, no, it's fine, this happens all the time, we just want to make sure you're okay.

Really?

Well, Pam was really worried about you, and she wanted me to call and make sure you hadn't been in a car accident or anything. Don't worry about it, says Toya. Walmart will be fine without me.

PART III

❧

COOKING

WAGES
Hourly: $7.25–$8.00

POST-TAX INCOME
Weekly: $247
Annually: $12,845

FOOD BILL
Daily: $4.74
Weekly: $33.19
Annually: $1,726

PERCENT OF INCOME SPENT ON FOOD
All food: 13.5%
Food at home: 7.7%
Eating out: 5.8%

CHAPTER 8

Kitchen Novice

"How are you with *controlled chaos?*" Freddie, the man sitting across from me in black chef togs embroidered with his name and the Applebee's logo, is choosing his words carefully. He's about my height, barrel-chested, with a complexion that could be southern European or South American—what used to be called swarthy. He looks at me, brow furrowed under a ladder of wrinkles that climbs to his hairline. The question remains: Can I handle chaos?

I can work fast, I say, eyeing the NFL championship replays on the screen behind him. We face each other over a high table in the bar, alone save for the population of Brooklyn athletes framed in posters on the wall. This is one Applebee's out of the twenty-one in New York City, a representative of the world's largest sit-down restaurant chain with two thousand outposts flung across the globe. Somewhere in Bahrain right now, another manager could be interviewing another potential worker in another oak-paneled bar crowded with locally relevant sports paraphernalia under another neon Applebee's sign. Here in Brooklyn, rain is pelting the sidewalk under a steel smudge of sky. Freddie continues with his questions.

Do you have a temper?

I hesitate.

You have a temper, huh?

Well, not too bad, I can handle myself, I say.

What sign are you?

I pause. Scorpio.

So you have a temper, then.

Not bad, I repeat evenly, but if somebody grabs my ass I'm gonna get pissed.

I see a glimmer of amusement flicker across Freddie's face.

We don't want that to happen.

Then we shouldn't have a problem.

We've already covered the basics: Yes, I speak Spanish, though only a little. ("Eh," said Freddie, "we only need a little.") I'm interested in kitchen work because I'm considering culinary school, but want to try working in an actual kitchen first—a statement that has been true in the past. Yes, I like providing good service, and to me that means working efficiently, without drama, and giving people what they want without burdening them with attitude.

My résumé, as at Walmart, lists college jobs—including some restaurant work—and then recent freelance copyediting, with a ten-year gap in between. When I ask about getting work in the kitchen, Freddie surprises me by asking what kind of prep I have done. Cutting up vats of stuff, I say, vaguely, hoping my stint at the Big Boy salad bar in high school will suffice.

So, bulk?

Yeah, bulk.

No portioning, though?

Not so much, no.

Well, with us it's almost all portioning, explains Freddie, but right now we don't need anybody in prep. My heart sinks. I'm desperate to see how the food America eats when we eat out is prepared. We certainly eat a lot of it: By 2010, Americans were spending 42 percent of our food budgets at restaurants.

We don't have any openings in prep, repeats Freddie. But I'm short an expediter.

I'm not sure what an expediter is, but I nod agreeably. I'm putting in applications at Applebee's all over town, and there's no reason to torpedo this option until I can find kitchen work at another store. OK, then, Freddie seems to be saying with the nod of his head and writing "Second Interview" across the top of my application in black marker. He looks up.

How are you at working with a lot of people?

A lot of people? I repeat. Pretty good, I'm pretty personable.

Freddie smiles efficiently and nods.

Can you come in tomorrow for a second interview? Around five o'clock?

I nod. Yeah, that's no problem.

Ask for Angelo, tell him I sent you.

Freddie stands, and I offer him my hand. We shake. I'll be back tomorrow.

* * *

After talking to Freddie, I begin applying to every Applebee's within an hour's commute of downtown Brooklyn. I spend hours traversing the city by subway, starting out from a quiet block in the borough's southern reaches—where I'm staying with friends until I find a place—and popping up in the middle of what feels like half of the city's neighborhoods. There are the tourist hubs of Times Square and the Financial District, which I'd expected, but also the humbler digs of Fordham Road in the Bronx, where the Applebee's is adjacent to a vacant hemodialysis center; the bustling shopping strip with a Salvation Army around the corner from the Astoria, Queens shop; and Restoration Plaza, a Bedford-Stuyvesant shopping center founded by Bobby Kennedy amid the urban redevelopment craze of the 1960s and '70s. By the time all is said and done I will have called and visited eleven Applebee's and applied to five of the six that tell me they are taking applications. My only failure on that front comes at the Harlem Applebee's. Over the phone, the woman had said they were taking applications and I should come in and fill one out. I walked in, "Fight the Power" playing in the entryway, and asked the three well-dressed African-American women at the hostess stand for an application. They took one look at me and said they were all out of applications.

In every Applebee's, even the tourist magnets of Midtown Manhattan, the patrons are mostly casually dressed Hispanics and blacks, not the pallid Midwestern tourists I expected. But if most of the faces in the Applebee's dining rooms I visit are brown and black, they reflect the fact that more than half of New York's are, too.

After another day and a half of job hunting, Freddie remains my best bet. I follow up with a visit to Angelo, who disarms me by asking about my hobbies (riding bikes, cooking, visiting with friends) and interests (traveling) before handing me a 150-question multiple-choice personality test. I ignore Angelo's suggestion to "answer honestly" and instead try to answer questions about authority as slavishly as possible, and with the requirements of kitchen work—working at high speed, coping with high stress, keeping cool under pressure—in mind.

Freddie calls me the next Thursday. They'll give me a try, he says. Can I come in tomorrow through Sunday?

I can work tomorrow and Saturday, but not on Sunday, I say, fumbling with an excuse about babysitting for friends. I actually just want to watch the Super Bowl.

All right, so can you stay a few extra hours on Friday?

Of course, and you can work me as hard as you want after that.

OK, cool, we'll make it work. We got to get you ready for Valentine's
Day, he says. We are going to get killed—

Awesome, I say, interrupting.

—in a good way, he finishes.

We both laugh.

Expediting, I am told at orientation, is the hardest job in the restaurant. The
primary responsibility of an "expo" is to coordinate the flow of food from
line to floor. To paraphrase Bernardo, the frenetic bear of a general manager
who runs my orientation session, everything I do keeps the restaurant moving. If I don't do my job right, the orders won't look right, and people won't
come back, and servers' tips will be lower, and the restaurant won't make as
much money, and it won't be able to afford to pay an expediter, which will
mean the servers will have to expo their food themselves, which is never a
good idea since it tends to result in the orders not looking right . . . and the
downward spiral into chaos and bankruptcy begins. I am the first domino
in line; if I fall, we all go down.

When I come back the next morning at 10:00, I don't start in the kitchen.
Instead, Freddie hands me a cup of coffee and a binder full of presentation
diagrams for every item on the menu and tells me to start memorizing: Do
hot wings get a ramekin of ranch dressing or blue cheese? Do they get a big
ramekin or a small one? Which sandwiches get a side of coleslaw? Which
dishes get sent out with wet naps? Which plates get lemons or limes? Tartar sauce? Cocktail sauce? Honey mustard? Sour cream? Mexi-ranch? There
are 151 different dishes on the menu, and nearly half require some degree
of dressing by the expediter. I spend several hours hunched over a table in
the back of the dining room, my hair pulled up under an Applebee's cap,
scribbling notes to help myself memorize. And then, around noon, as lunch
begins, Freddie puts me on the line.

The kitchen is big, a span of ruddy tile, white walls, and stainless steel
wrapped around its heart: the line, the place where meals are cooked and
readied for the dining room. I'd guess that the kitchen is just under half of
the dining room's size, a third of it dedicated to the line. The rest, explains
Freddie, is for storage and prep, where everything gets portioned out: bags
of French onion soup defrosted, sacks of Monterey cheese divvied up for the
line, bags of Alfredo sauce mixed with preshredded cheese, packs of Cargill
ground beef defrosted and formed into patties. Little of what he explains to
me sounds like cooking, but the line is all business nonetheless. Three cooks

whirl in the slice of space between sizzling cooktops and a long width of steel shelving, open on both sides and divided into three sections: the window. We stand on the other side, facing the cooks across the pass, a long low counter. A short, well-muscled man stands at its border, glancing up at a computer screen affixed to the top shelf, a tiny printer bolted underneath it. Fluorescent lights burn bright overhead.

Tony, this is Tracie, says Freddie. You're going to train her on expo, all right?

Yessirrr, says Tony.

He steps up, closer to the counter, and explains the line. The cooks put the food in the window, we dress it. Food moves down the pass from left to right, so ramekins are on the left of the pass, and then there's the expo line, a series of small refrigerated bins built into the pass, with all the sauces and garnishes tucked in place.

When food comes up you put the ramekin of sauce or slaw or whatever it is that goes with it, and send it out. Any questions?

What do you want me to do?

Before he can answer, the printer chortles and spits out a piece of paper. Tony tears it off, looks up at the computer screen, and presses a button, making the screen rearrange.

What did you just do? I ask.

Huh?

To the screen?

Oh, I bumped the ticket.

What do you mean?

Tony gives me a look equal parts teacher and irritated boss. It's not on the screen anymore, he says, already pulling plates out of the window and calling for sauces. I scoop them out and hand them to him. A server walks past, sees the plates, and barely pauses as he grabs them. The plates go out.

I soon realize that the computer is the nervous system of the restaurant, the circuitry that receives information, routes it through the brain, and enables the body to *do something* with it all. The cooks here never see paper tickets; instead, each station has its own computer screen. An order comes in and each dish crops up on the respective cook's screen—they don't know what else was ordered at the table. Simultaneously, the complete order, every dish and every last substitution of mashed potatoes for fries, eighty-six that onion on the Firepit burger, and all the rest, is listed on mine. Appetizers are supposed to be ready in seven minutes, entrees in fourteen, and each order has a time clock counting down next to it. When a cook finishes a dish, he hits a button—"bumps" it—and, on my screen, its text turns green. If an order is running over its allotted time, the top line gets highlighted in angry, blinking red.

Around 4:00, with the kitchen still slow, Claudette, a young black woman replaces Tony. She ties on an apron and sidles up alongside me, humming with energy, and starts barking at the cooks in English I don't yet fully understand: Where's that Cowboy? How long on that sweet-and-spicy for fifty-three? Is there an Orange Chick Bowl coming? Can I get a five-ounce? She tells me to get ranch for the barbecue wings, blue cheese for the hot ones, and a scoop of sour cream on top of those nachos, thanks. During the lulls, she breaks into Haitian Creole with Geoff, the dark-skinned cook on mid, swinging between coy laughter and sass. She bumps tickets with abandon, clears the screen as fast as it fills up, and bosses me around without being a bitch. I like her immediately.

She turns to me. You ever work in a kitchen before?

In college, a little. But that was ten, twelve years ago.

She stares at me. How old *are* you?

Thirty-three. Why, how old are you?

You look . . . a lot less than thirty-three.

How old are you? I ask.

Twenty-one.

You're just a baby, I tease, and she shoots me a look of disdain in return. I ain't no baby. I *got* a baby, she says, and turns back to the line.

We go on like this for a few hours, and then another manager, Matt, tells me to take my break a little before 6:00. They might send me home as early as 7:00 or 8:00, he says, but I might as well get some food; since I'm in training, I can order off the whole menu for free.

I put my order in for a Shrimp Island—skewers of grilled shrimp on a bed of rice seasoned with cilantro and citrus—and am waiting for it to come up, sipping on a soda in the back dining room, when I meet Hector. He's olive-skinned, tall, and broad-shouldered, his hair hidden by a trim black ski cap. He sits down at my two-person table, introduces himself, and explains that he was supposed to start at 5:00, but he has a bad headache so they're letting him wait until 6:00 since it's not too busy yet. I nod.

Do you like working here? I ask.

Well, the people here work with you, he says. Without skipping a beat, Hector tells me a long, involved—and heartbreaking—story about the personal struggles that landed him in a Brooklyn shelter with his three kids.

That sounds rough, I say, adding, truthfully, that my sisters and I were pretty much raised by a single dad, too, and I know it's really hard.

Hector nods back; there aren't a lot of programs for dads, he says, but that's changing. Anyway, he doesn't expect to stay in the shelter much longer; he's on a list for an apartment from the city, and should be able to move soon. As for working here, he repeats what he started with: They work with you.

Before we can get any further into conversation, Matt calls Hector into the kitchen and tells me my dinner is ready.

It was nice talking to you, Ma, says Hector and I nod back in agreement.

I finish my dinner and clock back in, swiping my employee card at a computer at the bar. An hour later, Matt sends me home and tells me to get ready for next weekend.

Now that I've found a job, I start looking for housing in earnest. One of the tricks to finding housing in New York is to understand that while finding nice, well-run apartments takes forever and frequently requires a broker, lowering one's standards—something that is easier for single, childless adults like me to do—can reduce the wait (and price) considerably. By now it's already after the first of the month, which makes things a little more difficult. I don't yet have my first check, but Freddie told me I'd be paid $8 an hour during training and $9 an hour after that, putting a month's take-home pay around $1,000. My startup fund of $925.10 has already been depleted by groceries and a public transit card and was too paltry to cover a deposit and rent besides; rents typically start around $500 a month for shared apartments, somewhat less if I loosen my one-hour-commute restriction. This pretty much relegates me to single-occupancy hotels or, preferably, an illegal sublet. In strictly financial terms, the most promising ad I find is for a room in the East Village. It's a three-bedroom, two-bathroom apartment, and the room is only $350. I just need to be an "open-minded female" who's comfortable with the male leaseholder *sometimes* walking around in his underwear and, *sometimes,* just letting "it hang out." Luckily, I find another ad that seems to hit the right balance: It's $500 a month, month to month is fine, no deposit required, it's furnished, and it's just two blocks from the subway station. It's also near Prospect Park, which means I'll have access to what, in Brooklyn, counts as luxury: outdoor recreation.

The streets are sleepy on Sunday morning, bright and cold in the winter sun. As promised, the park is two blocks away. There's also a sprawling discount supermarket called Western Beef three blocks away, its advertisements for specials on pigs' and cows' feet competing with the Popeye's, Wendy's, and McDonald's on the same corner. The neighborhood is unmistakably Caribbean. Storefronts hawk beef patties and vegetable roti under signs screaming in red and yellow; black iron barrels exude the scent of jerk chicken on the sidewalk; hair salons sell weaves and wigs with Indian hair. Across from the subway station, there's a discount store called Phat Albert's Warehouse ("We Guaranteed to Beat Any Price in Town") and the offices for the *Haitian Times*. As I cross Bedford Avenue, I can see the towers of the Ebbets Field Houses—a housing project built on the site of the old Brooklyn Dodgers field—a few blocks uphill.

The apartment itself is in a little two-family building on a wide street lined with the same. The entryway reeks of marijuana, enough that there's a faint buzzing at the back of my skull, but Dan—who's showing me the room—assures me it's just the downstairs neighbor. Upstairs, the apartment is a modest three-bedroom with a bay-windowed living room that looks out onto the street. Dan's leaving in a week, but the two twentysomething women who live here, Eve and Paula, will be staying for at least another month and a half until the lease runs out. There's a windowless bathroom and a tiny hallway of a kitchen crammed with a stove, sink, roughly two square feet of counter space, and a table in the corner with a window to the backyard. Paula, a video editor from Spain, has the big, sunny room in back, and Eve, a home economics teacher from New Mexico currently working at a day care center, has a glorified cubby off the living room.

My room shares a door with Paula's and has no window of its own. There's a double bed and a desk, and a huge wardrobe system, and, wafting up through the floorboards, the faint scent of weed. But the $500 includes utilities, the girls seem nice, and they both assure me the worst they've experienced in the neighborhood is some catcalls; nothing unusual, and half the time it's in Creole anyway. The neighborhood is changing, they say, more college kids moving in, and everyone's calling it Prospect-Lefferts Gardens instead of Flatbush. And it's hard to beat the rent: $1600 for the whole place.

I move in a week later.

My first day, with Tony and Claudette, concluded by 7:00 p.m. despite it being a Saturday, the busiest night of the week. But I work a full shift on my second night, a Thursday. The first couple hours are no problem. I'm working with Tony again, and he's mostly letting me work the line myself—it's slow enough for that. I have finally begun to remember which dressings and sauces go with which dishes. It's loose and easy, with Tony calling Geoff *Africano* and Geoff saying *pendejo* back to him and then beckoning me to the window to tell me he's going to call me Laura Ingalls because I've got my hair in braids. The cooks are being patient with my constant pestering. I ask Calixto on broil which sauce is on every plate of ribs—regular, sweet and spicy, or honey barbecue—and he answers me politely. I get Geoff, who's handling the flattop—or mid, the flat metal grill used to cook burgers, sandwiches, and quesadillas—to identify every plate he puts in the window, and he says, Looks like a Cowboy to me, Laura. And I pester Rico, on fry, with queries about which wings are which. When the computer spits out a ticket, I rip it off, I read it, I bump it from the screen, I pull the plates from the window—slowly and amid many questions, since I still can't recognize most of them—ladle the sauces, and assemble the order. Just before I send plates out, I squeeze the potato, rice, and vegetable sides out of the plastic bags they're heated in—the plastic, regrettably, typically degrades in the heat and flakes out onto the food, and I wipe what I can off the plate—and push it down the line. Easy.

Then the dinner rush begins.

At first, I don't realize what's happening. I notice, of course, that all four columns on the screen are suddenly full, but I don't yet understand the rhythm of the kitchen, that work passes through our hands as if from sea to shore. So I'm oblivious to what the wave of activity brewing behind the line means: I'm about to get slammed. Calixto is laying down a grid of ribs and steaks over the grill, there's a great gurgling hiss as Rico dumps another bag of frozen fries into boiling oil, Geoff is putting little curved plates in formation for the army of appetizers being cooked by Omar, who's slapping patties onto the flattop. Me, I just do what I've been doing: I stare at the screen, I wipe down the pass, I wait. And then it hits.

First one order turns green and then another, and then another, and another. I bump the orders and snatch the tickets as they begin to spiral down toward the food. I reach over to scoop sauces for the first order, and when I look up, there's, maddeningly, more green. I bump more tickets, stack them in my hand, and see that the orders on the screen are now blinking red. Tony is leaning against the bev station—the soda machine—behind me, flirting with a waitress.

Claudette comes through the kitchen—she's waiting tables tonight—and sees me facing down a window crammed with food that's rapidly congealing, cooling, and crusting over under the heat lamps. She turns to Tony: Would you help her?

Sink or swim man, says Tony, laughing. Sink or swim.

Claudette comes up alongside me.

You doing OK?

Does it look like I'm in the weeds, perhaps?

You look flustered, she says, then grabs the tickets out of my hand, and takes over.

Geoff, where's that Firepit? Did you see eighty-six on that sauce? Whitney, did your table want eighty-six on Tabasco or tomato? Where are those sweet-and-spicy ribs; these are regular. I need fries two, three, four times, Rico. That's four times, heard? Calixto, you got those ribs?

I mutely fill ramekins while Claudette all but clears the screen in five minutes flat.

You can take care of these, she says, handing me the last two tickets. I'm out.

She picks her order off the pass and flounces toward the dining room.

That was the first rush. Another comes an hour later. By then, Terry, another manager type, has replaced Tony. He's tall, heavy, and soft-spoken, lighter-skinned than Geoff, and offers the first bit of helpful advice I've gotten on expo: Ladle out your dressings in advance. When the second rush quiets down, he asks how long I've been here.

This is my second day, I say, and his eyes go wide.

And they put you here by yourself?

I nod. Yes.

You should have told me! I would have been training you. But this is only my third night here, so I don't know everybody yet.

I like to think I'll be more competent with practice, I say, grabbing an empty coleslaw bin, a casualty of the rush, and taking it to the dishwasher.

You're doing really good for your second day, offers Terry.

I get sent home around 10:30, and in my bathroom I can see the imprint of the kitchen on my face. My cheeks are red and blotchy, my eyes leaking tears from some unnamed irritant, and a raised rash has spread across my neck and chest. The caffeine I've ingested via the soda machine keeps me up for another few hours, and then I finally begin to drift off to sleep, the smell of fry grease still in my nostrils.

* * *

One thing I almost never see at Applebee's, not in my first week or anytime after, are customers. I hear the one-line stories dropped by waitstaff and managers between runs to the dining room, all of which inevitably skew toward the outrageous and scatological. ("So I take the birthday cake to the table, and her husband says she went to the bathroom and then her friend says, 'She's taking a shit.' I mean, what do you say to that?") But otherwise, I hear nothing, see nothing of the people who eat here apart from the plates sent back to be corrected by the cooks.

I poll my co-workers, though, about who's out there ordering all these shrimp-Parm steaks (sirloins topped with a handful of grilled shrimp and a dollop of Parmesan cream sauce), steak quesadilla towers (strips of grilled beef rolled up with cheese, onions, and peppers, burrito-style, then grilled, sliced in half, and arrayed vertically), and chicken-fried-chickens (a flat pancake of a chicken patty, breaded and deep-fried, served atop two mounds of mashed potatoes and flooded with a peppery gravy that's been nuked in a foam cup). So far as anyone can tell me, the typical table at our Brooklyn establishment is occupied by middle-class blacks and Latinos, interspersed with students from the college up the street plying the bar, a few after-theater drop-ins, and a more mixed lunch clientele from nearby businesses. There's no real way for me to know if "middle-class" means actually middle income or simply that most of those who show up don't *look* poor or rich. This is a place, after all, that probably constitutes a splurge for most folks, and our management knows it, reminding us that tax season is beginning, and people are looking to spend their refund checks on a treat.

Statistically speaking, the servers' assessment is probably right: Our patrons most likely come from the middle class or just below it. Applebee's doesn't publish demographic information about its customers,* but more broadly, full-service chains like it tend to draw their customers from the more affluent classes of America. In 2011, sit-down chains saw two-thirds of their guests coming from households earning $75,000 or more—and another 13 percent from households earning between $50,000 and $75,000. Even with deals like Applebee's "Two for Twenty," which feeds two adults for $20, a family of four could easily end up with a bill of $70 by the time tax and tip are taken care of. At that rate, lower-income families would spend down their "eating out" budget by visiting our tables almost twice

---

* While Applebee's declined to answer questions about proprietary data for this book, in 2006 the company's annual report noted that "a significant portion" of its clientele came from households earning less than $50,000 a year. (Applebee's 2006)

a month, while families earning more than $70,000 could do so every six days. But if I am surprised to learn of Applebee's middle-class appeal, even this far from the Midwestern highway exits and shopping-mall parking lots with which I associate the chain, that's only because I haven't been paying attention to the restaurant industry.

Restaurants like Applebee's are just a modern expression of a midcentury invention: the family restaurant. Fine dining has existed for the wealthy since the first formal restaurant opened in France in 1782. Quick, cheap food for workers, whether from peddlers' carts or tavern tables, is as old as modern civilization itself. But eating out wasn't introduced to the middle class until much later, around the turn of the twentieth century—and even then, it was modest. Then came the 1950s.

As the American middle class sprawled out after World War II and we became a nation transported by automobiles, eating out came within reach of far more Americans. First and foremost, we had more money. From 1947 to 1975, our incomes nearly doubled. And as our incomes rose, we spent more of our money on going out to dinner. In 1940, Americans spent about 15 percent of their food budget on eating out; by 1975 it was up to 28 percent, and by 2010 it was 41 percent. Families were heading for suburbia and adapting to car culture, making a family outing seem like less hassle. And more women were working outside the home, many of them lured to part-time work as a way to boost their living standards.

McDonald's gets all the attention as the premier chain of the 1950s (it opened shop in 1948), and it *is* the indisputable pioneer of turning meal preparation into an industrial activity. But its predecessors laid the groundwork for automated cooking. In the late 1800s, Fred Harvey tacked dining-car restaurants onto trains running between Kansas and New Mexico, staffed by uniformed Harvey Girls and serving a wide variety of freshly prepared meals. He pioneered the development of centralized menu planning and, importantly, the logistics management it required. But it wasn't until the 1940s, at Howard Johnson's, that centralized food preparation began to enter the mainstream, making it affordable to take the family out to dinner.

Howard Johnson's made its initial fortunes by selling meals to families traveling long distances on state turnpikes before World War II. Along the way, HoJo's did something even bigger: It figured out what could, and could not, be industrialized when trying to run a sit-down restaurant. At first, the restaurant used all the conveniences that modern industry had on offer to prepare meals. Its central commissaries used condensed bouillon, precooked chicken, margarine, and frozen vegetables to prepare massive quantities of chicken-pot-pie filling and clam chowder. The cooks froze great blocks of the stuff and shipped it out to be defrosted on site. Then, in the early 1960s, the chain started to experiment with improving its food quality, figuring out how to use modern culinary technology to its best advantage. The company was learning important lessons: If you remove the ultraperishable bellies from fried clams, you can ship breaded strips of the shellfish out to be fried on-site. Macaroni and cheese tastes better if it is portioned out at the commissary, frozen, and then baked at the restaurant. This was the kind of culinary research that required serious kitchen know-how, and for the key experimental stint during the 1960s, HoJo's employed real chefs for the task. Jacques Pépin, a celebrated French chef of 1960s New York, ran the central commissary in Queens, while his contemporary Pierre Franey took a post as vice president and traveled the country doing quality control for the company—even serving his gourmand friends reheated frozen meals on the sly as a way to test their quality. Within the next decade, Howard Johnson's research paid off—less for HoJo's than for emerging fast-food chains like Burger King, Kentucky Fried Chicken, and, naturally, McDonald's, all of which stripped down HoJo's techniques to offer food more quickly and cheaply. Throughout the 1960s and 1970s, eating out was more accessible to the middle class than ever before. Rising incomes were part of this, but so were the new food distributor networks cropping up to produce, store, distribute, and deliver a vast range of premade foods that could be cooked, reheated, or assembled from constituent parts into meals. It's no coincidence that Sysco, today the largest food supplier for restaurants in the country, went public in 1970.

By 1980, when the first Applebee's opened in Atlanta, Georgia, chain restaurants ruled the suburbs and highways. Sophisticated distribution companies that could manage a mix of perishable, frozen, and dry goods with ease were up and running—something critical to developing a standardized menu that went beyond burgers and could be replicated nationwide. Those networks could be hired to supply restaurants, or could provide a template for operators who wanted to run their own, providing a means of expanding singular restaurants into chains.

That's what happened at Applebee's, which started out as a neighborhood eatery headed up by Bill and T. J. Palmer. The eatery was so successful they sold it three years after opening their doors to the corporate giant W. R. Grace and Company, which turned it into a franchise—and then sold it to a pair of Applebee's franchise operators in Kansas City. By the time the company went public in 1989, there were one hundred Applebee's in the country; in 1999, there were one thousand all over the globe. Other full-service chains were doing the same, leveraging industrial economies of scale and advanced distribution technologies to move a great river of food down American highways to their myriad far-flung outposts. In 2009, Applebee's operated 2,008 restaurants, 140 of them abroad. You could get a Firepit burger in Lebanon or Brazil, a platter of riblets in Greece or Mexico. Eating at these places became a hallmark of American prosperity, a celebration of mainstream, middle-class success. When Applebee's opened a restaurant in the heart of Bedford-Stuyvesant, Brooklyn, in 2006, neighborhood leaders and city officials alike considered it a coup—a sign that the tide was turning for one of America's most infamous ghettos.

By the time I'm in the kitchen, though, it feels like America's rising fortunes have stalled. A quarter of New York City lives below the poverty line, and while it has always had more poor than the nation as a whole, that gap has narrowed—not just because more New Yorkers moved on up in the early 2000s, but because more of America got poorer over the same period. Even if the city's poverty rate has dropped, unemployment is peaking, stretching over 10 percent—and above 11 percent in Brooklyn. And yet, despite the faltering economy, they keep coming, flocking to Applebee's, families and couples and professional lunchers, waiting twenty, thirty minutes—even with some of the city's most lauded restaurants a ten-minute walk away. In one of my first weeks here, the denizens of Brooklyn, more than a third of them born on foreign shores, spent $122,000 at Applebee's, more than nine times the weekly sales of an average restaurant.

Applebee's doesn't sell itself as a cultural experience the way more self-conscious restaurants do, but I suspect that's just downmarket advertising at work. Our customers might not visit Ethiopia or Indonesia or a lush farm upstate by eating here, but it takes them somewhere else that's becoming just as rare: the twentieth-century American dream, when owning your own home and going out for a nice meal were within easy reach for so many of us. And that, oddly enough, makes my work at Applebee's gratifying in a way that I doubt I'd find in fine dining. Our customers aren't here for the food—not in any sophisticated culinary sense. They're here to take a night off from the daily grind.

* * *

YO, FRY GUYS, I need a five-ounce, NOW. Hector and Luis, the two fry cooks giggling back by the freezer, jump visibly at my command.

I smile sweetly, reposition my voice an octave higher, a significant number of decibels lower. Please?

What you need, sweetheart? asks Hector.

A five-ounce, please.

Aiight, Ma, I got you, says Luis, and the other cooks titter on the line.

That was mad sexy, says Geoff.

I *felt* that, says Rick, the server waiting on the five-ounce—slang for fries.

Well, you told me to bark, I say, pulling the five-ounce out of the window. Rick used to do expo before he served, so he tries to give me pointers when he sees me struggling. Pointers like, *They're not listening. You need to bark at them.*

It's Valentine's Day, a Sunday, and last night we were packed; I walked in the door at noon and didn't leave until midnight, going home just long enough to collapse into sleep and turn right back around. In at noon again, I'm working the line with Terry, who drives me mad by pulling appetizer trios—infuriating platters containing a made-to-order constellation of appetizers that change with every customer, some nightmare I suspect was dreamed up by an executive who's never worked the line during rush—and pushing them down to me at the far end of the line without the sauces. This means I have to double back and grab them out from under Terry, wasting time and energy. As the rush builds, Terry lets the printer tickets spiral down, down, down into the expo line, invariably dipping into the honey mustard. I grit my teeth every time he calls for a trio.

Otherwise, though, Terry and I are cool. During one of the rare thirty-second lulls where we can pause he says, You need to drink some water. You are *red*.

I've *been* drinking water, I say. This is just the color white people get when it's hot.

Really? I get blacker.

I learn something new every day here, Terry, I say. Every day.

And tonight, what I really learn—and not for the last time—is just how little I know when it comes to my job.

It starts around eight or nine o'clock. My eyes are burning—it's all the gas in the kitchen, explains Freddie, offering to give me some eyedrops—and I'm blinking and rubbing my eyes furiously as the screen starts to fill up. By now, I know my place. I'm not good enough to direct the line, but I'm getting better at helping it move.

Here we go, says Freddie. He and Terry start pulling tickets and barking out dishes: ribeyes, chopped steaks, shrimp islands with rice, kiddie hot dogs, bourbon and New York strip steaks, garlic herb salmon, chicken penne pasta, shrimp pesto bowl, quesadilla burgers, hot wings on the bone, and boneless honey barbecue wings. I duck in front of the managers, bending full over the pass so they can reach over me, and dress plates according to the laws I've managed to memorize: ribs get coleslaw, anything that swims gets a lemon, anything with quesadilla in the name gets salsa, chicken fingers get honey mustard, fried shrimp gets cocktail sauce, fish filets get tartar, baked potatoes usually—but not always, I have to check the ticket—take butter and sour cream, and salmon gets smeared with garlic butter.

Let's be clear: I'm no pro. For one thing, I don't have the hands for it, a function of not yet having enough calluses. My hands are so tender that I yelp in pain regularly during service, once so badly that Geoff comes around from behind the line and, without warning, grasps my hand and massages ice onto my thumb. I glare and tell him I'm fine, I'm a grown-ass woman. In response, Geoff flashes me a pair of bedroom eyes and says in a deep, even voice, Oh, I can see that. But the real reason I can't pull plates is because I can't identify dishes on sight and have to ask the cooks to tell me whether this steak is a ribeye or a nine-ounce.

At 9:30 I am shoved aside. The rush has slowed for the cooks, but it has migrated to the pass, a stampede of meals run amok. There are bowls of pasta teetering on top of each other; platters of ribs sitting in pyramids; towers of chicken baskets and trio plates hitting the top of the window. This food has to go out *now*. Calixto abandons broil to Damian, the other broil cook, and Omar leaves Geoff on mid to come work expo, and with a brusque, *Excuse me, Ma*, I'm ousted to the head of the pass, relegated to wiping down plates and checking orders against tickets before they go out. Terry's pulling from fry, Omar's talking to Geoff on mid, Calixto's grabbing plates from broil. Everyone's working their own tickets, calling for plates from every window, a furious flurry of arms and cheap porcelain flying up and down the line. I've heard line work described as being as graceful as dance, but this is harder, faster, hotter, meaner. What comes to mind is neither battle nor ballet, but a simultaneous expression of both—Capoeira.*

I work until 12:30—the kitchen officially closes at 1:00, so the danger of another hit has faded—but this time Calixto stops me as I walk to the back

* A mix of dance, sport, and music, Capoeira originated in Brazil in the sixteenth century, used as defense by runaway slaves who had formed their own societies in the country's undeveloped regions. Today, it is practiced as a martial art form on every continent. (Talmon-Chvacier 2008, 14–19)

to get my things.

Do you drink?

You mean, alcohol? Yeah, of course.

Bernardo gave us some Heinekens and Coronas. You want, you can have some with us in the back.

We can drink here?

Calixto laughs. Yes, we can drink here.

After I clock out and change my clothes, I go back into the kitchen to eat some of the rapidly congealing onion rings and fries Bernardo had the cooks put out for the staff tonight. We don't get staff meals like at fancy restaurants, but tonight they made an exception, equal parts generosity and an attempt to keep anyone from stealing off to take a break in the middle of the Valentine's Day rush. I inhale it by the fistful—I haven't eaten since I left home this morning—but Omar is waiting for me, back by the dry goods where Freddie is doing inventory. Freddie's counting our pasta, the powdered seasoning mix that goes on the broccoli, and the spongy focaccia bread that comes in disposable aluminum pans. Omar makes a drinking motion with his thumb and pinky before disappearing through the doors to the freight entrance.

That's between family, smiles Freddie. Tracie, you did a fucking great job tonight, I mean it.

Thanks, I say, opening the freight door.

There's nowhere to sit, so we stand on the landing, leaning against boxes and open stretches of wall, to-go cups of icy Corona in our hands. The only light comes from a fluorescent bulb at the base of the stairs casting us in long, weak shadow.

We talk about work, where these guys have worked before and where else they work now. Omar pulls shifts at another Brooklyn Applebee's; Calixto used to work at the Midtown flagship Applebee's—there, he says, they work off *two* screens, and during rush the whole thing is red, red, red. Geoff has worked at a number of kitchens around town, not just Applebee's, but the managers here offered him two dollars more than what he was making at some tourist spot in Manhattan, so he split. By now the exhaustion is creeping from my bones to my muscles, the beer finally counteracting the soda and coffee I've drunk. I'm smiling lazily, listening to their patter, when the conversation shifts to my side of the line.

Claudette, says Omar, never admits when she's wrong, and she talks too much—here, Geoff grins slyly. Bernardo runs things out too quickly and makes too many mistakes; they end up having to recook much of what he sends out. And Terry's too slow, can't ever move fast enough. But me, say Calixto and Omar and Geoff, I'm a natural, they can't believe how good I'm doing.

I'm not too far gone to realize that this is flattery more than fact, and I tell them so. But I feel a twinge of pride when Calixto counters, No, seriously. Everybody, all the cooks, *everybody* was saying, "You see that white girl work? *Damn,* she can *work.*"

At this, I smile and gulp down the last foamy bit of beer. I try, guys, I say. I try. But I gotta go home. I gotta be back here at two.

In a particularly sadistic (if lucrative) affront to restaurant workers everywhere, the calendar has placed Presidents' Day on the day after Valentine's Day, which fell the day after Saturday. Three straight days of whirling plates, high-strung servers, and endless fry grease. So while schoolchildren and office workers luxuriate in their day off, I head back to the kitchen on Monday.

By the time I finish my stint at Applebee's, I'll have learned how to spot the other members of my tribe on the subway: heavy-lidded eyes, blank stares, black pants specked with grease, hard-soled black shoes. I see them frequently on my commute, a scrappy crew of warriors heading to battle so that the rest of the city can eat. As a new inhabitant of the Applebee's kitchen, I can verify that my fellow workers live up to restaurant kitchens' reputation for being a haphazard melting pot. Luis, who runs trays of food out for servers, just came to the states from rural Oaxaca few months ago; the dishwasher Amadou used to run several businesses in his native Senegal; Tony was a musical theater devotee in high school in Puerto Rico; Hector ran an event production company with his wife before falling on hard times; Eric is paying tuition at a local college.

I'm the whitest of the bunch, one of a handful of nonimmigrants, and the only woman putting in regular hours with the line. Although whites make up 58 percent of restaurant workers, they only occupy 11 percent of lowly prep positions; out of the five white people on our staff of several dozen, two are managers. Women seem to do OK here;* there aren't any

---

* On average, women in the restaurant industry are paid significantly less than men, and the wage gap attributable to gender is larger than the one attributable to race. A 2009 survey of restaurant workers in New York City found that white women earned $4,508 less than men in front-of-the-house positions, and that women of color earned $5,795 less, a situation that creates a "gender tax" of 22 and 29 percent, respectively. Nonwhite workers as a whole earned an average of $2,895 less than their white counterparts, creating a "race tax" of 12 percent.

consistent female managers in our store, but a few come in from corporate now and then. The balance of management is black and Latino, though, which is noteworthy given how rare it can be elsewhere in the restaurant industry. In 2007, famed New York chef Daniel Boulud settled with Mexican workers who filed a federal discrimination case against him; a busser from Mexico claimed to have trained several French busboys and watched each get promoted ahead of him.

But even if I move up the ladder, from expo to line, it doesn't guarantee much improvement when it comes to wages. When Freddie hired me, he told me I'd make $8 an hour for training and $9 an hour after that, putting me on the lower end of kitchen workers, whose median wages range from $8.69 for prep to $10.09 for cooks. Geoff and Calixto tell me they earn around $12 an hour, which sounds like a lot until I calculate what it means in annual salary: $24,000.

The wages I hear about at Applebee's are fairly consistent, starting around $8 and going up into the low teens, and are always well within the law, but this reveals its status as a corporation more than it exposes any norms within restaurants. While Applebee's is the biggest "casual dining" operator in the country, the 1,868 American restaurants bearing its name in 2009 still represented less than 1 percent of America's full-service eateries, the majority of which are independently owned or are members of small restaurant corporations running a few boutique eateries. As in agriculture, enforcing labor laws among a vast, decentralized army of employers is difficult, making it easier for employers to skimp on pay.

There's one thing Applebee's has in common with smaller restaurants that cheat their workers, though. I am never given formal food safety training of any kind. This oversight is most common among employers who pay extra-low wages or cheat their workers out of overtime; restaurants that do this are twice as likely to skip out on food safety training, and nearly four times as likely to ask workers to perform jobs for which they haven't been trained, as those that do not. At first, I reason, maybe I'm not being taught anything about food safety because expo isn't charged with preparing the food, only serving it. They do, after all, tell me to change the bucket of sanitizing solution used to wipe down counters and plates every four hours—though there is no way that happens once rush hits.* Then I spend a couple days doing

_____

(Restaurant Opportunities Center 2009, 19–20)

* Failure to change buckets used for sanitation can be found in high-end restaurants, too. At

prep, and I conclude that the lack of food safety training is, at least where I'm concerned, an across-the-board kind of thing.

Mario Batali's Babbo, Bill Buford wrote in *Heat*, a bucket of soapy water sat in the kitchen for cooks to use to keep their hands clean, but "after an hour or so, the water was not something I wanted to look at . . . By the end of the evening . . . my hands seemed greasier after I washed them." (Buford 2007, 82–83)

CHAPTER 9

Kitchen Spy

I end up in the prep kitchen by making a deal with Freddie. After a couple weeks, he's begun talking about making me a "Neighborhood Expert," so I can train other people on expo. This comes after last week's staff meeting— held at 10:00 p.m. on a Tuesday, everyone standing awkwardly around the prep table—when I was among the dozen "Applestars" for the month, taking the not-terribly-competitive prize of Best Newcomer. (There were, by my count, two others eligible.) I figure this gives me some pull with Freddie, so I make a proposition: I'd like to learn how the kitchen works. He's mentioned wanting me to train people on expo, so I should know more about the kitchen, right? And since I typically work Friday to Sunday, racking up about thirty hours, I still have another ten before I hit overtime. Can I do some work in prep? Freddie doesn't hesitate. Can you come in on Wednesday at 9:00 a.m.? Definitely, I say. It's a deal.

I'm paired on my first morning with Denzel, a skinny kid who immediately sets me to scrubbing Idaho russets for baked potatoes. These go into a steamer, a metal box resembling an oven, along with a half-dozen redskins destined to be quartered and steamed with a sprinkling of spice powder for Weight Watchers herbed potatoes. As we load the potatoes into the steamer, Denzel tells me not to eat the mashed potatoes here because they only rinse those potatoes, they don't scrub them. They can't usually scrub every potato, he explains; the dust gets washed off, but the dirt stays on the skin.

About half my work for the day involves measuring out individual portions of food. I stand over a bin of cooked rice and divide four-ounce portions into plastic baggies. When I finish, I take a sticker gun and label each bag with the date when it should be thrown out. While I'm at it, one of the lunch cooks hands me a half-full tray of expired bags of rice and asks me to change their use-by date from yesterday to tomorrow.

Isn't that kind of gross? I ask Denzel.

You'll see all kinds of things here, he says. Throwing it out wastes money.

After the rice, there's linguine to portion out, and then penne pasta—all of it slightly undercooked, so that when the cooks on the line throw it in the microwave it doesn't get too soggy. Later on, there are endless trays of mashed potatoes that get divided into ten-ounce portions and bagged. Most of what we portion into baggies, I realize, is bound for the microwave.

Everything we make gets dated according to a chart on the wall that denotes the number of shifts before it should be thrown out. Followed closely, these directions remove the need for anyone to know what happened in the kitchen even an hour ago, or to be able to gauge whether food has rotted or not. The chart, the stickers, and the dates mean we don't have to know anything, really, other than how to read. Just as assembly lines pare down the skill and education needed by individual workers to, say, build a car, the structure of the Applebee's kitchen removes the need for culinary training. Even so, I get to make food.

Bro, let her make something, Freddie calls to Denzel as he walks through the back and sees me portioning out the penne. Have her *make* something.

So then I'm tasked with making garlic cherry tomatoes for one of the pasta bowls. I slice grape tomatoes into halves and portion one-quarter of a cup of them into a plastic baggie, adding one tablespoon of minced garlic that comes pre-chopped in a one-quart tub. I make fifteen bags; they're good for only one day, so they're made fresh every morning. These will get emptied onto the flattop and grilled, then scooped onto penne that's been nuked along with pesto scooped out of the plastic container it was shipped to us in, and Alfredo sauce defrosted from a bag.

Freddie keeps walking through and telling Denzel to give me a recipe. There's a thick binder on a shelf, filled with black-and-white photocopies, that lists ingredients and ratios to Applebee's specifications. The recipe for mashed potatoes: A sack of steamed redskins and a defrosted bag of garlic milk. For broccoli? Three 3-pound bags of florets, a quarter-cup of minced garlic scooped out of the plastic container it's shipped to us in, and one batch of dressing made from an envelope of powdered spice and thickeners mixed with warm water. It would free up Denzel if I had the recipe, instead of asking him how to do things, but Denzel tells me he doesn't like looking through the books. He'll just tell me the right way.

Next I make the Asian vegetable mix for the Orange Chick Bowl; the veggies will get nuked in their baggie and mixed with boneless wings out of the fryer and sweet-and-spicy sauce. I slice open pillowy bags of broccoli florets, their cut edges vaguely faded and parched, and mix them with fresh-cut strips of red pepper, preshredded carrots, presliced mushrooms, and defrosted snap peas. When I ask Emmet, a prep cook, where the vegetables are from, he shrugs: a warehouse somewhere. Then there's the filling for the chicken wonton taco appetizers. I dice several batches of chicken breast that had been defrosted from the cases in the freezer and grilled that morning, and mix it with a gelatinous sweet-and-spicy sauce poured from a plastic bag.

The last thing I make before being pulled onto expo for the lunch rush, summoned by Freddie with a "Tracie, come here, my love," is pesto Alfredo sauce. I scoop out pale sauce, thick like pudding, from a plastic bag and deposit it into small foam cups, then add a scoop of pesto, also premade and delivered to Applebee's, and some preshredded Parmesan cheese pulled from a big, square plastic bag in the walk-in. I put lids on the cups, date them, and head to the line, coming back an hour and a half later to portion out mashed potatoes until I go home.

Every ingredient arrives by the grace of Customized Supply Chain Services, LLC, a cooperative purchasing agent. Formed by Applebee's parent corporation, Dine Equity, in 2009, CSCS buys supplies for Applebee's and its sister company, International House of Pancakes. Combined, the two restaurants spend roughly $1.8 billion a year on the goods that come in through CSCS: the meat and bread, the spices, the soda syrup, the fish filets, the minced garlic tubs, the cartons of coleslaw dressing, not to mention paper towels and plastic gloves and sanitizing solution and all the rest. Everything arrives at our store in Brooklyn via CSCS, which negotiates with manufacturers to either purchase something they sell already—say, ranch dressing—or to make it for us to spec. By bringing those functions in-house, Dine Equity announced in 2011, the company expected to save 3 to 5 percent on operating costs.

Most restaurants don't go to the trouble of creating a separate purchasing arm, and instead contract with suppliers who do the negotiating for them. About 62 percent of restaurants outsource their fulfillment and distribution, typically using massive food service companies like Sysco—which supplies independent restaurants—or its affiliate, Sygma, which supplies chain restaurants and institutions. These kinds of companies operate as "broadliners," suppliers who can get you everything from Angus burgers to rubber gloves. These suppliers, in turn, negotiate contracts with the big food manufacturers, who provide incentives for ordering in bulk in the form of rebates. Critics call them kickbacks, but rebates are perfectly legal: If you buy enough, you get a discount.

These companies are dealmakers, negotiating purchases and sales, trying to leverage their massive buying power into lower prices for their customers. And once the deal is made, restaurant chains subcontract the tricky work of pickup and delivery to a logistics firm; Applebee's, by way of CSCS, uses an industry giant called ArrowStream to coordinate and transport its supplies. The ground beef we use at Applebee's may have carpooled on an ArrowStream truck with patties for Wendy's, or wontons for P. F. Chang's, or drumsticks for Church's Chicken; those restaurants use ArrowStream, too. So does Sygma. In all, ArrowStream coordinates the movement of food between more than four thousand food manufacturers, distributors, and restaurants, consolidating shipments and streamlining costs along the way.

There's no way for me to know the details of Applebee's relationships with CSCS, ArrowStream, or the manufacturers and distributors whose stock fill our shelves. I have no idea if Dine Equity gets rebates from the soda manufacturers for stocking their products, or from Cargill for buying its beef, or the precise terms of its deals for produce. But I can see why restaurants might balk at bringing in locally grown goods: Who could match the convenience of a broadliner paired with logistics and freight?

I manage to eke out only one more shift in the prep kitchen, this time under the tutelage of Emmet, who intersperses a tour of dry goods with his basic life story. He was born and raised in Queens, and over here is where we keep the powder for vegetable seasoning. This here's the powder for making gravy, and he spent a few years in Georgia but left when his girlfriend said she was going to call the police. I leave this nugget untouched, and instead ask whether we ever make anything from fresh ingredients here, a question that yields an incredulous look.

Nah, nah, nah, just add water, says Emmet. You'll learn, you'll learn.

The quality of the food being served here rarely comes up in the kitchen, and usually only if I prod gently by asking the cooks and servers about the other places they've worked. Then, a couple weeks later, Freddie's unlocking the office—a windowless cubby of a room across from the kitchen's ice machine—when he turns to me.

Tracie, I'm hungry, he says plaintively. But the food I want, we don't have it here.

What do you want?

Freddie's face goes a little soft.

I'm thinking fresh mozzarella, a little sundried tomato. His voice is pure

Brooklyn; I would have guessed he was Italian, straight from Bay Ridge, if I hadn't heard him talking about his Cuban temper.

I nod along. Oooh, buffalo mozzarella, in the water? Fresh vegetables? Freddie nods, casts a glance as if toward the heavens. Now you're talking!

One of my great weaknesses is kitchens. There are different ways to love a kitchen, of course: for the ease conferred by fine cookware, for the familiar lure of the meals shared within it, for being the final stop on the human animal's work of feeding itself. Yet what I love most about kitchens is the way they embody all of this lofty rhetoric while still being, at their core, deeply practical places. As much as we like to talk about humans as omnivores, just one more species selecting from nature's mind-boggling array of options, in truth, we're cooks.

Writers have noted cooking's deep cultural power for nearly two centuries, stretching back to Brillat-Savarin, a French gastronomist of the nineteenth century, who argued that it was through fire, and thus cooking, that man "tamed Nature itself." In the 1960s, Claude Lévi-Strauss called cooking the mark of our transition from nature to culture, and by the turn of the twenty-first century, the historian Michael Symons pinned "our humanity" on cooks. Yet it's Richard Wrangham whom I find the most persuasive.

A primatologist at Harvard University, Wrangham's work argues that apes did not evolve into man and then begin cooking, but that apes' acquisition of cooking skills is what turned them into humans—literally. By providing us with softer and more digestible foods, cooking reduced the amount of time dedicated to eating. In turn, this opened up time to spend on hunting, increasing the intake of meat and protein as well as cooked foods, all of which allowed our digestive tracts to shrink, relatively speaking, and our brains to grow. It also created an impetus for social structures that revolved around households and the sharing of food—practices that form the bedrock of human culture, rather than the everyone-for-himself ethos that rules most primate species when it comes to food. "We are not like other animals," writes Wrangham in *Catching Fire: How Cooking Made Us Human,* later adding, "we are cooks more than carnivores." We are cooks by evolutionary design; competence in the kitchen has *always* been key to our health.

In contemporary America, we've made saving time on food procurement into both art and science. Food processing techniques free us up even more, while increasing the calories we can absorb from our meals. Researchers have only recently begun to examine the connection between home cooking and obesity rates, but preliminary data suggest that people who take the time to prepare their own meals are less likely to be obese. Similarly, frequently eating out is correlated with higher BMI.* And it's this curious expression of an elemental evolutionary drive—to reduce the time put into cooking while maximizing the calories we derive from it—that I see on full display in the Applebee's kitchen. I'd come here with a vague notion that a restaurant kitchen would be a place where people cooked differently than time-strapped families throwing a Hot Pocket in the microwave. Certainly, it would be different than fast-food joints. But instead, I watch an endless assembly line, a large-scale mash-up that hits the sweet spot between McDonald's and Sandra Lee's *Semi-Homemade Cooking*.

Processed foods entered home kitchens decades before they arrived in restaurants. The first introduction of "convenience" foods for home cooks came in the 1930s, with Duncan Hines cake mixes in 1929 and Kraft Macaroni and Cheese in 1937; by the 1940s both Pillsbury and Betty Crocker were selling cake and pastry mixes. But it wasn't until the 1950s that full-on replacements for home-cooked meals, modeled on rations developed for the Naval Air Transport Service during World War II, were being hawked in grocery stores. Within a decade, convenience foods were so popular that the federal government undertook a four-city study analyzing their cost, quality, and preparation time, reprising the study in the late 1970s with the addition of a detailed taste comparison by government home economists. In 1979, convenience foods accounted for nearly half of all food bought for the home. By 2010, researchers found that nearly every dinner Americans prepared at home involved a convenience food product, a category that included everything from bagged salads to frozen dinners (but excluded basics like canned beans and plain bread). Today, despite all the concern about our reliance on fast food, only 14 percent of dinners eaten by two-parent families are fast food or other kinds of takeout; another 5 percent mix takeout with something made at home, and 3 percent are eaten at restaurants. But 70 percent are prepared in families' kitchens, and almost

---

* Social science research has only recently begun to examine the connection between home cooking and obesity rates. Partly this is because of the dearth of information available on Americans' cooking skills and the time dedicated to it. Research on the topic withered in the 1980s, and it was not until 2004 that the USDA began to collect relevant national data on time spent cooking through the American Time Use Survey. (Effland, date unknown; USDA Economic Research Service 2008)

always include some kind of convenience food.

As I become more comfortable in the kitchen at Applebee's, I'm over-whelmed with an eerie sense of déjà vu. It takes me a few days of thinking *I have been here before* before I make the connection: The kitchen I'm now in resembles the one I grew up in, writ large. Just like the meals my family lived on throughout my childhood, much of what's served at Applebee's actually wouldn't be that difficult, expensive, or time-consuming for a competent cook to make from scratch.

Discounting the stuff that comes out of the deep fryer,* most of what Applebee's serves is basic American fare that's easy to make: steak, chicken breast, potatoes, broccoli. Take, for instance, one of the lighter options on the menu, asiago peppercorn steak. It's a seven-ounce sirloin, grilled and topped with melted cheese and cracked pepper, served with steamed vegeta-bles. We sell it for $16.99, and between the time required to get to the res-taurant, ordering, and getting the meal, it probably takes forty-five minutes after leaving home before there's food on the table. A cook with solid, but basic, skills can probably match the time frame for preparation: cutting up vegetables, throwing them in a steamer, grilling the meat. Costwise, there's no contest. The ingredients for a comparable serving of steak, potatoes, and vegetables would be $3.72—a discount of nearly 80 percent for doing it, and the dishes, yourself. In strict dollars and cents, eating out costs four and a half times as much as eating at home.

The economics of something like Hamburger Helper are different, of course. The mix, milk, and beef required to make it cost $6.23 when I price it out at a store, and it takes 22 minutes from start to finish to make. Mak-ing a similar dish from scratch, though, costs $4.37 and takes 23 minutes to make. Most families eat more than beef and noodles at dinner, of course, and whether it's made entirely from scratch or thrown together with a few helpful kits, an average family dinner takes just under an hour to make. When researchers watched thirty-two two-income families cook dinner for four days, here's what they saw: It took people an average of fifty-two min-utes from the time they opened the refrigerator door to the time they sat

---

* Admittedly, removing the deep fryer from the equation changes the foodscape considerably. There were four basic items that came out of the fryer at Applebee's: french fries, chicken wings, chicken fingers, and fried shrimp. Of sixty-eight meals and appetizers offered, only nine were fried as a matter of course. Still, the nine steaks, three rib dinners, eight burgers, eight sandwiches, three slider meals, and the chicken tender basket were all served with french fries as a matter of course, and selecting a substitution cost $3.99. (Author's calculations, based on Dine Equity, 2010)

down at the table, whether they used a box kit like Hamburger Helper or cooked everything from scratch. The only difference was that meals cooked from scratch required about ten minutes more *active* time—minutes spent chopping and sautéing, for example—than box mixes.

Box meals don't save us time any more than going out to eat does, and they don't even save us money. What they do instead is remove the need to have to come up with a plan for dinner, something that's easy when you're a skilled cook—and bafflingly difficult when you're not. The real convenience behind these convenience foods isn't time or money, but that they remove one more bit of stress from our day.

And that's why Applebee's feels so familiar to me. The meals we serve here share a kind of social DNA with Hamburger Helper. Both are the fastest, easiest answer to the endlessly infuriating equation of health, time, money, and mental energy that American families calculate every day. And if we want to come up with a new solution, there has to be rejiggering of the equation itself; a changing, if you will, of the ground rules.

Today, most of us understand the planning of our eating lives as a zero-sum game. You can pay extra money for someone else to make your salad and bake your bread if you'd like to spend less time and energy while maintaining health. Or you can keep costs low by sticking to whole ingredients like heads of cabbage, sacks of onions, and bags of rice, but you'll spend far more time and energy to do it. The only variables we ever consider changing are time and money.* We forget that the final variable—energy, or the mental headspace—is just as fungible as the rest.

The key to getting people to eat better isn't that they should spend more money, or even that they should spend more time. It's making the actual

---

* In discussions of Americans' spending on food, it's important to remember that the United States has a limited array of universal public benefits like child care and health care in comparison to its peers. Americans often get derided for spending too little on their meals, with the observation that Americans spend about 13 percent of their take-home income on food, while, for example, the French spend about 20 percent. Only examining our food spending, however, glosses over the other expenses against which food must compete. The French may prioritize their meals, but that's possibly partly because their government provides quality child care, higher education, communication, and transportation at little or no out-of-pocket cost to its citizens, and mandates five weeks of paid vacation each year. While the average American family spends about 7 percent less of their paycheck on food than their French counterparts, they spend 7 percent more of it on education, housing, transportation, and health care. (Organization for Economic Cooperation and Development 2011; Organization for Economic Cooperation and Development 2006a; Organization for Economic Cooperation and Development 2006b)

cooking of a meal into an *easy* choice, the obvious answer. And that only happens when people are as comfortable and confident in the kitchen as they are taking care of the other endless chores that come with running a modern family—paying bills, cleaning house, washing the car. It only happens, in other words, when we can cook well. It doesn't take advanced culinary acumen to know that making a pasta-and-ground beef one-skillet dinner from scratch isn't actually any more difficult than using a box, but it does take education and training. Enough, at least, to convey that grilling a steak and steaming vegetables is just a basic household task.

Because, really, that's what I'm helping with back here amid the grease and the steam and the clang of tongs on metal: Coordinating a basic household task. There will be days for every person, every family, where it *is* worth paying four times more for the service. That's fine. But the longer I'm at Applebee's, the more I think everyone should be making that choice from equal footing: with easy access to fresh ingredients, and a solid ability to cook. Our health, as that of our ancestors, depends on it.

Even if I find Applebee's reliance on processed foods oddly familiar, the near absence of fresh food is unsettling. In our walk-in refrigerator, the produce takes up a small set of shelves, a stack of four or five roughly six feet wide and two feet deep. Primarily, this space is used for bags of produce already cut up in some far-off processing plant: precut broccoli florets, bags of shredded cabbage and carrots for coleslaw, bags of chopped romaine and baby spinach, shredded carrots, sliced mushrooms.

As far as whole produce, the stuff we cut up ourselves, there isn't much. I see a box of tomatoes, a few dozen heads of iceberg lettuce for burgers, grape tomatoes, a few sweet peppers, lemons and limes. The meat comes in frozen, but, save for the ribs and fried foods, uncooked; the Cargill ground beef gets portioned into hamburgers from the five-pound packs in which it is shipped. But *everything* else we have in the kitchen, every soup and sauce, every chicken wing with bone or without (the latter being, essentially, chicken nuggets) comes premade in a bag, often frozen. Even the seasonings come this way.

The lack of produce can be explained easily by one thing: cost, the cost of the produce itself and of the labor it takes to prepare it. Restaurant executives often sideline fruits and vegetables not just because of their high price tags, but because they are harder to store, can spoil and lead to waste, and undercut sales of more profitable items—like processed foods. Produce also gets sidelined because of the "special handling" it requires, which is to say it must be cleaned and chopped before it gets anywhere near the line.

The same economic calculus applies to the overwhelming presence of processed food, particularly preprepared foods like the chicken wings, which need only to be dropped into the fryer for reheating and crisping; the ribs, which come precooked and presmoked, reheated on the grill with a slathering of sauce; and the frozen Triple Chocolate Meltdown cake, nuked by Rico and Hector, thrown on a plate with a scoop of ice cream, and squirted with fudge sauce. None of this requires more than the most basic attention on the part of the cooks. And it saves incredible amounts of time and money. I never get a look at Applebee's inventory and cost documents, and food distributor data are notoriously hard to come by. But in 2007, *Slate* reporter Ulrich Boser found that an Angus country-fried steak from Sysco typically yields a five-dollar profit. This kind of faux cooking graces the white tablecloths of high-end restaurants as well as the booths of Applebee's. Thomas Keller, the renowned chef heading up the French Laundry, was using frozen fries in his kitchen in 2007, and the same year Belhurst Castle, a prestigious spa and inn lauded by *Wine Spectator,* was serving Sysco's Imperial Chocolate Cake, defrosted and garnished with fresh raspberries.

For what it's worth, the cooks I work with *know* the difference. On one of my first nights in the kitchen, Calixto chatted me up, asking about where I'd worked before, and had I ever been in a kitchen? I said not really, and asked him where he'd worked besides Applebee's.

Over at Junior's, he said, indicating a famous Brooklyn diner-style restaurant. And they've got a real kitchen over there, not like here.

What do you mean? Isn't this a real kitchen?

Nah, nah, he said. For onion soup, you cut up the onions and *make the soup,* he said, closing his eyes in reverie before snapping them back open. Not defrost a bag of it like here.

Due to both convenience and cost, Applebee's meals begin to feature prominently in my diet. As a kitchen employee, I get an eleven-dollar credit toward a meal every time I work, so I never bring food; I just order from the cheaper end of the menu. The seafood entrées are out of my price range, but salads and sandwiches are not. At first I try the salads, but the vegetables— having been precut and in bags—taste dry to me and, more important, I'm always starving again within the hour. Instead, I rotate between burgers, grilled chicken, and fish sandwiches matched with fries, baked potatoes, or broccoli.

Most of the kitchen staff do the same, though one afternoon I see Pedro, one of the cooks for mid, load a plate with Mexi-rice, dot it with pico de gallo, and then unload a Tupperware container of home-cooked pigs' feet onto it, a cold perfume of pork and cumin wafting up before he pops it in the microwave. Maria, a mother in prep, tells me she cooks big pots of stew, rice, and beans every few days for her two teenagers; Claudette cooks on her nights off.

At home, my local supermarket, Western Beef, dictates my diet. It's huge by New York standards, 42,000 square feet, and the parking lot—itself unusual in Brooklyn's real estate market—is separated from the doors by heavy metal fencing designed to keep shopping carts from leaving the premises. The aisles are crowded and narrow; shelves crammed with imported products from various Caribbean nations stretch to the ceiling. A few outlying aisles resemble a dollar store more than a supermarket, dedicated to the equipment of immigration and poverty: plaid, zippered bags that could encompass suitcases; crinkled cookware of heavy aluminum foil; tiny skyscrapers of patterned plastic dishware. A Trinidadian flag hangs from the rafters over the registers; soca blares from the speakers.

The produce section is solid, with the stuff trending toward Caribbean palates being the freshest: neon scotch bonnet peppers and glossy jalapeños, waxy yucca root, pineapples, avocados and garlic and squash. Stacks of corn tortillas still soft and pliable. Like the original Fairway, a higher-end market popular among the Manhattan's upper-middle class, Western Beef has an entire refrigerated room for its meat and dairy, hawking family-oriented specials like chicken legs and backs for thirty-eight cents per pound, sold in great, sloppy plastic bags of seven pounds or more. On average, New York City is more of a food desert than Detroit, with only 1.5 square feet of grocery store space per person, and my neighborhood is technically even worse. In 2010, a city analysis of supermarket access showed that Prospect-Lefferts Gardens had 1.0 square foot of supermarket space per person; I am lucky, then, to be so close to one of the neighborhood's few stores.

At first I cook myself wintry meals in the mornings before work: oatmeal turned creamy with peanut butter and a cooling splash of milk; huge, quartered squash with stringy orange flesh and hard green rinds, roasted and mashed to eat later; stews of chickpeas, chicken legs, spinach, and spices that I can freeze. But the longer I work, the more my home kitchen fades from my daily life. I've been put on Thursdays for expo, too, freeing Claudette up for another—and far more lucrative—shift on the floor. I find that by sleeping late, eating breakfast, taking care of laundry and such and then heading to work, I can keep my meal requirements to just two: late breakfast and then my free late-afternoon meal between the lunch and dinner rushes. I can feel apathy about my meals settling in, just as it did during my time at Walmart.

And just like at Walmart, I'm suddenly keen to take advantage of any more-affordable food options that come my way. I find that if there's any gnawing hunger between my meals, on workdays I can placate it with soda or "dead" food—a dish, usually a trio plate of wings, that has sat under the heat lamp too long to be saleable. Accordingly, my grocery bills plummet; in my second month, they average less than ten dollars a week, spent mostly on oatmeal, coffee, and the tortillas and crema that I've come to rely on as my postwork snack, usually washed down with a tallboy of Modelo from the bodega between the subway station and my house. I feel guilty spending my limited money on beer, but it's a cheap, easy way to counteract the lingering hyperkinesis of the kitchen.

All this thrift is being driven by economics, for I've run into some problems with Applebee's and my paycheck. Since I'd signed up for direct deposit, and kept forgetting to ask for my pay stub, it took me a week or so to figure out that I wasn't being paid what Freddie told me I'd be paid. The first problem came when I forgot to clock in on Valentine's Day, a twelve-and-a-half-hour day without a break; Matt said he'd fix it for me, and I saw him go to the computer, so I mistakenly assumed he did. Then I realized that my training wage is the state minimum—$7.25—instead of the $8 an hour Freddie had offered me. By my calculations, the combination yielded a paycheck that was short by $155. I mentioned both problems to Freddie, and he said he'd add some hours onto the next check for me. When I get my next paycheck, I can see that the difference in hours has been made up, and that I've been paid for the staff meeting, but my wages are still lower than they should be. I'm being paid $8 an hour for my work on expo instead of the $9 that I'd been told. This is a bigger deal, amounting to a steady and permanent underpayment of $30–40 a week. I mention it to Freddie and he explains that someone must have coded me in wrong; he'll look into it.

There's always food stamps, of course, but at my $8 an hour, I'm hovering at the borderline of being too affluent to qualify for them. At this rate, I'm not going to amass much in savings, but with diligent budgeting and some discipline, I figure I should be able to make rent.

Then my bank's fraud-detection department calls, and my financial picture falls apart. It takes hours to sort out, but $678.95 has been spent out of my account. They'll start investigating right away, but won't refund the money for weeks. I'm back to where I was with Walmart: Taking out an advance on a credit card, an errand that morphs into a three-hour odyssey involving two banks, one post office with a crazy woman waving a stack of money in a menacing fashion at her fellow patrons, and a tidy check-cashing spot housed in the building of a gas station. Workwise, though, things are looking up: I've relented to Freddie's entreaties, and today I start my training as a Neighborhood Expert.

No, no, you want to eat at a restaurant that's got *chefs*, not cooks, like we got here.

Vinnie, a heavyset, freckled Puerto Rican waiter, has slid into the booth with me and Kayla, a hostess, and is entertaining us with his ruminations on food. He grew up in the projects, he says, but now he lives near good restaurants in Brooklyn, and it's great. Eating healthy is too expensive, he continues. And you only live once. If I'm going to do something, I'm going to do it to the fullest, you know?

Kayla prefers to eat healthily, though she doesn't recommend the salmon here, and while she likes to cook, she hardly ever has time. We've been sitting here since 1:00, waiting for the expert training to start and wondering whether we're going to get paid for coming in. They said we don't need to clock in, so we're dubious.

Two hours go by before Maya from Apple Metro calls us into the bar along with a handful of servers and Emmet from prep. Rolando, a veteran server, is here to get recertified, and so is Rick, who tells me before we start that he wants to go to culinary school, too, though he's thinking he'll go into the navy first to pay for it. Michelle, another server, is exhausted in her Hunter College sweatshirt because she just handed in a paper for school that took all night.

We each sign a Neighborhood Expert agreement, agreeing to "approach the management team with solutions, not problems" and to "invest [our] time willingly and unselfishly so that others may succeed." There's a series of essay questions ferreting out our commitment to the company's approach, asking things like, "Which parts of the Applebee's service ethic make the most sense to you?" We get handed "finals," and at first Maya tells us to take them right now and disappears, leading to rampant cheating among all of us aspiring experts. Mine, for expo, focuses heavily on food presentation (What are the correct items on the Mozzarella Sticks and at what position? Correct answer: Marinara at 6:00, though, under Freddie's tutelage, we typically position it in the center). Then Maya comes back and tells us to just do the finals at home. There are a series of questions on mine suggesting that I may have missed some training: inquiries about the proper method for washing hands, temperatures at which foods may rot, protocol for sanitizing.

We listen to Maya extol how well the restaurant is doing, up to three trucks of food a week—it was just two a month before. And then, less than an hour later, she tells us she'll schedule another training in about a month. Class dismissed. We all look around, incredulous: That was *it?*

Later, I analyze my pay stubs and time cards to see if I was paid for the three hours I spent at Applebee's on my day off. My time cards never indicate that I was at the restaurant that day, and I'm never paid for my time. In the wonky terms of social science, this is a "partial nonpayment," or, optimistically, "a backlog." Either way, there's another word that researchers who examined New York City's restaurant industry in 2007 use to describe it that I find even more disheartening: common.

CHAPTER 10

Kitchen Fixture

The biggest difference between my job at Applebee's and the other jobs I've held over the last year is that I enjoy it. I take satisfaction in keeping the line moving; sending out food that's as good as it can be for the families we serve; and in noticing my own improvement. I *like* that everyone curses like sailors, that the nights evaporate in a timeless, headlong rush where pretension is an alien concept.

Most of all, I like the increasing sense that I know what I'm doing. Now, when a rush hits, I know to let an experienced manager man the tickets while I pull plates, and I spend the lulls between hits dishing out sauces. There's a deep, simple satisfaction in getting the answer right time after time: ribeye rare with mash and broc, shrimp Parm with fries and mash, Cowboy no onions. I know what they look like, I know where they'll be, and by pulling them immediately, the line keeps moving. I can see, in a concrete way that eludes me in the work of writing, that I'm actually doing something useful.

All of this makes it awkward for me to quit. Much of what's made the job enjoyable isn't the work itself, but the tone Freddie sets in the kitchen. It's not just that he heaps praise on me, either. In one of my first weeks here, he heard Luis calling me Mamí and intervened immediately. *Listen to me, her name is not Mamí, her name is Tracie. Do you understand me?* He'd been stern and serious, even when I told him I'd heard a whole lot worse, telling me that was not the point. And so I feel the unmistakable pall of guilt when I tell Freddie, who's just returned from a week of vacation, that I need to talk to him about something.

We sit in the back dining room, underneath a patch of wall filled with golf-themed signs, and I tell him my story: My grandmother's not doing well, and there's nobody to care for her, so I have to go back to Michigan. I can give them two weeks, as I have to be out of my apartment on the first, and I'm really sorry to quit on him 'cause I like the job and he's been great, but family's family.

Freddie looks at me calmly. OK, so you can give me two weeks?

Yes.

Is everything OK?

I sigh. It will be. I'd rather be in New York, but my family . . .

You know, life throws you a lot of curveballs, says Freddie.

I don't like them!

Yeah, I don't like them either. It's OK, he says kindly. I haven't had an easy life either.

Yeah, I mutter, lamely. There isn't much else to say. The lunch rush is building, the tables around us filling up, INXS playing on the stereo.

So here's what we're going to do, says Freddie, gears already turning in his head. We're going to have Becky work with us on Friday, Saturday, Sunday.

He's talking about a girl in prep, another single mom. She's quiet and tires easily, commuting all the way from Staten Island. Last week, we were working expo together when she walked out in the middle of rush, barely saying goodbye as she stripped her apron off and said it was too hot. (Later, I learn that she ended up in the hospital with pneumonia.)

I know she had a hard time before with that "It's too hot" business—Freddie rolls his eyes—but it's an opportunity for her, and we can figure this out.

OK. I pause. I'm sorry to quit on you.

It's OK. Feel better now? Freddie grins at me.

Yes.

You're, like, *phew,* right?

Yes. I nod emphatically.

We head back into the kitchen, and I've been working the line for about an hour when Freddie walks by me and shakes his head.

Now it's sinking in, he says. Two weeks. Shit. We're going to have to get drunk before you go.

When the kitchen slows down, I try, with occasional success, to lure the cooks into talking about food. One assessment is unanimous: We don't cook at Applebee's. We assemble.

This isn't stated outright so much as implied by the many little asides and comments from the cooks. This one place I worked, Geoff tells me one night, slamming the microwave door on a baggie of penne, we cooked the pasta *right,* pulled it right out of the water every time. Not like here. And the grill guys roll their eyes when I ask how a steak in the window is cooked. This one? asks Damian with disdain, pressing his finger onto the steaming flesh, gauging the give of the meat beneath his hand. That's medium.

But when it comes to talking about food, it's Claudette who can't say enough. Between her runs to the dining room, we talk about every meal we can: delicate pasta sauces, Asian noodle dishes, Haitian home cooking. I should be clear that we're not talking fine cuisine here. Claudette is a single mom, living on her own; her relationship with her parents went sour when she got pregnant, so here she is. And right now, *here* means four and five days a week at Applebee's, part-time classes at a local college—she dreams about owning a restaurant someday—and taking the baby, a little boy with big brown eyes, out on her days off.

At home, she cooks a lot of Haitian food, "but less greasy," and she's been experimenting with Asian fusion stuff, too. Her cooking happens on her days off; otherwise, like me, she cobbles together a diet from breakfasts and Applebee's meals, with the baby relying on formula and baby food.

When I come alongside her one afternoon to get a soda, she turns to me with a question: You ever think about having babies?

Not really, I say, getting an incredulous look. Not *ever?* asks Claudette. I brush her off with a vague response about how maybe someday I would, but not right now. Claudette's not buying it. She laughs.

Sorry, I thought all white people wanted to have babies.

I shake my head. They're so expensive, and a lot of responsibility.

Terry, who's expoing with me tonight, joins in.

It's not that expensive, he says. You make less than thirty thousand a year, right? You get free health care if you get pregnant. The kid gets free health care. And you get WIC for diapers and food until they're one.

I never thought of that, I say, truthfully. I find myself wondering if I might be able to qualify in my "real" life for this kind of help, if I might suddenly be in a much better position to have a family than I thought. It occurs to me that if wages are so low, and life is so hard, there's not much shame in taking a little help where I can get it.

Terry continues. He's got one kid himself, and the only hard part is babysitting—and that's not too hard if you have family around.

At this, Claudette rolls her eyes. Her family isn't much help to her, but she gets vouchers from the city to cover child care during the week, so there's someone to watch the baby while she's at class. That helps.

She fills her tray with soda and hoists it up to shoulder level.

They don't offer it on weekends, though, she says, and that's when I work. She balances her tray and darts out of the kitchen, striding at breakneck pace for the floor.

I clock out for lunch late in the afternoon and put in my order. By now I've developed a rule for which assembled meals I'll eat at work: anything off the grill, where the meat may have come in frozen but at least it's cooked fresh. I rotate between the burgers and fish sandwiches, and today I go for a blackened tilapia sandwich of unknown provenance, pairing it with a baked potato and broccoli. I'd had a late, light breakfast of coffee, toast, and oatmeal, knowing that I could have someone else cook for me at work, for free; I eat on my late afternoon break, pushing my "lunch" as close to the dinner hour as the kitchen will allow. There's some vague inkling that this isn't the best way to treat my body, a culinary critique simmering about the fish's sparse flavor, the soggy potato, the mushiness of the broccoli. But, assembled or not, this is a meal that meets my primary requirements: It is free, easy, and filling.

The happy hour crowd is starting to pour in, men flagging down the bartender, their dates perched on tall chairs and tapping manicured nails on the table tops. I get up from my table, hand my dirty plates to the bartender to send back, and clock back in. Someone drops money into the neon jukebox mounted on the wall, and a heavy hip-hop beat undulates into the room, Biggie Smalls's rolling boasts competing against the rising treble of bar chatter.

I walk away from the beat and head back towards the kitchen. I'm ready to move some food and feed these people.

The day after I tell Freddie I'm leaving, he brings in a new expo for me to train. Rafael is Calixto's cousin from Mexico and he doesn't speak any more English than I speak Spanish, leaving us stuck with the basics: *Grilled food is there, hamburgers are here, fried food is over there.* Instead I ask him about Mexico and whether he goes back much. Oh no, it's too dangerous with all the drug violence, better to stay here and work; besides, the borders are so tight that once you're here, you stay.

By now, everyone's heard that I'm leaving, so I'm juggling directives to Rafael in Spanish with pulling tickets and giving explanations of my plight. *Two fried shrimp,* and my grandmother's sick, *put cocktail sauce, Rafael,* and my mom died when I was a kid, *I need two honey samplers,* and I don't know when I'll come back.

Friday stays slow, but Saturday slams us hard. Rafael has worked in kitchens before, but he's not careful with the orders—or, possibly, he doesn't read English well—and things start to fall apart during the first hit around six o'clock. We're falling behind, Rafael pulling anything he sees out of the window and putting it in on the pass, and I'm unable to explain in Spanish what he's doing wrong.

Freddie appears out of nowhere. You with me?

With you.

Shrimp Parm mash and mash, garlic herb salmon, broc and rice, kid chicken sandwich.

Heard.

Bernardo comes through the kitchen, and Freddie turns to him: I am *not* doing this again next Saturday. I will walk out on you.

The line is falling behind, and by the time the second hit comes, at 7:30, we're in trouble. Hector and Luis over on fry are bumping orders before they're finished, so we start to pull a table's plates, thinking the order is ready, and find that we're missing the chicken fingers. Then we run out of soup, or rather, we run out of *defrosted* soup and have to hold up more orders. Freddie stations me on broil and mid, puts me in charge of checking tickets before we send orders to the floor. Everything's coming down in chaos, thrown off by Rafael, who's still pulling food just because it's ready and not grouping orders together. We slog through until the hit abates around 9:00.

Freddie turns to me, addressing his troops. From here on out, you *do not move* from down there, Tracie. And *nobody* takes food until *you have the ticket* and know what's going out. *Rafael,* says Freddie wearily in Spanish, *you have to match the ticket to the food.*

The bartenders bring back a round of Red Bulls for the line.

We get another hit at 10:00, and as it slows down around 11:00, Freddie catches me looking at the clock.

Tracie's like, when can I get out of here? he says.

I shake my head. Nah, I'm just like, how many more hits can we get?

At 11:45, Bernardo strides through the kitchen and looks at me. Tracie, go home.

I look at Freddie and he nods. I strip off the apron and turn to go clock out.

When you leave, Freddie says, shaking his head, I'm going to kill you.

* * *

My last weekend starts with Freddie handing me two photocopied pages. Study this, he tells me, we've got the AOA on Saturday, and you'll need to be prepared.

AOA is an Applebee's Operations Assessment, an inspection from corporate to make sure that we're doing everything according to spec, specifications, as decreed by the varying Applebee's manuals. It's never clear to me what the stakes are in this inspection, but Freddie and Bernardo are puttering around importantly, visibly stressed. I tuck the papers in my bag and study them on the train.

There are two sections on the handout, one set of general questions to be asked of kitchen staff and one set of queries specific to expo. The general questions are the most unsettling, because they reveal that I should have been getting food-safety training all along. Until reading this handout, I didn't know that the "food temperature danger zone" ranges from 41 to 140 degrees, and I didn't know that there was a specific order, top to bottom, in which to stack unprepared food in the coolers. There have been hints here and there: Freddie telling me to put the sani bucket on the bottom shelf in the kitchen (so that if it spills, it doesn't get into food); Emmet telling me to put the mashed potatoes on the top shelf in the walk-in, above the meats (so that no raw meat can contaminate them by dripping), the similarly unsettling questions on my expo "final." But nobody *told* me any of the kitchen stuff, not even the actually handy mnemonic device, LDIRTS: Label, Date, Initial, Rotate, Time, Shelf Life, for how to properly label prepared food.

There's also the introduction of a heretofore-unknown device: the "thermocouple," or thermometer, to check the temperature of food before it goes to the floor. In the two months I've been here, the thermometer has not come out once, but when I enter the kitchen on Saturday at eleven, one is sitting on the pass. You got to use this today, says Freddie. Check the meat temps against the wall chart, OK? This, I realize, is one more way that I don't need to know anything at all about food in order to do my job: Memorize the chart and compare temperatures, rather than gain skill enough to know a meat's doneness by touch and texture.

Early in the day, Julie, the inspector, corners me in the prep area while I change my apron. Terry's standing nearby, behind Julie, and prompts me with nods and shakes of his head, so I lie profusely, saying that yes, I'd had a trainer with me during all of my training; yes, I'd had a final, and she could find it in my file.

She comes into the kitchen a little later, and I watch from the pass as she quizzes the boys on the line. Pedro, one of the cooks on mid, has to run through LDIRTS. Rico has to explain how to minimize waste (follow recipes; follow LDIRTS; weigh portions properly). Damian has to identify the frill picks—toothpicks with colored cellophane knots at the top—associated with each rib sauce and temperature of meat (for the latter: red is rare, yellow medium-rare, green medium-well, and blue well-done). When Julie comes around to me, she asks me the same questions she asked all of them, effectively letting me cheat off what I just heard. When I identify all the frill picks correctly, Freddie beams. That's my girl!

Later, I hear Julie and Terry talking in the kitchen, and the words *management material* are being batted about.

When Julie turns to talk to Freddie, Terry comes over to me. You know, Julie thinks you'd make good management, he says. Stay here for a year and you could be a manager.*

I don't know, we'll see, I say. There are definitely worse things, I say. I could do a whole lot worse.

You're *good* at this, you know, says Terry.

Behind us, Freddie raises his voice just enough that it's easy to hear.

You know she's leaving me? And she's this good after just two months. Really?

Yes, really, says Freddie. I swear I feel him giving me a look.

I finish my stint at Applebee's on Palm Sunday, a wet rag of a spring day. It begins like most of my shifts, with shit-talking from broil.

When I ask Damian if he's got sweet-and-spicy baby backs coming for a table—I can see from the pass that the grill remains a vast, empty plain of hot metal—he rolls his eyes.

Do you *see* any ribs?

OK, baby, I say, I need you to drop one on the fly, OK? Please? By practicing my manners I've opened myself up, of course.

That's what she said last night, he says to Geoff, and they cackle together.

---

* My opportunities for advancement in the kitchen of an independent restaurant, as opposed to a corporate one like Applebee's, would likely be limited. On average, women are far rarer, and earn far less, in restaurant kitchens than their male counterparts. According to an 2010 survey of chefs, between eleven and eighteen percent were women, with women typically earning an average of $14,851 less than their male counterparts, or roughly nineteen percent. (Villaneueve and Curtis 2011)

I know why you're leaving, continues Damian. It's 'cause being close to me drives you crazy!

I nod. You've found me out, Damian. That's definitely the reason.

He grins triumphantly. I knew it.

We are deader than dead, even the postchurch rush barely filling the screens. Freddie walks in. I can't even *look* at you today; you're leaving me. We exchange smiles.

The kitchen gets pared down to the essentials pretty quickly; no sense in paying for staff we don't need. Damian goes home a couple hours after Calixto arrives, nodding goodbye as Calixto tells me he brought me something special; Becky floats between prep and expo.

Around eight o'clock, Calixto parades down the line from the freezer to broil. This is for you, *Mamí,* he says, displaying a bottle, frosted, of mezcal in his hands. We're drinking to you tonight!

Obvious drinking on the line has generally been restricted to Friday and Saturday nights, but tonight is different. Around nine, Geoff asks me if I want some tea and hands me a small to-go cup of vodka, Sprite, and fruit punch. It's strong, and I can feel a buzz start to course through my body. I look up from the line and Calixto winks at me as he unskewers shrimp into a pan.

The night wears on. We close at 11:00 on Sundays, and at 10:30 I turn around to see Calixto and Geoff standing at the head of the pass with three plastic to-go containers for sauce and the bottle of mezcal. Two cups are small, the size for ranch dressing on a salad; one is larger, the size for coleslaw. Calixto pours the liquor into each and hands me the largest.

Come on, baby, let's do a shot!

I smile. We count down and pound the fiery, smoky liquid together. I look up to see Hector staring at me from the fry side, eyes wide. You took that whole shot? I nod hazily. Whatever didn't splash out, I say.

I go back to work, messily organizing platters on the shelves beneath the pass. I'm about to stand up when I'm grabbed from behind and Rick pulls off my hat and crams a dish of whipped cream into my face. The whole staff is around me, laughing and giggling, showing me photos off their phones of my surprise before helping me wipe my face clean and pull my hair back up under my hat. I go to clock out, and when I come back into the kitchen Calixto is putting a platter on the pass, a broad yellow dish mounded with shrimp, lime, cilantro, garlic, and onion. Ceviche.

We made this for you, baby, he says, grinning. We all fall upon it, shoving bites of tender, citrusy fish in our mouths, fingers grabbing wildly. It's the first thing I've eaten here that tastes *fresh*. Geoff comes around from mid and joins us.

Take that hat off, he says. You're too gorgeous for this hat. You're smart, you're gorgeous, I'm gorgeous.

Thanks Geoff, that's sweet, I say, eating more ceviche, and from where he's doing inventory on the line, I hear Freddie call, That's right, Mumma, let your hair down.

I catch his eye and grin, can't help myself from playing along. I take the hat off and shake my hair down, then roll my eyes. Y'all happy? I laugh.

I'm still eating ceviche when Freddie comes around from inventory.

You know how I knew you were going to work out?

I shake my head, tipsy.

When you said that thing in the interview about not touching your ass! I knew it! He looks jubilant. He gives me a hug and tells me to call his cell phone if I ever need to pick up a shift.

Calixto taps me on my shoulder. This is for you, baby, he says, and points to a tiny to-go cup on the pass with a splash of mezcal and the worm in it.

For me? I say. I am drunk now, giddy with finishing my job, eager to be the girl who can keep up with the boys. One more splash won't hurt.

Aiight, I say, and knock it back in one fast gulp.

I *love* this girl, exclaims Geoff.

I leave the restaurant with a small posse of co-workers, trailing out the kitchen behind Calvin, one of the servers, Becky, and a few others. As we parade through the dining room on our way into the soggy spring night, Freddie and Tony look up from the table where they're doing paperwork.

Have fun, mama! says Freddie. And be safe.

Of all the things I enjoyed about my work at Applebee's—and there were many—I liked the kitchen banter the best. It was crass but not cruel to call a co-worker *pendejo*,* ballsy but not beyond the pale to inquire about my propensity for interracial dating ("So, do you like chocolate?"). I got a rush from feeling that I could hold my own amid the onslaught of innuendo that my gender and race inspired, that I was learning to give as good as I got. We were all in a hot, noisy kitchen, working together more or less as equals, and if we entertained ourselves with language and jokes inappropriate to the

---

* *Pendejo*, like most insults, can be used with a range of connotations from affectionate to enraged, but its most common usage translates to, roughly, *dumbass*.

office workers across the city, so be it. A little raunch ain't never hurt no one.

That was the fiction I sustained myself on, anyway, until my last night at Applebee's, which turned out to include sexual assault. I know this only by hearsay, though, as I don't remember much after leaving Applebee's. One of my co-workers drugged my liquor, in view of Hector, the fry cook—something I only learned weeks after the fact. In lieu of intervening directly, Hector urged Becky to keep an eye on me, never telling her that I had been drugged. Becky, in turn, did her best. We ended up drinking at Calvin's, where a friend of his, Mark, joined us. When the co-worker who had messed with my drink tried to take me home with him, Becky instead urged me to stay put.

In the meantime, I had caught the eye of Mark. As the party died down, I bade everyone goodnight and crawled into the only bed in the apartment clothed and alone; later, Becky and Calvin followed suit. In the wee hours of the morning, Becky awoke to find Mark stripping off my jeans; she told him to stop and fell back asleep, but he proceeded to approximately second or third base anyway, and left before any of us woke up. I gleaned most of the night's events though a series of phone calls with Becky, Calvin, and Mark. Becky proved to be far wiser than me, countering my initial, credulous recounting of the boys' version of events—which had included the observation that Mark, after all, has sisters—with, "What, like rapists don't have sisters? They think you stupid or something?"

These were the final dregs of my life at Applebee's, the last bit of my time as someone who had no better option than working in a hot, budget kitchen while fielding lewd asides from a half-dozen men. Someone, I realize, who wouldn't be expected to make a fuss; someone who would have nodded along with the other excuse Mark offered: "alcohol is an aphrodisiac." It occurs to me, in sequence, that this might be one reason women have been so rare in restaurant kitchens; that much of what kept my workplace bearable was not my own ability to roll with the punches but Freddie's personal interest in making sure I faced very few of them to begin with; and that this is possibly a glimpse of what life—not just work—is like for the vast sea of women born with fewer privileges than me.

I filed a police report, and Mark was arrested and then released. Without being able to remember anything, I found myself dependent on what everyone else said. The cop from the Special Victims Unit, who took my statement in the precinct kitchen as another officer microwaved his lunch behind us, made the point that, since I didn't remember anything, it was possible I had assaulted Mark—who could say, really? For the weeks before I talked to Hector, I was left to believe the story the cop had implied: I got too drunk, Mark took advantage, and what did I expect, anyway?

Before I left town, I called Hector, the fry cook. When I left Applebee's, he was about to move out of the homeless shelter, so I thought he might want some shelves I no longer needed; I also wanted to explain to him that I am actually a writer. I drove to his new place with the shelves, and when I told him about my "real" job, he took it in stride, asking if I'd be writing about how cooks drop food on the floor and serve it anyway—something I never observed. Then he asked how my last night went and proceeded to tell me he was worried after what he saw our co-worker put in my drink. It was only then that he told me he'd sent Becky along as a precaution. I was so shocked it didn't occur to me to ask for further details.

So why didn't Hector, who knew the precise degree of danger in which I was in, say something? I could never bring myself to call him and ask, but I suspect there were other things at play besides moral imperatives. Hector was one of the newest cooks in the kitchen, and still feeling out his place in it. For workers without job security, speaking out against a colleague carries real risk—particularly if you are supporting three kids while trying to move out of a homeless shelter, and particularly if it appears that an indirect intervention will take care of the problem. (Had it not been for Mark, after all, it would not have mattered that someone had drugged my drink, because Becky had served her intended purpose.) This is the unseemly rule that governs transgressions against established norms everywhere, whether it's something as abominable as sexual assault or as mundane as plastic flaking into food—something I never protested. Neither one is defensible, but it takes uncommon character—and an indifference to the consequences— to speak up when either one appears.

I never talked to my co-workers at Applebee's again, so I don't know if the full story of my last night ever made the kitchen rounds. By the time I was leaving town, I was so exhausted—by talking about the assault, by asking people questions about it, by arguing about whether I should have worn something different, by pointing out that getting drunk is stupid, yes, but that it's not the same thing as consent—that I couldn't bring myself to call the co-worker to see if it was true. I wanted nothing more than to have it all just *go away*, so I did what many victims of sexual assault do: I had a few sleepless nights. I talked to friends. I calmed down, albeit with a newfound reluctance to accept drinks from all but the closest of friends. And I thanked my stars that I had no reason to keep that job or ever go back to it. Without kids to support or "real" bills to pay with my check, I could do something that, for most women in my situation, would be unthinkable. I could just walk away.

A few months after I left New York, I found myself eating at a McDonald's. I was driving across country, and the tiny town I was passing through had no other options within sight of the gas station that lured me off the highway. So I tucked into a booth with a burger, fries, and soda, enjoying the air-conditioned respite from the sun-baked landscape outside. I was eating, I realized, a downmarket version of the Applebee's meals that sustained me through my days in the kitchen: industrial beef of unknown origin, fluffy white bread that likely arrived in a sheath of aluminum and plastic wrap, frozen shoestring potatoes recooked in the fryer, and a cool concoction of corn syrup, flavoring, and carbonation.

I had been wondering, since leaving New York, if I ate as well as I could have. I cooked on my days off, but maybe I could have done more. Instead of using a beer to counteract the buzz of a twelve-hour day infused with caffeine, I could have relaxed by cooking something simple from scratch. Or I could have been smarter about how I cooked, and done more of it in the mornings before I headed to Applebee's. I could have proposed to my roommates, Eve and Paula, that we share staple foods and pool resources the way conventional households do, or split up basic cooking duties. If I'd stayed longer, maybe we could have joined a community-supported agriculture club, or made a point of shopping at farmers' markets. There are so many seemingly small changes I could have made that I nearly get overwhelmed, first by the options and then by my own failure to make use of them. Then I take a breath, remember that I'm a reporter, and try to dispassionately observe my experience and use it to illustrate some greater truth.

So here is my story as an Applebee's worker, as I see it: I was a single woman earning $8 an hour, working forty or more hours a week, without health care or job security, trying to balance a life with room for friends and family, and did my best to eke out an existence that could afford me a few small luxuries. Here, I am talking bike rides and movies, for those are the things that began to seem luxurious; by then, beach vacations and expensive haircuts had morphed into the stuff of fairy tales. I remember tying myself in knots trying to figure out how to track down good produce that I could afford on a regular basis and how to make time for cooking it in my life.

On the days when the knots won, I typically consigned my diet to the category of "something I cannot change" and headed for the nearest fifty-cent bag of chips. I remember feeling frustrated, even angry, at the fact that my low wages meant that these basic functions of human life—procuring fresh food and having time to cook it—were nearly out of my reach, but I also felt ashamed, even guilty, for finding it such a struggle. Where, I sometimes wondered, are my *priorities*? And then I wonder if, in focusing solely on the contents of my plate, I am missing the forest for the trees.

The reason these things seem hard is because they *are*, at least for people like myself and my co-workers—not just at Applebee's, but at Walmart, and in the fields, and I suspect even for folks more affluent than that. Geography and the minute variations between the lowest rungs of our economy might change the details, but the healthiest route through the American foodscape is a steep and arduous path most easily ascended by joining its top income bracket. So far as I can tell, changing what's on our plates simply isn't feasible without changing far more. Wages, health care, work hours, and kitchen literacy are just as critical to changing our diets as the agriculture we practice or the places at which we shop.

Farms and fields are inextricably linked to my meals; I know this, probably, better than most. And yet none of it factored into my decision about my McDonald's lunch—or the ones I had on break at Applebee's, or the snacks I pulled out of the vending machine at Walmart, or even the meals I shared with my co-workers and landlords in California—because meals simply aren't the most urgent battle facing me, and with good reason. Before I can award them that place in my life as a matter of course, something has got to give: Either eating well needs to be easier, or the terms of my life need to be more forgiving. And no amount of intelligent analysis or principled argumentation will change those simple, pragmatic facts. I haven't landed here with my diet soda and mysterious beef patty because I, personally, haven't got the right priorities. I've landed here because, for a very long time, America has ignored a priority that should be one of its biggest: making sure its people can eat well, not just through the agriculture it practices but through the wages it pays, the work and education it provides, and the rules it keeps.

McDonald's, like Applebee's, is not a place I eat with any regularity in my "real" life, but it's a pretty good example of the kinds of meals we've made easy for most Americans to eat. Sitting here on a plastic bench and munching on french fries, I try to imagine an America where eating fresh food and cooking it is no more of a burden than the drive to McDonald's and back. What if eating well was the easy thing—and all this grease and corn syrup and salt were difficult? What if we really took the founders at their word and worked to build a nation where life and liberty were free in the fullest sense of the word, where health and sustenance were not considered luxuries, but were so common as to be unworthy of note? Where nobody bothered to brandish their food's local pedigree because it was simply unnecessary. Where chefs were more akin to race car drivers, doing for a profession what we all do by necessity, than to mysterious beings performing godlike acts of creation. Where not just farmers, but the people who worked for them, and the produce managers who chaperoned their goods, got the kind of appreciation they deserved for tending to what Barbara Kingsolver calls "the original human vocation": food. And where, once and for all, we could get past this childish notion that only rich snobs care about their meals, and everyone else is content with box meals.

That, I think, is the kind of America that could realistically grow from the one I visited for the year. It lies at the end of a long and tricky path paved in no small part with a faith that most Americans, when truly given the means and opportunity to make smart choices about their meals, will eat well. Building this America means shifting things that are a lot more resistant to change than our individual shopping carts, things like budgets and policies and culture. It means listening not just to the writers (myself included), but to the people who work at Walmart, and the people who cook our meals, and the people who pick our food, too; they are far more versed in what it will take for them (and the rest of us) to eat well than I am. And it means changing the way we talk about food, and remembering that it's one of the strongest bonds we have as humans; any foodies who can't see the common ground between themselves and an immigrant Mexican housewife might try reading a little Diana Kennedy or Rick Bayless. We have a long way to go before truly good food becomes the American way of eating, but I think we can get there. And there is frankly no more-fitting way for us to eat in the land of plenty than well.

CONCLUSION

A New American
Way of Eating

When I tell people that I spent a year working in the food system, most nod politely. When I go on to explain that I abandoned my life to work as a farmhand alongside migrant workers in California, then at Walmart grocery stores in Michigan, and finally at Applebee's in downtown Brooklyn, they perk up. And when I get to the parts about sixteen-dollar days and two hundred pounds of rotten asparagus and plastic melting into restaurant food, I almost invariably receive in response some permutation of the following: "Are you nuts?"

In the 2000s, I sometimes felt as if I might have been, in fact, crazy, as I heard people rhapsodize over spending $6 a pound on luscious farmers' market tomatoes. It felt very tempting to ignore all these farmers' markets and little farms, not because their proponents were wrong—about the importance of good food, or of developing sustainable ways of producing it—but because there seemed to be no grasp of the fact that many families struggled to afford *regular* tomatoes at the supermarket. I was reminded of one of my father's few maxims: It's not what you say, it's how you say it. In its very early stages, this book was intended partly as an experiment in translation. I wanted to see how and whether these new ideas about food might apply to a broader section of America, and try to locate common ground—in our meals, but also between our increasingly divided classes.

In the four years that have passed since I began developing this book, some common ground has emerged without any help from me. There is an organic garden on the White House lawn, and First Lady Michelle Obama has used it to illustrate the importance of access to affordable and healthy food—a concept at the heart of her campaign to end childhood obesity. At the same time, she's recruited grocers to her cause, and in mid-2011 presided over a press conference where Walmart, SuperValu, and other grocers committed to opening new stores in food deserts across the country. Farmers' markets all over the United States are beginning to take food stamps, and a growing number offer matching funds in-season to buy from local growers. Even celebrity chefs are getting serious about the social implications of their work: Jamie Oliver's television show, *Jamie's School Dinners*, has done the unthinkable and made the lunchroom meals at public schools into a topic of hot debate. What I suspected would be a hip fad for gourmands in 2006 has since gained a toehold in the public realm. Food isn't just in the lifestyle section; it's now considered a serious, mainstream issue. This is all the more striking because, for America, taking our food seriously is actually *new*.

Perhaps because this is largely new journalistic territory, I found myself less occupied with translating between classes than with simply observing mundane facts of life: that the food grown here is often picked by workers paid well below minimum wage and with very little oversight; that produce managers aren't necessarily given any better training to manage a town's fresh food supply than they are to stock sneakers; that food-safety training in a restaurant kitchen may be considered optional. Even the observations that I find unsettling would probably come as no surprise to anyone who has ever worked in the same jobs I held. Most farmworkers already know that their supposedly unskilled jobs take skill and time to learn and require hard work to be done well. Any restaurant worker can tell you that the manager under whom they work can make the difference between a kitchen, and the food it serves, being safe or dangerous. And anyone slogging through the depths of our economy on minimum wage or less, whatever their job, knows that their survival depends less on their own individual fortitude than the community of people they're able to draw around themselves for support.

When the poet and agriculturalist Wendell Berry wrote that "eating is an agricultural act," he was seeking to remind us of the inextricable link between the tending of our soil and our basic survival, and to reverse the broad denigration endured by farming as a trade, profession, and art. Our meals do begin with agriculture, but eating in a modern world is shaped by far more than that. I've come to think of the intricate linkages from farm to plate not as a food system, but as a foodscape, a lush, living, breathing world through which our meals travel. Farmers and chefs are the most visible of its inhabitants, but farmworkers and produce managers and stock clerks and prep cooks live there, too—and they are no less important to our meals. At the human end of the food chain, eating is not just an agricultural act, but a profoundly social one as well.

The night before I left California for Michigan, now nearly three years ago, I was fed like a queen. I had stopped at Rosalinda's to tell her family that I was in fact a writer. After Diego, her father, had taken me to talk with his friend Hector, we returned to the tiny two-bedroom apartment in which he was raising a family of eight. Diego pointed me to one of the ubiquitous stackable plastic lawn chairs that were, for all the families I had befriended in Greenfield, their primary furniture.

Have some food! he said.

I sat at the kitchen table, ready to eat dinner with everyone, but the six other kids stayed seated on the floor—they had no couch—watching a video from their older brother's visit back to Mexico. On the screen, their grandmother, wizened and barefoot, guided her teenage grandson on a tour of her house: dirt floors, rough walls, another plastic lawn chair, green hills sprawling outside the window. Only Rosalinda sat with me, while her mother cooked and Diego sat a few feet away, watching expectantly.

Claudia began to pile her wares on the scrap of table cleared before me: handmade tortillas, store-bought chimichangas freshly pan-fried; guacamole, carne asada, frijoles, watermelon. I tried to beg off, to no avail. By then my Spanish was strong enough that I knew Diego understood my pleas; he was just ignoring me. I turned to Rosalinda.

I really can't eat anything, I already ate today.

She looked at me, wary and unsure. And then I understood.

Is this, like, a Triqui thing? They're cooking all this for me?

She gave me a wan smile. Yeah, pretty much.

I ate to bursting and said my goodbyes. When I returned to Dolores and José's house, where I was staying, I found a similar spread, with a similar inspiration. I sat in another plastic chair and ate another massive meal.

These families were generous with me, I think, not just because of a tradition of hospitality, but because, as families eking out a living on very little, they understood the very basic role of food in their, and my, survival. They understood something that I vaguely knew but had never before articulated: that good, fresh food, like water, is a shared and precious resource.

Realizing this, for me, was akin to changing the focus on a camera. Adjust the lens in one direction, and only the meal on the plate will be clear. Adjust the lens again, and you can make out the contours of agriculture, with the rest a blur behind it. But make a final adjustment, so that the whole picture is sharp, and suddenly it becomes clear that our food is determined by far more than meals and fields. It's worthwhile, of course, to talk about food as a meal or as the product of a farm, but to engage with our meals solely on those terms is to ignore food's core essence. Food is not a luxury lifestyle product. It is a social good.

For a little more than a year, I had the opportunity to shift my perspective this way every few months, not just on our nation's meals, but on our way of life, too. Perhaps the most striking shift came at Walmart, when I realized my surprise at the extent and breadth of poverty among American whites—a fact that let me blend rather easily into my workplace and the communities in which I lived. That whites, too, are poor is easy to forget when my focal point is life in New York, where nearly all of the visibly poor faces are brown and black—a fact that also makes it easy to skim over the existence of middle-class strongholds in America's black and Latino communities. There's a world of scholarship on these topics, and I've read some of it, so in strictly intellectual terms I should not have been surprised. But the narrative trailing along in my subconscious was different, leaving me surprised by what are actually normal parts of American society.

I learned countless lessons from the people I met in the fields and in the kitchen at Applebee's, but insofar as the American way of eating goes, I find myself coming back again and again to Patti and Teri, the sisters I met at Detroit's Eastern Market. Both were white and didn't have much money, and though Patti lived near a supermarket she drove the fifteen miles to downtown Detroit because she could get a little extra money for produce. Eating fresh food was something Patti thought of as a luxury, but it was still important to her, so she drove to the city for the $20 worth of farm-fresh fruits and vegetables being offered to her on top of her food stamps. It's tempting to hold Patti up as a model for America to follow, a plucky and determined good eater. But I wonder if there isn't a different lesson to take from her. We're facing a dire public health problem related to poor diet. Is it really in America's best interest to maintain a food system where eating well requires one to either be rich or to drive a total of thirty miles? Nearly two years after leaving my job outside Detroit, I think the answer is no.

During my tenure in the fields, I made an effort to budget my money wisely. So I did what I had watched my father do every weekend as a child: I opened up the newspaper and looked for coupons. In very short order, I confronted the reality most families deal with every day: There were coupons for Reddi-wip, for Chef Boyardee ravioli in a can, for envelopes of Orville Redenbacher's microwave popcorn, for boxes of Tusconi cookies. If there was a food manufacturing company with goods to sell, there was a coupon for what it sold. But there were no coupons for something that America needs to eat far more of: produce, which is sold essentially in bulk and—with a few notable exceptions—doesn't carry a brand name. The Central Valley's bounty was all around me, fields of onions and carrots, almonds and oranges, but if I was looking for a deal I was left with Chef Boyardee.

This is just one of the myriad ways that eating well is difficult in America. In addition to coupons being of little use when one hopes to eat healthfully, we can add to the list our stagnating wages, skyrocketing income inequality, and mushrooming health care costs; agricultural policies that pay farmers to exhaust our soils by growing food not to be eaten, but to be burned; an increasingly monopolized food infrastructure that gives the people selling our food little incentive to keep it affordable; and a population so strapped for time, cash, and know-how that cooking dinner becomes a Herculean task rather than a simple and necessary chore. The list goes on and on, encompassing everything from changing our individual grocery lists to building new supermarkets to transforming entrenched government subsidy programs.

In pragmatic terms, there are two sides to this problem: supply and demand. Supply is restricted at both farm and retail levels. American farmers grow only enough fruits and vegetables to meet half of America's recommended daily servings of produce, and much of it comes from California's irrigated wonderland. Meanwhile, our richest farmland, in the prairie states, increasingly goes not to food that we eat but to grain destined for fuel tanks and cattle feed. Today, around 14 million Americans live in low-income neighborhoods with insufficient grocery stores. Yet it's hard to entirely fault the stores and the farmers, given the current state of demand: American shoppers don't eat anywhere near as many fruits and vegetables as they should. That kind of food costs more than processed foods, and preparing it is more complicated than most people feel comfortable with; it's not that they don't *want* the good stuff, but that they can't easily make it a regular part of the lives. The *demand* is there, but the means to exercise it is not.

There are simple fixes that could bring that demand out of hiding. One is to build on the success of programs such as the Double-Up Food Bucks program that lured Patti to Eastern Market and expand them to everyone— not just the poorest among us, who have no monopoly on the need to consume more fruits and vegetables. I haven't found research that shows the precise annual income at which the cost of food stops being a concern, but I can tell you from experience that it is far higher than the annual earnings of someone working full-time at the minimum wage. We need more jobs and higher wages; these goals are intrinsic, not additional, to any attempt to change America's food system. But we lose nothing if we keep health costs in check by making it easy for everyone to eat well. And one of the easiest ways to do that is to make eating well affordable; universal coupons for fresh produce would be a simple way to accomplish that.

Teri, Patti's sister, also suggested a second tactic that could boost demand for fresh food: cooking classes. If we managed to incorporate cooking into public education, we'd make sure the next generation could prepare healthy meals. It was my cooking skills, picked up as a kid and later as a nanny, that kept me from succumbing to a diet composed of Hot Pockets and Hamburger Helper. But leaving those skills to chance strikes me as shortsighted. Just as we have an interest in having kids who can read, we have a very strong public interest in having healthy kids. We recognize that the former is too important a skill to leave to parents alone, and therefore teach it in school; given the links between a healthy diet and knowing how to cook meals from scratch, we might want to try doing the same with cooking.

Yet it's worth asking whether we can then manage to *meet* all that demand, and I probably learned the most about the practice of agriculture not in the fields of California but in the once-vacant lots of Detroit. The lesson I've taken from people like Malik Yakini and Greg Willerer is not that urban agriculture will wholly replace larger-scale farming, but that it offers a phenomenal opportunity to experiment with new ways—which often draw on very old ways—of cultivating very good and healthy food. There are different terms for the kind of agriculture that I've seen in Detroit's modest farm plots, which rely on crop rotation, swap out chemical fertilizers for compost, minimize the use of costly machinery, and utilize mixed crop plans and intercropping. The most common referent is *agroecology*, a discipline that weds food production with an understanding of the ecological world. It came to international attention in early 2011 when the United Nations released a report arguing that agroecology, rather than the industrial agriculture promoted for decades, is key to solving hunger in Africa—and possibly in the world—due to its lower costs and long-term stability. Just as important, the diverse crop plans that define this kind of farming inherently mean a healthier diet, with fruits and vegetables as well as carbohydrates; they simply need to be studied and scaled up. I couldn't help but note, thinking back to my arm in the garlic fields, that a diversity of crops would mean a diversity of tasks—something good for workers, too, since their bodies bear the brunt of whatever tasks we leave to human hands.

It was also in Detroit, observing the phenomenal amount of food that came to the city but never arrived in its neighborhoods, that I realized we've focused our energies on cultivating a food supply without ever making sure it reaches our citizens. The food infrastructure that brings food into neighborhoods is in many ways just as important to our health as what goes on in the fields. Much of what has made modern supermarket prices so low has not been a drop in the cost of food itself, but the reduction in logistical costs achieved by stores that have brought distribution in-house. Supermarket food is cheap, in other words, because the big chains have their own storage and transportation infrastructure. We can, of course, keep leaving the management of our food supply to a handful of corporations on the basis that they provide us with low prices. Yet I wonder if this doesn't solve one problem by creating another that's even worse. Walmart already controls nearly one-quarter of our food; in 2011, it announced that it had opened up more than two hundred stores in underserved areas (where it would face little competition) and planned to do the same with another three hundred. As its market share grows, it's worth considering whether the company has any reason to keep its prices low.

Distributing our food solely through private networks makes sense only if you think of food as a consumer good, looking solely at the meal before you. But if you can change your perspective and see fresh food for what it is—a social good and a human right—it makes far more sense to have a little public control over its distribution. Just as we ensure that water and electricity gets to nearly every American, it makes sense to ensure that every American can access fresh and healthy food, too.

There's already some interest in and precedent for this. In 2010, the USDA began supporting local efforts to develop logistical systems and cooling and packing sheds in a few market areas around the country through its Food Hubs initiative; Detroit's Eastern Market is one of its models. Resources like that are inherently small-business friendly, since they let smaller stores compete against the big ones that can run trucking fleets. And they're farmer-friendly, too, helping solve the problem of the higher costs of well-produced farm products by aggregating shipments and sharing common facilities. Today, about 16 cents of every dollar Americans spend on food ends up back at the farm; the other 84 cents goes to the system that got it on our plates in the first place. The transportation, the packaging, the delivery, the supermarkets, even the cooks at restaurants, get everything else. If we managed to free up just a few cents of that dollar—something that would be easier to do if we had affordable, public food infrastructure—it stands to reason that we could pay farmers more, and in turn give farmworkers reasonable wages, without seeing our food costs skyrocket.

When I began this journey, I expected that I would observe some small, struggling subset of the American populace. But the reality is that I had plenty of company in the lower depths of our economy. Farmworkers are undeniably near the bottom with annual incomes that rarely reach far into five figures; for me, a year of farmwork would have reached just under $11,000. My other jobs, though, paid a little over minimum wage, putting me at just about the poverty line for a single person. Had I been able to secure full-time employment—something that eluded me, as it does so many other Americans—at $8 an hour, 40 hours a week, 52 weeks a year, I'd have earned almost $17,000; if I could be doubled into a couple, that would mean $34,000. More than one-third of American households earn less than $35,000 a year. With a little overtime luck, or if I'd ascended into management as I was encouraged to at Applebee's, I'd have been able to scratch my way into what is, in purely economic terms, our middle class: the third of households earning between $35,000 and $75,000. In much of the country, this is not a range of income that correlates with the kind of middle-class comforts enjoyed by previous generations—most notably the stability conferred by health care, pensions, and affordable housing.

I could make a practical financial pitch here about why it's critical that we address, head on, how food works for the poor by noting that obesity, diabetes, and other diet-related illnesses are most prevalent in the lowest depths of our economy and are thus more costly to the public purse. Or I could make an emotional one, beseeching readers to have more compassion for the poorest among us. Both of those appeals have their place. But I'm more interested in making a political one. In 2012, the working poor constitute arguably the largest, and fastest-growing, economic class within the American citizenry. Today, income inequality is on par with the levels that preceded the Great Depression, with 10 percent of America claiming half the nation's income; in 1976, the year of my birth, that same income bracket shared less than one-third of it.

America has been here before. In the early years of the twentieth century, a pragmatic visionary from Detroit faced a similar landscape. The richest tenth held 40 percent of the money; the other 90 percent scraped by on the rest. So Henry Ford set about designing a way of manufacturing cars that would make them affordable to average workers, even stealing inspiration from slaughterhouses disassembling animals into meat. When he started selling the Model T in 1908, it cost one-third less than most of the cars sold nationwide that year—and, unlike the industrialization of our food, offered a product of quality comparable to cars manufactured in a more artisanal fashion. In 1914, Ford began paying his workers $5 a day, doubling the average worker's wage and thus making his automobiles affordable to them. In the process, he built an empire that changed American society forever.

Ford was a capitalist, not a good Samaritan, yet his strategy contained a thread of brilliance that could appeal to both: He made it easy for most Americans to buy his products. Ford did eventually raise wages, but he never set out to sell his cars to a tiny cohort of elites. His founding conviction was that his success hinged on appealing to the struggling workers of America. Anyone serious about changing anything about the American way of eating—whether it's the way we grow our food, how we sell it, or how we eat it—will need to figure out how to do the same.

HOLY TED NUGENT,
WE'RE ALL FOODIES NOW

Many Americans care a lot about their food. But many also
find it difficult to improve the quality of what they eat.

A few years ago I bought a cookbook entitled *Kill It and Grill It* for my boyfriend, a Yale grad who hunted and fished. Admittedly, I offered the gift ironically. I'd been drawn to it by its cover photo of '70s rocker Ted Nugent and his wife, Shemane, each clad in a denim vest and clutching a rifle and a knife, respectively. As a native of rural Michigan, I saw the image as both funny and dismaying. They kind of look like families I grew up with, I thought. But who buys a cookbook with a gun on it?

And yet, thumbing through it at home, I found passages that were eerily similar to the books and articles on local food I was beginning to read with regularity. On page 121, I found something that could have been written by Michael Pollan. "The closer we can get to eating fruit from the tree, meat off the hoof, or vegetables from the ground, the better," wrote Shemane in the 2002 book.

Shemane also warns that, in analyzing food ingredients, "If you can't pronounce it, chances are it is not real food." Sound familiar? Pollan's Food Rule No. 7, formulated nearly a decade later, advises us to "Avoid food products containing ingredients a third-grader cannot pronounce."

It would be easy to dismiss this overlap as little more than a missed opportunity for a reality show: A boar-hunting battle between Nugent and Pollan, or a cook-off between Alice Waters and Shemane. There is plenty on which ardent pro-gun supporters and the marquee names advocating for local and sustainable food do not agree. And yet, maybe that's precisely the point.

One reason those imagined contests are funny is that we tend to think that taking food seriously is the exclusive domain of those who are affluent, well educated, and—let's be honest—liberal. These assumptions are made by all sides, whether it's Alice Waters insisting that some people don't eat

well because they prefer "to buy Nikes, two pairs," or Sarah Palin tweeting that Michelle Obama's efforts to make school food healthier represent a "nanny state run amok!"

Both comments are painfully far removed from the reality of most Americans' lives. I know this not from my daily life as a writer in New York, but because, in 2009 and 2010, I worked—and ate and lived—undercover researching America's food system for a book. I made use of food banks alongside indigenous Mexicans I met in California fields, shared lunch breaks with single moms on my shift at a Michigan Walmart, and ate with my fellow kitchen workers at a New York City Applebee's. If there's one thing I learned, it's that Palin and Waters are missing a very important fact: Many (and I would guess most) Americans care quite a lot about their food and health. The problem is that many of them find it incredibly difficult, because of time and money and access, to do much to improve the quality of what they eat.

It was Patti Good, a Kmart cashier from a declining Detroit suburb, who drove that point home for me. I was interviewing people who receive federal food assistance and participate in a matching-funds program called Double Up Food Bucks at the city's Eastern Market, a bustling retail and wholesale farmers' market spread across five massive sheds that have stood there for 150 years. Patti had driven thirteen miles to get an extra $20 for produce. "You can't afford stuff like that all the time," she said of oranges, adding that last year, with Double Up's help, she'd been able to afford a real splurge: a pineapple.

Eastern Market is a bright spot in Detroit's food landscape. City residents there have only about 1.6 square feet of grocery store per person; industry metrics consider 3 feet per person to be necessary to facilitate a sufficient food supply.

Nationwide, 23.5 million Americans live in "food deserts"—neighborhoods with insufficient grocery stores. The traditional explanation for food deserts is that there is insufficient demand for groceries in some neighborhoods, but Patti made me wonder if this isn't a semantic hiccup. People everywhere have to eat; there is always demand for food, just as there is always demand for water. The challenge isn't that people don't want fresh food; rather, it's how to get it to them at affordable prices. Supermarkets are one way, though their absence in communities, one expert told me, is an example of a "market failure." Eastern Market offers another—and one, I noticed, that kept prices competitive by nixing the middleman.

Between Patti and the Nugents, I've lost any patience for the idea that caring about food is elitist; that's just culture-war posturing. Now, when people spout off about foodie pretensions or the poor's misplaced priorities, I tell them about Patti, or I urge them to read the first few pages of *Kill It and Grill It*.

"It is good to know exactly where one's food comes from," writes Ted. "We sure as hell wouldn't waste good hunger or any one of our much-anticipated family mealtimes on fast food or junk food."

So is Nugent a foodie? Given the term's liberal, urban connotations, I doubt it. But the ideas he shares with the people who are offer a compelling reminder that good food is something on which most Americans already agree.

ACKNOWLEDGMENTS

It's common to think that the author of a book is the person responsible for it, but in the last three years I've learned publishing's dirty little secret: A book is a collective effort. That only my name appears on the cover of this one makes it the grandest bait and switch I've ever pulled. If you've read this far, you've not only been parsing my words on the page, but the expertise and skill of the dozens of people who made it possible in the first place, either by producing work that I've drawn from or by giving me the means to write a book in the first place. So please, dear reader, indulge me in this laundry list—and anyone I've forgotten, please excuse the (utterly unintentional) slight.

Initial thanks go to the families, roommates, and co-workers who appear in this book, only a few of whom I knew well enough to disclose my "real" job to at the end; I learned more in my time with them than I could have gleaned from a thousand books. They're followed quite closely by the three talented young journalists who chose—in addition to holding their own full-time jobs—to work for me, earning only glory in exchange for the exhaustive reporting they conducted on my behalf: Dorothy Hernandez, Clarissa León, and Katie Rose Quandt contributed facts to nearly every page of this book. Completing it without their intelligence, talent, and dedication would have been impossible. Similarly, I was lucky to have an investigative reporter even more detail-oriented than me, Jennifer Block, check my work; all errors were added after she finished cleaning up my mess.

I am not a particularly religious person, but I can think of no other word than *blessed* to describe my luck in landing at Scribner. Editor Alexis Gargagliano is not only talented, thoughtful, and wickedly intelligent, but incredibly patient—something shared by her assistant, Kelsey Smith. Rex Bonomelli designed a cover so phenomenal that I still catch my breath when I look at it, going so far as to manufacture labels for the gorgeous cans of food that you see. Lauren Lavelle and Cody Gertz went the extra mile to make sure people heard about the book. And I never would have met any of them without the creativity and support of my agent Rebecca Friedman, first at Sterling Lord and now at Hill Nadell, who listened to me suggest one book ("something about supermarkets") and then asked me a dangerous question: What do you *really* want to write about?

The answer—how food works in the lives of most Americans, not just hip young things and professionals in New York—sent me on a journey that led me to speak with dozens of experts. The bibliography is a thank-you list of sorts, but I'd be remiss if I didn't single out the people who repeatedly shared their expertise and talents with the random woman (and her assistants) querying them on the other end of the phone.

For the reporting on farms and farm labor, Sandy Brown and Jim Cochran of Swantonberry Farm walked me through the intricacies of farm labor from a small grower's perspective. California Rural Legal Assistance introduced me to the world of farmwork, and I'm particularly indebted to Luis Jaramillo for championing my work, and then Fausto Sanchez, Mariano Alvarez, Ephraim Camacho, Mike Courville, Jésus Lopez, Michael Marsh, and Mike Meuter for continuing to help. I would never have been able to learn about farmwork if Jessica Culley, José Manuel Guzman, and Richard Mandelbaum of CATA had not introduced me to workers while writing the proposal for this book. Vera Chang's work compiling an overview of America's farm labor system meant I didn't have to do it myself. For a national picture, Farmworker Justice in Washington, D.C., provided historical and political context. Brad Gleason, Gregorio Jacobo, and Frank Maconachy offered valuable insights about large-scale agriculture. Amanda Pomicter plumbed the depths of America's agricultural history on my behalf. At the United Farm Workers, I benefited greatly from the expertise of Irv Hirschenbaum and Roman Pinal.

For the twin issues of supermarkets and urban agriculture, I drew on a vast sea of knowledge that began with Brahm Ahamdi, Will Allen, Ian Marvey, and Bryant Terry, who were among the first to suggest to me that even poor people wanted good food. John Ameroso and Bob Lewis clued me in to the importance of both extension and agricultural marketing when it comes to bringing healthy food into neighborhoods. Ashley Atkinson, Patrick Crouch, and Malik Yakini patiently answered my endless questions about urban agriculture despite having other things to do with their time. Jonathan Bloom's work on food waste relieved me of doing that reporting on my own. Dan Carmody, Randall Fogelman, and Kami Pothukuchi fielded more questions than were probably necessary about regional food systems in Michigan. Tracey Deutsch deconstructed the early years of the supermarket. Alicia Glenn, Harvey Gutman, and Fran Spencer provided valuable insights on the challenges of bringing supermarkets into underserved areas. Shane Hamilton made me rethink the importance of transportation in the American diet, and the curious political expressions of class in America. James Johnson-Piett gave me lessons in the nitty-gritty of bringing produce into neighborhoods where it was hard to find. Roberta Cook shared her exhaustive knowledge on the American produce industry.

In delving into America's kitchens, I was fortunate to find Bonnie Azab Powell, Maisie Greenawalt, and Helene York of Bon Appétit Management Company, who shared their knowledge of the economics of commercial kitchens with me. Ulrich Boser's work on Sysco was a boon for a reporter without extensive private industry contacts. Megan Elias plumbed the depths of American home economics so I didn't have to. Andrew Haley generously shared his expertise on American restaurants. Saru Jayaraman and JoAnn Lo patiently explained the experiences of restaurant workers, most of whom work for independent restaurants, instead of chains like Applebee's; I look forward to Jayaraman's forthcoming work on the subject.

There are also sources who fall into a miscellaneous category and I'll recognize them here. Mark Arax was selfless in sharing his endless knowledge of California's Central Valley. Jim Roan of the Smithsonian Institute's National Museum of American History Library fielded endless inquiries. Curt Guyette, Meghan O'Neill, Brian Smith, Sandra Svoboda, and Travis Wright shared invaluable expertise and sourcing about Detroit; their colleagues Justin Rose, Corby Winer, Paul Kroll, and Rudy Pokorny were invaluable, too. Jacob Hodes counseled me in the many uses of spreadsheets to organize my reporting, an experiment that yielded a digital beast I've called the Barretizer (in honor of my old mentor). Briana Kaya pulled exhaustive census data for me, which is woven into countless sections of the book. Christian Paiz and Aimee Stowe patiently fielded translation queries. Proyecto Linguistico de Quetzalteco de Español in Guatemala gave me the gift of Spanish even if I've yet to make it my own. As of writing this, I can count four-dozen sources from the USDA among my contacts, but Elizabeth Frazao, Phil Kaufman, Sheri Kosco, Ephraim Liebtag, Hayden Stewart, and Richard Volpe fielded more than their share of queries with generosity and patience.

Sources are one thing; backers are another. In addition to the generosity of Scribner, I relied on crucial support from a coterie of people and institutions who can only be described as patrons. The Fund for Investigative

Journalism, as well as the Food and Environmental Reporting Network, supported some of the more nuanced farm labor reporting you've read here; the Mesa Refuge gave me a spectacular break from Detroit's wintry streets to finish a key section of the manuscript; and the Louis M. Rabinowitz Foundation covered the cost of fact-checking. The friendship and professional colleagueship offered me by Annia Ciezadlo and Mohamad Bazzi has been unparalleled, often bordering on familial, but their formal support of my work was key to it ever getting done; the generosity of Oscar Owens and Elissa Berger, whom I've been blessed to count as friends for half my life, was similarly indispensable. And as the first iteration of the book went to press, Melissa Lutdke and Florence Graves at the Schuster Institute for Investigative Reporting gave me a boost by naming me a Senior Fellow there.

More than grants and loans, I relied heavily on in-kind support, particularly DIY writer's retreats: the homes of people generous enough to share theirs with me. Turning eight hundred pages of typed reporting notes into a narrative took several months of writing in a trailer nestled among the pines of northern New Mexico, a feat I never would have accomplished without the generosity first of Camille and Larry Owens, and then their neighbors, Jim Horn and Jane Fritz. Completing the heavy historical and industry reporting once I had a narrative required finding housing and office space, and in Detroit I found both. An angel named Jessie Doan provided the former, made possible with the support of her colleagues on the board of the La Salle Cooperatives in downtown Detroit, particularly Toby Barlow, John Canzano, and Christian Unverzagt. Similarly, the Detroit Metro Times gave me a temporary professional home via a new author fellowship, under the brainstorming of their talented editor W. Kim Heron, publisher Chris Sexton, and assistant editor Michael Jackman. The myriad medium-term stays this book required were covered in Los Angeles by Aaron Chappell and Cora Neumann and Andras Rosner; in Oakland by Jessica Warner and Jason Saunders; in Manhattan by Keene Berger; in Brooklyn by Oscar Owens and Elissa Berger, Michael Rabinowitz and Elana Karopkin, and Indrani Sen and Clay McLeod; in Detroit by Colleen Burke, Christina and Martina Guzman, and Sean Mann. The patient staff of Pratt Area Community Council, particularly Stephanie Blue and Suzette Brown-Scotland, made sure my nomadic lifestyle didn't mean losing Brooklyn forever.

As if that weren't enough, home-cooked meals, cocktails, and the occasional overnight stays took their toll on a number of friends scattered across the country. I'm forever indebted to the guest rooms, sofas, and kitchen tables of: Shomial Ahmad's family in Fort Worth, Texas; Marvin, Kay, and Will Barkis in Louisburg, Kansas; Jessica Basta and Ben Getting in Los Angeles; Jared Bunde in Brooklyn; Francesca Cecchi and Adam Meyers-Spector, and their lovely daughters, in Forest Hills, Queens; Heidi Chua in Brooklyn; the Faissals in Longmont, Colorado; Sabrina Fecher and her daughter Naomi in Philadelphia; Paul Fitzgerald and Andrea Hill-Fitzgerald in Chicago; Mel Gallagher and David Williams Phillips in New Orleans; Johanna Gilligan, Owen Henkel, Kristy Magner, and Abby Feldman also in New Orleans; Lloyd and Stephen Goding outside of Las Vegas, New Mexico; Gabriel Guerrero in Detroit; Amanda Hickman and Noah Budnick in Brooklyn; Meredith Hines-Dochterman and family in North Liberty, Iowa; Meghan Kline in Kalamazoo, Michigan; Geoff Kurtz and Alyson Campbell and their two darling children in Brooklyn; Richard and Susan Lindeborg in Las Vegas, New Mexico; Robert and Ivy Nichols, and their three lovely kids, in Phoenix, Arizona; Matt Pacenza, Julie Stewart, and their two boys in Salt Lake City, Utah; Stephanie Rosenblatt in Long Beach, California; Estelle Davis, Jessica Shearer, Bela Walker, and Jennifer Flynn-Walker in Brooklyn. And Taliah Lempert in Brooklyn gets props for offering something just as valuable as a place to stay: wine and her unparalleled creative talents.

I never would have known how to be such a welcome guest without the training I received overseas under the phenomenal hosting talents of Mario and Stella Cecchi in Milan, Italy; Eliott Fishman and Damon Rao in Melbourne, Australia; Trish Proudman and her sister Barb in Kawhia, New Zealand; Patnarin Stirapongsasuti and Noy Thrupkaew in Bangkok, Thailand; Célia Schneider in Paris; Claire Whitmer and Emmanuel Bridonneau in Nantes, France. Back stateside, I am also obliged to thank the talented junkyard mechanics who've kept my car running without sending me to the poorhouse. The Ulibarris of Las Vegas, New Mexico, not only fixed my car but sent me home with homemade goat cheese and an elk roast. Further mechanical assistance came from Manuel of Mexicantown in Detroit; Ben of Michael's Auto Service in Kalamazoo; and the good-hearted family of Alicia and Chad Van Slyke, who rescued my car from decrepitude on a state highway in Pratt, Kansas. Reaching even further back, I'm particularly indebted to three families. Two of them hired a college kid from the rural hinterlands and let her loose in their kitchens: Jay Kriegel, Kathryn McAuliffe, and Tessa and Caitlyn Roush treated me like family and endured culinary experiments at their expense. Diana Burroughs deserves thanks for similarly letting me loose in her Edgarton kitchen; Sanford, Jackson, and Samantha get kudos for eating what I came up with. The third family welcomed me to a crumbling block of Brooklyn as my superintendent and his family, but by the time I left that block Milton Saunders, his wife, Gobi, and their grandchildren Destiny, Denzel, Dynasty, Daeshawn, and Diamond had become true friends, too. Samantha gets kudos for eating what I came up with. The third family welcomed me to a crumbling block of Brooklyn as my superintendent and his family, but by the time I left that block Milton Saunders, his wife, Gobi, and their grandchildren Destiny, Denzel, Dynasty, Daeshawn, and Diamond had become true friends, too. And before I even made it to New York, a long line of Holly, Michigan's excellent public school teachers encouraged me to write and think well. I had many great ones, but it's Julie Grimes-Frank, Bev Mackenzie, Amy Aleo, Kaye Thorsby and Irene Peavey who stick out the most.

There are two things one needs to write a book like this: confidence in your reporting skills and the belief that you are, in fact, a writer. In acquiring the former, I've had some of the best teachers and coaches around. Wayne Barrett, LynNell Hancock, and Alyssa Katz, all multiplied the instruction I got from New York University's journalism department into a career. They taught me more than it's actually possible to know; all my mistakes are indications of the lessons I either failed to learn or have simply forgotten. If it took three talented teachers to make me think I was a reporter, it took far more attention from professionals to persuade me I was a writer. In addition to the funders mentioned earlier, I'm humbled and inspired to have had my work commended by the Harry Chapin Media Awards at WHYHunger, the James Aronson Social Justice Journalism Awards, the Livingston Awards for Young Journalists, the Casey Medals for Meritorious Journalism, the Wesleyan Writer's Conference, and the University of Maryland Journalism Fellowships in Child and Family Policy.

I might never have thought this was possible were it not for the encouragements of other writers, editors, and other professionals of varying stripes who've provided me with encouragement and criticism, support and advice—and, where applicable, inspired editing—wherever they can. (I'm also lucky enough to count many of them as friends, too.) Sincere thanks thus go out to Allison Arieff, Warren Belasco, Emily Biuso, Jennifer Bleyer, Haven Bourque, Dana Bowen, Bill Buford, Ava Chin, Rico Cleffi, Cathy Carron, Kate Crane, Paula Crossfield, Catherine diBenedetto, Erin Edmison, Barbara Ehrenreich, Daniel Engber, Cathy Erway, Barry Estabrook, Nina Fallenbaum, William Finnegan, Charles Fishman, Frank

Flaherty, Nick Fox, Ann Friedman, Dan Fromson, Barry and Joan Gaberman, Denise Gaberman and Dan O'Reilly-Rowe, Anthony Garrett, Matt Haber, Christy Harrison, Oran Hesterman, David Kamp, Sarah Karnasiewicz, Andrea King Collier, Beth Kracklauer, Corby Kummer, Francis Lam, Anna Lappé, Tara Lohan, Barry Lynn, Isabel MacDonald, Kate Manchester, Douglas McGray, Debbie Nathan, Zora O'Neill, James Oseland, Tom Philpott, Michael Pollan, Janet Poppendieck, Matthew Power, Jennifer Prediger, Yael Sadan, Jonathan Schell, Eric Schlosser, Indrani Sen, Larry Smith, Naomi Starkman, Josh Viertel, Bill Wasik, Seth Wessler, Rachel Wharton, JuliAnne Whitney, and Charles William Wilson.

I'm also deeply indebted to the friends and colleagues who took the time to read various drafts of the manuscript. Some of them are mentioned earlier for their support, but they bear repeat mention. Annia Ciezadlo, Claire Cox, Jessica Daniel, Nina Fallenbaum, Rob Fetter, Hilary Goldstein, Owen Henkel, Michael Jackman, Douglas McGray, Jessica Shearer, Jessica Warner, and Toya Williford all gave me the incredible gift of criticizing my work so that it might be better. The flaws that remain are most likely things I've been too lazy to fix.

Finally: Family, whose primary contribution to the work you hold in your hands was the formation of *me*. Mike and Sue Eby of Fenton treated and fed me like one of their own after I befriended their daughters Kate and Amanda. (Amanda's husband, E. J. Hammacher, isn't too bad, either.) My sisters, Johanna and Shana, let me crash on their couches at all hours and eat their food, as did their partners, Matt Warra and Matt Ramsey. Catherine Hull—who might as well be a McMillan—has done the same, and her parents, Dick and Betty Hull, have fed me more than a nonrelative has any responsibility to do. Jennifer Metz disproves the notion of an evil stepsister, and her husband, Rob, and my niece, Kaitlyn, have proven to be kind and loving hosts. Gordon and Dorothy Huston have been generous to a fault with me, and I'm lucky to have added them as grandparents; the same sentiment can be extended to Pam and Jack Akey, their daughters, Chris and Lauren, and their respective families. The extended web of Nichols, McCandlesses, and Barleys that reaches beyond my immediate family gets kudos, too.

The tight nuclear center of all this family, though, is inhabited by my father, John McMillan, my stepmother, Bonnie McMillan, and my grandparents, all of whom taught me key lessons: the importance of thank you and of listening before speaking; the necessity of hard work and to never,

WHAT I SPENT ON FOOD

On average, I spent about 19 percent of my income on food, with 10 percent spent on groceries and 9 percent spent on meals away from home. This varied dramatically depending on my earnings, though: As a farmworker I spent more than a quarter of my earnings on food, while as a restaurant worker I was spending half as much.

I earned the least as a farmworker but spent the most on food. New to economizing on my meals and incredibly hungry besides, I spent more than $7 a day feeding myself, above the national average per person. By the time I'd moved into work at Applebee's, food ran me less than $5 a day.

		AVERAGE	FARMING	SELLING	COOKING
FOOD SPENDING AS SHARE OF INCOME	Food as % Income	18.74%	25.57%	17.23%	13.43%
	% Food, At Home	10.22%	11.76%	11.25%	7.65%
	% Food, Out	8.52%	13.81%	5.98%	5.79%
DAILY SPENDING	Food Budget, Single Adult	$4.74	$7.44	$5.44	$4.74
WEEKLY INCOME AND SPENDING	Income	$223.85	$203.62	$220.91	$247.03
	Food Spending	$41.10	$52.06	$38.06	$33.19
ANNUAL INCOME AND SPENDING	Income	$11,640.25	$10,588.07	$11,487.26	$12,845.41
	Food Spending	$2,137.35	$2,706.97	$1,979.32	$1,725.76

NOTES

Daily food budget based on average spending on food for duration of project; weekly income based on weeks actually worked; weekly food spending based on actual expenditures; annual income and food spendings are projections, based on weekly figures projected for 52 weeks; food as share of income, and spending at home and out, based on weekly figures.

WHAT AMERICANS SPEND ON FOOD

Although the average American household spends about 11 percent of their income on food, the numbers break down very differently depending on income.

Take the 10 percent of American households earning between $10,000 and $15,000 a year. They spend 36 percent of their income on food. Meanwhile, the richest families—the top 10 percent, who earn $70,000 a year or more—spend just 9 percent of their income on food.

		AVERAGE	$10k-$14,999	$40,000-$49,000	$70,000+
FOOD SPENDING AS SHARE OF INCOME	Food as % Income	10.62%	35.84%	13.44%	8.90%
	% Food, At Home	6.21%	29.55%	8.96%	4.88%
	% At Home, Fruits and Vegetables	16.65%	14.56%	16.35%	16.89%
	% Food, Out	4.41%	6.29%	4.48%	4.02%
DAILY SPENDING	Food Budget, Household of 4	$24.50	$13.88	$16.84	$24.50
	Food Budget, per Person	$6.13	$3.47	$4.21	$6.13
WEEKLY INCOME AND SPENDING	Income	$1,620.13	$271.81	$879.67	$2,453.00
	Food Spending	$171.98	$97.42	$118.23	$218.42
ANNUAL INCOME AND SPENDING	Income	$84,247.00	$14,134.00	$45,743.00	$127,556.00
	Food Spending	$8,943.00	$5,066.00	$6,148.00	$11,358.00

NOTES

All data on income and food spending drawn from annual figures reported by the Bureau of Labor Statistics for 2009.

ever forget (or look down on) where I—or anyone else—came from. They were focused on making sure I was a good person, but I like to think that these lessons have made me into a good journalist, too. I'm eternally grateful that my dad, my stepmother, and my grandmother, Katheryn C. Weddle—who was my first teacher in the kitchen—get to see how their efforts translate into my work. I wish my mother, Charyl K. McMillan, and my other grandparents, Donald E. Weddle, John A. McMillan, and Margaret M. McMillan, had lived to see it, too. This book is dedicated to them.

CHEAP FOOD?

One of the goals of this book was to see what it took to eat well on a budget. You can see on the next two pages how my spending broke down over time in each job, and how it compares to the average spending for American families at different income levels. There is no data for the spending of single adult households at varying income levels, and I would naturally spend less as a single adult than as a parent, so the most comparable numbers are the percentages. Detailed documentation of my spending, including receipts and the like, can be found at www.americanwayofeating .com. Judged by the numbers, I faltered badly at eating economically in the beginning but got much better about it as time went on.

Take, for instance, my time in the fields, where I was spending more than one-third of my meager income on food. Unwilling to buy processed junk food, unaccustomed to weathering bouts of intense hunger, and living in shared homes where I felt uncomfortable using the kitchen, I repeatedly purchased pre-made food instead of cooking my own. I also relied heavily on the meals my landlords would share with me. On many days, I spent as much as $3, $4, even $5 on fresh sandwiches and coffee, when $1 would have gotten me something off the dollar menu at the local McDonald's. On average, I spent more than $7 a day on my meals as a farm worker, a foolish practice for someone earning $150 a week. This strategy would also have failed me in the long run, since I was digging into savings to cover the cost of these extravagant meals.

The dollar figures being tossed around above may sound unusually low to anyone who's been following the national debate over our meals. Today's conventional wisdom holds that Americans spend too little on what they eat, often bolstered by statements that Americans spend only 7 (or, some-times, 10 or 12) percent of their income on food. The lower numbers are usually drawn from estimates of Americans' average grocery bill—which represents just over half of what we spend on food overall. We spend nearly as much on meals someone else prepares for us, whether it's at a sit-down restaurant or a drive-through window. So a truly accurate picture of what we spend on food includes both at-home and away-from-home meals.

When accounting for meals at restaurants and at home, Americans spend an average of 13 percent of their income on food, but the key word here is average; spending breaks down very differently depending on how much money you earn. In 2009, households earning less than $30,000 a year spent between 21 and 36 percent of their income on food, while families earning $70,000 or more spent just 9 percent. (Interestingly, all families spend between 14 and 18 percent of their grocery budget on fruits and veg-etables, with the greatest share being spent not by the affluent but by those families earning between $15,000 and $19,999 each year.) That the rich spend less, as a proportion of income, is actually proof of a very old law in economics, Engel's law, which stipulates that as income rises, the propor-tion dedicated to food will decrease—even if the actual dollar amount rises.

That's because, as income rises, people who've established a basic diet begin to spend their money elsewhere. Even though my weekly income increased by 42 percent between the fields and Applebee's, my other expenses, particularly rent, had as well. Had I continued to spend exactly the same amount of money on my meals in New York as I had in California, food would have represented about 21 percent of my income. But in Cali-fornia, with lower income, food took up 26 percent of my budget.

Here, this reminds me of my brief exchange in Detroit with Brenda, Christina's sister. She talked about switching to Walmart for her groceries as her income dropped after a divorce, saving a quarter here and a three dimes there. Before embarking on this project, I'd have raised an eyebrow: an extra couple bucks each week? But these days, I'm right there with her.

NOTES

Most original documentation and author's calculations
can be viewed online at www.americanwayofeating.com.

INTRODUCTION: EATING IN AMERICA

2 "It is nothing of the kind." (Kingsolver 2008, 16)

4 "I love Popeye's. I love McDonald's" . . . "I've got to live my life." Unpublished reporting from Dec. 11, 2003. (B*Healthy 2003)

4 one by one, directly into her mouth. (McMillan 2004)

5 good, fresh food tends to cost more, especially in cities. A national study on pricing in poor urban communities found that grocery stores were consistently smaller and more expensive in lower-income, urban neighborhoods. Typically, stores were 2.5 times smaller in lower-income neighborhoods than in affluent ones; at smaller stores, 67 of 132 items surveyed were more expensive than those at large ones. (Fellowes 2006)

6 seventeen square feet . . . just 3 percent. In 2000, Washington Heights (zip code 10040) had a per capita income of $13,297, and in 2003 had .58 square of grocery store space per person. Soho (zip code 10014) had a per capita income of $40,820 in 2000, and 17.32 square feet of grocery store space per person three years later. (McMillan and Woodward 2004)

6 after the urban riots. For a discussion of the role of twentieth-century riots in supermarket development, see Gutman 2011a; Deutsch 2010; Sexton, Jr. 1973.

6 far more customers. For a discussion of the supermarket industry's relationship with the suburbs, see Spencer 2011; Gutman 2011a; Ortiz 2011; Andrew Smith 2004a; Sexton, Jr. 1973; Charvat 1964.

6 there wasn't anyone to deliver produce to them. For corner stores seeking to stock produce, self-supply is typically cited as the most accessible and economical option. Soft drinks and snacks such as chips are typically delivered to stores and stocked in shelves by the manufacturer, and semi-perishable goods such as muffins are typically delivered by small-scale wholesalers, but there is no equivalent for produce, a problem that has hindered efforts to boost WIC clients' consumption of fruits and vegetables. (Berkenkamp 2010; Andreyeva et al. 2011; Ashbrook et al. 2008; Gleason et al. 2011)

6 technological black hole. When New York eliminated the paper coupons and switched to electronic benefit transfer cards in 2001, farmers didn't have the technology to process them. By 2003, a few vendors at markets around the city had joined a federally funded pilot program testing wireless terminals that can process the cards. (McMillan 2004)

8 Obesity may soon outpace tobacco as the deadliest health threat in America. By 2008, the quality-adjusted life-years lost in America to obesity exceeded those lost to smoking, a first. In 1993, for example, obesity equaled roughly half the number of years of life lost

to smoking; by 2008, obesity exceeded it. (Haomiao and Lubetkin 2010)

8 **nearly two-thirds of Americans are overweight or obese.** From 1987 to 2007, the fraction of adults who were overweight or obese increased from 44 percent to 63 percent; almost two-thirds of the adult population now falls into one of those categories. The share of obese adults rose from 13 percent in 1987 to 28 percent in 2007. (Congressional Budget Office 2010)

8 **cost America $75 billion per year** . . . A 2004 analysis of American medical spending in the journal *Obesity Research* showed annual US obesity-attributable medical expenditures to be $75 billion, and of those, $21.3 billion was spent in Medicaid, or twenty-eight percent of obesity spending. (Finkelstein, Fiebelkorn, and Wang 2004) In 2004, the Centers for Medicare and Medicaid reported that there were 45.8 million Americans enrolled in Medicaid, while the U.S. population stood at 293.7 million, ranking Medicaid enrollees at 15.59 percent of the U.S. population. (Ellis, Vernon K. Smith, and Rousseau 2005; U.S. Census Bureau 2004)

8 **but attitude."** (Kingsolver 2008, 31)

8 **the freshest ingredients."** (Kingsolver 2008, 127)

8 **Americans spend** . . . **the French** . . . **20 percent.** According to national surveys of domestic spending, in 2007, Americans spent 13.3 percent of their income out-of-pocket on food, while the French spent 19.6 percent. Meanwhile, Americans spent 5.7 percent out-of-pocket on health care, compared to 3.5 percent by the French; 17.6 percent on transportation compared to 14.6 percent by the French; 2.1 percent on education compared to the French's 0.8 percent; and 32.0 percent on housing compared to 31.4 percent by the French. (Author's calculations, based on Bras et al. 2009; Bureau of Labor Statistics 2009a; Pannuzi 2010)

8 **five weeks of paid vacation.** In France, parents are entitled to up to three years of paid parental leave. In addition, mothers receive 16 to 26 weeks of paid, job-protected leave around the birth of their child, and fathers eleven days. French law also requires workers receive 25 statutory vacation days each year. (Organization for Economic Cooperation and Development 2006a; Ray and Schmitt 2007)

9 **as much as 32 percent.** An *American Journal of Public Health* study found that for every additional supermarket in a census tract, black Americans consume an average of 32 percent more fruits and vegetables, while white Americans average an increase of 11 percent. (Morland 2002)

9 **spending less time preparing and eating our food.** Although social science research is just beginning to examine the link between time spent cooking and health, a recent survey of the existing literature on the topic found that Americans—and particularly low-income Americans—have been spending less time cooking and cleaning up while consuming more prepared foods and snacking more since the 1970s. Similarly, other research suggests that the less skilled we are in the kitchen, the less healthfully we eat. (Kolodinsky 2008; Guthrie, Lin, and Frazao 2002)

9 **as much as five and six times** . . . **otherwise done without.** In 2009 and 2010, the Wholesome Wave Foundation backed SNAP one-to-one matching programs at 148 farmers' markets across the country, including sites in Chicago, IL, Baltimore, MD, Providence, RI, and San Diego, CA. Introduction of the matching funds preceded increases in redemption of SNAP at every market; notably, several markets that had accepted SNAP prior to the matching funds saw increases far higher than the matching funds alone would account for. In Chicago, roughly $1100 in SNAP benefits was spent

at the 61st Street Farmers' Market in 2009; by 2010, it was up to $10,000. In Armory Park, Rhode Island, the farmers' market saw $600 in SNAP redemption in 2008; after introduction of the benefit, SNAP increased to $5,652. Additionally, among matching fund clients who responded to a survey, 73 percent said they would not have come to the market without the incentive program. (Wholesome Wave 2010).

9–10 "the climate requires indispensably a free use of vegetable food . . . inexcusable." (Foley 1900, 904) For a further discussion of Jefferson's thoughts on agriculture, see *The Founding Gardeners.* (Wulf 2011)

10 aptly dubbed this the "paradox of plenty." (Levenstein 1993, 237–53)

10 across the globe. For an excellent, detailed look at the spread of this American paradox, see *Stuffed and Starved.* (Patel 2008, 1–19)

10 deposited there by our aid programs, our philanthropists, and international institutions. In the 1960s, America's "Green Revolution" technologies, using high-yield hybridized seed and fertilizers developed by American companies, were introduced to Africa with support from the Ford and Rockefeller Foundations. (Hazell 2009)

10 Walmart . . . isn't only the largest grocer in the United States, but in the world. In 2010, Walmart was the top grocer in the United States, representing 24 to 26 percent of all food retail sales in the country (Author's calculations, USDA Economic Research Service 2010; Walmart Stores, Inc. 2010; Euromonitor International 2011); in 2008, the most recent year for which reliable data is available, it was also the largest food retailer in the world, accounting for 6.1 percent of global food sales. (de Schutter 2010) Supermarket retailing began to spread to developing countries in the 1990s, with supermarkets rising from 10 to 20 percent of food retail to as much as 75 percent. In many countries beginning to adopt supermarkets, Walmart is a market leader, typically residing in the top three or five retailers for the country. (Balbi and Joseph 2010; Roe, Shane, and Somwaru 2005; Reardon and Berdegué 2002)

10 The American way of eating is on track to become that of the world, too. As an example, in 2008, between 60 and 70 percent of all food sales in Argentina and Brazil occurred through supermarkets. (de Schutter 2010a, 2)

11 of the $18.3 billion we allocated in 2009 for federal agricultural subsidies. According to the Environmental Working Group, the USDA spent $7.686 billion on farm commodity subsidies in the calendar year 2009. In addition to commodity subsidies, which accrue primarily to grains, the USDA spent another $5.425 billion on crop insurance; $4.030 billion on conservation; $0.244 billion on disaster subsidies; and $0.825 billion on specialty crops. Out of this total of $18.3 billion, specialty crops accounted for 4.5 percent of America's agricultural subsidies, while commodities received 42 percent. (Hamerschlag 2010)

11 more than two-thirds of the food we eat at home. In 2009, 67.1 percent of Americans' at-home food was bought at supermarkets, 18.1 percent was bought at supercenters, 8.1 percent at drug stores and other retailers, and 5.2 percent through other outlets. (USDA Economic Research Service 2011a)

11 just over 1 percent of America's groceries. "In 2009, the USDA reported that 1.1 percent of at-home food sales were made through direct marketing channels such as farmers' markets and buying shares in a farm's crop through community-supported agriculture projects. More detailed research based on 2007 data put the share lower, at 0.4 percent. (U.S. Department of Agriculture, Economic Research Service 2011a; Martinez et. al 2010)

12 next three biggest competitors combined. In 2009, American grocery sales totaled

roughly $628.6 billion, and Walmart sales $137.8 billion, giving Walmart approximately 22 percent of the U.S. grocery market, and ranking its sales well above the 15 percent market share of its next three largest competitors combined. (Author's calculations, based on Kaufman 2011; Walmart Stores, Inc. 2010) As a side note, industry groups typically rank Walmart's market share higher, between one-quarter and one-third of U.S. food sales; this reflects the use of retailers' sales from all store departments, rather than restricting for sales of supermarket and grocery merchandise.

CHAPTER 1: GRAPES

17 Most personal budgetary calculations shown here are drawn from the appendix, "Cheap Food?" All annual calculations are projected, based on my average earnings. Further documentation, including select receipts, paystubs and the like can be found on www .americanwayofeating.com.

19 **came to $10.34.** Receipts available on www.americanwayofeating.com.

23 **bear fruit for twenty-five years or more.** (Lockwood 2011)

23 **watching it rot on the vine.** In 1975, California passed a law extending union rights to farmworkers in response to pressure from the United Farmworkers. (Martin 2001) Much of the UFW's early success can be traced to the crop on which it focused, grapes. Because grapes take seven years from first planting to first harvest, and must be picked while ripe and shipped immediately, growers were especially vulnerable to strikes, since they could lose years of investment in a just a few weeks. (Ganz 2009, 111)

24 **the premiums vary, usually an incrementally higher wage along with the promise of more hours.** (Pinal 2011)

25 **a brand, I later find out, of Giumarra Vineyards.** Nature's Partner is a brand founded and run by Giumarra Vineyards in 2000. Under this label, Giumarra sells grapes grown in Chile, Mexico, and California. (Giumarra 2011) Giumarra claims itself one of the nation's largest growers of table grapes, overseeing more than 10,000 acres in the foothills of the Sierra Nevada mountains of California. (Nature's Partner 2011)

28 **about 16 percent . . . experts call marketing.** In 2008, 15.8 cents of every dollar Americans spent on food accounted for its farm value; the other 84.2 percent went to marketing. (Canning 2011)

29 **increase the average American family's produce bill by about sixteen dollars a year.** Comprehensive research on the impact of higher farm wages on consumer prices is scarce, but UC Davis agricultural economist Philip Martin explains that labor costs vary widely, from 1 or 2 cents per pound for harvesting oranges and tomatoes to 20 or 30 percent of production costs for apples and lettuce. On average, however, if farm wages were allowed to rise 40 percent, and all the costs were passed on to consumers, Martin estimates the cost to the average household at a maximum of $16 a year. (Martin 2011a) Even raising wages more broadly, rather than merely within agriculture, is unlikely to raise food prices significantly. In 2000, the USDA estimated the impact of a minimum wage hike of 50 cents an hour on food prices. This would likely have a far greater impact on food prices than raising agricultural wages in specific, since off-farm labor accounts for more than one-third of food prices. The researchers found that food prices for groceries would increase by less than 1 percent, while the price of eating out would increase by a full 1 percent. (Lee, Schluter, and O'Roark 2000)

29 **to work in the fields at all.** According to farm labor economist and expert Philip Mar-

tin, "during the summer of 1963, Congress held often emotional hearings on the need for Bracero farmworkers. Witnesses argued that Bracero workers were necessary to keep fruit and vegetable prices "reasonable" and to help the United States maintain "food security" during the Cold War. *The California Farmer* wrote that "all agree that the state will never again reach the 100,000 to 175,000 acres [of processing tomatoes] planted when there was a guaranteed supplemental labor force in the form of the bracero . . . The industry sees no hope of filling the [labor] gap in tomatoes from the domestic ranks even if competition for workers drives wages up to the average factory wage." (Martin 2007)

29 **the lettuce companies went back to paying pickers what they'd always been paying them.** Margaret Visser provides a succinct and compelling history of labor in the lettuce fields, including abandoned attempts to mechanize it. (Visser 1986, 205–214)

30 **"Every time the unions raised their flags . . . in about 13 months.** (Maconachy 2011)

30 **they would drown.** California heat stress regulations require work sites in farm fields to provide sufficient shade to accommodate one-quarter of workers present while standing, and one quart of water per hour, per worker when temperatures are 85 degrees or above. (Rosenberg 2008, Maconachy 2011)

30 **When the bracero program ended.** See James F. Thompson and Blank 2000.

30 **selecting for traits like durability and an ability to ripen well after being picked, rather than flavor.** Although processing tomatoes would surely have been bred to withstand mechanical harvesting, explains University of Florida tomato cultivation expert Harry Klee, "nobody cares because with processing tomatoes, the only thing they care about . . . is sugar . . . so yes they've bred them to be firmer to withstand the machinery and that would affect your sensory response to them, but it's irrelevant because nobody eats them that way. What's important to the flavor of a tomato are the volatile oils you perceive, and the first thing you do to a processing tomato is you boil it, and those chemicals are lost." (Klee 2011) For an excellent discussion of the tension between fresh tomatoes' flavor and industrial marketability, see Estabrook 2011, 139–152.

31 **95 percent of all farms used the new machine.** (James F. Thompson and Blank 2000)

31 **a drop of more than three-quarters.** In 1960, it took 5.3 hours to harvest a ton of tomatoes; in 1997, it took .4 hours. (Ibid.)

31 **Yet prices didn't drop nearly as much . . . saving us the other 34 cents.** Prices are expressed in 2011 dollars, as per the Bureau of Labor Statistics inflation calculator. (Author's calculations, based on USDA Economic Research Service 1970; USDA Economic Research Service 2011b) and can be found on www.americanwayofeating.com.

32 **I spend $25 . . . make about $23 . . .** On June 23, 2009, I purchased a twelve-pack of Gatorade ($7.99, plus $0.60 in returns), a twenty-four pack of Coca Cola ($8.99, $1.20 in returns) and a Sprite Fridge Pack (twelve cans, $4.99, $0.60 in returns) for $25.13 (including tax). Selling thirty-six cans of soda at $1 each, and twelve Gatorades at $1.50, would yield $54 gross and about $29 net profit. Original receipts can be seen on www .americanwayofeating.com.

CHAPTER 2: PEACHES

42 **tent communities in the hills.** Photographer David Bacon has documented the presence of farmworkers' tent communities in southern California, including expensive homes in a new development overlooking the "La Gallinita" camp, made by indigenous Mix-

tec and Zapotec farmworkers from Oaxaca, on a hillside outside Oceanside, California. (Bacon 2011)

44 **heat poses the most immediate danger.** Maria Isabel Vasquez Jimenez, 17, collapsed in a Farmington, California, vineyard on May 14, 2008, and died of heat stroke two days later. She was working for a now-closed farm labor contractor called Merced Farm Labor. The vineyard in which she was picking, owned by Bronco Winery, was one of the vineyards producing Two Buck Chuck. (Goodyear 2009)

46 **2.2 cents a pound.** On July 13, my co-sorter, Carlos, explained that each *cajón*—crate— gets you $22 for the crew, and each crate is 1,000 pounds. By that rate, we are paid 2.2 cents per pound of fruit to pick it. To see a copy of my typed reporting notes, go to www.americanwayofeating.com.

46 **ten and twelve viajes a day.** On July 14, I noted that we had completed twelve *viajes* that day. To read a transcript of my reporting notes, visit www.americanwayofeating.com.

48 **to fill one and a half.** On July 16, I noted that it took us from 10:00 a.m. to 1:30 p.m. to fill one and a half trailer loads of peaches. To read a transcript of my reporting notes, go to www.americanwayofeating.com. (McMillan 2009)

50 **"water has exactly the value of blood."** (DeVoto 1951, 73)

51 **Meadows of wildflowers . . . than forty feet.** In early California, wrote Mark Arax and Rick Wartzman, "Tulare Lake was the most dominant feature on the California map, an immense sheet of water that extended out over the desert for 800 square miles . . . The oyster-shaped inland sea was so shallow, two or three feet deep in many parts and never more than forty feet at its deepest, that a fierce northwest wind would whistle through the reeds and blow the water another mile or two across the savannah." (Arax and Wartzman 2003, 46)

51 **the soil . . . organic matter is below .75 percent.** According to USDA data, the field in which I sorted peaches consisted of Delhi sand (6.7 percent), Delhi loamy sand (34.8 percent), Hesperia sandy loam (27.6 percent) and Hesperia fine sandy loam (30.9 percent). The soil organic matter was less than .75 percent. (National Cooperative Soil Survey 1997, USDA Natural Resources Conservation Service 2011)

51 **less than the 1 to 2 percent. . . .** The .75 percent soil organic matter in the fields I worked would typically be problematic for food cultivation, explained Jonathan Hempel, director of the National Soil Survey Center, a division of the USDA's Natural Resources Conservation Service. "You have to regionalize and say that a decent organic matter content in desert or arid soil is 1 to 2 percent; in the prairie, it's 3 to 5 percent; in the timbered east, it's probably 1 to 3 percent," he told me, That said, added Hempel, "at the minimum you want 3 percent, and if you want to talk about a healthy soil, you want to be up around 5." (Hempel 2011a)

51 **not a drop of water . . .** In 2009, California's climate division 5 (San Joaquin Valley) got .82 inches of rain in May; one one-hundredth of an inch in June and July; and no rain at all in August and September. (Stephens 2011)

51 **full third of its farmland.** In 2007, California farm land constituted 34.2 percent of all farmed land in the United States and 51.7 percent of all irrigated farm land. (National Agricultural Statistics Service 2007) Calculations available at www.americanwayofeating.com.

51 **one way to accomplish that Herculean feat: irrigation.** When I asked soil quality experts what the likely productivity of the Central Valley would be without irrigation and fertilizers, the rough estimate—offhand, nonscientific—was one-quarter. (Hempel 2011b)

51 **The initial efforts . . .** I'm referring primarily to settlers coming from the east in the nineteenth century. Missionaries in California did practice small-scale agriculture, par-

ticularly viticulture (grape growing) prior to the wave of settlement that came in the nineteenth century. (Arax and Wartzman 2003, 48)

51 "subsidized monopolization of California." (Didion 2003)

51 California outpaced the Midwestern bread basket. In the nineteenth century, writes the journalist Mark Arax, "the acres devoted to grain production kept increasing through the 1870s and '80s until California led the nation in wheat production—57,420,188 bushes by 1884." (Arax and Wartzman 2003, 76)

51 "bonanza farms" In his seminal account of California farms in the 1930s, the writer Carey McWilliams noted that "William Godwin Moody, visiting the State at the time, wrote an interesting piece called 'Bonanza Farms,' which, in the title, aptly describes the great wheat ranches." (Carey McWilliams 1935)

52 are for the long haul. For a primer on the economics of farming and water in contemporary California, see the series on California agriculture from Grist.org, California Dreaming. (Jenkins 2011)

52 Peaches . . . more than three acre-feet of water a year. Interview with Maxwell Norton, farm advisor, UC-Davis and Merced County Cooperative Extension. (Norton 2011)

53 a hundred thousand acres now lie fallow. The Westlands Water District is an icon of California water battles, constituting one of the largest irrigated agricultural districts in the nation. In the mid 2000s, the district fallowed its land after water dried up, productivity climbed, and salinity rose. (Westlands Water District 2001; Jenkins 2011; Editorial Writer Desk 2001; di Croce 2011)

53 the consequences of irrigation . . . Mesopotamia became "a backwater." For an excellent discussion of Mesopotamian agriculture and irrigation's role in its demise, both *Dirt: The Erosion of Civilizations* by earth scientist David Montgomery, and *Out of the Earth: Civilization and the Life of the Soil* by environmental scientist Daniel Hillel, are instructive. (Montgomery 2008; Hillel 1991)

54 one-quarter of America's food . . . (Gonzales and McChesney 2011)

54 The Central Valley's grand bounty . . . List of produce grown in Central Valley taken from California Agricultural Resource Directory. (California Department of Food and Agriculture 2010)

CHAPTER 3: CUTTING GARLIC

60 union office up the highway. The foreman was most likely referring to a processing plant for Dole in Soledad, on North Sunborne Road, where 90 percent of the employees are represented by Teamsters Local 890. (Diaz 2011)

61 $300, with six weeks left to go. By my third week, after spending $300 on rent to stay with Dolores and José, the remaining balance in my "start-up fund" was $287.28. Receipts and other primary source material can be found on www.americanwayofeating .com.

62 one morning of *limpiando*. On July 27, 2009, I spent five hours weeding beans and chiles for Dominguez Farms, a labor contractor based in Greenfield, where I was paid minimum wage. Copies of my pay stub and other primary materials can be viewed at www.americanwayofeating.com.

65 with much success. José G. Lopez, the owner of El Bajío Packing and G.T.O. Packing— both of which were registered as farm labor contractors with the California Department of Labor and Industrial Relations in 2009—has been successful enough to launch an

arts foundation, Casa Guanajuato, which promotes the culture of his home state of Guanajuato. In 2007, Lopez served on a delegation to a summit for successful immigrant leaders in Mexico. (Secretaría de Desarrollo Social y Humano; Guidestar 2008; California Department of Industrial Relations, 2009a-b; López 2007)

66 **ten buckets** My first *tarjeta,* dated July 30, 2009, shows that I arrived at 5:30 a.m. and left at 2:00. That day, I picked ten buckets but forgot to hand over my *tarjeta* to the company. When I explained this during work the next day, on August 1, Rosa told me she would add the rest of the day's buckets to my card from the day before. Therefore, my first *tarjeta* shows that I picked 18 buckets, while my second accounts for the buckets I had picked before explaining the situation to Rosa. *Tarjetas* and other primary source material can be found on www.americanwayofeating.com.

69 *If you're having girl problems, I feel bad for you, son; I got ninety-nine problems, but a bitch ain't one.* (Jay-Z 2003)

69 **more than one-third on rent.** From my third week in the fields (my time in Greenfield), I dedicated on average 21 percent of my spending to food, and 35 percent to rent. An itemized list of my spending while in California and other source material can be found on www .americanwayofeating.com.

72 **that information isn't printed on the check.** According to California law, all paychecks for unsalaried workers must be accompanied by an accounting of the total hours worked; the piece-rate paid; all deductions made; net wages earned; dates of the pay period; and applicable hourly rates. (California Department of Industrial Relations 2011a)

72 **comes to $54.40.** My initial paycheck, dated Aug 7, 2009, covered my first calendar week of work, from July 30 to August 1 and came from the Wells Fargo payroll account for El Bajío Packing, Inc. My paychecks and other source materials can be found on www.americanwayofeating.com.

73 **I just signed it, like all my co-workers.** According to my reporting notes, on July 31, I noticed that the *mayordomo* was wearing a safety vest that said *La Seguridad es Primera.* (McMillan 2009)

73 **three feet off the ground.** California regulations for shade in the fields require that shade structures be high enough for adults to stand under, a provision intended to discourage growers from using trucks and other heavy machinery for shade. (Marsh 2011)

73 **I'm cutting . . .** *Tarjetas* listing my productivity for each day of work can be found, along with other source materials, on www.americanwayofeating.com.

74 **My thighs . . . my right arm.** Photos of me, my hand, and my leg after my first few days in the field are available along with other source material on www.americanwayofeating .com.

75 **the numbers never match the information on their tarjetas.** On July 31, Diego showed me several pay stubs for himself and his family, each of which indicated they had worked between two and five hours when they had worked eight- and nine-hour days. My full reporting notes can be found at www.americanwayofeating.com.

75 **If Rosalinda picked . . . she'll be paid that amount minus social security and taxes.** On August 1, 2009, Diego showed me several of his paychecks and those for Rosalinda. One check covered three days, during which he had worked roughly twenty-six hours and picked thirty-nine buckets. Minimum wage would have yielded around $208, and piece rate would yield $49.60; his check was for about $65, the equivalent of about eight hours of minimum wage. The same befuddling math was at work on Rosalinda's checks, too, where she had worked for two days, filling twelve buckets; her check paid her $19, and clocked her hours at slightly over two. Full reporting notes can be found at www

.americanwayofeating.com.

75 **The Garlic Company and Christopher Ranch . . .** Photos documenting the companies I worked for, and conditions in the field, can be found on www.americanwayofeating .com.

76 **hired their own harvest company.** Both Christopher Ranch and the Garlic Company contract with Rava Ranch to grow garlic to their specifications in the Salinas Valley, and then hire a separate labor contractor to conduct hand-harvesting. (Layous 2011; Codiga 2011)

76 **the state's 1,200 labor contractors.** As of August 3, 1011, there were 1,227 farm labor contractors registered in the state of California. (California Department of Industrial Relations 2011b)

76 **not working in an area known for garlic.** In 2009, garlic production in California provided nearly all of the garlic grown in the United States. Of the 22,230 acres of garlic harvested that year, 20,900 were in California, accounting for 97.5 percent of the value of garlic grown in the U.S. that year. (California Department of Food and Agriculture 2010)

76 **about eighty miles north.** The distance between the location of the Bella Vista ranch and Gilroy is 81.5 miles. (Google Maps 2011b)

76 **half of the fresh garlic we eat comes from American farms, with the balance coming from abroad—and most of it from China.** In 1998, American fresh-market production accounted for just over 81 percent of U.S. consumption, imports represented 19 percent, with Chinese garlic at just over one-tenth of 1 percent. By 2010, Chinese imports to the United States were at 270 times their volume in 1998. That year, roughly 49 percent of fresh garlic sold in the United States came from U.S. farms. The same year, Chinese imports accounted for 41 percent overall, with other imports making up the last 10 percent of the market. (Author's calculations, based on National Agricultural Statistics Service 2009a; Foreign Agricultural Service 2010; Foreign Agricultural Service 2011; National Agricultural Statistics Service 2011)

76 **imports from China accounted for less than 1 percent of it.** In 1998, China exported 255 tons of garlic to America. That year, Americans consumed about 192,986 tons of fresh garlic. (Ibid.)

76 **80 percent of the fresh garlic . . .** Based on rough estimates of America's production of fresh, rather than processed, garlic, the United States grew 156,648 tons of fresh garlic in 1998, and 78,771 tons of it in 2010. Over the same period, imports more than doubled, increasing by 82,000 tons—69,000 of which came from China. (Ibid.)

76 **a flat bald spot instead.** American garlic is typically sold with root hairs still at the base; Chinese garlic is cleanly shaven of its roots. (Cline 2007)

76 **plant fields on a grand scale that would never make sense anywhere else in America.** Notes on logic of industrial garlic drawn from interview with John Duffus, The Garlic Company. (Ehn 2011; Duffus 2011)

76 **five packer-shippers.** The five major packer-shippers of American fresh garlic are Sequoia Packing, Harris Fresh, The Garlic Company, George Chiala, and Christopher Ranch; all but Christopher Ranch have extensive dehydration operations in addition to their fresh garlic processing. (Duffus 2011; Ehn 2011)

77 **other half of America's garlic.** There are no numbers available for the share of the U.S. harvest that went to processing for 2009, but in 2007, U.S. farms harvested 26,172 acres of garlic; 14,285 for processing (54.5 percent) and 11,887 fresh (45.5 percent). In 2002, the United States harvested 32,398 acres of garlic; 13,058 for processing (40 percent). In 1997, the United States harvested 33,842 acres of garlic, but there's no indica-

tion of how much went for processing. (National Agricultural Statistics Service 2009a)

77 **grow and harvest it themselves.** Christopher Ranch emphasizes the family roots of its farm in its marketing materials, and the founding farmer's pioneer background; The Garlic Company emphasizes the firm's roots in the south Central Valley and hence their proximity to their fields. (Christopher Ranch 2011; The Garlic Company 2011)

77 **The Garlic Company prides itself . . .** On The Garlic Company's website, the company explains the superiority of its product by appealing to consumers' concerns that an agribusiness may not know much about the food it is selling: "This closeness to the fields gives us better oversight over every aspect of garlic production, from the first planting to harvest, storage, and processing. We're one of the few garlic companies that actually controls everything, from field to shelf." (The Garlic Company 2011)

CHAPTER 4: GLEANING GARLIC

79 **thirty-one acres of land.** According to county agricultural maps, the field we were picking in, part of the Bella Vista Ranch in San Lucas, California, was 30.7 acres. (Monterey County Agricultural Commission 2009b)

80 **thirty miles.** From my house in Greenfield to the field we picked at just outside San Ardo, it is 32.4 miles. (Google Maps 2011a)

80 **"leave them for the poor and the stranger."** (Leviticus 19:9–10, KJV)

81 **forty-two** *cajones.* On August 5 and 6, I noted that when the "double-trailered semi leaves, it is carting four dozen *cajones*, stacked with a double row of five on each trailer, with the two extras place firmly in the center of the top row." Photographs from the field confirm that crates are typically stacked two high, with the extras on top, giving a total of forty-two, rather than the four dozen I indicate in my notes. (McMillan 2009) Original reporting notes can be found on www.americanwayofeating.com.

81 **in this case, The Garlic Company.** (Ibid.)

82 **where more than half of American garlic ends up.** In 2007, a total of 22,177 acres of garlic were grown in California, accounting for 84.8 percent of all American garlic, nationwide 54.6 percent went to processing, while approximately 56 percent of California did. (Author's calculations, based on National Agricultural Statistics Service 2009a)

82 **$51.20 per hundredweight . . . it cost to fill them at minimum wage.** In 2009, the USDA reported that the average price of a cwt (hundredweight) of fresh garlic grown in California was $51.20. Our twelve buckets would yield about 300 pounds, for a market price of $153.60, while paying four workers for eight hours at minimum wage would cost $256, meaning that it cost more to harvest the garlic than the farmer will earn selling it. (National Agricultural Statistics Service 2011)

82 **netted sleeves of heads from . . . go for $1,104.** In my first days at a Walmart outside of Detroit, I later see loose heads of Garlic Company garlic sold in Walmart for $3.38 per pound. In Greenfield, I noted that the La Princesa market sold five-head sleeves, a little less than a pound, from Christopher Ranch garlic for $1.99. (McMillan 2010c; McMillan 2009)

82 **but spending $824.89.** Figures here represent spending from my fourth through seventh weeks in the fields, as well as a month's rent paid in week three. Income includes all earnings from garlic, as well as my final check from peaches. All documentation of spending can be found at www.americanwayofeating.com. (McMillan 2011)

83 **wage after taxes.** Fifty forty-hour weeks paid at $8 an hour would yield a gross income

of $16,640. Discounting California and federal income taxes would adjust that income to $13,476—or a monthly income of $1,124. (McMillan 2011)

83 **55 percent of my grocery budget . . . $44.93 a week.** During my first four full weeks in Greenfield, my food spending was $38.39, $46.56, $36.40 and $59.66, a total of $181.11, for an average of $45.28. (McMillan 2011)

85 **a two-quart jar of half-sour pickles** My original notes from the food drop can be found on www.americanwayofeating.com.

88 **seventeen buckets of garlic.** To see my *tarjetas* and paychecks from the fields, go to www.americanwayofeating.com.

90 **lettering with "Christopher."** Photos of the fields I picked in, along with other source materials, can be viewed at www.americanwayofeating.com.

90 **There's a big semi . . . club stores like Costco.** Discussion of factory process for garlic industry taken from interviews with representatives from the Garlic and Onion Research Advisory Board, The Garlic Company, and USDA Cooperative Extension of Monterey County in California. (Richard Smith 2011; Ehn 2011; Duffus 2011)

91 **85 percent of the food we buy.** In 2009, 67.1 percent of Americans' grocery spending was at traditional food retailers, and 18.1 percent was done through supercenters and warehouses. (USDA Economic Research Service 2011a)

91 **any repetitive grasping.** Paperwork related to the original diagnoses and subsequent visits can be found on www.americanwayofeating.com.

95 **Every day I cut garlic . . .** My third paycheck totaled $154.40. One day of that work was gathering, paid at minimum wage. I worked 8.5 hours on each of the four other days, and was paid a total of $94.40. On August 10, I was paid $22.40 for picking fourteen buckets; the check said I worked for 2.5 hours. On August 11, I was paid $25.60 for picking sixteen buckets; the check said I was present for three hours. On August 12, I was paid $27.20 for picking seventeen buckets; the check said I worked for three hours. And on August 13, I was paid $19.20 for twelve buckets; the check said I worked for two hours. My paychecks and *tarjetas* can be viewed at www.americanwayofeating.com.

96 **the average fine levied against companies that cheat farmworkers.** From 2000 to 2008, the average fine for a violating the Agricultural Worker Protection Act was $342, about a third of the maximum penalty available. On average, violators pay about 75 percent of fines, due to both compromises by enforcement agencies and a lack of enforcement. (Goldstein, Howe, and Tamir 2010)

96 **"the exploding Pinto theory of labor management."** (Heller 2011)

CHAPTER 5: GROCERY

101 **top ten states for fruit and vegetable production.** Michigan is ranked tenth for fresh produce and floral production, employing 5,028 people with wages of $114,688,291 and generating sales of $718,952,057. (Means 2009)

101 **I knew it was bad before coming here . . .** In 2009, Michigan had the highest average unemployment rate in the country, at 13.5 percent, followed by Nevada, which posted an unemployment rate of 12.5 percent for the year. (Bureau of Labor Statistics 2009b)

103 **founded the company in 1962.** (Walmart Stores, Inc. 2011a)

104 **Their first supercenter . . . to claim the top spot.** Walmart opened its first supercenter, a grocery store combined with the discount warehouse retail store, in 1988. (Walmart

Stores, Inc. 2011) In January 2001, Supermarket News, a trade publication for supermarkets and supercenters, reported that Walmart had become the nation's largest food retailer, a fact then-CEO of Walmart, Lee Scott, heralded in the company's 2001 annual report. (Merrefield 2000; Supermarket News 2001; Walmart Stores, Inc. 2001)

104 **half the company's sales.** In fiscal year 2011, Walmart reported that 54 percent of its $260.3 billion in sales at its U.S. stores, and 55 percent of its $49.5 billion in sales at Sam's Clubs, came in grocery. (Walmart Stores, Inc. 2010b)

104 **sell 22 percent of all groceries in America.** Calculating grocery market share can be tricky, and depends on whether a company's sales of nongrocery items (like Walmart's extensive electronics section) are included. Some industry publications, such as Supermarket News, choose this route, which overstates the company's role as a grocer. Other industry publications, like Progressive Grocer, are more selective, weeding out electronics and other general merchandise with the use of private data. Here, I've chosen to use publicly available information—Walmart's annual reports, and the USDA's estimate of all food retail sales in 2009—and to select for grocery sales only. The company's annual report filed with the Securities and Exchange Commission puts Walmart's FY2010 (calendar year 2009) overall sales at its U.S. stores at $259.9 billion with 53 percent of sales coming from grocery, giving their supercenters annual grocery sales of $137.8 billion. The USDA puts all food retail sales for 2009 at about $629.6 billion, giving Walmart a market share of 22 percent. (Author's calculations, based on Walmart Stores, Inc. 1998; Kaufman 2011; USDA Economic Research Service 2010; Euromonitor International 2011)

104 **next *three* largest grocers, who accounted for 11 percent of all grocery sales in 2009.** In 2009, the top four supermarket chains in the United States accounted for 37.0 percent of grocery sales. If Walmart accounted for 26.1 percent, that leaves the next three stores with 10.9 percent of sales. (Ibid.)

104 **had been there before.** From the mid-1990s to the early 2000s, twenty-nine supermarket chains declared bankruptcy; Walmart was the catalyst for twenty-five. (Fishman 2006)

104 **world's first supermarket.** There is some dispute over whether King Kullen was the first "supermarket." Today, King Kullen is recognized as the first supermarket by the Smithsonian Institution, and founder Cullen's marketing model is closest to that used by modern markets. However, Clarence Saunder's Piggly Wiggly introduced the self serve format in 1916. For a discussion of the history of King Kullen and its role in the formation of the American supermarket industry, *The Super Market* by M.M. Zimmerman is an authoritative text. (Zimmerman 1955)

105 **parceling out goods from bulk.** Cullen's model had significantly lower operating costs than traditional stores. In a letter to George Hartford of A&P in 1934, he urged the company to adopt his model for its lower cost: "In other words, it is costing you seven percent to wait on this customer, and how do you expect to live when a super market can do exactly the same work for four percent." (Cullen 1934)

105 **"high-priced houses of bondage"** ... **"a riot" at his doors.** In a letter outlining his marketing vision to a Kroger vice-president in 1930, Cullen wrote, "When I come out with a two-page ad and advertise 300 items at cost and 200 items at practically cost, which would probably be all the advertising that I would ever have to do, the public, regardless of their present feeling toward Chain Stores, because in reality I would not be a Chain Store, would break my front doors down to get in. It would be a riot. I would have to call out the police and let the public in so many at a time. I would lead the public out of the high priced houses of bondage into the low prices of the house of the promised land." (Cullen 1930 in Zimmerman 1964)

105 **a few household items.** Cullen's initial proposal to Kroger involved a business model centered on $12,500 a week in sales ($163,216 in 2010), with 68 percent of that slated to come from dry grocery, 12 percent from produce, and 20 percent from meats. (Ibid.)

106 **hydrogenated fats . . . invented by the French.** Hydrogenated oil was invented in 1905 by Paul Sabatier, a French chemist who won the Nobel Prize in chemistry for his discovery that nickel and platinum were good catalysts for hydrogenation. (Ettlinger 2007, 99–100)

106 **its capacity to extend shelf life.** For a discussion of the preservative properties of corn syrup, see (Ettlinger 2007, 64)

106 **a sore spot for many customers.** Historian Tracey Deutsch provides an interesting angle on the appeal of self-service stores, pointing out that the absence of clerks in supermarkets was considered a selling point in their early years. In addition to the convenience of avoiding a clerk, it also made it easier and more comfortable for, say, African Americans to shop in stores where they might encounter racism, or for women to avoid having their shopping preferences discussed by neighbors. Business historian Richard Tedlow provides a helpful discussion of clerks' traditional role: not to serve, but to sell. (Deutsch 2010, 50–55; Tedlow 1996, 230)

107 **enabling the retailer to compete against other manufacturers.** In 1930, A&P ran seventy private food manufacturing plants, including coffee-roasting, bakeries, food factories, creameries, and a salmon cannery, for which it operated its own fishing fleet. (Tedlow 1996, 213)

107 **variety of sellers.** In 1918, more than half of the American cities with populations over 30,000 maintained municipal markets. Of the two hundred thirty-seven markets scattered throughout these cities, one hundred seventy-four were retail, fourteen wholesale, and forty-nine a mix of the two; sixty-seven of them had been founded since 1914. (Goodwin 1929, 27–28, in Tedlow 1996, 188)

107 **in turn sold to more peddlers.** Food historian Harvey Levenstein provides an authoritative discussion of food distribution in the early twentieth century across America; American historian Tracey Deutsch provides a closer look at the distribution system in place in Chicago during the same period. (Levenstein 1988, 42; Deutsch 2010, 13)

107 **still sold in neighborhood butcher shops.** In the early twentieth century, even A&Ps lacked self-service and meat counters; meat was sold only by neighborhood butchers. (Tedlow 1996, 42)

107 **seven cents elsewhere.** A *Businessweek* article on the rise of "cheapy" food stores in the American east compared prices at King Kullen to other stores, finding that ten-cent drug items at most stores could be bought in Cullen's store for 9 cents; tomato soup that cost 7 cents at most stores would cost 4 cents at King Kullen; and general electric vacuum cleaners going for $35 in most stores would ring up at $11.94 at King Kullen. (*Businessweek* staff 1933, 11, in Charvat 1964, 18) Similarly, early circulars from King Kullen show produce prices that are markedly lower than those advertised at A&P. At King Kullen, six pounds of sweet potatoes cost 10 cents, while just two pounds would cost 15 cents at A&P; ten pounds of potatoes from Kullen cost 15 cents, while five pounds at A&P cost 10 cents; and three heads of lettuce would run a customer 10 cents at Kullen, while one head would cost 5 cents at A&P. (King Kullen 1930 in Audacity 1997, 16; A&P 1930, 15)

107 **underselling every grocer in town . . . legislation to shut him down.** In the early 1930s, the New Jersey Assembly introduced a bill to outlaw selling at or below cost, and in 1933 the U.S. Senate resolved to investigate supermarkets. (Zimmerman 1964, 52) By

then, Cullen was not the only retailer experimenting with his brand of retail, spurring legislators to examine the issue. In New Jersey, for example, the store Big Bear pursued a similar model with much success, and large food retail had cropped up in California as well. (Tedlow 1996, 240)

107 **forty-five stores.** In June 2011, King Kullen listed forty-five locations throughout New York City and Long Island. (King Kullen 2011)

108 **positioning the company as a leader in grocery.** As early as 2001, Walmart executives were prioritizing grocery as one of the company's strategic growth areas, and the segment has seen fairly consistent growth even as the retailer's overall sales fell. In 1998, the company sold so little in grocery that it did not even mention the category in its annual report; by 2011 it represented more than half of Walmart's U.S. sales. (Zwiebach 2001; Walmart Stores, Inc. 2010b, 8, 12)

109 **have to price every single thing.** In March 2011, the Michigan Legislature passed the Shopping Reform and Modernization Act, effective September 2011, which relieved retailers of the requirement that all items for sale in a store must bear a price tag. (Office of the Attorney General 2011)

111 **Cold breakfast cereal . . .** During the late 1880s and 1890s, a number of independent manufacturers experimented with ready-to-eat breakfast cereals, one step removed from "granula," a nugget-like grain product invented at a sanatorium in upstate New York that was too hard to chew unless it soaked in liquid for at least twenty minutes. The Kelloggs built on this to develop granola and then flaked cereals, founding the Kellogg Corn Flake Company in Battle Creek, Michigan in 1906. (Progressive Grocer 1999, 25; Santlofer 2004, 200)

114 **my first two weeks of grocery shopping.** Notes and receipts from my grocery shopping in Kalamazoo can be found on www.americanwayofeating.com.

115 **"planning ahead is a measure of class."** "Planning ahead is a measure of class," wrote Gloria Steinem in 1980. "The rich and even the middle class plan for future generations, but the poor can plan ahead only a few weeks or days." (Steinem 1980, cited in; Steinem 1995)

116 **gap between grocery bills and paychecks.** In a 2008 survey, thirty-seven percent of low- and middle-income households surveyed used credit cards to cover basic living expenses such as rent, mortgages groceries, utilities and insurance. The average credit card debt held by families earning less than $35,000 in 2005 was $7,170. (García and Draut 2009, 4, 7)

117 **In King Kullen's early days . . .** Michael Cullen outlined this pricing structure—selling 300 items at cost, 200 at 5 percent markup, 300 at 15 percent markup and another 300 at 20 percent markup—in his original letter pitching the model to a vice-president at the Kroger Grocery and Baking Company. (Zimmerman 1964, 44–45)

117 **—for sake of argument—** Specific pricing data is considered proprietary within the supermarket industry; as such, these are hypothesized prices chosen to illustrate a point and do not reflect actual profit data. "Nobody will give you the numbers," said John Stanton, a professor of food marketing at Saint Joseph's University. "In the business it's almost top secret . . . 'best left unspoken' is the motto." (Stanton 2011)

117 **low prices will lead people into the store.** While there is no definitive history of the use of loss leading in food, there is no discussion of it prior to King Kullen. For a more detailed look at the use of mass marketing and loss leading techniques within the grocery industry, see Ellickson 2007; Tedlow 1996, 182–258; Zimmerman 1955; Zimmerman 1964.

117 **A typical supermarket sells . . .** Supermarkets typically carry anywhere from 15,000 to

60,000 stock-keeping units, or SKUs, depending on the size of the store; the national average is 38,718. Stores may offer a service deli, a service bakery, and/or a pharmacy. By comparison, in 2011, Walmart supercenters averaged 142,000 items. (Food Marketing Institute 2010; Walmart Stores, Inc. 2011d)

118 **function as what Walmart calls a trip-driver.** The lure of food, particularly produce, is well-understood at Walmart. In early 2010, less than a year before the company announced a major initiative to boost its sales of produce, the company's internal magazine explained, "Fresh is a trip-driver—it brings in customers." The same issue reported that 95 percent of people coming to Walmart come in for produce/food. (Walmart Stores 2010a, 15)

118 **tell its suppliers what price will be paid . . .** As an example: In the late 1990s, Walmart began selling gallon jars of Vlasic Pickles for $2.97, just a few dimes more than small jars of sliced pickles, and a price so low that both Vlasic and Walmart only made one or two cents per jar. Sales volume skyrocketed, but profits for Vlasic dropped by 50 percent. At the same time, a crippling share of Vlasic's business now depended on selling through Walmart; terminating the relationship would have imperiled the company financially. (Fishman 2006, 79–83)

118 **economists call it a monopsony.** A specific analysis of Walmart within the context of monopsony can be found in (Fishman 2006, 83).

118 **"so large that it can defy the laws of supply, demand, and competition."** (Fishman 2006, 82)

118 **they're transportation and distribution systems, too.** In 2009, an OECD panel on global investment and concentration in the food industry explained that "Today, retailers act as sellers who sell their services to suppliers, who are obliged to buy these services if they want to sell their products to retailers." (Konig 2009, 4)

118 **". . . replicates the power once enjoyed by our nation's biggest railroads."** (Lynn 2010, 70)

118 **the five biggest chains alone sold more than half of the produce in America.** In 2005, the top five grocers sold fifty-two percent of produce in the United States, up from twenty-six percent in 1995. (Produce Marketing Association 2008, 1)

118 **probably around one-quarter.** Walmart doesn't report its sales figures publicly, but in 2010 its annual report indicated that grocery sales at its U.S. Stores totaled $137.8 billion. Taking into account that the average American family's grocery budget allocated 10.7 percent to fresh fruits and vegetables, that gives a rough estimate of $14.7 billion in produce sales. (Walmart Stores, Inc. 2010b)

118 **produce consumed by 26.3 million American families each year.** In 2009, the average four-person family spent $560 a year on fresh fruits and vegetables. Given the estimate of Walmart's annual produce sales at $14.7 billion, that means 26.3 million American families could be fed through Walmart's produce section. Extrapolated out to the number of Americans, not just families, 105.3 million Americans eat from Walmart's produce section. (Author's calculations, based on Bureau of Labor Statistics 2009a; Walmart Stores, Inc. 2010b; Chanil and Major 2010)

118 *five hundred* **largest cities.** In 2010, the cumulative population of America's 500 largest cities was 103,650,679.(Author's calculations, based on U.S. Census Bureau 2011)

119 **throng of women.** An early King Kullen circular, done in the style of a tabloid paper and undated, was reprinted in (King Kullen 1930 in Audacity 1997)

120 **collective gross income well into the billions.** Apart from indicating that "the majority" of its associates work full-time, and that the average wage of full-time associates in 2009 was $11.24, Walmart does not release information as to the specifics of its workforce. If

60 percent of its workforce of 1,454,599 worked full-time at 34 hours a week, full-time associates alone would collectively earn $16.7 billion. (Author's calculations, based on Walmart Stores, Inc. 2009)

121 **drive the thirty miles . . .** The distance from my home in Kalamazoo to Decatur, MI, where the Christmas party at the potato farm was held, is 29.9 miles. (Google Maps 2011a)

125 **in the low twenties.** The snowstorm hit Kalamazoo from the night of December 9 through the night of December 10; the high temperature on December 11 was 22.5 degrees, the low 9. (Weather Underground 2009)

125 **two feet of snow.** From December 9, 2009, to December 11, between twelve and sixteen inches of snow fell across much of southwestern Michigan. (National Weather Service 2009)

126 **spend nearly 40 percent.** Households in my income bracket of $10,000–$14,999 a year spend roughly 39.8 percent of their income on food; there are no statistics available for single adults arranged by income class. (Bureau of Labor Statistics 2011a, Table 1)

126 **$408 a month.** The income cut-off for single adults to receive Medicaid in Michigan ranges from $341 to $408 a month. (Rosso 2011)

CHAPTER 6: PRODUCE 101

129 **"you still have to eat."** (Ciezadlo 2011, 8)

129 **its population of 714,000.** The 2010 Census put Detroit's population at 713,777, considerably lower than population estimates from both private market sources and the public American Community Survey, which put the city's 2009 population between 850,000 and 913,000. Like their counterparts in New York City, Detroit officials announced plans in early 2011 to contest the census count. (U.S. Census Bureau 2005a; Social Compact 2010, 8; Seelye 2011; Wattrick 2011a)

129 **closing up shop as the city's economic prospects fell.** (Joel J. Smith and Hurst 2007)

130 **make do with about half.** In 2010, Detroit had 1.59 square feet of grocery store space per resident, while supermarket industry executives typically seek to achieve three square feet per resident in a market. (Social Compact 2011)

130 **New Orleans and Washington, D.C. . . . 25 percent.** In 2008, researchers found New Orleans residents to have 2.09 square feet of grocery store space per resident. In 2010, analysis of Washington, D.C.'s food environment found residents to have 2.11 square feet per person. (Social Compact 2008; Social Compact 2010b)

130 **"fringe" retailers.** A 2007 report commissioned by LaSalle Bank found that 92 percent of food stamp retailers in Detroit are "fringe" retailers, while 8 percent are supermarkets; the study did not provide numbers on food stamp sales by type of store. (Mari Gallagher 2007).

130 **Every store in the food stamp program.** According to the USDA, which administers the food stamp program, food stamp retailers must carry at least three varieties of qualifying foods in each of four staple food groups, with perishable foods in at least two of the categories: meat, poultry or fish, bread or cereal, vegetables, fruits, and dairy products. (Food and Nutrition Service 2011b)

130 **WIC . . . has a more demanding grocery list to fill.** When WIC rules were revised in 2009, retailers became required to stock fruits, vegetables and whole grains in addition to the traditional array of breads, eggs, low-fat milk, and canned fish. (Food and Nutrition Service 2011a)

130 **triple the national average.** Nationally, 85 percent of SNAP benefits were redeemed at

supermarkets and supercenters in 2009, according to federal data. Convenience stores, by contrast, accounted for 4 percent of food spending among SNAP clients nationwide, while Detroit's SNAP clients patronize convenience stores more frequently, spending just over 13 percent of their food stamps there, one-third higher than in Wayne County, where Detroit is located, and more than double the state average. (Author's calculations, based on Food and Nutrition Service 2009; Pierce and Kent Wells 2011)

131 **on his itinerary.** Supermarkets, particularly during the Cold War, became a typical stop for visiting dignitaries. Chinese leader Deng Xiaoping visited a Texas supermarket on a diplomatic visit in 1979, giving rise to a flurry of Chinese media marveling at America's wealth. Soviet Premier Boris Yeltsin's visit to a Houston supermarket in 1989 is credited with spurring a fit of anger and disillusionment with the prospects for his country. (Bogert 1993; Becker 1997; Sperling 1990)

131 **estimated $200 million—nearly one-third of their grocery budgets—at suburban supermarkets.** A city-sponsored study of food access suggested unmet demand for full-service grocers totaling $200 million in the Detroit study area. Existing full-service grocers capture 69 percent of residents' expenditures, indicating that about 31 percent is spent outside the city. (Social Compact 2011)

131 **these weren't their markets or their customers.** (Cynthia Stewart 2011; Spencer 2011; Gutman 2011a; Ortiz 2011)

132 **Crime and poverty rates there were among the highest in Manhattan.** In 2000, 35.9 percent of residents in the East Harlem zip code of 10029 were poor, as were 43.7 of residents in neighboring 10035. Citywide, the poverty rate that year was 21.2 percent. Comparative crime rates, as opposed to raw numbers, are not readily available by zip code, but news accounts around the time of the Pathmark's opening confirm that crime rates in Harlem were significantly higher than elsewhere in the city. (U.S. Census Bureau 2010a, 2000b, 2000c; Siklos 1997; Kirby 1997)

132 **highest-grossing stores . . . beacon for other cities looking to replicate its success.** (Pristin 1999; Hubert 2010)

132 **"land of opportunity."** (King 1995)

132 **a bit steep for Detroit.** Median contract rent in Detroit, i.e. rent for full apartments or houses, was $534 in 2005–2009, according to the 2010 Census. Shared housing is often much lower, around $200-$300 per person plus utilities. (U.S. Census Bureau 2005a; Metzger 2011)

132 **sometimes less.** Apartment listings typically showed apartments starting around $300, with some just under that. (Anon. 2011a; Anon. 2011b; Anon. 2011c; Anon. 2011d)

132 **city that's lost nearly 1 million residents . . .** Detroit's population peaked in 1950, at 1,849,568, dropping to 710,777 in 2010, according to Census Bureau statistics. Local officials put the population higher, between 800,000 and 825,000, and in early 2011 announced plans to challenge the 2010 census count. (Bureau of the Census 1993, Table 46, pp. 593–594; Metzger 2011; Wattrick 2011a)

132 **average of 1,200 residents a month.** Based on a 2010 population of around 800,000, Detroit lost about 150,000 in 10 years, putting the decline at 15,000 per year, or about 1,200 per month. (Metzger 2011)

133 **50 percent higher than the country's as a whole.** In May 2010, Detroit's seasonally adjusted unemployment rate was 14.7 percent, and Michigan's was 13.6 percent, compared to the national rate of 9.7 percent. (Bureau of Labor Statistics 2010c; Bureau of Labor Statistics 2011b)

133 **cavernous steel plants.** For a discussion of Mexican immigration to Detroit, see (Baba

and Abonyi 1979, 50–75; Skendzel 1980, 14–15)

133 **Guzman family history.** (Guzman 2011)

133 **shuttered for years.** Four factories, now all closed, ring the southwest section of the city, stretching from the neighborhood's northern edge at Michigan Avenue and Clark, and then down along its southern edge on Fort Street heading into the next neighborhood, Delray. Just over the city line, in Dearborn, sits the River Rouge plant, once the world's largest factory, now used to build Ford pickups. (Hernandez 2011b)

135 **citywide network of food gardens . . . 80 percent returning . . . each year.** Information on the Greening of Detroit's urban agriculture efforts taken from (Atkinson 2011)

136 **Onions, potatoes, zucchini, and oranges are all *cheaper.*** In January 2011, I conducted an item-by-item comparison of a shopping list based on the USDA Food Plan (designed for clients of SNAP). Of twelve common produce items, La Colmena was cheaper on four of them. For green peppers and cantaloupe, La Colmena was within 10 percent of Walmart's price; for iceberg lettuce it was thirteen percent less; the remaining five prices were more than one-third higher than at Walmart. (Author's calculations, drawn from Hernandez 2011c; Hernandez 2011d)

136 **issue contracts to food manufacturers.** In 2010, "nearly one in every four items sold in . . . supermarkets, drug chains, and supermarkets" were private-label goods. While there are a number of ways to supply private-label products, the majority of options involve contracting with manufacturers rather than coordinating production in-house. (Private Label Manufacturer's Association 2011a; Private Label Manufacturer's Association 2011c)

136 **it was ConAgra . . . that first issued the recall, not Walmart.** (Associated Press 2007a; Associated Press 2007d)

137 **it cleans La Colmena's clock when it comes to processed foods.** In January 2011, the cost of a 29-ounce Great Value can of pears at Walmart was 99 cents, a per-ounce cost of 3.4 cents. The same month, a 15-ounce can of Dole pears at La Colmena was $1.99, a per ounce cost of 13.3 cents. (Hernandez 2011c; Hernandez 2011d)

137 **between 14 and 16 percent on price.** A 2008 Walmart-backed study found that consumers could have saved 13.81 percent overall in grocery bills by shopping at Walmart instead of competitors. This research corroborates an academic paper from 2005 showing that a market basket of 54 grocery items was priced 15.65 percent less at Walmart than at other local supermarkets, and gives a lower estimate than other research, which puts the range of price differences between traditional stores and Walmart anywhere from 5 to 48 percent, depending on the item. (Lauritano and Sangwan 2008; Volpe and Lavoie 2005; Hausman and Leibtag 2005)

137 **the produce and fresh meat.** (Lauritano and Sangwan 2008, 1)

137 **categories in which Walmart is . . . least able to compete.** A 2004 paper examining price differences between a shopping basket of 24 goods found "no obvious pattern" in pricing difference between Walmart and other food retailers, noting that there were "relatively small effects for ground beef, apples, and bananas" but significant effects for lettuce, and tomatoes. A more recent study of food prices at Walmart and competing supermarkets in New England found that the difference between prices at supercenters and conventional supermarkets was negligible in the meat department; around 11 percent for produce; 25 percent for grocery; and 35 percent for dairy. (Hausman and Leibtag 2005, 18; Volpe and Lavoie 2005, 20–21)

137 **2 or 3 percent.** Absolute price difference between Walmart and "Big Three" supermarket chains is about 2 to 3 percent, considerably lower than price difference between all

competitors, according to a 2005 study. (Basker and Noel 2007, 14–15)

138 **contracting out their own food manufacturing.** For a discussion of the benefits of bringing distribution infrastructure within the function of a company, i.e. vertical integration, see (Stiegert and Sharkey 2007; Ellickson 2006)

138 **22 percent.** As reported earlier, Walmart market share is based on author's calculations and Walmart's annual report, and should be considered more of a back-of-the-envelope calculation than pure social science. (Walmart Stores, Inc. 2010b; USDA Economic Research Service 2010; Kaufman 2011)

138 **low prices are good for everyone.** When Walmart's Senior Vice President of Sustainability Andrea Thomas appeared at a press conference with Michelle Obama in January 2011, she explained the company's interest in building stores in food deserts by saying, "But in a larger sense—by impacting the entire marketplace—we believe that our initiative can make healthy, affordable food more accessible in the nation's food deserts. The reality is that as more people start eating healthier, healthier eating becomes more affordable to all." (Thomas 2011)

138 **drop in local grocery prices of between 1 and 8 percent.** In 2005, researchers estimated that the presence of a supercenter resulted in a decrease in local grocery prices of between 6.4 and 7.8 percent; a 2007 study put the impact much lower, at between 1.0 and 1.2 percent (and half that for larger stores); and a 2011 study found that a supercenter reduced local food prices by between 2.6 and 6.0 percent. (Volpe and Lavoie 2005; Basker and Noel 2007; Courtemanche and Carden 2011)

139 **no discernible effect on local prices at all.** In examining the effect of a new supercenter on twenty-three markets over a period from 1993 to 2003, an agricultural economic study found that "the market share of supercenter food sales and the marginal impact of supercenter entry did not have a significant impact on food prices." (Stiegert and Sharkey 2007)

139 **in 2009 they accounted for 37 percent.** In 1958, the top four grocery firms accounted for 21.7 percent of the market: the top eight were 27.5 percent, and the top twenty were 34.1 percent. In 1992, the top four represented 16.8 percent of the market, the top eight were 26.4 percent, and the top twenty were 39.2 percent. That number increased steadily, with a huge jump in 1999, presumably from Walmart's new focus on grocery. By 2009, the top four represented 37 percent of the market share food retail in the United States, with the top eight commanding 49.6 percent of the market, and the top twenty representing 64.2 percent. (Kaufman 2011; Census of Retail Trade 1958)

139 **more than five million.** In twenty-nine American cities, Walmart represents 50 percent or more of grocery sales, ranging from 50 percent to 71 percent. City size ranges from 768,200 down to 75,500, and the total population of these cities combined is 5,667,000. Among the nation's one hundred largest metropolitan areas, however, Walmart typically maintains a smaller share, even in the thirteen in which it is the market leader. (Anon. 2011a; MMR 2010)

140 **not by estimating future reductions to Walmart's.** Confirmation of this calculation was drawn from a discussion with company spokesperson Lorenzo Lopez. Notably, Walmart also said they would not lower prices by pressuring its suppliers, i.e. farmers, to accept lower prices. In a press release announcing their healthy food initiative, Walmart indicated it planned to save customers approximately $1 billion per year on fresh fruits and vegetables through a variety of sourcing, pricing, and transportation and logistics initiatives that will drive unnecessary costs out of the supply chain. Executive Vice President for Corporate Affairs Leslie Dach told the *New York Times* that this would cut into prof-

its, but could be made up for by increasing sales volume. "This is not about asking the farmers to accept less for their crops," said Dach. (Gay Stolberg 2011; Lopez 2011)

140 **downward pressure on wages out.** A number of studies have linked Walmart to lower overall wages, and increased poverty rates in communities where the retailer is present, and many cities and states have considered or passed legislation designed to mitigate the retailer's impact in their communities, either by prohibiting stores of its size or, more typically, by requiring higher wages or increased spending on health insurance. (Arindrajit, Lester, and Eidlin 2007; Goetz and Swaminathan 2004; All About Cities staff 2006; Council of the District of Columbia 2007; Miller 2004; Walters 2011)

140 **"our mission of 'save money, live better.'"** Both Andrea Thomas and Bill Simon spoke at the January 20, 2011 press conference with Michelle Obama about Walmart's new healthy eating initiative. (Thomas 2011)

145 **life-support system.** The five elements of produce life support are respiration, temperature, moisture/water supply, light, and nutrients or food, according to the *Produce Operations* CBL. (McMillan 2010a, 5/20, 10:34 a.m.)

145 **made on impulse.** Seventy to 80 percent of items in produce are sold on impulse, according to the "Merchandising" segment of the *Produce Operations* CBL. (McMillan 2010a, 5/20, 11:05 a.m.)

145 **profits can be considerably higher in produce.** Profits are 1.6 times higher in produce than in other store departments, according to *Walmart World* magazine. It's unclear how this is calculated, however, and most grocers agree that *gross margins* are larger in produce—though profit varies. Margins are wider in produce because of the labor costs to manage it and the natural "shrink," i.e. waste from spoilage that occurs. A well-managed produce department, then, will be able to keep most of that margin in the store's pocket, while a poorly managed one could easily run through most of that margin. (Walmart Stores, Inc. 2010a, 15; Gutman 2011b)

146 **in arcane detail, what I am to be taught.** The handout is called "Sales Associate—Food (Fresh/Cost) Training Plan Acknowledgment," and charts out tasks that are to be learned within seven, fourteen, twenty-one and twenty-eight days of my training period. To view my training documents and other primary source material, see www.american wayofeating.com.

147 **number-one item in the section.** "Bananas are your number-one volume item," according to the Produce Operations CBL I completed during my training at Walmart. For hand-written notes and other primary source material, visit www.americanwayofeating .com.

150 **95 percent of our fruits and vegetables.** In 2006, 95 percent of American produce sales occurred in supermarkets, grocery stores, supercenters and wholesale clubs, with conventional supermarkets selling 56 percent, supercenters 20 percent, wholesale clubs 16 percent, and grocery stores 3 percent. (Means 2009, 8)

150 **roughly one of every four dollars Americans spend on fresh produce ends up at Walmart.** Walmart does not publish sales data for specific categories, and declined to answer questions for this book, so this calculation is a rough estimate. Walmart produce sales are calculated by taking its 2011 annual U.S. and Sam's Club sales of $309.7 billion, and the share of sales it attributed to grocery in each format (54 and 55 percent, respectively) to get an estimate of annual grocery sales: $167.7 billion. The average share of grocery bill dedicated to fresh fruits and vegetables in 2009 was 10.7 percent; when applied to Walmart's grocery sales, this gives us estimated produce sales at Walmart of $17.6 billion in 2009. The same year, American produce sales—excluding

Walmart, which does not report figures publicly—totaled $48 billion. Combining these two figures gives a rough estimate of national retail produce sales of $65.5 billion, with Walmart's share of that at 26.8 percent. (Author's calculations, based on Walmart Stores, Inc. 2010b; Bureau of Labor Statistics 2011a, Table 39; Chanil 2010)

150 **"we're in the distribution business."** (Lillo 2003)

150 **6.3 million [farms].** In 1930, there were 6.3 million farms at an average of 157 acres. (National Agricultural Statistics Service 1964, Tables 6, 9)

150 **half of which grew fruits and vegetables.** In 1929, the only year for which vegetable figures are available, 628,540 farms in the U.S. (10 percent of farms) harvested vegetables for sale; in 1930, 2,751,018 farms harvested fruits, nuts, grapes, or coffee for sale. Combined, these two figures put the cumulative number of farms producing fruits, vegetables, nuts, grapes, or coffee at 3,379,558—more than half of America's 6.3 million farms. (Ibid.)

150 **public markets and jobbers, small stores and wholesalers, peddlers and vegetable stalls.** A 1940 paper published by the GPO deconstructs the volume of produce moving through New York City's markets in 1936. The data show 42,000 freight cars coming from farmers' markets and130,000 coming through the Washington wholesale market—and all of their produce going through "independent retailers, fruit and vegetable stands, hucksters, pushcarts, restaurants, etc.," accounting for 70 percent of the 245,000 freight cars entering the city; the remaining 30 percent went through chain stores. (Hoffman 1940, 8 in Tedlow 1996, 196)

151 **the more things people actually bought.** Nutritionist and food industry expert Marion Nestle explains, "Supermarkets want to expose you to the largest possible number of items that you can stand to see, without annoying you so much you run screaming from the store. This strategy is based on research proving that 'the rate of exposure is directly related to the rate of sale of merchandise.' In other words, the more you see, the more you buy." (Nestle 2006, 19)

151 **as much as 60 percent on operations costs.** In the 1980s, supermarkets realized that they could afford to sell a wider array of products—and generate more sales—if they built in-house distribution networks. By 1998, 49 of the top 50 supermarket firms were operating their own distribution networks; operations costs dropped from 25 to 60 percent for firms operating self-distribution. (Kochersperger 1997 in Ellickson and Misra 2008)

152 **average American farm is 418 acres.** In 2007, the U.S. Census of agriculture reported that 125,478, or 5.69 percent, of the nation's 2,204,792 farms accounted for 75 percent of farm sales, at an average acreage of 2,216 acres. One square mile contains 640 acres, making this farm size equivalent to three and one-half square miles. The average size for all farms in the United States that year was 418 acres. (National Agricultural Statistics Service 2007, Table 40)

152 **"the small landholders are the most precious part of a state."** (Jefferson 1785 in Boyd et al. 1950 in Monticello 2011)

152 **maximum acreage per family at 160 acres.** In 1862, Abraham Lincoln signed the Homestead Act into law. It "offered settlers up to 160 acres of land for only a small fee. In return, the settlers had to live on and improve the property." (Jason Porterfield 2005, 4–8)

152 **Reclamation Reform Act in 1982.** Arax and Wartzman provide a thorough discussion of California and U.S. politics related to irrigation policy in *The King of California*. (Arax and Wartzman 2003, 194–95; 359)

154 **by 2008, private-label salads represented 15 percent of the market.** (Cook 2008)

154 **marked up 85 percent.** According to inventory documents, a case of six ten-ounce bags of chopped romaine lettuce from Dole cost Walmart $8.12, or $1.35 each, and were sold for $2.50, a markup of 85 percent. (Walmart Stores, Inc. 2010c, 1) To see images of the inventory documents and a spreadsheet charting costs, go to www.americanwayofeat ing.com.

155 **half an entire town's produce supply.** In 2011, there were three stores selling groceries and produce in Belleville: Walmart, Meijer (a regional competitor to Walmart) and Belle Foods. While sales data for each store was not available, market analysts often use square footage as shorthand for market concentration. Under that metric, Walmart and Meijer are both large, supercenter-format stores, while Belle Foods is a small market of 7,500 square feet. Thus, it is a safe ballpark estimate to assume that Walmart represents roughly half the town's produce supply. (Hernandez 2011a; Deacon 2011)

157 **the same proportion as today.** While the share of students taking home ec has remained relatively stable, the gender of those students likely has not. In 2002–03, home ec students were 37 percent male and 63 percent female. In 1959, 99 percent of secondary home ec students were female, and half of all female secondary students took home ec that year, compared to just one percent of males. (Carol Werhan and Wendy L. Way 2006)

157 **pass their knowledge on to their children.** A 2006 Betty Crocker survey of women in their twenties and forties found that while 64 percent of the twentysomethings had mothers who had worked outside the home full-time, only thirty-eight percent of the fortysomethings had. (Anthony 2006)

157 **than their mothers and grandmothers.** According to a survey done by the Consumer Research Network, in 1996, 53 percent of Americans felt they had less knowledge and fewer cooking skills than their mothers and grandmothers. (Yankelovich Partners 1996)

157 **two-thirds of eighteen- to twenty-four-year-olds said they could not fix a meal.** A Land O' Lakes survey found that only 30 percent of adults aged eighteen to twenty-four were comfortable preparing a full meal, compared 46 percent of those aged thirty-five to forty-four and nearly half of those aged fifty-five to sixty-four. (Brewstter 2007)

157 **evidence of America's waning cooking skills . . .** (Sagon 2006)

157 All price citations from Walmart are drawn from inventory documents for the produce section of the store at which I worked, and can be viewed at www.americanwayofeating .com. (Walmart Stores, Inc. 2010c)

158 **easy for such problems to spread far and wide.** The dangers of even bagged lettuce became clear in 2006, after an E. coli outbreak sickened twenty-six people in three different states, and could be traced back to the same lot of bagged lettuces. In 2010, Consumer Reports analyzed a small sample of packaged salads and found that 38 percent had unacceptable levels of bacteria that typically indicate fecal contamination. (Lea Thompson 2006; Consumer Reports 2010)

158 **about three-quarters of Americans' sodium intake.** A study of sixty-two adults, widely considered authoritative on the subject, found that 77 percent of sodium intake in the United States comes from processed foods. (Mattes and Donnelly)

158 **A box of . . . 40 percent.** Nutrition information and cooking times drawn from packaging of Hamburger Helper and a frozen bag meal from Great Value. (General Mills 2011; Great Value 2011)

159 **saving money on their grocery budget.** Cooking Matters, a national nonprofit that develops and runs low-income cooking classes with chefs and low-income parents, has tracked the results of its classes in twenty-eight cities. When their students learned to

cook, and learned how to do it on a budget, they saved money and prepared more of their food at home. As an example, a Cooking Matters class in Elmira, New York, found that 79 percent of students reported eating more healthfully; 63 percent reported saving money on food; 63 percent paid more attention to health and nutrition; and 60 percent were cooking and eating new foods more frequently after completing a class. This tracks with academic studies which suggest that people with a greater knowledge of nutrition eat a healthier mix of vegetables than people with less nutrition education. (Cooking Matters 2009; Wakerly 2007; Condrasky and Hegler 2010)

159 **more capable of planning healthy, affordable meals.** Participants in a South Carolina Cooking With A Chef program, upon being surveyed after the class, said that they felt "encouraged . . . to do more chopping" and had the "confidence to try new things and not be afraid of failing;" that the "program is helpful for figuring out how many vegetables to buy for the week" and "kids asked for a salad instead of macaroni and cheese;" and that they felt "more confident with spices." (Condrasky et al. 2010)

160 **new law passed in Arizona . . . similar one being considered in Michigan.** On June 11, 2010, State Rep. Kim Meltzer introduced "legislation to secure Michigan's borders . . . similar to what Arizona has in place." (State News Service 2010)

160 **economic downturn nearly as bad as Michigan's.** In 2009, a year when Michigan posted the highest unemployment rate in the country at 13.3 percent, California was just three states behind with an unemployment rate of 11.3 percent. (Bureau of Labor Statistics 2009c)

CHAPTER 7: PRODUCE 201

161 **pizza and beer with friends:** In spring 2010, I spent a total of $112.45 on food "out," for an average of $14.06 a week; this represented roughly one-third of my food budget. The "Food-Out" category included coffee and snacks when I was away from home and got hungry, as well as things like pizza, beer, and tacos. Going out for a meal or a drink, not just grabbing a snack, took up $70.19, or 22 percent, of my overall food budget: Tostadas with a friend on May 1 ($2.79); tacos with friends on May 2 ($5); two beers after soccer on May 3 ($7.50); a Subway Value Meal at orientation on May 18 and again on May 21 ($10.60); more Subway on May 27 ($5.30) and pizza and beer after soccer ($15); a burger and beer on June 2 ($13); tacos on June 5 ($3); and beer after soccer on June 14 ($11). Copies of most receipts, and a full accounting of my budget, can be found on www.americanwayofeating.com.

164 **corn, still in its husk, became too consumed with mold.** Photos available on www.americanwayofeating.com.

165 **can no longer be ignored.** On May 30, I arrived to find Mary doing returns on some carts piled with damages and giving off the smell of rotting produce. Mary asked me if I knew it was supposed to be done daily—it had clearly been sitting for longer than one day—and when I said yes, but I didn't know how to do it and there wasn't anyone in charge to ask, she replied, Nobody is ever in charge over here. (McMillan 2009)

165 **begin to number in the dozens.** In my last two nights, no returns were done, leading to a backlog. According to photos I took, there appeared to be at least three dozen crates left in the dry storage and back rooms. Photos available on www.americanwayofeating.com.

165 **Chilean plums and grapes through New York, Honduran melons through Miami.**

Interview with Dominic Russo, Jr. of Rocky Brother Produce. (Russo 2011)

165 **Detroit had four wholesale markets.** In 1963, the USDA performed a detailed assessment of Detroit's food infrastructure, charting out the possible need for a new produce terminal. The report identified four wholesale markets: Eastern Market, Western Market, the Union Produce Terminal, and Twelfth Street Terminal. Since then, the Twelfth Street Terminal and Western Market have closed. (Blackmore and Clowes 1963, 16–28)

165 **seen their market districts erode as property values shot up.** In late 2005, New York City's Fulton Street Fish Market moved from its 175-year home in Manhattan's rapidly redeveloping financial district to the Bronx, a shift, wrote *New York Times* columnist Dan Barry, that would remove a "barnacle to development" and hasten "the gradual transformation of the neighborhood into an Old New York outlet mall." Similarly, the New York City Terminal Market in the Bronx considered leaving New York City as it neared the expiration of its lease in 2011, due in part to operating costs; as this book went to press, it had signed a short-term lease to cover its bases while negotiating for the long-term. (Barry 2006; Semple 2008; Fickenscher 2011)

166 **nobody keeps an eye on the volume of sales.** Most of the nation's fifteen terminal markets still in operation do not track market wide sales. The USDA tracked this information until 1998, when it realized that the scale of private distribution networks was so vast that tracking sales through terminals was moot without adding in private data—something which it has no power to demand from retailers. (USDA Agricultural Marketing Service 2011; Maxwell 2011) However, before Philadelphia built a new produce terminal in 2011, it gauged the scale of business it was doing at the time: over $1 billion in produce each year, the equivalent of 1.1 million families' average annual produce budget. That food travels to stores up to 500 miles from Philadelphia's heart, cities as far-flung as Pittsburgh and Washington, D.C. The new facility expects to see business expand to $1.6 billion, the equivalent of 2.8 million families' produce budgets. (Lloyd 2010; Stilwell 2011; author's calculations of annual produce budget for a family of four, based on Bureau of Labor Statistics 2011a, Table 39)

166 **the market itself is little more than a landlord.** Interview with Ben Vitale, president, National Association of Produce Market Managers. (Vitale 2011)

166 **more than one-third of the residents have no car.** In 2000, 38 percent of the households in zip code 48202 did not have a car. (U.S. Census Bureau 2000a)

167 **$16 million market . . . created by these vouchers.** In 2010, roughly $12.1 million in WIC vouchers for fruits and vegetables were redeemed in Michigan, or 75.4 percent of the $16 million in vouchers that had been issued. Comparable national figures are currently unavailable, as the federal government does not require states to report redemption rates of these vouchers. (Shannon 2011)

167 **slowly redeveloping small-food infrastructure.** See Ashbrook et al. 2008; Andreyeva et al. 2011; Gleason et al. 2011.

167 **rat-infested Dumpsters and Porta-Pottys.** In 2007, the Los Angeles affiliate of NBC ran an investigative piece on that city's produce terminal market. (Grover 2007)

168 **lost nearly two-thirds of the produce wholesalers it had eighty years ago.** As a general rule, the more retailers there are in competition, the healthier the competition in the marketplace. By this measure, America's independent wholesale market looks to be less vibrant than it was a century ago. In 1929, each wholesaler in the United States served an average of 21,630 Americans; in Detroit, the figure was 14,006—meaning that Detroit had *more* wholesalers per person. By 2007, the most recent year for which figures are available, both saw wholesalers decline in relationship to

the population they served. America's wholesalers had diminished while its population expanded, reducing the ratio of wholesalers to people. That year, each wholesaler served 58,444 people; in Detroit, where population shrank and fewer supermarket chains had opened up shop, there were 21,847 people per wholesaler. (Author's calculations, based on U.S. Census Bureau 2007, 2010b, 2011c; Bureau of the Census 1993, Tables 14, 46)

168 **the city today is about half the size it was in 1930.** In 1930, Detroit's population was 1,568,662, while the 2010 Census put the city's population at 713,777, indicating a drop in population of 54.5 percent. (Author's calculations, based on Wattrick 2011a; Bureau of the Census 1936)

168 **4.3 million residents.** According to the 2010 Census, the Detroit Metropolitan Statistical Area is home to 4.3 million residents in its six counties: Lapeer, Livingston, Macomb, Oakland, St. Clair, and Wayne. (U.S. Census Bureau 2011c–h; U.S. Census Bureau 2000)

169 **usually to stores in the suburbs.** Detroit's Eastern Market has been leading a local effort to link growers at their market with retail venues throughout the region. In recent years, they have helped to establish a wholesale food box program modeled after community supported agriculture projects; a fleet of mobile produce trucks; and a range of farmers' markets around the city. (Carmody 2011)

170 **29 percent higher than that of conventional fruits and vegetables.** According to a report backed by the USDA, organic price premiums for ten common produce items in 2004 ranged from 9 percent for oranges to 78 percent for potatoes, with an average of 29 percent. (Stevens-Garmon, Huang, and Lin 2007)

171 **standard soil test.** Growers selling food through the city's existing urban farm cooperative are required to get, and pass, a soil test before selling anything through the network. (Atkinson 2011)

171 **the most prodigious among them . . . Grown in Detroit grossed $60,000 in produce sales in 2010.** This sales figure reflects Grown in Detroit sales through November; full annual sales were closer to $60,000. (Atkinson 2011)

172 **greens and vegetables all summer long.** In addition to the produce, Willerer has also pioneered an idea he calls "farm fast food," where he includes homemade sauces like pesto or salad dressings to make it easy for his customers to prepare the produce quickly. (Willerer 2011)

172 **next to Willerer on Saturdays.** Rising Pheasant Farms' Leadley and Vandyke, a couple, first began experimenting with urban agriculture in 2009, but didn't take their work to a retail level until 2011. (Leadley 2011)

172 **establish large-scale commercial farming in the city.** (Whitford 2009; Lewis 2009)

172 **Recovery Park, an agriculture, housing, and community development project designed to employ recovering addicts and other residents.** (Wozniak 2010)

172 **one of economic development and job creation.** (Chase 2010)

172 **outstripped the cash aid distributed to the city's poor.** Founded in 1894, the Pingree patches grew $30,998-worth of food in 1896, compared to $23,729 distributed by the poor commission. (Holli 1969, 72)

172 **79 percent of all homes are single-family.** In 2005–2009, 78.95 percent of Detroit dwellings were single-family detached, single-family attached, or mobile homes. (Department of Housing and Urban Development 2009)

172 **a federal program that set aside money to encourage food production in urban settings.** David Malakoff provides a thorough discussion of the history and demise of the

federal Urban Gardening Program in his work for *Community Greening Review.* (Mala-koff 1994, 4–12)

173 **revived a link . . . and urban soil.** Prior to the Urban Gardening Program, extension offices in cities typically focused on home economics, leaving agriculture to the rural offices. Thus, UGP presented the first link between extension's agricultural practices and urban centers. (Ibid.)

173 **agricultural efforts became strictly rural affairs.** Congress created the extension program primarily to focus on the issues affecting rural communities and to boost agricultural production, though as extension has grown, its health, nutrition, and home economics lessons have become strongholds in urban offices, too. Urban agriculture has not typically been an area of focused research for extension. (National Institute of Food and Agriculture 2011)

173 **defined by the way they already farm.** The case of organic strawberry production is a good example of this. In the 1970s, farmer Jim Cochran and agroecologist Stephen Gliessman, approached the UC Extension Service for help with growing strawberries organically. "They told us it was impossible," says Gliessman. It wasn't. Gliessman, a professor at UC–Santa Cruz, and Cochran kept experimenting and eventually developed a way to grow organic strawberries on a commercial scale—all with little help from extension. Twenty years later, Cochran's practices are in use by major berry growers around the United States and the world, and in the fall of 2011, UC-Davis published its first handbook on organic strawberry cultivation—signaling its acceptance in the canon of American agricultural practices. (Gliessman 2011)

173 **Truthfully, it's left . . . or making small-scale growing profitable.** There are few books detailing the more recent history of American agricultural extension. The history depicted here draws primarily on basic information from the USDA as well as interviews with national experts on the topic. (Gliessman 2011; Yee 2011; Lantagne 2011)

174 **gazebos, after all, take away growing space.** During a reporting visit with Ameroso while writing a profile on him in 2010, he watched a crew of volunteers building a roofed structure. "Oh, please, why are you making gazebos?" he muttered. "Why do they build structures on these things that take away growing area?" (McMillan 2010b)

174 **two acres tucked within a massive city park on the city's northwest side.** D-Town Farms is located in Detroit's Rouge Park. Details about the history of the farm taken from Malik Yakini. (Yakini 2011b)

174 **"inventory shrinkage."** (Yakini 2010)

175 **"strong Detroit bees that'll make it through the winter."** (Ifeoma 2010)

175 **Currently very little . . . people's home refrigerators.** (Atkinson 2011)

175 **"We need to work much more on the infrastructure."** (Yakini 2011a)

176 **Nearly half the non-tropical fruit . . . and three-quarters of their vegetables . . .** In 2010, Detroit had 4,848 vacant acres owned by public entities—cities, counties, land banks. The same year, a 2010 Michigan State University study found that farming 263 acres biointensively, or 1,660 acres conventionally, could supply 31 percent of the fresh vegetables and 17 percent of the fresh, non-tropical fruit Detroiters eat each year. With storage and season extension, researchers projected that 568 acres of biointensive farming, or 3,602 acres of conventional, would yield 76 percent of vegetables and 42 percent of fruit. (Colasanti, Litjens, and Hamm 2010)

176 **843 acres.** (Central Park Conservancy 2011)

176 **"We want it looking like Manhattan."** (Wattrick 2011b)

177 **started growing food for himself and his neighbors.** Details on Mark Covington's

work at Georgia Street are drawn from an interview with him in July 2011. (Covington 2011)

177 **"Urban agriculture won't save Detroit."** (Covington 2010)

178 **surprise audit.** Eric Johnson, co-manager of Belleville Walmart, received a responsive document regarding a COOL violation, dated June 23, 2010. The non-complying item was corn on the cob. The store provided the necessary documentation and was not fined. (Emmer-Scott 2010)

178 **after a month.** As noted earlier, there was a leak in the walk-in cooler when I arrived at Walmart, and it continued for nearly a month, fixed just before I left in mid-June. Photo documentation of this can be found at www.americanwayofeating.com.

180 Price of garlic at Walmart drawn from reporting notes; price of garlic at La Colmena drawn from copies of receipts on June 10, 2010. See receipts at americanwayofeating.com.

180 **canned goods are always cheaper.** On June 9, 2010, I bought a jar of La Costeña pickled jalapeños from the Honey Bee market for $1.99. On June 16, I bought a jar of Great Value (the Walmart house brand) pickled jalapeños for $1.24. See receipts at americanwayofeating.com.

180 **redder, riper and less wrinkled.** On April 26, I purchased 1.9 pounds of stem tomatoes for $1.99 per pound at La Colmena. On my last night at Walmart, my receipt indicates that tomatoes are typically priced at $2.18 a pound, but were on sale that day for 99 cents. At 99 cents, they look to be selling for less than they cost; a shipment of tomatoes on the vine inventoried on May 26, 2010, cost Walmart $1.11 a pound. (Walmart Stores, Inc. 2010c) See receipts at americanwayofeating.com.

181 **one-fifth of Detroiters living without a car.** According to American Community Survey 2005–2009 estimates, 65,610 of Detroit's 317,734 households, or 20.6 percent, were without a car. (U.S. Census Bureau 2009a)

CHAPTER 8: KITCHEN NOVICE

186 **42 percent of our food budgets.** By 2009, food away from home constituted 41.5 percent of our food spending, down from 44 percent in 1990. (USDA Economic Research Service 2011c)

187 **Restoration Plaza.** In 1964, Senator Robert F. Kennedy included plans for the Bedford Stuyvesant Renewal and Rehabilitation Corporation and the Development Services Corporation in the Economic Opportunity Act of 1964. The project was intended to serve as a model for community development. (Bedford Stuyvesant Restoration 2011)

187 **applied to five.** I visited eleven Applebees locations in 2010: Bedford-Stuyvesant on January 19; Long Island City, Queens on January 20; downtown Brooklyn; two Midtown locations—42nd Street and 50th Street—and the Battery Park/Financial District location on January 21; Sheepshead Bay and Triangle Junction on January 22; and Riverdale, Fordham Road, and Harlem on January 28. Only five accepted applications from me. (McMillan 2009)

187 **more than half of New York's are, too.** In 2009, New York City's population was estimated to be 44.5 percent white, non-Hispanic. (U.S. Census Bureau 2010a)

188 **There are 151 . . . expediter.** Of 151 dishes listed in the Applebee's expo guide, sixty-three dishes (about 42 percent of the menu) require dressing by the expediter. (Applebee's IP, LLC 2010b)

191 **My start-up fund of $925.10 . . . At minimum** wage of $7.25, working forty hours a week, I would earn $290.00 a week, monthly of $1,160, or an annual salary of $15,080. At that income, the state tax rate of 5.25 percent and federal income tax rate of fifteen percent would result in a tax rate of 20.25 percent, giving me a monthly take-home monthly income of $925.10. (Author's calculations)

191 **just letting "it hang out."** An ad posted on January 31, 2010, on New York Craigslist advertised with the headline "$350 OPEN MINDED FEMALE ROOMY WANTED AVAILABLE TO MOVE IN ASAP !!! (Lower East Side)," indicating that "as owner of the apt I like to be comfortable in my own home so I walk around in my boxers sometimes and i sometimes just let it 'hang out.' If this may be even a minor issue the [sic] this is not the room for you so don't reply." (Anon. 2010)

192 **unmistakably Caribbean.** The neighborhood I lived in was home to 88 different ancestries in 2000, with West Indian, a collective term identifying Caribbean heritage, the largest group at 36.3 percent. The neighborhood was also 4.2 percent African, 6.1 percent self-identified American; 38.4 percent of the neighborhood was categorized as "other" ancestry, a grouping that represented about sixty different ancestries (U.S. Census Bureau 2010i).

192 **old Brooklyn Dodgers field.** The Ebbets Field Houses are on the old site of Ebbets Field, former home of the Brooklyn Dodgers. The field, torn down in the late 1950s, was replaced by housing in the early 1960s. To view photos of the neighborhood in which I lived, including the housing projects now on the site of the old field, go to american-wayofeating.com. (Kuntzman 2007)

195 **don't *look* poor or rich.** In 2009, the median family income for Brooklyn, as a borough, was $48,751, about 22 percent less than the U.S. median of $62,363. (U.S. Census Bureau 2010i)

195 **chains like Applebee's tend to draw their customers from more affluent classes of America.** In 2011, industry researchers estimated that 64 percent of patrons at full-service chain restaurants came from households earning $75,000 a year or more, and 13 percent from households earning $50,000 to $75,000 a year. Households earning less than $50,000, despite making up around 60 percent of America, accounted for 23 percent of such sales. (Samadi, 13; DeNavas-Walt, Proctor, and Jessica C. Smith 2010, 40)

195 **Even with deals . . . taken care of.** Presumed bill of $67 from $20 for two adults' meals; $6.99 each for two kiddie meals; one alcoholic beverage per adult ($6 x 2); and a dessert to split among the four ($7). = $53 flat plus tax ($4) = $57. Plus tip of $10 = $67. (Author's calculations)

196 **At that rate . . . every six days.** At Applebee's, a family of four urbanites could easily end up with a bill of $70 by the time tax and tip are taken care of. Using that $67 tab as a baseline, families of four earning between $20,000 and $30,000 a year—who, on average, would spend around $1,787 eating out each year—would spend down their "eating out" budget at our tables after two visits each month. Families of four earning more than $70,000—who spend, on average, $5,134 eating out each year—would have to eat at Applebee's six times a month, roughly every five days, to exhaust their "eating out" funds. (Author's calculations, based on Bureau of Labor Statistics 2011a)

196 **in France in 1782.** La Grande Taverne de Londres in Paris, which opened in 1782, is widely considered the first fine-dining restaurant. (Kamp 2006, 32)

196 **incomes nearly doubled.** In 1947, the median American income was $25,460 in 2009 dollars. By 1975, it was $49,729 in 2009 dollars. In 2009, median income had climbed further still, to $60,088. (U.S. Census Bureau 2009b, Table F-7)

196 **more of our money on going out to dinner.** The share of Americans' food budget spent at home and away-from-home is reported annually by the USDA. (USDA Economic Research Service 2011d)

196 **the logistics management it required.** For a discussion of Fred Harvey's role in developing chain restaurant techniques, see Mariani 1991, 42–47; Jason D. Porterfield 2004, 590–591; Haley 2011.

196 **Howard Johnson's . . . clam chowder.** For a discussion of Howard Johnson's contributions to the American restaurant scene, see Levenstein 1993, 47–49; Kamp 2006, 78–79; Bassett 2004, 691.

197 **HoJo's employed real chefs.** For a discussion of Franey and Pépin's roles in the evolution of Howard Johnson's, see Bassett 2004, 691; Kamp 2006, 78–89; Franey 2010, 156–59; Pépin 2003, 117–19.

197 **quickly and cheaply.** New quick-service restaurants like McDonald's, Burger King, and Kentucky Fried Chicken modeled new techniques on Howard Johnson's concepts. (Bassett 2004, 691)

197 **went public in 1970.** In Sysco's first year, it saw sales of $115 million. By 2008, annual sales were $37 billion. (Sysco, Inc. 2011)

198 **Greece or Mexico.** In 2009, Applebee's operated fifty-six restaurants in Mexico, nine in Brazil, one in Lebanon, and eight in Greece. (DineEquity 2010, 45)

198 **tide was turning for one of America's most infamous ghettos.** In 2003, Bedford-Stuyvesant community leaders began talking with national chains to bring in restaurants like Applebee's. When the Bedford-Stuyvesant Applebee's opened three years later, Brooklyn Borough President Marty Markowitz told news channel New York 1 that he considered it a sign that the neighborhood was attracting serious investment, enough that there might be concerns about gentrification and displacement. "There is investment coming into the community. The challenge for people like me and others in government is to ensure that the area not only maintains its racial balance, in terms of racial diversity, but also that it maintains income diversity," said Markowitz. (Kapadia 2006; Pristin 2003)

198 **more of America got poorer** Since the 1970s, New York City's poverty rates have been consistently higher than the national average, typically around six percentage points higher. From 2002 to 2009, however, the national poverty rate rose by two percentage points, from 12.4 percent to 14.3 percent. Over the same period, New York's poverty rate fell by 3.4 percentage points, from 21.2 to 18.7 percent (Gaines 2011)

198 **over 11 percent in Brooklyn.** In Oct. 2009, unemployment hit 10.1 percent, its highest national rate since June 1992 when it peaked at 7.8 percent. Brooklyn's unemployment rate peaked in January 2010 at 11.1 percent, the highest it had been since July 1997, when it had reached 11.3 percent. (Bureau of Labor Statistics 2010c)

198 **In one of my first weeks . . .** At the staff meeting on February 23, 2009, the general manager told us that "last week alone we did $122,000 in sales, just last week alone. The only better week that you did last year was graduation week." In 2009, there were 251,467 full-service restaurants in the United States. The same year, full-service restaurant sales totaled $168,589,000,000. Therefore, the average full service restaurant grossed $670,422 a year, or $12,893 a week, $1841/day. (Author's calculations, based on Technomic 2010, Exhibits 1–2)

201 **We don't get staff meals . . .** According to an a comprehensive survey of low-wage work in New York City, "lack of meal breaks, or erratic meal breaks, is a pervasive problem." New York State law requires that workers putting in six hours or more (extended over

midday) are entitled to at least thirty minutes off for lunch; workers beginning their shift before 11:00 a.m. and working past 7:00 should be given a second break of at least thirty minutes between 5:00 p.m. and 7:00 p.m. (Bernhardt, McGrath, and DeFillipis 2007, 56; Division of Labor Standards 2007)

202 **a scrappy crew of warriors.** By 2004, New York's restaurant industry employed about 169,500 workers, more than hospitals or manufacturing. This represented just under five percent of NYC workers. (Kharbanda and Ritchie 2005, 4)

202 **one of a handful of non-immigrants.** In the last three decades, the presence of immigrant groups has steadily increased in kitchens. From 1980 to 2000, the share of white workers in restaurants dropped from 51.8 percent to 27.0 percent, a decrease of twenty-five percentage points, while the share of Hispanics increased by 14 percentage points and the share of Asians by 10 percentage points. (Kharbanda and Ritchie 2005, 6)

203 **The balance of management . . .** Although demographics on positions within the restaurant industry can be difficult to come by, management within the entire food chain—including agricultural and processing work—is overwhelmingly white, with 74 percent of management positions held by whites, who constitute 58 percent of food workers, and people of color holding 26 percent of management positions, despite constituting 42 percent of the workforce. (Yen Liu and Apollon 2011, Figs. 3, 7)

203 **promoted ahead of him.** In July 2007, Daniel Boulud settled a federal lawsuit accusing him of discrimination against nonwhite employees, bringing to end a two-year battle. José Arenas, a Mexican busboy, a plaintiff in the case, had alleged that he had trained three French busers who were then promoted ahead of him. (Ellick 2007; Severson 2007)

203 **median wages** Median hourly wages for restaurant cooks in 2010 were $10.65 (annual salary of $22,140), while food prep workers' median wage was $9.18 (annual salary of $19,100). This places both occupations well below the wages considered sufficient to support a family of three, which range anywhere from $14.97 in rural Ohio, for example, to $29.91 in Brooklyn. (Bureau of Labor Statistics 2009b; Pearce 2011, 8; Pearce 2010, 7)

203 **norms within restaurants.** Wage and hour violations are especially common at high-end "white tablecloth" restaurants and independent family-style and ethnic restaurants. (Bernhardt, McGrath, and DeFillipis 2007, 55)

203 **less than 1 percent.** In 2009, Applebee's had 2,008 restaurants, one hundred forty of which operated in other countries. The same year, there were 251,467 full-service restaurants in the U.S., 21,034 of which belonged to companies listed in the Technomic Top 100. Applebee's thus constitutes .07% of all American restaurants, and just under 9 percent of those run by large chains. (DineEquity 2010, 28; Technomic 2010, Appendix J-2)

203 **a few boutique eateries.** Applebee's, according to the most recent data available, is the nation's largest full-service chain, representing about 3 percent of all full-service restaurant sales. As such, it is a leader of a pack that, in aggregate, represents more than half of all restaurant sales. In 2009, 56 percent of restaurant sales occurred at full-service chains listed in industry tracker Technomic. It's important to note, however, that even small chains, such as Danny Meyer's Union Square Hospitality Group in New York, get classified as chains, despite operating at far lower volume than a place like Applebee's. (Technomic 2010, Appendices I1, I2; Restaurants and Institutions 2009)

203 **for which they haven't been trained.** A survey of more than five-hundred New York City restaurant workers found that, of those who reported working under multiple labor

violations, 66 percent also reported not receiving any health or safety training, as compared to 34 percent of those who experienced few labor violations at work. Similarly, 11 percent of those working under poor labor conditions were forced to do a job for which they were not trained (compared to 3 percent) and 18 percent reported being forced to cut corners that might have endangeredthe healthy or safety of customers (also compared to 3 percent). (Restaurant Opportunities Center 2010, 3)

CHAPTER 9: KITCHEN SPY

207 **sanitizing solution and all the rest.** In 2009, Applebee's parent company Dine Equity formed Centralized Supply Chain Services, a purchasing cooperative, to leverage the combined purchasing power of Applebee's and its sister company, International House of Pancakes, to get better deals with suppliers and streamline management. CSCS spends roughly $1.8 billion each year purchasing 95 million pounds of chicken; 78 million pounds of soy oil; 70 million pounds of beef; 57 million pounds of pork; 30 million pounds of cheese, and 5.6 million gallons of soft drinks. (Centralized Supply Chain Services, LLC 2010)

207 **expected to save 3 to 5 percent on operating costs.** In a call with industry analysts discussing the fourth quarter of 2010, Julia Stewart, Chairman and CEO of Dine Equity, Inc., told reporters that, "Over the longer term we expect 3 percent to 5 percent savings out of the co-op, and I think they're well on their way to doing that, and they quantify that for their members once a month on each of the brands." (Fair Disclosure Wire 2011)

207 **about 62 percent outsource . . .** According to a 2009 survey of supply chain executives at food service companies, just under 4 percent of respondents did not use outsourcing for any of their supply chain needs—meaning that 96 percent outsource. For those who outsource aspects of supply chain management, most outsource at least part of their logistics and transportation (82 percent) and/or fulfillment and distribution (62 percent). (ArrowStream, Inc., 2009)

208 **streamlining costs along the way.** Information on client list and length for ArrowStream is drawn from promotional materials. (ArrowStream 2008; ArrowStream 2010)

209 **"tamed Nature itself."** "Cooking is also, of all the arts, the one which has done the most to advance our civilization," wrote Brillat-Savarin in 1825, "for the needs of the kitchen were what first taught us to use fire, and it is by fire that man has tamed Nature itself." (Brillat-Savarin 2009, 283)

209 **transition from nature to culture.** "Not only does cooking mark the transition from nature to culture," wrote Lévi-Strauss in 1964, "but through it and by means of it, the human state can be defined with all its attributes." (Lévi-Strauss 1983, 279)

209 **"our humanity" on cooks.** (Symons 1998, 213, 223 in Wrangham 2009, 13)

209 **apes' acquisition of cooking skills is what turned them into humans—literally.** Writes Wrangham, "according to the evidence carried in our bodies, it would take the invention of cooking to convert habilines into *Homo erectus*, and launch the journey that has led without any major changes to the anatomy of modern humans." (Wrangham 2009, 103)

209 **reduced the amount of time dedicated to eating.** According to calculations by Wrangham, cooking reduces the amount of time spent on chewing by about four hours per day. This calculation is based on comparisons with observational studies of great apes

and humans, which routinely show that humans spend between one-tenth and one-fifth as much time eating/chewing as do primates. (Wrangham 2009, 136–142)

209 **opened up time to spend on hunting . . . brains to grow.** (Wrangham 2009, 142–46)

210 **the connection between home cooking and obesity rates.** No peer-reviewed studies have proved a direct link between home cooking and good health, but a number of studies suggest that people who spend more time preparing and eating their food are less likely to be obese. Other studies have documented a link between fatness and restaurant patronage: a 2000 study found that source of food (that is, restaurants versus home) is a significant determinant of BMI, with women significantly affected by eating at fast-food places and men by eating out generally; and a 1999 study found that a frequency of restaurant consumption was associated positively with body fatness. A 2006 report on Chicago neighborhoods found that obesity rates increased when fast-food restaurants were closer than supermarkets. (Kolodinsky 2008; Binkley, Eales, and Jekanowski 2000; McCrory et al. 1999; Gallagher 2006, 31)

210 **selling cake and pastry mixes.** Duncan Hines introduced cake mix in 1929, with Pillsbury and General Mills following suit by the late 1940s. (Andrew Smith 2004b, 606)

210 **replacements for home-cooked meals.** Frozen prepared foods, i.e. chicken a la king, were introduced in 1939, but did not become popular until after the war. Frozen dinners were introduced throughout the 1940s, initially derived from meals developed for the Naval Air Force, and the first "TV dinner," from Swanson, was introduced in 1953. (Andrew Smith 2004c)

210 **detailed taste comparison:** In 1963 and 1979, the USDA published studies comparing the cost, convenience and taste of convenience foods against home-prepared foods. The verdict: Of twenty-four items compared in the 1979 study, four received critical marks. Homemade cheese fondue, the only scratch preparation with poor marks, was deemed too runny, while frozen strawberries were "mushy and weak in flavor," canned Sloppy Joe "runny and lacked meat flavor," and stuffed potatoes were "dry and hard." (Traub and Odland 1979)

210 **accounted for nearly half of all food . . .** In 1978, convenience foods accounted for nearly half of all foods sold for consumption at home; 58 percent of them were more expensive in convenience form, 24 percent were less expensive, and 18 percent were about the same. (Traub and Odland 1979, iii)

211 **almost always include some kind of convenience food.** A 2007 UCLA study of thirty-two dual-income families found that less than 14 percent of family dinners consisted solely of takeout or fast foods; 5 percent combined takeout food with food prepared at home; 5 percent were eaten at restaurants; and 3 percent were eaten at someone else's home. A full 70 percent were prepared at home, nearly all of which involved some kind of convenience food product. Other market research shows that 90 percent of Americans use convenience foods. (Beck 2007; Harris and Shiptsova 2007)

211 **forty-five minutes . . .** Here, I'm assuming fifteen minutes of travel time, fifteen minutes to be seated and place meal orders, and fifteen minutes before food is served. (Author's calculations)

211 **a discount of nearly 80 percent . . . for doing it . . . yourself.** Based on USDA food price data, to prepare an Asiago Peppercorn steak would require one-half cup cooked potato ($.085), one-half cup cooked broccoli ($0.315) and one-half cup cooked carrots ($0.16), plus 7 oz. of grade-A boneless sirloin steak (7 oz at $0.37/oz = $2.59), and 1 oz. Asiago cheese ($0.57/oz) = $3.72. I have not included the cost of salt, pepper, or butter. (USDA Economic Research Service and Bureau of Labor Statistics 2011; Hayden

Stewart et al. 2011; Yahoo shopping 2011)

211 **economics of something like Hamburger Helper.** In 2011, I prepared Hamburger Helper Beef Stroganoff, spending $2.68 on the box mix, $3.26 for a pound of ground beef, and calculated that the two cups of milk required for the recipe cost $0.29. The meal, which is supposed to yield five servings, took twenty-two minutes to make, the last ten of which were waiting for the dish to cook. To make a simple ground beef gravy-and-noodles dish, I spent $0.83 on the requisite amounts of onion, garlic, butter, low-sodium bouillon, flour, mustard, noodles, and Worcestershire sauce—and used the same amount of milk and meat—yielding a cost of $4.38. The meal took 23 minutes to prepare, though it's worth noting that it required active cooking the entire time. See www.americanwayofeating.com for details.

212 **ten minutes more *active* time . . .** A 2007 survey of thirty-two dual-income families' meals over four days found that home-cooked meals took an average of thirty-four minutes' active time to prepare, and fifty-two minutes total to prepare. Using convenience foods did not reduce the time it took to prepare a meal, but rather saved cooks ten to twelve minutes of active cooking time. (Beck 2007)

213 **Restaurant executives . . . "special handling."** In 2009, ABC news reported that an 2009 *American Journal of Preventive Medicine* study surveying restaurant executives indicated that restaurants are wary of using healthy items, like fruits and vegetables, because they cost more, are harder to store, frequently spoil and lead to waste, and require special handling, the executives said. And they may take business away from more profitable items. "We don't want to serve an item that's going to take dollars away from a more profitable item," one executive said. (ABC News 2009)

214 **frozen fries in his kitchen.** In 2007, *New York Magazine* reported that Thomas Keller favored frozen french fries at his Bouchon bistros. (Maurer 2011)

214 **Belhurst Castle . . . fresh raspberries.** In 2007, *Slate* magazine reported that "each reheated Angus country fried steak [from Sysco] will bring in almost $5 in profits," and that Edgar's Restaurant at Belhurst Castle uses Sysco's Imperial Towering Chocolate Cake. (Boser 2007)

214 **out of my price range.** Sandwiches and burgers range in price from $7.99 to $10.99, while seafood entrees range in price from $12.49 to $15.99. Typically, making a substitution for french fries—baked potato, steamed vegetables—is supposed to increase the cost by $3.99, but I never notice additional money being taken from my check. (Applebee's IP, LLC 2010a)

215 **huge by New York standards.** The Western Beef supermarket on Empire Boulevard in Brooklyn, New York, is 42,000 square feet, according to the New York State Department of Agriculture and Markets, which regulates food retailers. (Kara Jones 2011)

215 **Trinidadian flag . . .** For images from the Western Beef supermarket, see americanway ofeating.com.

215 **sloppy plastic bags of seven pounds or more.** On February 25, 2010, I bought groceries at Western Beef for $37.51. This included a 7.54-pound bag of chicken leg quarters at 48 cents per pound, minus a 75-cent discount for a total cost of $2.87, or 38 cents per pound. To see receipts and a list of my expenses, see www.americanwayofeating.com.

215 **one of the neighborhood's few stores.** In 2010, a study of supermarket access in the five boroughs commissioned by the New York City Department of Public Health showed that Prospect-Lefferts Gardens residents have 1.0 square feet of grocery store space per capita, putting it at one-third of the industry standard. (AECOM 2010)

216 **a paycheck that was short by $155.** My first check from Applebee's, dated February 26,

2010, covered my first two weeks of work. My first week of work, from February 8 to 14, constituted training. I was told I would be paid $8 an hour for training, but my paycheck put my training wage at $7.25; the 12.5 hours I had worked on Valentine's Day were not added to my check despite my having informed a manager. My next check, covering February 15 to 21, paid me an hourly wage of $8 an hour—compared to the $9 at which I had been hired—and did not include additional hours. Had I been paid for Valentine's Day at my stated wages, I should have grossed $677.24 on my check dated February 26. Instead, that check grossed $521.66, a difference of $155.58. My next check paid me for about fifteen hours more than I had actually worked, indicating that Danny had added hours to my check to cover Valentine's Day (12.5 hours) and that I was paid for the staff meeting (about 2.5 hours). To see copies of my paychecks and time cards, see www.americanwayofeating.com. (McMillan 2009)

217 **$678.85 has been spent . . .** On March 2, there were two unauthorized charges made to my checking account, one for $125 (Fry's Grocery, Phoenix) and $263.38 (a medical company from which I have received prescriptions in the past). On March 3, charges for $69.29, $72.54 (both to a Circle K in Phoenix) and $77.17 (1146 N. 23 Avenue, also in Phoenix) were made without authorization. On March 4, there was a charge of $62.91 (Circle K) and $8.66 (McDonald's). These seven charges totaled $678.95. My bank refunded $482.38 of the charges on March 22, and the remaining $196.57 on April 14. To see documentation of the unauthorized charges on my account, see www .americanwayofeating.com. (McMillan 2009)

218 **I may have missed some training.** In my expo "final" of twenty-four questions, two addressed hand washing, two addressed protocol with sanitizing solution, one addressed expiration date protocol, and one addressed holding temperatures for food. To see a copy of my expo final, go to www.americanwayofeating.com. (Applebee's IP, LLC 2009)

218 **never paid for my time.** My Neighborhood Expert training at Applebee's occurred on March 9. My time cards, printed out at Applebee's, indicated that from March 8–14, I worked 32.2 hours, and from March 15–21, I worked 42.58 hours, for a total of 74.78 hours. My paycheck covering the period from March 8–21 accounted for 74.83 hours, slightly less than I had clocked in for. Had I been compensated for the three hours I spent at Applebee's for the Neighborhood Expert training, the extra hours would have shown up either on the timecards (which never indicated I was at Applebee's on March 9) or my paycheck. To see my time cards and paychecks, go to www.americanwayofeat ing.com.

218 **find even more disheartening: common.** In a 2007 report, New York University Law School researchers documented the terms of work in thirteen different industries in New York City and found that "the fundamental legal protections in the workplace that were hard-fought and hard-won in the last century do not apply." For restaurant workers, they found that nonpayment of wages, partial nonpayment, and several months' backlog of pay were common, particularly among kitchen staff and dishwashers. (Bernhardt, McGrath, and DeFillipis 2007, 2, 56)

CONCLUSION: A NEW AMERICAN WAY OF EATING

233 **America's increasingly divided classes.** In 2011, writes the Nobel Prize–winning economist Joseph Stiglitz, "The upper 1 percent of Americans are now taking in nearly a quarter of the nation's income every year. In terms of wealth rather than income, the top 1

percent control 40 percent. Their lot in life has improved considerably. Twenty-five years ago, the corresponding figures were 12 percent and 33 percent." (Stiglitz 2011)

233 **campaign to end childhood obesity.** In February 2010, Michelle Obama announced the Healthy Food Financing Initiative with a goal "to eliminate food deserts in America completely in seven years," coupling it with her Let's Move campaign. (Obama 2011)

234 **grocers committed to opening new stores in food deserts.** On July 20, 2011, seven retailers announced commitments, made via First Lady Michelle Obama's Let's Move campaign, to open or expand more than 1,500 supermarket stores in food deserts. These retailers are Supervalu (250 new Save-A-Lot stores), Walgreens (bringing produce and healthy options to 1,000 stores), Walmart (275–300 stores to be opened or expanded), California Freshworks Fund ($200 million for healthy food retailing in California), Brown's Super Store (one new store in Philly and expanding one in Chelthenham), Calhoun Food (ten new stores in Alabama and Tennessee), and Klein's Family Markets (Baltimore, one new store). (Obama 2011)

234 **farmers' markets . . . are beginning to take food stamps.** In 2009, roughly nine hundred farmers' markets and farm stands across the country accepted SNAP benefits. (Wasserman et al. 2010)

234 **matching funds in-season.** In 2010, Wholesome Wave Foundation operated SNAP matching coupon programs at 160 farmers' markets in twenty different states, while the Fair Food Network backed the Double-Up Food Bucks program at farmers' markets across the state of Michigan. (Nischan 2010; Fair Food Network 2011)

234 **"eating is an agricultural act."** (Berry 1990, 145–49)

236 **nearly all of the visibly poor faces are brown or black.** In 2009, while the poverty *rates* among blacks and Hispanics were markedly higher than among whites—26, 25 and 9 percent, respectively—45 percent of America's poor were reported that they were white; 22 percent were black; and 26 percent were Hispanic or Latino. In Michigan, whites constitute the majority of the state's poor at 58 percent, while blacks represent 29 percent, and Hispanics 8 percent, of the poor. In New York City, by contrast, whites accounted for just 21 percent of the poor, while blacks make up 28 percent of those in poverty, Hispanics 42 percent, Asians 12 percent, and "other" or "two races" make up 25 percent of the city's poor. Please note that percentages here reflect the share of responses received against the population, and may not add to one hundred due to respondents indicating more than one race. (National Poverty Center 2009; Author's calculations, based on U.S. Census Bureau 2009c)

237 **There were coupons for . . .** To see images of the local circulars offering coupons for food, go to www.americanwayofeating.com.

237 **our stagnating wages.** In 2009, inflation-adjusted earnings for the median male worker were lower than in the early 1970s, and median earnings for women have generally stagnated since 2001 after having risen for the four preceding decades. (Greenstone and Adam Looney)

237 **skyrocketing income inequality.** According to an analysis by UC-Berkeley economist Emmanuel Saez, in 2007, the share of American income earned by the top 10 percent was 49.7 percent, "a level higher than any other year since 1917, and even surpasses 1928, the peak of the stock market bubble in the 'roaring' 1920s." In the 1970s, by contrast, the top ten percent earned roughly one-third of the nation's income. Wealth, as opposed to income, has also become more concentrated. In 2011, the top 1 percent of Americans took controlled 40 percent—compared to 33 percent twenty-five years earlier. (Saez 2009; Stiglitz 2011)

237 **mushrooming health care costs.** In 1965, America's health care spending was $187 billion (in 2005 dollars). By 2005, it had risen to roughly $1.9 trillion. (Orszag 2008)

237 **but to be burned.** This succinct description of biofuels should be attributed to Raj Patel. For a concrete discussion of the role biofuels play in heightening food insecurity, see the work of Princeton's Tim Searchinger, whose review of international reports on the dynamics that led to the 2008 food crisis concluded that "Biofuels have contributed significantly to crop price increases and food insecurity in the early 2000s, and will continue to cause higher crop prices, but the magnitude of impacts will be smaller in the future as markets adjust." (Patel 2009; Searchinger 2008)

237 **grow only enough fruits and vegetables to meet half of America's recommended daily servings of produce.** In 2006, the USDA reported that to grow enough produce to meet the 2005 daily guidelines for fruit and vegetable consumption, the United States would need to increase the acreages in fruit production by 117 percent and its vegetable production by 137 percent, more than double the acreage dedicated to fresh produce from 1999–2003. Similarly, a study published in the American Journal of Preventative Medicine found that from 1970 to 2007, "the country's food supply has been failing to provide diets consistent with federal recommendations on a number of key components for the past several decades," with the U.S. food supply containing just 30 percent of the vegetables required for Americans to meet recommended consumption levels, and less than half the recommended amount of fruits. (Buzby, Hodan Farah Wells, and Gary Vocker 2006; Krebs-Smith, Susan, Reedy, and Bosire 2010)

237 **much of it comes from California's irrigated wonderland.** In 2007, California agriculture accounted for 34 percent of all fruit and vegetable acreage that was harvested—but for 52 percent of irrigated cropland dedicated to fruits and vegetables. (National Agricultural Statistics Service 2007)

237 **our richest farmland . . . goes to . . . grain destined for fuel tanks and cattle feed.** In 2007, the United States dedicated 30 percent of its farmland to corn for both grain and silage; 20 percent to forage, typically used for feeding livestock; and just 3 percent to fruits and vegetables. In the prairie states of Iowa and Nebraska, corn and forage accounted for 65 percent of all farm land harvested that year, while less than one-tenth of 1 percent went to fruits and vegetables. (National Agricultural Statistics Service 2007)

237 **around 14 million Americans lived in low-income neighborhoods with insufficient grocery stores.** The USDA Food Desert Locator defines a food desert as a low-income census tract where at least one-third of residents live one mile from the nearest large grocery store in urban areas, or ten miles in rural areas. Using 2000 census figures, the USDA in 2011 identified 6,500 census tracts as food deserts, with 13.5 million residents. (Breneman and Ver Ploeg 2011)

237 **American shoppers don't eat anywhere near as many fruits and vegetables as they should.** In 2009, an estimated 32.5 percent of U.S. adults consumed fruit two or more times per day, while the percentage of adults who consumed vegetables three or more times per day was 26.3 percent, This fell significantly below the CDC's target of having 75 percent of Americans eating fruit twice a day, and 50 percent eating vegetables three times a day, by 2010. (Grimm et al. 2010)

238 **simple way to accomplish that.** Research from the USDA suggests that coupons are more effective in promoting fruit and vegetable consumption than simple price reductions., A 2010 study by the agency found that people with coupons for 10 percent off produce would buy 2 to 11 percent more fruits and vegetables, compared to a 5 to 6 percent increase for just price drops. (Diansheng and Leibtag 2010)

238 **United Nations released a report arguing that agroecology . . . simply need to be stud-ied and scaled up.** In addition to citing the benefits of diverse crop plans, the report from the Special Rapporteur on the Right to Food noted that urban farming is a good model for smaller-scale efforts. It also called for additional investment in extension ser-vices, training and efforts to scale-up effective practices—something for which urban agriculture is well-suited. (de Schutter 2010b)

239 **another three hundred.** In July 2011, Walmart announced that it had opened 217 stores in food desert areas since 2007 and planned to open another 275–300 in similarly dis-advantaged communities by 2016. (Walmart Stores, Inc. 2011c)

239 **Detroit's Eastern Market is one if its models.** In 2010, the USDA Agricultural Market-ing Service highlighted Detroit's Eastern Market as a model for addressing food access issues, citing its comprehensive food hub approach as a "business development model [that] can be expected to bring good things to Detroit." (Tropp 2010)

239 **16 cents . . . ends up back at the farm; the other 84 cents.** According to the USDA 2008, 15.8 percent the cost of farm commodities—the food grown on farms, rather than the food industry as a whole—went to the farm; 84 percent went to marketing. (Canning 2008)

240 **annual incomes that rarely reach far into five figures.** In a 2005 study of agricultural workers, the average wage earned by crop workers was $7.25, and the average annual days worked was 190. Estimating an eight-hour day, that would put farm workers at an average annual income of $11,020. (Carroll et al. 2005)

240 **the poverty line for a single person.** In 2009, the official poverty rate for a single adult was $11,161. (National Poverty Center 2011)

240 **full-time employment . . . eluded me.** In June 2010, when I was finishing my work at Walmart, 8.9 million Americans were employed part-time "for economic reasons," meaning they wanted full-time work but could not find it. A year later, the figure had dropped to 8.7 million. (Bureau of Labor Statistics 2011b)

240 **the third of households earning between $35,000 and $75,000.** In 2009, 32.2 percent of American *households* earned between $35,000 and $74,999; 31.6 percent earned more than $75,000 and 36.2 percent earned less than $35,000. (DeNavas-Walt, Proc-tor, and Jessica C. Smith 2010, 33–39, Table A-1)

240 **most prevalent in the lowest depths of our economy.** In 2005–2008, the rate of obesity among American adults living below the federal poverty line was 22 percent higher than among those living at 400 percent of the poverty line or above; the rate of heart disease was 40 percent higher; and the rate of diabetes was twice as high. (National Center for Health Statistics 2011)

240 **more costly to the public purse.** A 2004 study found that Americans spent $75 bil-lion on obesity-related health problems, with Medicaid accounting for 28 percent of that.(Finkelstein, Fiebelkorn, and Wang 2004) At the time, the 41.3 million Americans on Medicaid represented an estimated 14.5 percent of the population. (Author's calcula-tions, based on Ellis, Vernon K. Smith, and Rousseau 2005; U.S. Census Bureau 2004)

240 **working poor constitute arguably the largest, and fastest-growing, economic class within the American citizenry.** I say arguably to buffer any complaints that a household income of $40,000 is not poor, but an income that can provide basic needs to a family of three such that they do not need outside help from the state or family—self-sufficiency, in other words—typically hovers around $45,000, though at the low end it can be as low as $27,196 (as in rural Ohio) or as high as $ $91,552 (as in south Manhattan, New York City). In any event, marketing experts have been exhorting retailers to focus their

outreach strategies on households earning $35,000 a year or less; that income class is the fastest-growing one in the country. From 2000 to 2015, the share of the U.S. population earning under $35,000 is projected to go from 36.5 percent to 38.9 percent, while the share between $35,000 and $55,000 will stagnate from 20 percent to 19.9 percent, and households earning over $55,000 will go from 43.5 percent to 41.3 percent. (Pearce 2010; Pearce 2011; Information Resources, Inc. 2009).

241 **America has been here before . . . scraped by on the rest.** In 1917, the earliest year for which data is available, the richest decile of America held 40.5 percent of the nation's income. By 1928, the wealthy's share of income had climbed to 49.3 percent of the nation's income—the highest share they would hold until 2007, when they reset their record, reaching a pinnacle of 49.7 percent. (Saez 2009)

241 **one-third less than most of the cars sold nationwide that year.** In 1908, the American automobile industry sold 63,500 cars, with 43 percent selling for less than $1,375. In 1916, two years after Ford raised wages, sales had climbed to 1,535,600, with 91 percent selling for less than $1,375. And by 1920, sales were at 1,905,600 and with 68.2 percent selling for less than $1,375. (Tedlow 1996, 130, Table 3–3)

241 **making his automobiles affordable to them.** In January 1914, Ford announced a $5 a day wage, and a reduction of the work day from nine to eight hours, more than doubling the average auto worker's wage. (Ford Motor Company 2011b)

241 **not a good Samaritan.** Among the critiques made of Ford are his use of the Ford Service, a violent private security force; his involvement with the Nazi movement in Germany, particularly through his business dealings with Hitler; and his use of racial tensions in Detroit to thwart unionization attempts. The tycoon served as inspiration for *The Flivver King: A Story of Ford-America,* Upton Sinclair's follow-up to the *The Jungle,* and is the subject of numerous biographies; *The People's Tycoon* and *Henry Ford and the Jews* being two of the more recent. (Sinclair 1937; Watts 2006; Baldwin 2002)

241 **easy for most Americans to buy his products.** In his definitive history of American mass marketing, Richard S. Tedlow describes Henry Ford's approach to his work: "The course he set for himself was to build a 'car for the common man,' for the 'great multitude,' a 'universal' car that would be sufficiently versatile to serve for every occasion. This car would be durable and it would be inexpensive both to purchase and to operate." (Tedlow 1996, 120–122)

APPENDIX: CHEAP EATS?

251 **spent just nine percent.** Household food spending patterns are documented each year by the Bureau of Labor Statistics. In 2009, the most recent year for which data were available at the time of publication, households earning between $10,000 and $14,999 spent 35.5 percent of their post-tax income on food; those earning between $15,000 and $19,999 spent 25.5 percent; and those earning between $20,000 and $29,999 spent 21.2 percent. (Author's calculations, based on Bureau of Labor Statistics 2011a, Table 39)

251 **all families spend between 14 and 18 percent of their grocery budget on fruits and vegetables.** Consumer spending data for 2009 indicate that families earning between $15,000 and $19,999 spent 18.3 percent of their grocery bill on fruits and vegetables. Families in the next-lowest income bracket, $10,000 to $14,999, spent 14.6 percent, while all other income brackets spent between 16.1 percent and 16.9 percent of their grocery budget on fruits and vegetables. (Author's calculations, based on Bureau of

Labor Statistics 2011a, Table 39

BIBLIOGRAPHY

254 Even though my weekly income . . . 26 percent of my budget. In the fields, I spent an average of $52.06 each week on food and earned a weekly average of $203.62. At Applebee's, my weekly income climbed to $247.03. So $52.06 represented 21.1 percent of my income as an expediter. (McMillan 2011)

251 Information in this appendix, "Cheap Food?," is based on 2009 Bureau of Labor Statistics data. Comparative data on household spending elsewhere in the book is drawn from 2007, the most recent year available for France. Thus, numbers here differ from those With dited exception, *all source material* will be available annotated and online at www.americanwayofeating.com, thanks in part to the wonderful folks at DocumentCloud—an online document source repository that's designed with investigative reporters in mind.

As such, all original reporting documents, such as Walmart inventory sheets and *tarjetas* from the fields, along with photographs and detailed accounts of my spending from each job, will be available online. Much of the reporting in this book required independent calculations; all the relevant spreadsheets will be available online, along with the primary documents providing the source data. And I'll of course provide links to material already available online, directing readers—whenever possible—to the exact page with the relevant information.

A&P. 1930. "A&P Advertisement." *Hempstead Sentinel*, August 28.

ABC News. 2009. "Healthy Food? At a Restaurant? Are You Serious?" *ABC News*. February 25. Accessed August 13, 2011. http://abcnews.go.com/print?id=3056708.

AECOM. 2010. *NYC Full Service Grocery Store Analysis*. New York: New York City Department of Health and Mental Hygiene.

Agricultural Worker Health Project. 2011. "Farmworker Transportation." *California Rural Legal Assistance*. Accessed February 17, 2011. http://www.agworkerhealth.org/RTF1.cfm?pagename=Transportation.

Aguirre International. 2005. *The California Farm Labor Force Overview and Trends from the National Agricultural Workers Survey*. Burlingame, CA: Aguirre International. June.

All About Cities staff. 2006. "San Diego passes anti-Wal-Mart legislation." *All About Cities*. November 30. Accessed July 15, 2011. http://allaboutcities.ca/san-diego-passes-anti-wal-mart-legislation/.

Andreyeva, Tatiana, Ann E. Middleton, Michael W. Long, Joerg Luedicke, and Marlene B. Schwartz. 2011. "Food retailer practices, attitudes and beliefs about the supply of healthy foods." *Public Health Nutrition* 14 (6) (February 16): 1024–31.

Anon. 2010. "$350 OPEN MINDED FEMALE ROOMY WANTED AVAILABLE TO MOVE IN ASAP !!! (Lower East Side)." *Craigslist.org*. Accessed January 31. http://craigslist.org/newyork/.

Anon. 2011a. Walmart market share, 29 select MSAs.

Anon. 2011b. "295/month large studio apartment." *Craigslist.org*. Accessed August 7. http://detroit.craigslist.org/.

Anon. 2011c. "8740 HERITAGE PLACE Near Joy/Grand River 1 bd $275 and up." *Apartments.com*. Accessed August 7, 2011. http://www.apartments.com.

Anon. 2011d. "Detroit W—Chicago/Lodge 1bd quiet secure apt $300mo." *Apartments.com*. Accessed August 7, 2011. http://www.apartments.com.

Anthony, Mark. 2006. "Toops Scoops: Young cooks look for 'easy wow.'" *Food Processing*. February 1. Accessed July 12, 2011. http://www.foodprocessing.com/articles/2006/030.html.

Applebee's. 2006. *Applebee's International, Inc. 2006 Annual Report & Form 10-K*. Overland Park, KS: Applebee's, Inc.

Applebee's IP, LLC. 2009. "Conducting the Daily Inspection: Expo." Applebee's IP, LLC, December.

———. 2010a. "Applebee's Menu." DineEquity.

———. 2010b. "Applebee's Expediting Manual." Applebee's IP, LLC. February.

Arax, Mark, and Rick Wartzman. 2003. *The King of California: J. G. Boswell and the Making of a Secret American Empire*. New York: Public Affairs.

Arindrajit, Dube, T. William Lester, and Barry Eidlin. 2007. *A Downward Push: The Impact of Wal-Mart Stores on Retail Wages and Benefits*. Research brief. University of California-Berkeley Labor Center. December.

ArrowStream, Inc. 2008. *ArrowStream Logistics*. ArrowStream, Inc.

———. 2009. *Supply Chain Insights Survey: A Foodservice Industry Perspective*. ArrowStream, Inc.

———. 2010. *Supply Chain Excellence from Point A to Z*. ArrowStream, Inc.

Ashbrook, Alexandra, Kristin Roberts, and Social Compact. 2010. *When Healthy Food Is Out of Reach: An Analysis of the Grocery Gap in the District of Columbia*. Washington, DC: Social Compact and D.C. Hunger Solutions.

Ashbrook, Alexandra, Kristin Roberts, Allison Karpyn, and James Johnson Piett. 2008. *Creating Healthy Corner Stores in the District of Columbia*. D.C. Healthy Corner Store program. October.

Associated Press. 2007a. "Peanut Butter Is Recalled As 300 Fall Ill." *New York Times*. February 16.

———. 2007b. "National Briefing Washington: Cantaloupes Are Recalled." *New York Times*. February 17.

Atkinson, Ashley. 2011. Director of Project Development and Urban Agriculture, Greening of Detroit. Telephone interview by author, transcribed. July 11.

Audacity staff. 1997. "Reprint in magazine." *Audacity*.

B*Healthy. 2003. B*Healthy cooking class. Reporting notes from author. December 3.

Baba, Marietta Lynn, and Malvina Hauk Abonyi. 1979. *Mexicans of Detroit*. Peopling of Michigan Series. Wayne State University Press.

Bacon, David. 2011. "Living Under the Trees: 14 San Diego." Accessed February 16, 2011. http://dbacon.igc.org/Imgrants/sd14.html.

Balbi, Maria Julia, and Ken Joseph. 2010. *Argentina: Retail Food Sector*. Global agricultural information report. Washington, DC: U.S. Department of Agriculture, Foreign Agricultural Service. May 1.

Baldwin, Neil. 2002. *Henry Ford and the Jews: The Mass Production of Hate*. New York: Public Affairs.

Barry, Dan. 2006. "Just Scents and Memories, Wafting on the Breeze." *New York Times*. August 5.

Basker, Emek, and Michael Noel. 2007. *The Evolving Food Chain: Competitive Effects of Wal-Mart's Entry into the Supermarket Industry*. Discussion paper 2007–03. San Diego: University of California-San Diego, Department of Economics. June.

Bassett, Linda. 2004. "Howard Johnson's." In *The Oxford Encyclopedia of Food and Drink in America*. New York: Oxford University Press.

Beck, Margaret E. 2007. "Dinner preparation in the modern United States." *British Food Journal* 109 (7): 531–47.

Becker, Jasper. 1997. "Jiang's journey into a new world." *South China Morning Post.* October 27.

Bedford Stuyvesant Restoration. 2011. "History." *Bedford Stuyvesant Restoration Plaza.* Accessed March 2, 2011. http://www.restorationplaza.org/about/history.

Bellows, Anne C., Adam Diamond, Benjamin Onyango, and William K. Hallman. 2008. "Understanding Consumer Interest in Organics: Production Values Vs. Purchasing Behavior." Journal of Agricultural and Food Industrial Organization 6 (2).

Berkenkamp, JoAnne. 2010. Local foods program director, IATP. December 16.

Bernhardt, Annette, Siobáhn McGrath, and James DeFilippis. 2007. *Unregulated Work in the Global City.* New York: Brennan Center for Justice at New York University School of Law.

Berry, Wendell. 1990. "The Pleasures of Eating" in *What Are People For?* New York: North Point Press.

———. 2009. "Nature as Measure." In *Bringing It to the Table: On Farming and Food.* Berkeley, CA: Counterpoint.

Binkley, J. K., J. Eales, and M. Jekanowski. 2000. "The relation between dietary change and rising US obesity." *International Journal of Obesity* 24 (8) (August): 1032–39.

Blackmore, W. Edward, and Harry G. Clowes. 1963. *Detroit Wholesale Food-Distribution Facilities.* Marketing research report. Washington, DC: U.S. Department of Agriculture, Agricultural Marketing Service, Transportation and Facilities Research Division. August.

Bloch, Matthew, Jason DeParle, Matthew Ericson, and Robert Gebeloff. 2009. "Food Stamp Usage Across the Country." *New York Times.* November 28.

Bloom, Jonathan. 2010. *American Wasteland: How America Throws Away Nearly Half Its Food (And What We Can Do About It).* Cambridge, MA: De Capo Press.

Bogert, Carroll. 1993. "The Russian evolution." *Vancouver Sun.* July 3.

Bon Appétit Management Company Foundation and United Farm Workers. 2011. *Inventory of Farmworker Issues and Protections in the United States.* Bon Appétit Management Company Foundation. March.

Boser, Ulrich. 2007. "How Sysco came to monopolize most of what you eat." *Slate.* February 21. Accessed July 5, 2011. http://www.slate.com/id/2160284/.

Bouchard, Maryse F., Jonathan Chevrier, Kim G. Harley, et al. 2011. "Prenatal Exposure to Organophosphate Pesticides and IQ in 7-Year Old Children." *Environmental Health Perspectives* 119: 1189–95.

Boyd, Julian P., Charles T. Cullen, John Catanzariti, and Barbara B. Oberg. 1950. *The Papers of Thomas Jefferson.* 33 vols. Princeton, NJ: Princeton University Press.

Bras, Marie-Annick, Olivier Pégaz-Blanc, Monique Di Franco, Delphine Kocoglu, Françoise Martial, and Patricia Roosz. 2009. *La France en Bref Édition 2009.* Institut National de la Statistique et des Études Économiques.

Breneman, Vince, and Michele Ver Ploeg. 2011. "Definition of a Food Desert." *United States Department of Agriculture.* Accessed July 23. http://www.ers.usda.gov/data/fooddesert/documentation.html.

Brewstter, Elizabeth. 2007. "Cooking Up Change: Land O'Lakes gets back to culinary basics." *Food Processing.* March 1.

Brillat-Savarin, Jean Anthelme. 2009. *The Physiology of Taste: Notes on Transcendental Gastronomy.* New York: Alfred A. Knopf.

Buford, Bill. 2006. *Heat: An Amateur's Adventures as Kitchen Slave, Line Cook, Pasta-Maker and Apprentice to a Dante-Quoting Butcher in Tuscany.* New York: Vintage Books.

Bureau of Labor Statistics. 2009a. *Consumer Expenditure Survey, 2007.* Washington, DC: U.S. Department of Labor. Accessed July 25, 2011. http://www.bls.gov/cex/.

———. 2009b. "OES Industry-Specific Occupational Employment and Wage Estimates: Full Service Restaurants." *Bureau of Labor Statistics, Occupational Employment Statistics.* February 19. Accessed July 17, 2011. http://www.bls.gov/oes/2007/may/naics4_722100.htm.

———. 2009c. "Unemployment rates by State, seasonally adjusted, Nov. 2009." *Local Area Unemployment Statistics.* November. Accessed August 5, 2011. http://www.bls.gov/lau/lastrk09.htm.

———. 2010a. *Numbers of nonfatal occupational injuries and illnesses by industry and case types, 2009.* Industry injury and illness data. Washington, DC: U.S. Department of Labor.

———. 2010b. *Incidence rates of total recordable cases of nonfatal occupational injuries and illnesses, by quartile distribution and employment size, 2009.* Industry injury and illness Data. Washington, DC: U.S. Department of Labor.

———. 2010c. "Local Area Unemployment Statistics, Kings County seasonal unemployment rate." *Bureau of Labor Statistics Data.* Accessed September 22, 2011. http://data.bls.gov/pdq/SurveyOutputServlet.

———. 2010d. "Regional and State Employment and Unemployment—June 2010." U.S. Department of Labor, July 20.

———. 2011a. *Consumer Expenditure Survey, 2009.* Washington, DC: U.S. Department of Labor. Accessed July 25. www.bls.gov/cex.

———. 2011b. *Employed Persons by Class of Worker and Part-Time Status.* Household data. Washington, DC: U.S. Department of Labor. July 8. Accessed July 25. http://www.bls.gov/news.release/empsit.t08.htm#cps_empsit_a05.f.3.

———. 2011c. "Labor Force Statistics from the Current Population Survey." *United States Department of Labor.* Accessed July 16. http://data.bls.gov/pdq/SurveyOutputServlet.

Bureau of the Census. 1936. *Statistical Abstract of the United States.* Washington, DC: U.S. Department of Commerce.

———. 1993. *1990 Census of Population and Housing Population and Housing Unit Counts United States.* Washington, DC: U.S. Department of Commerce and Bureau of the Census.

Businessweek staff. 1933. "The Cheapy Thrives." *Businessweek.* February 8.

Buzby, Jean C., Hodan Farah Wells, and Gary Vocker. 2006. *Possible Implications for U.S. Agriculture from Adoption of Select Dietary Guidelines.* Economic research report. Washington, DC: U.S. Department of Agriculture, Economic Research Service. November. Accessed July 23, 2011. http://www.ers.usda.gov/publications/err31/.

Buzby, Jean C., Hodan Farah Wells, Bruce Axtman, and Jana Mickey. 2009. *Supermarket Loss Estimates for Fresh Fruit, Vegetables, Meat, Poultry, and Seafood and Their Use in the ERS Loss-Adjusted Food Availability Data.* Washington, DC: U.S. Department of Agriculture, Economic Research Service, March.

California Department of Food and Agriculture. 2010. *California Agricultural Resource Directory, 2010–2011.* California: California Department of Food and Agriculture.

California Department of Industrial Relations. 2011a. "Paydays, pay periods, and the final wages." *California Department of Industrial Relations.* Accessed August 14. http://www.dir.ca.gov/dlse/faq_paydays.htm.

————. 2011b. "Farm labor contractors license database: Full list." *California Department of Industrial Relations*. Accessed August 3. www.dir.ca.gov/.

————. 2009a. "Farm labor contractors license database: El Bajío." *California Department of Industrial Relations*. Accessed August 3. www.dir.ca.gov/.

————. 2009b. "Farm labor contractors license database: GTO Packing." *California Department of Industrial Relations*. Accessed August 3. www.dir.ca.gov/.

California Employment Development Department. 2010. "Quarterly Census of Employment and Wages (QCEW)—Major Industry." *Employment Development Department, State of California*. Accessed July 14. http://www.labormarketinfo.edd.ca.gov/qcew/CEW-Major_NAICS.asp.

Canning, Patrick. 2008. *Food Dollar Series: Food Dollar Application*. Washington, DC: U.S. Department of Agriculture, Economic Research Service. Accessed February 25, 2011. http://www.ers.usda.gov/Data/FoodDollar/app/.

————. 2011. *A Revised and Expanded Food Dollar Series: A Better Understanding of Our Food Costs*. Economic research report. Washington, DC: U.S. Department of Agriculture, Economic Research Service. February.

Carmody, Daniel. 2011. Executive director, Eastern Market Corporation. Telephone interview by author, transcribed. February 7.

Carroll, Daniel, Russell Saltz, and Susan Gabbard. 2009. "The Changing Farm Workforce: Findings from the National Agricultural Workers Survey presented at the Immigration Reform and Agriculture Conference." Washington, DC. May 21.

Carroll, Daniel, Ruth M. Samardick, Scott Bernard, Susan Gabbard, and Trish Hernandez. 2005. *Findings from the National Agricultural Workers Survey 2001–2002: A Demographic and Employment Profile of United States Farm Workers*. Washington, DC: U.S. Department of Labor, Office of Programmatic Policy. March.

Census of Retail Trade. 1958. *Market shares, 1958–1992, of 4, 8, 20 and 50 leading grocery chains*. Washington, DC: U.S. Department of Agriculture, Economic Research Service.

Central Park Conservancy. 2011. "The Official Website of Central Park—FAQ." *Central Park Conservancy*. Accessed July 27, 2011. http://www.centralparknyc.org/visit/general-info/faq/.

Centralized Supply Chain Services, LLC. 2010. "About CSCS." *CSCS*. Accessed August 13, 2011. http://www.cscscoop.com/cscs/cscspublic1.nsf/web/about?opendocument.

Chanil, Debra. 2010. "Fertile Ground." *Stagnito Media*. October. Accessed August 8, 2011. http://www.progressivegrocer.com/inprint/article/id1266/fertile-ground/.

Charvat, Frank J. 1964. *Supermarketing*. New York: Macmillan.

Chasarik, Krisann. 2011. E-mail to author. "Your staffing/inspection questions." February 18.

Chase, James. 2010. Vice president, marketing and communications, Majora Carter Group. Telephone interview by author, transcribed. May 7.

Christopher Ranch. 2011. "The Ranch." *Christopher Ranch*. Accessed February 24. http://www.christopherranch.com/index.htm.

Ciezadlo, Annia. 2011. *Day of Honey: A Memoir of Food, Love, and War*. New York: Free Press.

Clarke, Cynthia M. 2009. *Workplace Injuries and Illnesses in Grocery Stores*. Washington, DC: U.S. Department of Labor, Bureau of Labor Statistics. December 19. Accessed August 6, 2011. http://www.bls.gov/opub/cwc/sh20031216ar01p1.htm#10a.

Cline, Harry. 2007. "Quality, flavor keeping California garlic competitive." *Western Farm Press*. June 2.

Codiga, Janette. 2011. Spokesperson for Christopher Ranch. Telephone interview by author, transcribed. August 12.

Colasanti, Kathryn, Charlotte Litjens, and Michael Hamm. 2010. *Growing Food in the City:*

The Production Potential of Detroit's Vacant Land. C.S. Mott Group for Sustainable Food Systems at Michigan State University. June.

Community Water Center. 2011. *Water & Health in the Valley: Nitrate Contamination of Drinking Water and the Health of San Joaquin Valley Residents.* Health and drinking water series. Visalia, CA: Community Water Center.

Condrasky, Margaret D., and Marie Hegler. 2010. "How Culinary Nutrition Can Save the Health of a Nation." *Journal of Extension* 48 (2) (April).

Condrasky, Margaret D., Sara G. Griffin, Patricia Michaud Catalano, and Christine Clark. 2010. "A Formative Evaluation of the Cooking with a Chef Program." *Journal of Extension* 38 (2) (April).

Congressional Budget Office. 2010. *How Does Obesity in Adults Affect Spending on Health Care?* Economic and budget issue brief. Washington, DC: Congressional Budget Office. September 8.

Consumer Reports. 2010. "Bagged salad: how clean are packaged salads?" *Consumer Reports.* March. Accessed August 10, 2011. http://www.consumerreports.org/cro/magazine-archive/2010/march/recalls-and-safety-alerts/bagged-salad/index.htm.

Cook, Roberta. 2008. "Trends in the Marketing of Fresh Produce and Fresh-cut Products." Presentation from the University of California-Davis Department of Agriculture and Research Economics. September.

Cooking Matters. 2009. *2009 Annual Review: September 1, 2008—August 31, 2009.* Operation Frontline/Share Our Strength.

Council of the District of Columbia. 2007. Legislation No: B17-0098—Large Retailer Accountability Act of 2007. *Council of the District of Columbia.* February 6. Accessed July 15, 2011. http://www.dccouncil.washington.dc.us/lims/legislation.aspx?LegNo=B17-0098&Description=%22LARGE+RETAILER+ACCOUNTABILITY+ACT+OF+2007%22.&ID=18201.

Courtemanche, Charles, and Art Carden. 2011. "Supersizing supercenters? The impact of Walmart Supercenters on body mass index and obesity." *Journal of Urban Economics* 69: 165–81.

Covington, Mark. 2010. Visit to Georgia Street community garden. Interview by author, transcribed, Detroit, Michigan. May 5.

———. 2011. Follow-up with Mark Covington. Telephone interview by author, transcribed. July 13.

Cowan, Tadlock. 2005. *California's San Joaquin Valley: A Region in Transition.* Congressional Research Service. December 12.

Cullen, Michael. 1930. Letter to vice president, Kroger Grocery and Baking Company.

———. 1934. To Mr. George L. Hartford, Great Atlantic and Pacific Tea Company. December 10.

Deacon, Bradley N. 2011. Freedom of Information Act Request: Belleville food stores, via Department of Agriculture and Rural Development, State of Michigan. April 27.

DeNavas-Walt, Carmen, Bernadette D. Proctor, and Jessica C. Smith. 2010. *Income, Poverty, and Health Insurance Coverage in the United States: 2009.* Current population reports: consumer income. Washington, DC: U.S. Census Bureau. September.

DeParle, Jason, and Robert Gebeloff. 2009. "Food Stamp Use Soars, and Stigma Fades." *New York Times.* November 28.

Department of Housing and Urban Development. 2009. *American Housing Survey.* Washington, DC: U.S. Census Bureau. Accessed July 26, 2011. http://www.census.gov/hhes/www/housing/ahs/ahs.html.

Deutsch, Tracey. 2010. *Building a Housewife's Paradise: Gender, Politics, and American Grocery Stores in the Twentieth Century.* Chapel Hill: University of North Carolina Press.

DeVoto, Bernard. 1951. "Two Points of a Joke." *Harper's Magazine.* October.

di Croce, N. 2011. "Don't let growers grab water with their distortions." *Sacramento Bee.* June 26, p.E5

Diansheng, Dong, and Ephraim Leibtag. 2010. *Promoting Fruit and Vegetable Consumption: Are Coupons More Effective Than Pure Price Discounts?* Washington, DC: U.S. Department of Agriculture, Economic Research Service. June.

Diaz, Veronica. 2011. Dole processing plant/Teamsters. Telephone interview by Clarissa León. July 11.

Didion, Joan. 2003. *Where I Was From.* New York: Vintage Books.

DineEquity. 2010. *DineEquity Inc. 2010 Annual Report.* DineEquity.

Division of Labor Standards. 2007. "Guidelines for Meal Periods." New York State Department of Labor, September. Accessed August 12, 2011. http://www.labor.state.ny.us.

Duffus, John. 2011. Garlic company practices. Telephone interview by author, transcribed. April 4.

Duggan, Daniel, and Nate Skid. 2011. $4.2 million in incentives key in Whole Foods deal. *Crain's Detroit Business.* July 27. http://ow.ly/6GvOW.

Editorial Desk. 2010. "Forced Labor." *New York Times.* September 8. p.A26.

Editorial Desk. 2001. "Keep Water Deal Flowing." *Los Angeles Times.* October 16, p. 16.

Effland, Anne B. W. Date unknown. "USDA's Historical Studies of the Use of Time by Homemakers presented at the USDA Economic Research Service, Washington, DC."

Ehn, Bob. 2011. California garlic industry. Telephone interview by author, transcribed. April 1.

Ellick, Adam B. 2007. "Boulud Settling Suit Alleging Bias at a French Restaurant." *New York Times.* July 31.

Ellickson, Paul B. 2006. "Quality Competition in Retailing: A Structural Analysis." *International Journal of Industrial Organization* 24 (3): 521–40.

———. 2007. "From A&P to Wal-Mart: The Evolution of the Supermarket Industry." Presented at the Fair Trade Commission. Washington, DC. May 24.

Ellickson, Paul B., and Sanjog Misra. 2008. "Supermarket Pricing Strategies." *Marketing Science* 27 (5) (October): 811–28.

Ellis, Eileen R., Vernon K. Smith, and David M. Rousseau. 2005. *Medicaid Enrollment in 50 States: June 2004 Data Update.* Kaiser Family Foundation. September.

Emmer-Scott, Valerie L. 2010. Documents regarding COOL violation at Belleville Walmart. June 23.

Employee, Michigan Department of Health and Human Services. 2011. Michigan workers' compensation. Telephone interview by Clarissa León, transcribed. January.

Engel, S. M., J. Wetmur, J. Chen, C. Zhu, D. B. Barr, R. L. Canfield, and Mary S. Wolff. 2011. "Prenatal exposure to organophosphates, paraoxonase 1, and cognitive development in childhood." *Environmental Health Perspectives* 119 (April): 1182–88.

Estabrook, Barry. 2011. *Tomatoland: How Modern Agriculture Destroyed Our Most Alluring Fruit.* Riverside, NJ: Andrews McMeel.

———. 2009. "The Price of Tomatoes." *Gourmet.* March.

Ettlinger, Steve. 2007. *Twinkie, Deconstructed: My Journey to Discover How the Ingredients Found in Processed Foods Are Grown, Mined (Yes, Mined), and Manipulated into What America Eats.* New York: Hudson Street Press.

Euromonitor International. 2011. *Grocery Retailers—US*. Country sector briefing. July.

Fair Disclosure Wire. 2011. "Event Brief of Q4 2010 DineEquity Earnings Conference Call—Final." *Fair Disclosure Wire*. March 3.

Fair Food Network. 2011. "About Us." *Double Up Food Bucks*. Accessed July 20, 2011. http://www.doubleupfoodbucks.org/about?phpMyAdmin=ZAR8MegLORXw1X9vhTYvia CNN67.

Fellowes, Matt. 2006. *From Poverty, Opportunity: Putting the Market to Work for Lower Income Families*. Brookings Institution.

Fickenscher, Lisa. 2011. "Hunts Point Market signs 3-year lease extension." *Crain's New York Business*. June 1. Accessed August 11, 2011. http://www.crainsnewyork.com/article/20110601/REAL_ESTATE/110609980.

Finkelstein, Eric A., Ian C. Fiebelkorn, and Guijang Wang. 2004. "State-Level Estimates of Annual Medical Expenditures Attributable to Obesity." *Obesity Research* 12 (1) (January): 18–24.

Fishman, Charles. 2006. *The Wal-Mart Effect*. New York: Penguin.

Fleming, John. 2007. "Walmart presentation to Carbon Disclosure Project September 24." Accessed August 11, 2011. http://walmartstores.com/pressroom/news/6735.aspx.

Foley, John P., ed. 1900. *The Jeffersonian Cyclopedia*. 1st ed. Funk and Wagnalls. Google Books edition, 2011.

Food and Nutrition Service. 2009. *End of an Era: Benefit Redemption Division 2009 Annual Report*. Washington, DC: U.S. Department of Agriculture.

———. 2011a. "WIC Food Package Regulatory Requirements." *United States Department of Agriculture*. Accessed August 7, 2011. http://www.fns.usda.gov/wic/benefitsandservices/foodpkgregs.HTM.

———. 2011b. "SNAP Monthly Benefit Issuance Schedule." *United States Department of Agriculture*. January 3. Accessed July 11 2011. http://www.fns.usda.gov/snap/ebt/states/michigan.htm.

———. 2011c. "Supplemental Nutrition Assistance Program Store Eligibility Requirements." *United States Department of Agriculture*. August 4. Accessed August 7, 2011. http://www.fns.usda.gov/snap/retailers/store-eligibility.htm.

Food Marketing Institute. 2010. "Supermarket Facts: Industry Overview 2010." *Food Marketing Institute*. Accessed August 6, 2011. http://www.fmi.org/facts_figs/?fuseaction=superfact.

Ford Motor Company. 2011a. "The Model T Put the World on Wheels." *Ford Motor Company*. Accessed August 6, 2011. http://corporate.ford.com/about-ford/heritage/vehicles/modelt/672-model-t.

———. 2011b. "Henry Ford's $5-a-Day Revolution." *Ford Motor Company*. Accessed July 24, 2011. http://corporate.ford.com/about-ford/heritage/milestones/5dollaraday/677-5-dollar-a-day.

Foreign Agricultural Service. 2010. "Garlic Imports, 1995–2010." *United States Department of Agriculture*. Accessed July 7, 2011. http://www.fas.usda.gov/gats/ExpressQuery1.aspx.

———. 2011. "Garlic Exports, 1998–2011." *United States Department of Agriculture*. Accessed August 3, 2011. http://www.fas.usda.gov/gats/ExpressQuery1.aspx.

Franey, Pierre. 2010. *A Chef's Tale: A Memoir of Food, France, and America (At Table)*. Lincoln, NE: Bison Books.

Gaines, Leonard. 2011. Special tabulation provided to Dorothy Hernandez. *Poverty rates, US, NYS, NYC and Kings County, 1969–2009*. Washington, DC: U.S. Census Bureau.

Gallagher, John. 2011. "Urban Farms Waiting to Root." *Detroit Free Press*, March 29, sec. Real estate.

Gallagher, Mari. 2006. *Good Food: Examining the Impact of Food Deserts on Public Health in Chicago*. Chicago: Mari Gallagher Research and Consulting Group.

———. 2007. *Examining the Impact of Food Deserts on Public Health in Detroit*. Chicago: Mari Gallagher Research and Consulting Group.

Ganz, Marshall. 2009. *Why David Sometimes Wins: Leadership, Organization and Strategy in the California Farm Worker Movement*. New York: Oxford University Press.

García, José, and Tamara Draut. 2009. *The Plastic Safety Net: Findings from a 2008 National Household Survey of Credit Card Debt Among Low- and Middle-Income Households*. Demos.

Garden Resource Program Collaborative. 2011. "Garden Resource Program Collaborative: About Us." *Detroit Agriculture*. Accessed July 27, 2011. http://www.detroitagriculture. org/GRP_Website/About_Us.html.

Gay Stolberg, Sheryl. 2011. "Wal-Mart Plans to Make Its House Brand Healthier—NYTimes. com." *New York Times.* January 25.

General Mills. 2011. Hamburger Helper Beef Stroganoff nutrition facts. General Mills.

Giumarra. 2011. "Grapes." *Giumarra*. Accessed May 26, 2011. http://www.giumarra.com/ products/grapes/9.

Gleason, Stacy, Ruth Morgan, Loren Bell, and Jennifer Pooler. 2011. *Impact of the Revised WIC Food Package on Small WIC Vendors: Insight from a Four-State Evaluation*. Altarum Institute. March.

Gliessman, Stephen. 2011. Extension and organic strawberries. Telephone interview by author, transcribed. July 29.

Goetz, Stephen J., and Hema Swaminathan. 2004. *Wal-Mart and County-Wide Poverty*. Department of Agricultural Economics and Rural Sociology, Pennsylvania State University. October 18.

Goldstein, Bruce, Barbara Howe, and Iris Tamir. 2010. *Weeding Out Abuses: Recommendations for a law-abiding farm labor system*. Farmworker Justice and Oxfam America.

Gonzales, Richard, and John McChesney. 2011. "California's Central Valley." *National Public Radio*. February 27. http://www.npr.org/programs/atc/features/2002/nov/central_valley/.

Goodwin, Arthur E. 1929. *Markets: Public and Private*. Seattle, WA: Montgomery Printing.

Goodyear, Dana. 2009. "Drink Up: The rise of really cheap wine." *New Yorker*. May 18.

Google Maps. 2011a. Kalamazoo to Decatur, MI. *Google Maps*. Accessed July 8. http://maps. google.com/.

———. 2011b. Greenfield, CA 93927 to Garlic, San Ardo. *Google Maps*. February 23. Accessed July 5. http://maps.google.com/.

———. 2011c. Gilroy, CA to Bella Vista Ranch. *Google Maps*. Accessed February 24. http:// maps.google.com/.

———. 2011d. Woodward Ave & W Jefferson Ave, Detroit, MI to Walmart Supercenter, Dearborn. *Google Maps*. Accessed August 8. http://maps.google.com/.

GPO. 1873. *Historical Statistics of the United States, Colonial Times to 1970*. Washington, DC: GPO.

Great Value. 2011. Great Value Italian Sausage and Rigatoni nutrition facts and cooking instructions. Walmart Stores.

Greenstone, Michael, and Adam Looney. 2011. "Women in the Workforce: Is Wage Stagnation Catching Up to Them Too?" *Brookings Institution. Up Front Blog*. April 1. http:// www.brookings.edu/opinions/2011/0401_jobs_greenstone_looney.aspx.

Griffioen, James. 2011. "Yes There Are Grocery Stores in Detroit." *Urbanophile* blog. January 25. http://www.urbanophile.com/2011/01/25/yes-there-are-grocery-stores-in-detroit-by-james-griffioen/.

Grimm, K. A., K. S. Scanlon, L. V. Moore, L. M. Grummer-Strawn, and J. L. Foltz. 2010. "State-Specific Trends in Fruit and Vegetable Consumption Among Adults—United States, 2000–2009." *Morbidity and Mortality Weekly Report* 59 (35) (September 10): 1125–30.

Grover, Joel. 2007. "Gross-ceries at the 7th Street Market." *Dateline NBC—KNBC.com.* March 25. Accessed July 25, 2011. http://www.msnbc.msn.com/id/17789410/ns/dateline_nbc/.

Guidestar. 2008. "Casa Guanajuato del Condado de Monterey." *Guidestar.org.* Accessed August 3, 2011. http://www2.guidestar.org/organizations/26-0562233/casa-guanajuato-del-condado-demonterey.aspx.

Guthrie, Joanne F., Biing-Hwan Lin, and Elizabeth Frazao. 2002. "Role of Food Prepared Away from Home in the American Diet, 1977–78 versus 1994–96: Changes and Consequences." *Journal of Nutrition Education and Behavior* 34 (3) (June): 140–50.

Gutman, Harvey. 2011a. Former executive at PathMark stores. Telephone interview by author, transcribed. January 11.

———. 2011b. Produce margins, etc. Telephone interview by author, transcribed. July 16.

Guzman, Christina. 2011. Guzman family specifics. Telephone interview by author, transcribed. July 15.

Haley, Andrew. 2011. Restaurant history. Telephone interview by author, transcribed. March 7.

Hamerschlag, Kari. 2010. *Farm Subsidies in California: Skewed Priorities and Gross Inequities.* Environmental Working Group.

Hamilton, Shane. 2009. "Supermarket USA Confronts State Socialism: Airlifting the Technopolitics of Industrial Food Distribution into Cold War Yugoslavia." In *Cold War Kitchen: Americanization, Technology, and European Users.* Cambridge, MA: MIT Press. March, 143–46.

Haomiao, Jia, and Erica I. Lubetkin. 2010. "Obesity-Related Quality-Adjusted Life Years Lost in the U.S. from 1993 to 2008." *American Journal of Preventive Medicine* 39 (3) (September): 220–27.

Harris, Michael J., and Rimma Shiptsova. 2007. "Consumer Demand for Convenience Foods: Demographics and Expenditures." *Journal of Food Distribution Research* 38 (3) (November): 22–36.

Hausman, Jerry, and Ephraim Leibtag. 2004. *CPI Bias from Supercenters: Does the BLS Know that Wal-Mart Exists?* Working paper. Cambridge, MA: National Bureau of Economic Research. August.

———. 2005. *Consumer Benefits from Increased Competition in Shopping Outlets: Measuring the Effect of Wal-Mart.* Working paper. Cambridge, MA: National Bureau of Economic Research. December.

Hazell, Peter B. R. 2009. *The Asian Green Revolution.* IFPRI discussion paper. International Food Policy Research Institute. November.

Heller, Mark. 2011. Farm labor background. Telephone interview by author, transcribed. July 27.

Hempel, Jonathan. 2011a. Soil organic matter. Telephone interview by author, transcribed. July 5.

———. 2011b. E-mail correspondence with author. "Reporter inquiry re: Soil map for CA Central Valley." July 15.

Hernandez, Dorothy. 2011a. Telephone interviews with twenty-three food retailers registered in Belleville with the Michigan Department of Agriculture.

———. 2011b. Closed plants in SW Detroit. *Google Maps*. Accessed January 19. http://maps.google.com/.

———. 2011c. Thrifty Food Plan shopping list, Walmart. January 19.

———. 2011d. Thrifty Food Plan shopping list—La Colmena. January 19.

Hillel, Daniel. 1991. *Out of the Earth: Civilization and the Life of the Soil.* New York: Free Press.

Hoffman, A. C. 1940. *Large-Scale Organization in the Food Industries.* Monograph. Washington, DC: Temporary National Economic Committee.

Hollenbach, Barbara. 1998. A Cultural Sketch of the Copala Trique. *Summer Institute of Linguistics in Mexico.* Accessed July 5, 2011. http://www.sil.org/mexico/mixteca/triqui-copala/A001-CulturalSketch-trc.htm#Marriage.

Holli, Melvin G. 1969. *Reform in Detroit: Hazen S. Pingree and Urban Politics.* New York: Oxford University Press.

Hubert, Diana. 2010. "Rebuilding Harlem." *Epoch Times.* September 19.

Human Rights Watch. 2010. *Fields of Peril: Child Labor in US Agriculture.* New York: Human Rights Watch. May.

Ifeoma, Aba. 2010. Tour of D-Town Farms. Interview by author, transcribed, Detroit Michigan. May 14.

Information Resources, Inc. 2009. *The Lower Income II Report: Serving Budget-Constrained Shoppers in a Recessionary Environment.* Symphony IRI Group. February.

Jay-Z. 2003. "99 Problems." *The Black Album.* Roc-A-Fella, Def Jam, April 27.

Jefferson, Thomas. 1785. Letter to James Madison. October 28.

Jenkins, Matt. 2011. "Where Westlands water flows, California's agriculture follows." News magazine. *Grist.org.* Accessed February 17. http://www.grist.org/article/food-2011-01-26-where-westlands-water-flows-californias-agriculture-follows.

Johanon, Lisa. 2011. Executive director, Central Detroit Christian Community Development Corporation. Telephone interview with author, transcribed. July 11.

Jones, Kara. 2011. Western Beef market square footage. Telephone interview with Clarissa León. June 6.

Jones, Samuel. 2011. E-mail correspondence with Katie Rose Quandt. "Info request re: COOL." January 11.

Kamp, David. 2006. *The United States of Arugula: How America Became a Gourmet Nation.* New York: Broadway Books.

Kapadaia, Milaness. 2006. "Restaurant Grand Opening Celebrates New Food, Jobs In Bed-Stuy." Video. *Top Stories.* NY1. February 22.

Kaufman, Phil. 2011. *Top 4, 8, and 20 firms' share of U.S. grocery store sales, 1992–2009.* Washington, DC: U.S. Department of Agriculture, Economic Research Service.

Kavanaugh, Kelli B. 2007. "Great Groceries." *Model D Media.* December 11. http://www.modeldmedia.com/features/groceries12307.aspx.

Kharbanda, Remy, and Andrea Ritchie. 2005. *Behind the Kitchen Door: Pervasive Inequality in New York City's Thriving Restaurant Industry.* Restaurant Opportunities Center. January 25.

Khoka, Sasha. 2008. "Teen Farmworker's Heat Death Sparks Outcry. *All Things Considered.*" June 6. Accessed August 2, 2011. http://www.npr.org/templates/story/story.php?storyId=91240378.

Kimmelman, Noam. 2011. "Get Fresh Detroit: About Us." Accessed July 25. http://www.getfreshdetroit.com/.

King, Angela G. 1995. "Retailers return to the city / Merchants' land of opportunity." *USA Today.* February 20.

King Kullen. 1930. King Kullen circular.

———. 2011. "King Kullen Grocery Company Weekly Circular Locator." *King Kullen.* Accessed June 10, 2011. http://kingkullen.mywebgrocer.com/Store Locator. aspx?s=160569075&g=25ffa1c6-0a0e-48ee-be19-2a5b28696bbe&uc=370A037&f =cir.

Kingsolver, Barbara. 2008. *Animal, Vegetable, Miracle: A Year of Food Life.* New York: Harper Perennial.

Kirby, Joseph A. 1997. "New stores, tourists kindle Harlem's hopes; Businesses seek to tap underserved market." *Chicago Tribune.* March 16, sec. C1.

Klee, Harry. 2011. Tomatoes and flavor. Telephone interview with author, transcribed. July 7.

Klonsky, Karen. 2011. *Comparison of Production Costs and Resource Use for Organic and Conventional Produce Systems.* Davis: University of California-Davis.

Kochersperger, R. H. 1997. *Food Industry Distribution Center Benchmark Report.* Washington, DC: Food Marketing Institute and Food Distributors International.

Kolodinsky, Jane. 2008. "Obesity and Time Use—A First Look Using ATUS Data." *Consumer Interests Annual* 54: 161–62.

Konig, Gabor. 2009. "The Impact of Investment and Concentration Among Food Suppliers and Retailers in Various OECD Countries." In *Session 2.2 Promoting Responsible International Investment in Agriculture,* 16. OECD. December 7.

Krebs-Smith, Susan, Jill Reedy, and Claire Bosire. 2010. "Healthfulness of the U.S. Food Supply: Little Improvement Despite Decades of Dietary Guidance." *American Journal of Public Health* 38 (5) (May): 472–77.

Kuntzman, Gersh. 2007. "Ebbets Field memories are being preserve . . . at local McDonalds." *Brooklyn Paper.* September 29. Accessed March 2, 2011. http://www.brooklynpaper. com/stories/30/38/30_38ebbets.html.

Kurlansky, Mark. 2002. *Salt: A World History.* New York: Penguin Books.

Laitner, Bill. 2010. "Fighting to Farm." *Detroit Free Press.* November 21.

Lantagne, Doug. 2011. Extension history and priorities. Telephone interview with author. July 29.

Lauritano, Mark, and Hemant Sangwan. 2008. *A Cost Comparison of Shopping for Food Categories at Wal-Mart and Other Grocery Stores: A Business Planning Solutions Briefing.* Global Insight. August 15.

Layous, John. 2011. Series of e-mail correspondence with author. "Garlic Company response." August 11–25.

Leadley, Carolyn. 2011. Rising Pheasant Farms. Telephone interview by author, transcribed. July 27.

Lee, Chinook, Gerald Schluter, and Brian O'Roark. 2000. *How Much Would Increasing the Minimum Wage Affect Food Prices?* Agriculture Information Bulletin. Current Issues in Economics of Food Markets. Washington, DC: U.S. Department of Agriculture, Economic Research Service. May.

Leibtag, Ephraim, Catherine Barker, and Paula Dutko. 2010. *How Much Lower Are Prices at Discount Stores?* Economic Research Report. Washington, DC: U.S. Department of Agriculture, Economic Research Service. October.

Levenstein, Harvey. 1988. *Revolution at the Table.* New York: Oxford University Press.

———. 1993. *Paradox of Plenty: A Social History of Eating in America.* New York: Oxford University Press.

Lévi-Strauss, Claude. 1983. *The Raw and the Cooked: Mythologiques, Volume One*. Chicago: University of Chicago Press.

Lewis, Mark. 2009. "Businessman pitches urban farm proposal for Detroit." *Crain's Detroit Business*. April 2.

Leviticus 19:9–10. King James Version of the Bible. Google books edition.

Lillo, Andrea. 2003. "Wal-Mart gains strength from distribution chain." *Home Textiles Today*. March 24. Accessed July 16, 2011. http://www.hometextilestoday.com/article/495437-Wal_Mart_gains_strength_from_distribution_chain.php?intref=sr.

Linn, Robert. 2011. "The Food Grasslands of Detroit." *Mapping the Strait: Exploring Detroit through maps and diagrams*. June 6. Accessed July 5. http://mapdetroit.blogspot.com/.

Lloyd, Linda. 2010. "New Shelter for Food." *Philadelphia Inquirer*. December 26.

Lockwood, David. 2011. E-mail correspondence with Clarissa León. Vineyard longevity. June.

Lopez, Lorenzo. 2011. Walmart produce prices. Telephone interview with author, transcribed. August 12.

López, Roberto C. 2007. "Figuran guanajuatenses como líderes de migrantes." *Correo*. May 11. http://www.correo-gto.com.mx/notas.asp?id=24856.

Luginbuhl, R. C., D. N. Castillo, L. L. Jackson, and K. A. Loringer. 2008. "Heat-Related Deaths Among Crop Workers—United States, 1992–2006." *Journal of the American Medical Association* 300 (9) (September 3): 1017–18.

Lundqvust, J., C. de Fraiture, and D. Molden. 2008. *Saving Water: From Field to Fork—Curbing Losses and Wastage in the Food Chain*. SIWI policy brief. Stockholm International Water Institute.

Lynn, Barry. 2010. *Cornered: The New Monopoly Capitalism and the Economics of Destruction*. New York: Wiley.

Maconachy, Frank. 2011. Lettuce harvesting machines. Telephone interview with author, transcribed. July 13.

Malakoff, David. 1994. "Final Harvest: How the federal government's Urban Gardening Program, which served 23 of America's poorest inner-cities, flourished—then faltered." *Community Greening Review*.

Mariani, John. 1991. *America Eats Out: An Illustrated History of Restaurants, Taverns, Coffee Shops, Speakeasies and Other Establishments That Have Fed Us for 350 Years*. New York: William Morrow.

Marsh, Michael. 2011. Farm labor contractors. Telephone interview with author, transcribed. May 9.

Marshall, Ray. 1981. "The Labor Department in the Carter Administration." *United States Department of Labor*. January 14. Accessed August 1, 2011. http://www.dol.gov/oasam/programs/history/carter-esa.htm.

Martin, Philip. 2001. "Labor Relations in California Agriculture." In *The State of California Labor, 2001*. University of California for Labor and Employment, University of California-Berkeley. Escholarship version.

———. 2007. "The Real Farm Labor 'Shortage.'" *Front Page*. November 14. Accessed August 1, 2011. http://archive.frontpagemag.com/readArticle.aspx?ARTID=28829.

———. 2011a. *Farm Exploits and Farm Labor: Would a raise for fruit and vegetable workers diminish the competitiveness of U.S. agriculture?* Briefing paper. Washington, DC: Economic Policy Institute. March 21.

———. 2011b. "California Hired Farm Labor 1960–2010: Change and Continuity. In Washington, DC. April 30.

Martinez, S. et al. 2010. *Local Food Systems: Concepts, Impacts, and Issues*. U.S. Department of Agriculture, Economic Research Service.

Massey, Daniel. 2011. "Walmart hunts for a way into the city." *Crain's New York Business*. June 20.

Mattes, R.D. and Donnelly, D., 1991. Relative contributions of dietary sodium sources. *Journal of the American College of Nutrition*, 10(4), pp.383–393

Maurer, Daniel. 2011. Keller Cops to Using—No!—Frozen Fries. *Grub Street New York*. May 28. Accessed July 5, 2011. http://newyork.grubstreet.com/2007/01/in_his_cookbook_bouchon_thomas.html.

Maxwell, Barbara. 2011. Produce terminal tracking, USDA. Telephone interview with Katie Rose Quandt. July.

McCrory, M. A., P. J. Fiss, N. F. Hays, A. G. Vinken, A. S. Greenberg, and S. B Roberts. 1999. "Overeating in America: association between restaurant food consumption and body fatness in healthy adult men and women ages 19 to 80." *Obesity Research* 7 (6) (November): 564–71.

McGray, Douglas. 2006. "The Invisibles." *West*. April 23.

McMillan, Tracie. 2004. "The Action Diet: New York's food justice movement aims to change more than what kids eat." *City Limits*. August.

———. 2009. Reporting Notes, 2009–2010. June.

———. 2010a. Reporting notebook, Wk @ WM, 4/28–5/21.

———. 2010b. "An Urban Farming Pioneer Sows His Own Legacy." *New York Times*. May 18.

———. 2010c. WM Notes 2010. June.

———. 2011. Budget transcript, June–Aug 2009. (Also see Appendix.)

McMillan, T. and Karah Woodward. 2004. "InfoGuide: Where to Grab A Bite." *City Limits*. Accessed August 3, 2011. http://ow.ly.7ivln.

McWilliams, Carey. 1935. *Factories in the Field: The Story of Migratory Farm Labor in California*. Berkeley: University of California Press.

McWilliams, James. 2009. *Just Food: How Locavores Get It Wrong and How We Can Truly Eat Responsibly*. New York: Little, Brown.

Means, Kathy. 2009. U.S. Produce Industry: By the Numbers. August 24.

Merrefield, David. 2000. "Top 75: How They Change." *Supermarket News*. January 24. Accessed August 6, 2011. http://subscribers.supermarketnews.com/mag/top_change/index.html.

Metzger, Kurt. 2011. E-mail correspondence with author "Re: Response." January 24.

Miller, George. 2004. *Everyday Low Wages: The Hidden Price We All Pay for Wal-Mart: Wal-Mart's Labor Record*. Democratic Staff of the Committee on Education and the Workforce, U.S. House of Representatives, February 16. http://www.mindfully.org/Industry/2004/Wal-Mart-Labor-Record16feb04.htm.

Mills, Paul K., Jennifer Dodge, and Richard Yang. 2009. "Cancer in Migrant and Seasonal Hired Farm Workers." *Journal of Agromedicine* 14: 185–91.

Mines, Richard, Sandra Nichols, and David Runsten. 2010. *California's Indigenous Farmworkers*. California Rural Legal Assistance. January.

Mintz, Sidney W. 1985. *Sweetness and Power: The Place of Sugar in Modern History*. New York: Penguin Books.

MMR. 2010. "Big food retailers augment position: Top 100 Markets." *MMR*. June 14.

Mogk, John. 2011. "Exempt cities from Right to Farm Act?" *Detroit Free Press*. March 3, sec. Opinion.

Monterey County Agricultural Commission. 2009a. *Notice of completion, Bella Vista Ranch.* State of California Pesticide Use Report. Monterey County Agricultural Commission. August 14.

————. 2009b. *Notice of completion, Gallagher Ranch.* State of California Pesticide Use Report. Monterey County Agricultural Commission. August 18.

————. 2009c. *Ranch #23—Bella Vista Ranch.* Pesticide use map. Monterey County Agricultural Commission. August 26.

Montgomery, David R. 2008. *Dirt: The Erosion of Civilizations.* Berkeley: University of California Press.

Monticello. 2011. Quotations on Agriculture. *Thomas Jefferson's Monticello.* Accessed August 10, 2011. http://www.monticello.org/site/jefferson/quotations-agriculture#_ref-2.

Morales Waugh, Irma. 2010. "Examining the Sexual Harassment Experiences of Mexican Immigrant Farmworking Women." *Violence Against Women* 16 (3): 237–61.

Morland, Kimberly. 2002. "The contextual effect of the local food environment on residents' diets: the atherosclerosis risk in communities study." *American Journal of Public Health* 92 (11) (November): 1761–67.

Nadal, Alejandro. 2002. *Corn in NAFTA: Eight Years After.* Research report. North American Commission for Environmental Cooperation. May.

National Agricultural Statistics Service. 1964. *1964 Census of Agriculture.* Washington, DC: U.S. Department of Agriculture.

————. 1997. *1997 Census of Agriculture.* Washington, DC: U.S. Department of Agriculture.

————. 2007. *Census of Agriculture.* Geographic Area Series, Part 51. Washington, DC: U.S. Department of Agriculture.

————. 2009a. "Quick Stats (Vegetables)." *United States Department of Agriculture.* Accessed July 8, 2011. http://www.nass.usda.gov/QuickStats/PullData_US.jsp.

————. 2011. *Vegetables 2010 Summary.* Washington, DC: U.S. Department of Agriculture. January.

National Center for Health Statistics. 2011. *Health, United States, 2010: With Special Feature on Death and Dying.* Washington, DC: U.S. Department of Health and Human Services. February.

National Climatic Data Center. 2011. "Climatography No 84 (Bakersfield), 1971–2000." *National Oceanic and Atmospheric Administration.* Accessed February 18. http://www.ncdc.noaa.gov/DLYNRMS/dnrm?coopid=040442.

National Cooperative Soil Survey. 1997. Official Series Description - HESPERIA Series. Accessed July 14, 2011. https://soilseries.sc.egov.usda.gov/OSD_Docs/H/HESPE RIA.html.

National Institute of Food and Agriculture. 2011. "Extension." *United States Department of Agriculture.* Accessed August 11. http://www.csrees.usda.gov/qlinks/extension.html.

National Poverty Center. 2009. "Poverty in the United States: Frequently Asked Questions." *National Poverty Center.* Accessed July 23, 2011. http://www.npc.umich.edu/poverty/.

National Weather Service. 2009. "Snow Totals from the Latest Storm." *National Oceanic and Atmospheric Administration.* December 12. Accessed August 7, 2011. http://www.crh.noaa.gov/news/display_cmsstory.php?wfo=grr&storyid=44128&source=2.

Nature's Partner. 2011. "Farmer Details: Giumarra." *Nature's Partner.* Accessed February 18. http://www.naturespartner.com/ThePeople/Giumarra/.

Neavling, Steve. 2011. "Detroit can map out its future with census data." *Detroit Free Press.* April 3.

Nestle, Marion. 2006. *What to Eat: An Aisle-by-Aisle Guide to Savvy Food Choices and Good Eating*. New York: North Point Press.

New York Times, the Editors. 2011. "Forced Labor." *New York Times.* May 26.

Newman, Andy. 2011. "Poll Finds Modest Rise in Support for Bike Lanes and Wal-Mart." *City Room, New York Times.* Accessed July 28. http://cityroom.blogs.nytimes.com/2011/07/28/poll-finds-modest-rise-in-support-for-bike-lanes-and-wal-mart/?scp=3&sq=walmart&st=cse.

Nischan, Michel. 2010. Telephone interview by author, transcribed. October 5.

Norton, Maxwell. 2011. E-mail correspondence with Dorothy Hernandez. "Reporter query about growing peaches." June 13.

Nugent, Ted. 2005. *Kill It and Grill It: A Guide to Preparing and Cooking Wild Game and Fish.* Washington, DC: Regnery.

Obama, Michelle. 2011. "First Lady Michelle Obama Announces Nationwide Commitments to Provide Millions of People Access to Healthy, Affordable Food in Underserved Communities." Accessed July 20. http://www.whitehouse.gov/the-press-office/2011/07/20/first-lady-michelle-obama-announces-nationwide-commitments-provide-milli.

Office of the Attorney General. 2011. "Michigan's New Scanner Law: The 2011 Shopping Reform and Modernization Act." *Michigan.gov.* March. Accessed July 12. http://www.michigan.gov/ag/0,1607,7-164-34739_20942-134114—,00.html.

Oosting, Jonathan. 2011. "Could Meijer build two stores in Detroit? Gary Brown says they're looking at Redford High site." News. *MLive.com.* June 30. Accessed August 7, 2011. http://www.mlive.com/business/detroit/index.ssf/2011/06/could_meijer_build_two_stores.html.

Organic Materials Review Institute. 2011. "OMRI Generic Materials List." *Organic Materials Review Institute.* Accessed August 4. http://www.omri.org/omri-lists.

Organization for Economic Cooperation and Development. 2006a. "Annex E, France," in *Starting Strong II, Early Childhood Education and Care.* Paris, France: Organization for Economic Cooperation and Development.

———. 2006b. "Annex E, United States," in *Starting Strong II, Early Childhood Education and Care.* Paris, France: Organization for Economic Cooperation and Development.

———. 2011. "Annex E, Italy" in *Starting Strong II, Early Childhood Education and Care.* Paris, France: Organization for Economic Cooperation and Development.

Orszag, Peter R. 2008. *CBO Testimony: Growth in Health Care Costs.* Washington, DC. January 31.

Ortiz, Larissa. 2011. Larissa Ortiz Associates. Telephone interview with author, transcribed. January 24.

Pannuzi, Nicola. 2010. *Households Consumption Expenditure Year 2009.* Rome, Italy: Italian National Institute of Statistics.

Patel, Raj. 2008. *Stuffed and Starved: The Battle for the World Food System.* New York: Melville Press.

———. 2009. "The World Food Crisis." Panel discussion presented at Slow Food Nation. August 29. San Francisco, CA.

Patel, Raj, and Gisele Henriques. 2004. *NAFTA, Corn and Mexico's Agricultural Trade Liberalization.* IRC Americas Program Special Report. Americas Program of the Center for International Policy. February 13. Accessed August 3, 2011. http://www.cipamericas.org/archives/1009.

Paul, Pamela. 2011. "The Rich Lack Empathy, Study Says." *New York Times.* January 2.

Pearce, Diana. 2010. *The Self-Sufficiency Standard for New York State 2010*. New York State Community Action Association, Inc., and Wider Opportunities for Women. June.

———. 2011. *The Self-Sufficiency Standard for OHIO 2011*. Center for Women's Welfare. May.

Pépin, Jacques. 2003. *The Apprentice: My Life in the Kitchen*. New York: Houghton Mifflin Harcourt.

Pierce, Shelly, and Kent Wells. 2011. "Special tabulation, SNAP redemption by store type." U.S. Department of Agriculture, Food and Nutrition Service. March 1.

Pinal, Roman. 2011. Structure of farm labor. Telephone interview by author, transcribed. May 31.

Porterfield, Jason. 2005. *The Homestead Act of 1862: A primary source history of the settlement of the American heartland in the late 19th century*. New York: Rosen Publishing.

Porterfield, Jason D. 2004. "Harvey, Fred." In *The Oxford Encyclopedia of Food and Drink in America*. New York: Oxford University Press.

Pristin, Terry. 1999. "Harlem's Pathmark Anchors a Commercial Revival on 125th Street." *New York Times*. November 13.

Private Label Manufacturer's Association. 2011a. "Market Profile: Store Brands Achieving New Heights of Consumer Popularity and Growth." *Private Label Manufacturer's Association*. Accessed August 7, 2011. http://plma.com/storeBrands/sbt11.html.

———. 2011b. "Market Update." *Private Label Manufacturer's Association*. Accessed August 7, 2011. http://plma.com/storeBrands/facts11.html.

Produce Marketing Association. 2008. *Retail Fresh Produce Industry Sales*. Fact sheet. Newark, DE: Produce Marketing Association.

Progressive Grocer staff. 1999. "The PG 100: The Most Influential People, Products and Events of the 20th Century." *Progressive Grocer*. May.

Rauh, V., Srikesh Arunajadai, Megan Horton, Lori Hoepner, and Dana B. Barr. 2011. "Seven-Year Neurodevelopmental Scores and Prenatal Exposure to Chlorpyrifos, a Common Agricultural Pesticide." *Environmental Health Perspectives* 119 (April): 1196–1201.

Ray, Rebecca, and John Schmitt. 2007. *No-Vacation Nation*. Washington, DC: Center for Economic and Policy Research. May.

Reardon, Thomas, and Julio A. Berdegué. 2002. "The Rapid Rise of Supermarkets in Latin America: Challenges and Opportunities for Development." *Development Policy Review* 20 (4): 371–88.

Relinger, Rick. 2010. "NAFTA and the U.S. Corn Subsidies: Explaining the Displacement of Mexico's Corn Farmers." *Prospect* (April).

Restaurant Opportunities Center. 2009. *The Great Service Divide: Occupational Segregation & Inequality in the New York City Restaurant Industry*. Restaurant Opportunities Center. March 31.

———. 2010. *Serving While Sick: High Risks and Low Benefits for the Nation's Restaurant Workforce, and Their Impact on the Consumer (Executive Summary)*. New York: Restaurant Opportunities Center. September 30.

Restaurants and Institutions. 2009. "R&I 2009 Top 400 Restaurants Chains." *Restaurants and Institutions*. July 15. Accessed August 12, 2011. http://www.rimag.com/article/print/372414-R_I_2009_Top_400_Restaurants_Chains.php.

Roe, Terry, Matthew Shane, and Agapi Somwaru. 2005. "The Rapid Expansion of the Modern Retail Food Marketing in Emerging Market Economies: Implications to Foreign Trade and Structural Change in Agriculture." Presented at the American Agricultural Economics Association annual meeting in Providence, Rhode Island. July 24.

Rosenberg, Howard. 2008. "Battling Heat Stress in the 2008 Legal Context." *AgSafe Newsletter.*

Rosso, Colleen. 2011. Medicaid eligibility range in Michigan. Telephone interview with author, transcribed. September 23.

Russo, Dominic. 2011. Detroit Produce Terminal suppliers. Telephone interview by author, transcribed. July 14.

Saez, Emmanuel. 2009. *Striking It Richer: The Evolution of Top Incomes in the United States (Update with 2007 Estimates).* University of California-Berkeley. August 5.

Sagon, Sandy. 2006. "Cooking 101: Add 1 Cup of Simplicity." *Washington Post.* March 18.

Samadi, Nina. *Chain Full-Service Restaurants in the U.S.* Industry report. IBISWorld.

Santlofer, Joy. 2004. "Cold Cereal." In *The Oxford Encyclopedia of Food and Drink in America.* New York: Oxford University Press.

de Schutter, Olivier. 2010a. *Addressing Concentration in Food Supply Chains: The Role of Competition Law in Tackling the Abuse of Buyer Power.* New York: United Nations. December.

———. 2010b. *Report submitted by the Special Rapporteur on the right to food.* Human Rights Council, sixteenth session, agenda item 3. United Nations General Assembly. December 20.

Searchinger, Tim. 2008. *Summaries of Analyses in 2008 of Biofuels Policies by International and European Technical Agencies.* German Marshal Fund of the United States. November 18.

Secretaría de Desarrollo Social y Humano. "Migrantes." *Guanajuato Gobeierno del Estado.* Accessed August 3, 2011. http://www.guanajuato.gob.mx/migrantes/soledad.htm.

Seelye, Katharine Q. 2011. "Detroit Census Confirms a Desertion Like No Other." *New York Times.* March 22.

Semple, Kirk. 2008. "Bronx Produce Co-op Says Market May Leave the City." *New York Times.* June 12.

Severson, Kim. 2007. "A Top Chef's Kitchen Is Far Too Hot, Some Workers Say." *New York Times.* January 17, sec. F1.

Sexton, Jr., Donald E. 1973. *Groceries in the Ghetto.* Lexington, MA: D.C. Heath.

Shannon, Alan. 2011. E-mail correspondence with Katie Rose Quandt. FY10 WIC program cost/redemption information. July 22.

Siklos, Richard. 1997. "Dorothy Pitman Hughes Is Selling Shares in Her Business to Help Her Expand—Just as Big Business Is Cottoning on to the Immense Potential of New York's Most Downtrodden Neighborhood." *Financial Post.* September 20.

Sinclair, Upton. 1937. *The Flivver King: The Story of Ford-America.* Charles H. Kerr Publishing. Google books edition.

Skendzel, Eduard Adam. 1980. *Detroit's Pioneer Mexicans: A Historical Study of the Mexican Colony in Detroit.* Grand Rapids, MI: Littleshield Press.

Smith, Andrew. 2004a. "Grocery Stores: Supermarkets." In *The Oxford Encyclopedia of Food and Drink in America.* New York: Oxford University Press.

———. 2004b. "Wheat." In *The Oxford Encyclopedia of Food and Drink in America.* New York: Oxford University Press.

———. 2004c. "Freezers and freezing." In *The Oxford Encyclopedia of Food and Drink in America.* New York: Oxford University Press.

Smith, Joel J., and Nathan Hurst. 2007. "Grocery closings hit Detroit hard." *Detroit News.* July 5.

Smith, Richard. 2011. Garlic industry questions. Telephone interview by author, transcribed. July 7.

Social Compact. 2008. *New Orleans, LA Grocery Gap*. Washington, DC: Social Compact and the O.C. Haley Boulevard Merchants and Business Association.

———. 2010. *When Healthy Food Is Out of Reach*. Washington, DC: Social Compact and D.C. Hunger Solutions.

———. 2010a. *City of Detroit Neighborhood Market Drilldown: Catalyzing Business Investment in Inner-City Neighborhoods*. Washington, DC: Social Compact. December.

———. 2011. *Detroit Grocery Gap*. Washington, DC: Social Compact.

Spencer, Fran. 2011. Former director, Retail Chicago. Telephone interview by author, transcribed. January 27.

Sperling, Godfrey. 1990. "Gorbachev and Khrushchev." *Christian Science Monitor*. June 19, sec. Opinion.

Stanton, John. 2011. Supermarket pricing practices. Telephone interview with author, transcribed. September 23.

State News Service. 2010. "Meltzer introduces immigration changes to secure Michigan's borders." *State News Service*. June 11.

Steinem, Gloria. 1980. "The Time Factor." *Ms*.

———. 1995. *Outrageous Acts and Everyday Rebellions*. New York: Henry Holt.

Stephens, Scott. 2011. E-mail correspondence with author. Quick reporter inquiry re: rainfall. February 23.

Stevens-Garmon, John, Chung L. Huang, and Biing-Hwan Lin. 2007. "Organic Demand: A Profile of Consumers in the Fresh Produce Market." *Choices: The Magazine of Food, Farm, and Resource Issues*. Accessed February 17, 2011. http://www.choicesmagazine.org/2007-2/grabbag/2007-2-05.htm.

Stewart, Cynthia. 2011. International Council of Shopping Centers. Telephone interview with author, transcribed. January 14.

Stewart, Hayden, Jeffrey Hyman, Jean Buzby, Elizabeth Frazão, and Andrea Carlson. 2011. *How Much Do Fruits and Vegetables Cost?* Economic Information Bulletin. Washington, DC: U.S. Department of Agriculture, Economic Research Service.

Stiegert, Kyle W., and Todd Sharkey. 2007. "Food Pricing, Competition, and the Emerging Supercenter Format." *Agribusiness: An International Journal* 23 (3): 295–312.

Stiglitz, Joseph. 2011. "Of the 1%, by the 1%, for the 1%." *Vanity Fair*. May.

Stilwell, Eileen. 2011. "New produce market a cut above old one." *Courier-Post*. June 15.

Stoll, Steven. 1998. *The Fruits of Natural Advantage*. Berkeley: University of California Press.

Supermarket News. 2001. "Supermarket News Top 75." *Supermarket News*. January 15. http://subscribers.supermarketnews.com/mag/sn_top/index.html.

Symons, Michael. 1998. *A History of Cooks and Cooking*. Urbana and Chicago: University of Illinois Press.

Sysco, Inc. 2011. "The Sysco Story." *Sysco*. Accessed March 9. http://www.sysco.com/about-sysco.html.

Talmon-Chvaicer, Maya. 2008. *The Hidden History of Capoeira*. Austin: University of Texas Press.

Tamayo, William. 2000. "The Role of the EEOC in Protecting the Civil Rights of Farm Workers." *U.C. Davis Law Review* 33: 1075.

Tannehill, Reay. 1973. *Food in History*. New York: Stein and Day.

Technomic. 2010. *Top 500 Chain Restaurant Report: Full Service Restaurants*. Technomic Information Services.

Tedlow, Richard S. 1996. *New and Improved: The Story of Mass Marketing in America*. Boston, MA: Harvard Business School Press.

The Garlic Company. 2011. "California Difference." *The Garlic Company.* Accessed August 3. http://www.thegarliccompany.com/california-difference.

The Week Fact Sheet. 2010. "Walmart's 'aggressive' new convenience-store strategy." *The Week.* September 22. Accessed August 7, 2011. http://theweek.com/article/index/207329/ walmarts-aggressive-new-convenience-store-strategy.

Thomas, Andrea. 2011. "Making Food Healthier and Healthier Food More Affordable." Prepared remarks presented at the press conference. January 20.

Thompson, James F., and Steven C. Blank. 2000. "Harvest mechanization helps agriculture remain competitive." *California Agriculture* 54 (3) (June): 51–56.

Thompson, Lea. 2006. "Unseen danger in bagged salads." Television. *Dateline NBC.* NBC. April 30. Accessed August 10, 2011. http://www.msnbc.msn.com/id/12536902/ns/ dateline_nbc/t/unseen-danger-bagged-salads/#.TkM2oL-r9cA.

Traub, Larry G., and Dianne D. Odland. 1979. *Convenience Foods and Home-Prepared Foods: Comparative Costs, Yield and Quantity.* Agricultural economic report. Washington, DC: U.S. Department of Agriculture, Economics, Statistics, and Cooperatives Service.

Trop, Jaclyn. 2010. "Meijer plans to build its first Detroit store." *Detroit News.* October 27.

Tropp, Debbie. 2010. "Detroit's Eastern Market: A Food Hub in a Food Desert." *Know Your Farmer Know Your Food Blog.* December 17. Accessed July 24, 2011. http://kyf.blogs. usda.gov/2010/12/17/detroit%E2%80%99s-eastern-market-a-food-hub-in-a-food-desert/.

U.S. Census Bureau, 2000a. 48202—Fact Sheet. *American Fact Finder.* Accessed July 27, 2011. http://ow.ly/7iwLq.

———. 2000b. 10029—Fact Sheet. *American Fact Finder.* Accessed July 15, 2011. http:// ow.ly/7iwEB.

———. 2000c. 10035—Fact Sheet. *American Fact Finder.* Accessed October 30, 2011. http://ow.ly/7iwFn.

———. 2004. "American Community Survey: United States—General Demographic Characteristics." *U.S. Census Bureau.* Accessed July 24, 2011. http://ow.ly/6FJYa.

———. 2005a. "Detroit city, Michigan—ACS Demographic Estimates." *U.S. Census Bureau.* Accessed August 7, 2011. http://ow.ly/6FJYM.

———. 2007. "Fresh fruit and vegetable merchant wholesalers, Table 1. Selected Industry Statistics for the U.S. and States." *Economic Census.* Accessed August 11, 2011. http:// factfinder.census.gov/.

———. 2009a. "American Community Survey: Households without vehicles." *U.S. Census Bureau.* Accessed August 11, 2011. http://ow.ly/6FJWx.

———. 2009b. *Current Population Survey, 2009: Annual Social and Economic Supplements.* Washington, DC: U.S. Census Bureau.

———. 2009c. "Table B17001: Poverty Status in the Past 12 Months by Sex by Age." *American Community Survey.* Accessed July 23, 2011. http://ow.ly/63Sk6.

———. 2010a. "New York City, New York—Fact Sheet. *American FactFinder.* Accessed July 15, 2011. http://factfinder.census.gov/.

———. 2010b. "Economic Census: Sector 42, Wholesale Trade." *American FactFinder.* Accessed August 11, 2011. http://factfinder.census.gov/.

———. 2010c. "Livingston County QuickFacts." *U.S. Census Bureau State & County Quick Facts.* Accessed August 11, 2011. http://quickfacts.census.gov/.

———. 2010d. "Macomb County QuickFacts." *U.S. Census Bureau State & County Quick Facts.* Accessed August 11, 2011. http://quickfacts.census.gov/.

———. 2010e. "Oakland County QuickFacts." *U.S. Census Bureau State & County Quick Facts.* Accessed August 11, 2011. http://quickfacts.census.gov/.

———. 2010f. "St. Clair County QuickFacts." *U.S. Census Bureau State & County Quick Facts.* http://quickfacts.census.gov/qfd/states/26/26147.html.

———. 2010g. "Wayne County QuickFacts." *U.S. Census Bureau State & County Quick Facts.* Accessed August 11, 2011. http://quickfacts.census.gov/.

———. 2010h. "Lapeer County QuickFacts." *U.S. Census Bureau State & County Quick Facts.* Accessed August 11, 2011. http://quickfacts.census.gov/.

———. 2010i. "American Community Survey: Brooklyn Borough, Kings County, New York." *U.S. Census Bureau.* Accessed March 8, 2011.

———. 2011. "Population Change for Places of 50,000 or more presented at the Operational Press Briefing, March 24, Washington, DC." Accessed August 8. http://2010.census.gov/news/press-kits/operational-press-briefing/march-24-2011.html.

U.S. Department of Agriculture, Agricultural Marketing Service. 2011. "Fruit and Vegetable Market New Portal: Terminal Market." *United States Department of Agriculture.* Accessed July 25, 2011. http://marketnews.usda.gov.

U.S. Department of Agriculture, Economic Research Service. 1970. *Table 79: Tomatoes, canned, Retail price, farm value, farm-retail spread, and farmer's share of retail price, 1947–70.* Unknown. Unknown. Washington, DC: U.S. Department of Agriculture, Economic Research Service.

———. 2008. "Eating and Health Module (ATUS)." *USDA/ERS Data Sets.* Accessed January 4, 2011. http://www.ers.usda.gov/Data/ATUS/.

———. 2010. "Food Marketing System in the U.S.: Food Retailing." *USDA/ERS Briefing Room.* Accessed June 4, 2011. http://www.ers.usda.gov/Briefing/FoodMarketingSystem/foodretailing.htm.

———. 2011a. *Food-at-home sales by Type of Outlet, 1999–2009.* Food expenditures tables: table 14. *USDA/ERS Briefing Room.* Accessed August 1. http://www.ers.usda.gov/briefing/cpifoodandexpenditures/data/Expenditures_tables/table14.htm.

———. 2011b. *Individual food—processed fruits and vegetables.* Farm-to-retail price spreads. Washington, DC: U.S. Department of Agriculture, Economic Research Service.

———. 2011c. "Food CPI and Expenditures: Table 10." *ERS/USDA Briefing Room.* Accessed July 13. http://www.ers.usda.gov/Briefing/CPIFoodAndExpenditures/Data/Expenditures_tables/table10.htm.

———. 2011d. "Food CPI and Expenditures: Table 7." *ERS/USDA Briefing Room.* July 13. http://www.ers.usda.gov/Briefing/CPIFoodAndExpenditures/Data/Expenditures_tables/table7.htm.

U.S. Department of Agriculture, Economic Research Service, and Bureau of Labor Statistics. 2011. *Livestock, Dairy and Poultry Outlook, Aug. 2010—Jan. 2011.* Summary of retail prices and price spreads. Washington, DC: U.S. Department of Agriculture, Economic Research Service. February 17.

U.S. Department of Agriculture, Natural Resources Conservation Service, 2011. Custom soil resource report for Eastern Fresno Area, California, Selma Site. February 24.

U.S. Department of Labor, Office of the Assistant Secretary for Policy, and Office of Programmatic Policy. 2005. *Findings from the National Agricultural Workers Survey (NAWS) 2001–2002. A Demographic and Employment Profile of United States Farm Workers.* Research report. March. Accessed May 11, 2011. http://www.doleta.gov/.

U.S. Equal Employment Opportunity Commission. 1999. "EEOC and Tanimura & Antle settle sexual harassment case in the agricultural industry." *U.S. Equal Employment*

Opportunity Commission. February 23. Accessed August 3, 2011. http://www.eeoc. gov/eeoc/newsroom/release/2-23-99.cfm.

———. 2005a. "Jury orders Harris Farms to pay $994,000 in sexual harassment suit by EEOC." *U.S. Equal Employment Opportunity Commission.* January 21. Accessed August 3, 2011. http://www.eeoc.gov/eeoc/newsroom/release/1-21-05.cfm.

———. 2005b. "Rivera vineyards settles EEOC suit alleging sexual harassment, retaliation, job segregation." *U.S. Equal Employment Opportunity Commission.* June 15. Accessed August 3, 2011. http://www.eeoc.gov/eeoc/newsroom/release/6-15-05.cfm.

United Farm Workers. 2009. "CA Heat." *UFW: The Official Web page of the United Farm Workers of America.* Accessed February 19, 2011. http://www.ufw.org/_board. php?mode=view&b_code=cre_leg&b_no=5629&page=1&field=&key=&n=8.

Value, Joe. 2011. Michigan Department of Labor. Overtime. Interview by Clarissa León. Seattle, Washington. July 5.

Villanueve, Francoise, and Laura Curtis. 2011. "Chef Salaries and Hospitality Industry Salaries." *www.starchefs.com.* May. Accessed July 17, 2011. http://www.starchefs.com/ cook/features/chefs-salary-report.

Villarejo, Don, and Marc Schenker. 2007. *Environmental Health Policy and California's Farm Labor Housing.* Environmental Infrastructure Policy Papers Grant Program. University of California-Davis John Muir Institute for the Environment. May.

Villarejo, Don, Marc Schenker, Ann Moss Joyner, and Allan Parnell. 2010. *(Un)Safe at Home: The Health Consequences of Sub-standard Farm Labor Housing.* California Rural Legal Assistance, Inc. June 3.

Visser, Margaret. 1986. "Lettuce: The Vicissitudes of Salad." In *Much Depends on Dinner: The Extraordinary History and Mythology, Allure, and Obsessions, Perils and Taboos of an Ordinary Meal.* New York: Collier Books, 191–223.

Vitale, Ben. 2011. President, National Association of Produce Market Managers. Interview by author. Detroit, Michigan. July 15.

Volpe, Richard J. 2011. Food prices. Interview by author. Detroit, Michigan. August 7.

Volpe, Richard J., and Nathalie Lavoie. 2005. "The Effect of Wal-Mart Supercenters on Grocery Prices in New England." Paper presented at the American Agricultural Economics Association annual meeting, Providence, Rhode Island. July 24.

Wakerly, Susanne. 2007. *Share Our Strength's Operation Frontline Program in Elmira, NY, Presents the 2007 Long-Term Survey Project.* Food Bank of the Southern Tier. April 25.

Walmart Stores, Inc. 1998. *1998 Walmart Stores, Inc. 10-K Annual Report.* Bentonville, AR: Walmart Stores, Inc. April 23.

———. 2001. *2001 Walmart Annual Report.* Bentonville, AR: Walmart Stores, Inc.

———. 2008a. *Your 2008 Associate Benefits Book: Summary Plan Description.* Bentonville, AR: Walmart Stores, Inc. January 1.

———. 2008b. *Summary of Material Modifications: Amendment to Associates' Health and Welfare Plan.* Bentonville, AR: Walmart Stores, Inc. July 20.

———. 2009. *2009 Global Sustainability Report.* Bentonville, AR: Walmart Stores, Inc.

———. 2010a. "A Fresh Emphasis." *Walmart World.*

———. 2010b. *2011 Walmart Stores, Inc. 10-K Annual Report.* Bentonville, AR: Walmart Stores, Inc. March 26.

———. 2010c. "Warehouse Receiving Detail Report." Walmart. May 26.

———. 2011a. "About Us." *Walmart Corporate.* Accessed August 6. http://walmartstores. com/AboutUs/.

———. 2011b. "Walmart Organic Solutions by State." Walmart Stores. March 17.

———. 2011c. "Walmart to Open up to 300 Stores Serving USDA Food Deserts by 2016; More than 40,000 Associates Will Work in These Stores." *Walmart Corporate*. Accessed July 20. http://walmartstores.com/pressroom/news/10635.aspx.

———. 2011d. "State Information." *Walmart Corporate*. June 5. Accessed July 5. http://walmartstores.com/pressroom/StateByState/State.aspx?st=MI.

Walters, Dan. 2011. "Anti-Wal-Mart bill clears Senate committee." *Capitol Alert Blog*. April 6. Accessed July 15. http://blogs.sacbee.com/capitolalertlatest/2011/04/anti-wal-mart-bill-clears-sena-1.html.

Ward, Mary H., Theo M. deKok, Patrick Levallois, Jean Brender, Gabriel Gulis, Bernard Nolan, and James VanDerslice. 2005. "Workgroup Report: Drinking-Water Nitrate and Health—Recent Findings and Research Needs." *Environmental Health Perspectives* 113 (11) (November): 1607–14.

Wasserman, Wendy, Debra Tropp, Velma Lakins, Carolyn Fogley, Marga DeNinno, Jezra Thompson, Nora Owens, and Kelly Williams. 2010. *Supplemental Nutrition Assistance Program (SNAP) At Farmer' Markets: A How-To Handbook*. Washington, DC: U.S. Department of Agriculture, Agricultural Marketing Service. June.

Wattrick, Jeff. 2011a. "Mayor Dave Bing says Detroit must challenge Census count, confront reality." *Detroit News*. March 22. Accessed July 15. http://www.mlive.com/news/detroit/index.ssf/2011/03/mayor_dave_bing_says_detroit_m.html.

———. 2011b. "Despite objections from gardeners, Detroit City Council committee recommends land sale to independent business." *MLive.com*. June 9. Accessed July 27. http://www.mlive.com/news/detroit/index.ssf/2011/06/post_65.html.

Watts, Steven. 2006. *The People's Tycoon: Henry Ford and the American Century*. New York: Random House.

Weather Underground. 2009. "Weather Station History." *Weather Underground*. December. Accessed August 7, 2011. http://www.wunderground.com/weatherstation/WXDailyHistory.asp?ID=KMIKALAM1&month=12&day=12&year=2009.

Weiner, Tim. 2002. "In Corn's Cradle, U.S. Imports Bury Family Farms." *New York Times*. February 27. Accessed August 3, 2011. http://www.nytimes.com/2002/02/26/world/manzanillo-journal-in-corn-s-cradle-us-imports-bury-family-farms.html?src=pm.

Werhan, Carol, and Wendy Way. 2006. "Family and Consumer Sciences Programs in Secondary Schools: Results of a National Survey." *Journal of Family and Consumer Sciences* 98 (2): 19–25.

Westlands Water District, 2001. Why Land Retirement Makes Sense for Westlands Water District, Westlands Water District.

Whitford, David. 2009. "Farming: One way to try and save Detroit." *Fortune*. December 29. Accessed July 26, 2011. http://money.cnn.com/2009/12/29/news/economy/farming_detroit.fortune/.

Wholesome Wave. 2010. "Draft results of partial market data and consumer surveys." *Wholesome Wave*. December 19.

Wilkinson, Mike. 2011. "Pockets of growth show in Detroit." *Detroit News*. May 2, sec. Metro.

Willerer, Greg. 2011. E-mail to author. July 27.

Wozniacka, Gosia. 2011. "Latino-indigenous Mexican divide stirs Salinas Valley town." *San Jose Mercury News*. August 13. Accessed August 14. http://www.mercurynews.com/rss/ci_18675758?source=rss.

Wozniak, Gary. 2010. Chief development officer, SHAR Foundation and RecoveryPark. Interview by author, transcribed, Detroit, Michigan. May 13.

Wrangham, Richard. 2009. *Catching Fire: How Cooking Made Us Human.* New York: Basic Books.

Wulf, Andrea. 2011. *The Founding Gardeners: The Revolutionary Generation, Nature, and the Shaping of a Nation.* New York: Alfred A. Knopf.

Yahoo shopping. 2011. "Asiago Cheese." *Shopping, Yahoo.* March. Accessed March 7. http://shopping.yahoo.com/dairy-eggs/asiago—cheese-type/.

Yankelovich Partners. 1996. American Meat Institute. Accessed July 17, 2011. http://www.meatami.com/ht/d/ReleaseDetails/i/286.

Yakini, Malik. 2010. Visit to D-Town Farm. Interview by author, transcribed, Detroit, Michigan. May 14.

———. 2011a. Interview with Malik Yakini. Interview by author, transcribed, Detroit, Michigan. May 19.

———. 2011b. History of D-Town Farm. Interview by author, transcribed, Detroit, Michigan. July 10.

Yee, Larry. 2011. Agricultural extension and sustainability. Interview by author, transcribed, Detroit, Michigan. July 29.

Yen Liu, Yvonne, and Dominique Apollon. 2011. *The Color of Food.* Oakland, CA: Applied Research Center. February.

Zimmerman, Max Mandell. 1955. *The Super Market: A Revolution in Distribution.* New York: McGraw-Hill.

———. 1964. "The Trading Post Comes to the City: The Origin of the Supermarket." In *Business Decisions That Changed Our Lives.* New York: Random House, 33–55.

Zwiebach, Elliot. 2001. "A First for Wal-Mart: Supercenter Sales Lead." *Supermarket News.* November 5. Accessed August 6, 2011. http://subscribers.supermarketnews.com/mag/first_walmart_supercenter/.

Q&A WITH AUTHOR TRACIE MCMILLAN

On What Drives People's Food Choices

Q: Tell us a little about your general food philosophy and what drove you to start writing this book.

A: I think everybody mostly wants to eat healthy. I honestly believe that the only people who think that poor people don't care at all about their diet—and only eat fast food because they're too stupid to know any better—are people who don't know any poor people, who have never actually talked to working people about how their meals work and how their lives work and what's important to them and their families. Working people are not running around screaming, "I want diabetes! I think it would be awesome, and I'm not going to eat anything but McDonald's and soft-serve ice cream because that would be cool."

The basic rules of good nutrition have been the same since my grandma was a kid: Eat fruits and vegetables; don't eat a lot of fat; don't eat a lot of salt; don't eat a lot of sugar. Those are really basic, and they've held true. I think we can trust that most people will follow them if it's relatively easy for them to do that—and instead we've built this whole society that doesn't make any of that easy. No wonder people are eating junk.

Q: Usually the media frames any discussion about food choices as one of "nutrition," but your reporting puts it in the context of everyday life.

A: The more that I worked on the book, the more flummoxed I was by the fact that all of our public and journalistic work to change how people eat has been aimed at nutritional information. To say, "If we just tell people the right mix of fruits and vegetables, the right thing to do, they'll do it." We've clearly been pursuing that path at least since I was a kid, and it hasn't worked out very well. So maybe we need to take a broader view of how people are actually making decisions about their food. Not what they know in a general sense, which is salad is good, burger is bad; I would argue you can have a burger every once in a while. But you know that people understand that . . . so it's not a matter of getting them to figure that out, much less the seasonal, local stuff. I feel like the seasonal stuff is really easy to make an argument for. Eat food when it's cheap.

Q: That's one of the things that interested me most about your book—the way nutritional choices aren't presented as a lifestyle choice but as the way we live as a society.

A: I really feel like how we eat reflects the bigger choices that we're making in terms of what we want America to be like—and we've made it really, really easy for people to eat poorly and not exercise and not have time with their families. That's sort of the de facto state that we've built in the U.S., and if we want people to be able to spend more time on their food, we've got to figure out some things that we can change about the way American life works right now. I keep coming back to wages. It's really interesting if you look at what Americans versus the French are spending on food as a portion of their income—so this isn't comparing dollar prices. When you're comparing overall budgets, the French spend about 19 or 20 percent of their budget on food, while Americans spend about 12 or 13 percent. So depending on how you line up the numbers, it's roughly a 6 or 7 percent difference, and if you look at the overall budgets, we spend that 6 percent less on food—but we spend 6 percent more on health care, education, housing. And all of those are things that the French government subsidizes and takes out of their tax base and puts back into communities. The French spend . . . I think it's 28 percent of their GDP on social programs, and we spend about 15 percent.

On Getting By

Q: Many food policy people live upper-class lives.

A: That's true, and the upper-class connotations of food writing have always made me cringe. But I have to be really honest, their work is what makes mine possible. Most people care about food, and would be totally down with the idea of getting farm-fresh food if they had the means to do that. So if we really care about people eating well, we have to talk about wages and work life, we have to talk about how life works for typical American families. We don't get very far as a country if we confine discussion of food to well-intentioned, very intelligent, talented chefs and food writers.

Q: Has the experience of living on limited means changed you?

A: Oh, my gosh, I've gotten so much better at budgeting—more, I would say, from the way I had to live while I was working on the book, writing the book, than when I was reporting it. I had to learn how to hustle really fast, and learn how to sort of pare down my expenses, so now I'm really good about, like, keeping my pantry all stocked, and then every week I just buy fruits and vegetables.

Q: Talk a little bit about your pantry. How well-stocked is it?

A: My pantry is sort of overstocked. I make sure that I have every kind of bean that I might want to cook, and I have every kind of rice. I've got lots of grains, a lot of canned fish. I've got a bunch of different oils and vinegars, because I want the building blocks so I'm able to cook well when I feel like it. I have cornmeal, whole wheat flour, white flour, white sugar and brown sugar, molasses. I have all these things because the secret to being able to cook well with fresh ingredients is a) having really good condiments, and b) learning how to use everything that I eat, and not throwing things away. For instance, onion skins are really good to keep in the freezer, to put away to make stock with when I need to make veggie stock.

Q: Does the media too often vilify fast food and chain supermarkets and dismiss the people who shop and work there as ignorant?

A: It's not just the media. In American culture, and in coastal cities in particular, there tends to be a real disdain for people who shop at Walmart or people who go to McDonald's. The belief is that these people really don't care.

It was a little jarring for me when I had my book launch and called together a panel of what I kind of thought of as anti-foodie foodies. The topic was basically "Do you have to be a hipster to care about food?" There was an audience question saying, "Those people who shop at Walmart aren't very thoughtful," and someone on my panel just reflexively said, "Yeah, those people at Walmart don't care about their food." It reminded me what a bubble most people in New York live in.

A quarter of America buys their groceries at Walmart, and less than 2 percent of food spending is done at farmers' markets. If people are really concerned about making big changes, maybe we should look at engaging with the 25 percent of Americans who shop at Walmart. I love farmers' markets and fresh food. Low-income people love fresh food, too. But there are all these other reasons that getting fresh food for them is quite difficult.

On Journalism

Q: Can you tell us a little bit about how you started the reporting for the book and how you chose the places you would work?

A: Most of the help came from California Rural Legal Assistance. They helped me figure out a place to stay and try to find work. They don't have media resources, so they just said, "Go talk with a community worker for an hour and good luck." And, through a community worker, I met friends of friends and was able to find work and a place to stay. The supermarket section of the book was meant to explore what happens to the food between farm and plate. We talk a lot about the farm to the table, but nobody understands what happens between the farm and the table.

Walmart made sense because such a huge percentage of the population shops there. I decided to go to Michigan because that's where I'm from and because I didn't want the book to be just about the coasts. A lot of people don't know this, but Michigan has an incredibly diverse agricultural economy. It produces lots of fruits and vegetables. And Detroit is a really fascinating city going through a really interesting time right now. It's known throughout the country as a food desert, and so I thought that would be a good place to understand how food distribution works.

Q: What did you bring with you when you went undercover?

A: I brought a notebook, a tiny Dell laptop I bought for $300, a camera, and an audio recorder. It's kind of amazing to think about, but in 2009 smart phones weren't the way they are now. By the time we got to the point where I was doing promotional work for the book, (publisher) Scribner said, "Do you have video?" I didn't have a smart phone that could do video three years ago. The same farm workers I worked with then now have crappy little phones that can do video.

Q: Wouldn't it have been difficult to shoot video?

A: Not really. In the fields, nobody is paying attention to you. Nobody gives a crap about these workers. It's not like they have a big problem with undocumented workers giving them trouble.

Q: Wouldn't video have complicated things ethically, though?

A: There's a whole set of ethics for using video and photos when you're undercover. I was basically just using the camera to document things to help me remember. Kate Boo did this really interesting thing with her book *Behind the Beautiful Forevers*. She gave flip video cameras to kids in the slum and had them run around and film their lives. I think that's really great and works perfectly for her book.

Q: How did you take notes?

A: For the farm work, I have the best notes because I was driving to and from work sites often by myself, and I would just narrate into the audio recorder. I took tons of really short audio notes instead of just one long one. That really helped me with the transcription later.

Q: Were there things that you wanted to capture exactly, like things people said? When you were surrounded by people, in Applebee's or Walmart, that must have been difficult.

A: The kitchen at Applebee's was the hardest. I would work a twelve-hour shift in the kitchen, and I couldn't remember everything that happened. I was taking the subway, and I'm not the kind of person who feels comfortable talking to myself on the subway. The only reason I was able to make that work was because of luck. I had met William Finnegan from *The New Yorker* maybe five or six years ago and said, "Could you look at my clips and help me figure out what to do, because I just left my job?" He paged through who knows how many thousands of words of welfare stories and gave me some advice. So I had remained in touch with him. I knew that Bill Buford did a phenomenal job writing about what goes on in a kitchen in *Heat*—which started as a feature he wrote while on staff at *The New Yorker*.

So I got in touch with Finnegan, and he put me in touch with Bill Buford. He had this method of keeping track of significant events through the night. You boil something that happened down to a headline and you assign it to a finger. He said, "I can usually keep five to seven in my head, and when I go home, I write those down. They will work as a little string sticking out of a sweater; you pull it out and you'll find that everything comes out with it." I tried it, and he was right.

Q: What was the toughest part of going undercover?

A: This was the first time I had gone undercover to do work like that, because I believe very strongly in the importance of being up-front with people about what you're doing and who you are, and I am not a good actress [laughs]. So in the place where I was culturally the least good a fit, in the fields, I was really protected by the fact that I didn't speak the language. I just seemed like a kind of dumb white girl, and that was really helpful.

The first thing was getting over my anxiety about doing that kind of project and coming to terms with it. It meant that I had to be dishonest with my coworkers. I don't really care so much that I'm not honest with the companies. It's very interesting—the same year that I was working at Walmart during the holiday season, Stephanie Rosenbloom at the *New York Times* went and worked for a day at a Walmart with the company's permission, and she had a very different experience than I did.

And that's why you go undercover. Companies and supervisors do not treat you the same, and coworkers won't be as honest with you, or as open. I've come out of this very convinced that undercover work is worthwhile, but it's also complicated. There's a tendency to think, "I can totally do this, and how else can I get this information?" but I also understand why people react badly to it sometimes.

The other hard thing was finding the right balance between my narrative and talking about the people I was with. It's not supposed to be about me—a white girl doing this work. The idea is that I can only tell my story and what I observed, but I'm using that to get to the stories of the people around me.

Q: What has changed about your relationship with food since you wrote this book?

A: I have so much more appreciation of and respect for the fact that the reason I get to be a journalist is that there are thousands and millions of people working around the world to feed me. It was very humbling to have such a concrete lesson in how much labor there still is around food.

On What We Can Do to Change Things

Q: What can people do to change the way they eat and how the system works?

A: One really important thing people can do is cook more. That's an important piece of self-sufficiency. It builds your ability to care for yourself and your family and keep everyone healthy; it also means you gain the knowledge to decide, "I'll pay for this fancy tomato because it tastes better," or "I don't need top-shelf for this dish, I can economize." And that's really powerful.

Something even easier to do is, if you shop at a farmers' market, ask your farmer about their labor practices the same way you ask them about their growing practices. Ask what they're paying their workers and where their workers are from and what their relationship with them is; that doesn't get asked. The only way you know is if you ask—and the only way farmers know it matters is if you ask.

Organic and local have *nothing* to do with labor practices. Absolutely nothing. In fact, labor has always been the source of a deep rift in the organic community. Most growers argue against including labor rules as part of organic certification, and usually use the rationale that workers on organic farms are exposed to fewer pesticides, which is probably true. But organic work is a lot worse in terms of musculoskeletal injuries because farmworkers do all this work by hand. There's a short-handled hoe that's been banned since the 1970s; it was considered a landmark victory for farm-workers' rights because it's a tool that requires you to bend over full at the waist so your torso is almost parallel to your legs and hobble along a row while you use it. It will literally cripple you. I talked to a legal advocate who knew some workers on an organic farm who had been told to use the hoe, and organic growers have said, "But I'm an organic grower and organic growers get a hand-weeding exemption."

Asking about labor practices is a really easy thing for anybody who's sort of already on the local and sustainable bandwagon to do. Just start asking the questions; there's no harm in that.

Q: But doesn't that make food more expensive? How do you talk about making food accessible to everyone when you're arguing that people should be paid more?

A: In the book I write about how it's possible to pay farm workers a better wage without making our food unaffordable, but the real point here is to understand that good food is not elitist, though most of the arguments made in its favor have been. That's a critical difference.

Q: You write, "When cooking instruction is paired with basic nutrition education, Americans cook more and eat more healthfully—even when money is tight." What's your prescription for battling kitchen illiteracy?

A: Almost everything people are eating at home involves some degree of convenience foods. Those kinds of things usually tend to have a lot of salt and preservatives in them. But it's actually no more time-intensive to do a Hamburger Helper kind of thing from scratch, and it's actually cheaper.

The thing that sucks about a box isn't that it's quick—it's that if you don't already know how to cook, you think you can't make a cake without a box.

We need to start thinking about cooking as a basic life skill, not something that's optional. Incorporating that into public education to me seems like a smart idea. It can be a really great way to teach people other stuff. It's great for math. And for reading comprehension. Or learning to write recipes. It's an important survival skill.

We don't want to be raising kids who depend on corporations to tell them what to eat and how to eat. People talk all the time about a nanny state, but there's the corporate nanny, too. And I don't like that, either! If we want people to be self-sufficient, we need to include cooking as part of public school education.

Q: What's missing from the food discussion in the media?

A: There are very few staff reporting jobs now. Freelance rates were never luxurious, but they've dropped below subsistence at this point. So, increasingly, the people who go into journalism are people from affluent families, and that changes the way media view the world. If you couple that with food-writing tradition, based in gourmandism, you can begin to understand why our public discussion around food seems so skewed. Lambasting food writers for writing to elite audiences doesn't make sense, because that's where the tradition comes from.

Q: But you're clearly working from a different kind of background.

A: There's a much smaller tradition of really engaging with food in all its sociopolitical contexts, like with George Orwell and A.J. Liebling, but one thing I really found, doing the investigative research side of the book, is that there's no set protocol for how to do this kind of reporting.

Q: How so?

A: In Detroit, for instance, I kept hearing people cite this statistic that Detroiters spend 60 percent of their food stamps at corner stores on stuff like liquor and junk food, with just enough normal food spending to get certified. That's a powerful statistic that really indicts the food system in Detroit. So, I asked where that number was from, and they're like, "Oh, I don't know, I just heard it."

Someone finally said it came from a book someone had written years earlier, so I asked the author where they got the number from. They told me they couldn't find any real statistics, so just wrote that there are more corner stores than supermarkets in Detroit, so people must spend more food stamp money at corner stores than grocery stores. Which is crazy!

It took me and a research assistant thirty phone calls and emails and two months to track down a good statistic after that, and we found that the real number was 14 percent. Which is still double the national average, so is significant, but it's not 60 percent! So there's a lack of real reporting on this kind of stuff, which I'm hoping will change soon.

Q: What do you think has stopped that kind of reporting from getting more attention?

A: Well, it's depressing stuff, writing about problems with food. But still, people respond to food in a way that people don't respond to writing about poverty.

Food is this universal experience we've all had. Everyone's been hungry, even if it's a very safe hunger where you just haven't had time to eat yet, so people can identify with the idea that being hungry would really suck. By comparison, people who aren't poor don't really experience the problems of not being able to pay bills, and just absolutely not being able to scrape by.

TEACHING GUIDE FOR TRACIE MCMILLAN'S

The American Way of Eating

Jonathan Deutsch, Ph.D., Kingsborough Community
College, CUNY and CUNY Graduate Center

1. How does McMillan's Midwestern and working-class upbringing as described in the introduction inform her perspective on the food system? Think about your own childhood. In what ways does it shape your attitudes toward food?

2. McMillan writes, "Like all myths, the idea that only the affluent and educated care about their meals has spread not because it is true, but because parts of it are." How does this statement hold up across other public health issues? Support or refute with an example.

3. McMillan writes in the introduction, "Fancy food was for the rich; box meals were for the rest of us, and there was no point in making a fuss about it." What factors, forces, and structures do you think led to this understanding?

4. Many activists point to supermarket availability in "food deserts" as a solution to improve public health nutrition. What are some arguments for and against policies that subsidize the placement of supermarkets in food deserts?

5. Do you agree with McMillan's assertion that "Everyone wants good food"? Support or challenge using the book and outside examples.

6. Summarize the argument against simply encouraging Americans to spend a larger percentage of their dollar on food as the French and others do in order to improve nutrition and working conditions for food workers.

7. Critique the argument that "Food is a choice made from equal footing—a vote, if you will, with our fork."

8. Summarize Levenstein's paradox of plenty and explain how it frames McMillan's work.

9. Were McMillan's undercover journalism methods ethical? Why or why not? How would you have improved her methods with regard to human subjects protections?

10. McMillan works in three segments of our food system—farm, retailer, and restaurant—to "learn how the whole machine works." What is she missing? What other reporting would be needed to paint a more complete picture?

11. Compare and contrast McMillan's methods with those of an anthropologist or sociologist studying the same topic.

12. McMillan writes, "In each job, I lived and ate off the wages I earned, paying rent and buying groceries as if it were, in fact, my real life." How is that distinction important to her methodology, narrative, and analysis?

13. How has the food world changed between McMillan's reporting and the book's publication? Where do you see things going next?

14. In what ways is this a women's studies book?

15. Distinguish between a food system and a foodscape in McMillan's conception.

16. Address the reflexivity of the writing. How does the "character" of Tracie McMillan develop over the course of the book?

17. Explain what McMillan means when she writes, "Food is not a luxury lifestyle product. It is a social good." Provide an example beyond the text to illustrate.

18. Identify a specific concern McMillan raises in the book and propose a national food policy to address it. How would it work, and what do you anticipate the implications would be for consumers, labor, business, and health?

19. In the conclusion, McMillan distinguishes between viewing food as a consumer good and as a social good. What are the policy implications of each view?

20. After reading this book, could you argue, as the industry does, that there are positive aspects to entry-level work in the food industry?

21. Beyond personality, explain the possible motivations for the generosity that Pilar, Lorena, and other farm workers show Tracie.

22. What did McMillan learn from working undercover that would have eluded her if she limited her methods to observation and interview?

23. Summarize the process that McMillan underwent to secure entry-level work in each part of the food industry. How did those experiences differ from your preconceptions?

24. Will having read this book change the way you view or interact with food workers? How so?

25. Re-imagine an anecdote in this book if McMillan were a man. Rewrite the anecdote to that imaginary character's experience and reflect on the changes you made and why you made them.

26. Re-imagine an anecdote in this book if McMillan were Latina. Rewrite the anecdote to that imaginary character's experience and reflect on the changes you made and why you made them.

27. Citing examples from the book, what are some implications from the world McMillan describes for the safety of our food supply?

28. How does McMillan's own diet illustrate the paradox of poverty and obesity?

29. Comment on the juxtaposition of stories of food work with accounts of workers' meals. What points is McMillan implying or explicitly making?

30. How does the reputation of Detroit as the country's largest food desert relate to McMillan's experiences in the city? What are the implications for policy, planning, and public health?

31. How does the type of "cooking" that happens at Applebee's relate to this larger discussion of our food system?

32. It seems to sit uncomfortably with McMillan that so many foods in the Applebee's kitchen are heat and serve. How would the story and its implications change if she did her reporting at Junior's as Calixto mentions?

Recommended Reading from Scribner:

Random Family by Adrian Nicole LeBlanc
Our America by Lealan Jones & Lloyd Newman
Other America by Michael Harrington
Just Like Us by Helen Thorpe

ABOUT THE AUTHOR

Tracie McMillan writes about food, travel, and class for a number of publications including the *New York Times, Saveur, Harper's,* and *Slate.* Her writing and reporting have earned numerous awards, including the Harry Chapin Media Award; the James Aronson Award for Social Justice Journalism; and finalist nods from the James Beard Journalism Awards and the Livingston Award for Young Journalists. In 2011, McMillan was named a senior fellow at the Schuster Institute for Investigative Journalism at Brandeis University, and is a 2013 Knight-Wallace Journalism Fellow at the University of Michigan. She lectures widely on food and class from her home base in Brooklyn, with frequent stays in Detroit, Oakland, and New Mexico. She can be reached via www.traciemcmillan.com.